Visions of Cannabis Control

Visions of Cannabis Control

JON HEIDT AND JOHANNES WHEELDON

Great Clarendon Street, Oxford, OX2 6DP,
United Kingdom

Oxford University Press is a department of the University of Oxford.
It furthers the University's objective of excellence in research, scholarship,
and education by publishing worldwide. Oxford is a registered trade mark of
Oxford University Press in the UK and in certain other countries

© Jon Heidt and Johannes Wheeldon 2023

The moral rights of the authors have been asserted

First Edition published in 2023

All rights reserved. No part of this publication may be reproduced, stored in
a retrieval system, or transmitted, in any form or by any means, without the
prior permission in writing of Oxford University Press, or as expressly permitted
by law, by licence or under terms agreed with the appropriate reprographics
rights organization. Enquiries concerning reproduction outside the scope of the
above should be sent to the Rights Department, Oxford University Press, at the
address above

You must not circulate this work in any other form
and you must impose this same condition on any acquirer

Public sector information reproduced under Open Government Licence v3.0
(http://www.nationalarchives.gov.uk/doc/open-government-licence/open-government-licence.htm)

Published in the United States of America by Oxford University Press
198 Madison Avenue, New York, NY 10016, United States of America

British Library Cataloguing in Publication Data

Data available

Library of Congress Control Number: 2023943118

ISBN 978-0-19-887521-5

DOI: 10.1093/oso/9780198875215.001.0001

Printed and bound by
CPI Group (UK) Ltd, Croydon, CR0 4YY

Links to third party websites are provided by Oxford in good faith and
for information only. Oxford disclaims any responsibility for the materials
contained in any third party website referenced in this work.

Foreword

Don't Believe the Hype is not only the name of a hugely popular song by the hip-hop group Public Enemy but also something I wish more politicians, policymakers, and media pundits had taken into account when crafting, considering, and debating cannabis and its regulation. Had they done so, in my humble opinion, our world would be in a much better place.

It was Richard Nixon who declared drug abuse "public enemy number one" at a press conference in 1971 and suggested it was "necessary to wage a new, all-out offensive" to "defeat the enemy." With those statements, the "war on drugs" was officially launched, bringing billions of dollars (cumulatively, perhaps a trillion dollars to date in the United States alone) to bolster law enforcement and the proliferation of the prison industrial complex. In doing so, innumerable lives have been destroyed, families torn apart, and communities left in tatters.

Of course, our prohibitionist approach to drugs and the people who use them dates back much further than Nixon's declaration. Non-medical use of opium was criminalized in Canada and the United States early in the twentieth century, and cannabis followed shortly thereafter. American anti-drug crusaders took their fight to the world stage, resulting in the adoption of the United Nation's Single Convention on Narcotic Drugs in 1961. The international treaty controls activities surrounding specific narcotics and stipulates a set of regulations for their medical and scientific uses.

Initial intentions aside, the global prohibitionist mindset formalized by the Single Convention has had the dual effect of exacerbating social inequalities and hampering scientific inquiry. Here, the American example is telling. As the most commonly used illegal substance in the United States, cannabis is a gateway drug: not necessarily a gateway to harder drug use, as common wisdom would have it, but a gateway into the criminal justice system for the nation's most marginalized populations. Despite increasing state-level legalization, there were well over 500,000 cannabis arrests a year (the majority of which were for possession) in the United States between 2010 and 2018, with Black people more likely than White people to be arrested, even though their past-year cannabis use rates are similar.[1]

---

[1] ACLU (2020).

As I have documented extensively,[2] it is disproportionately Black, Brown, and otherwise marginalized Americans who are targeted by the police for cannabis-related offences, irrespective of the fact that its use cuts across racial groups and social classes. The burden of cannabis prohibition is unduly borne by the oppressed. At the same time, the classification of cannabis as a Schedule 1 substance under the Controlled Substances Act (meaning it is deemed to have a high potential for abuse and no currently accepted medical use) severely restricts its access by scientists wanting to study its effects—both positive and negative. Immense stigma around the plant and those who consume it remains.

Signs of change are not only on the horizon but also firmly at many of our doorsteps. Writing from Canada, where cannabis is legal, some of the problems associated with prohibition are no longer present in my country, yet many remain. The path to this point, and the lingering problems, are well charted by Heidt and Wheeldon in this book—a much-welcome contribution to the literature.

Visions of Cannabis Control presents a fascinating blend of social commentary, theoretical consideration, and regulatory analysis to guide the reader through the past to a possible future. Our route to the present has not been straightforward when it comes to cannabis, and the path(s) to legalization are likewise not simple. Regulators face a host of challenges inherent in bringing an illegal substance out of the shadows. They must address broad issues. These include public health and safety concerns along with the more practical matters that influence related outcomes, such as modes of production and distribution, age restrictions, possible tetrahydrocannabinol (THC) limits, the types of products that will be made available, taxation schemes, and measures intended to address the disproportionate harms of prohibition. Heidt and Wheeldon guide the reader through prominent existing models and consider their respective strengths and weaknesses.

From my vantage point, it is not a matter of whether cannabis will be legalized in most countries around the world but when it will be legalized. Decriminalization has taken hold on continents worldwide, and legalization is sure to follow. While not perfect, the Canadian model demonstrates that cannabis can be legalized without the sky falling in.

---

[2] Owusu-Bempah & Rehmatullah (2023).

As criminologists, we should be mindful of our discipline's role in sustaining cannabis criminalization, thus contributing to the militarization of policing and the growth of the prison industrial complex. Both have caused untold devastation. As we look forward, we should chart research agendas that are mindful of the past and that help shape the future of cannabis regulation in a more thoughtful, empirically driven, and caring fashion. *Visions of Cannabis Control* shows us how this can be done.

Professor Akwasi Owusu-Bempah
Toronto, Canada
March 2023

Preface

This book examines how labeling, stigmatization, and racism have informed cannabis policies since their inception. These ideas grew out of earlier papers and research studies undertaken over the past five years in this area by both authors. The original inspiration for the initial studies was witnessing the proliferation of unregulated cannabis dispensaries in British Columbia that started roughly a decade prior to the passage of the Cannabis Act in 2018. Despite the fact that cannabis was still illegal, law enforcement seemed to allow dispensaries to do business with recreational consumers often posing as medical users—these lines are often blurred to begin with. The disjuncture between policy and practice was incredibly intriguing and begged for further inquiry and more rigorous theoretical analysis.

This book is also, in part, a reaction to this activity and the new webs of control that are by-products of drug policy reform. Popular views on drug use seem to be shifting—what was once viewed as criminal and deviant behavior is now being redefined as a mental health issue or, in some cases, a recreational activity less harmful than drinking alcohol. Before cannabis prohibition officially ended, there seemed to be a vacuum in terms of cannabis control in many jurisdictions. Police were not enforcing cannabis law, and when they did, prosecutors would not prosecute or judges dismissed cases. Eventually, unregulated dispensaries opened and started to sell illicit cannabis. Coincidentally (or not), within in a few years of these shifts, research on the connection between cannabis and schizophrenia started to be heavily circulated in the news media. After a while, this narrative changed, and more recently, cannabis has been correlated with psychosis and violence.

New concerns related to public health have emerged in recent years. Initially, there was great concern from the public over the possibility that more people would now be smoking cannabis and driving. Police were less concerned with this as they were aware that, since cannabis law had not been consistently enforced for years in many areas, there were *already* many people driving around while high. Many were also concerned about public smoking and consumption. Would families at the beach be subjected to massive clouds of cannabis smoke? Would children be inhaling second-hand smoke and getting intoxicated? Many universities (including my own University of the Fraser Valley) formed committees to address the possibility that students would smoke cannabis on campus. This is somewhat ironic because, at many universities, copious amounts of cannabis were smoked on campuses while it was illegal, and no serious efforts were made to stop this. Cannabis legalization was just the motivation that was needed to institute the long-discussed cigarette-smoking bans on campus—the difference now was that they would also apply to legal cannabis.

In Canada, cannabis legalization can be a considered a mixed success at best. While it is laudable that people who use cannabis are no longer officially labeled as criminals, there is still a stigma that remains firmly in place. Further, access is still an issue in some areas that have chosen to outlaw dispensaries, and illicit markets still attract many medical and recreational users. According to recent reports, over 40 percent of Canadian consumers are still opting for illicit markets. It appears there is much work to be done in the realms of both policy and research.

Jon Heidt
Mission, British Columbia, Canada
March 31, 2023

Acknowledgments

The path to writing and publishing *Visions of Cannabis Control* was neither direct or obstacle-free (the phrase *What a Long Strange Trip its Been* comes to mind), and because of this we have incurred many debts along the way. The authors would like to thank Marcos Baudean, Akwasi Owusu-Bempah, Neil Boyd, David Brewster, Gale Buford, Heith Copes, Dominic Corva, Yvon Dandurand, Emily Dufton, Niamh Eastwood, Peter Kraska, Rosario Queirolo, Sveinung Sandberg, Stan Shernock, Alex Stevens, and Gino Vumbaca their thoughtful feedback on early drafts of chapters and manuscripts. Thanks also to Adrienne Chan, Irwin Cohen, Michele Giordano, Hayli Millar, and Martin Silverstein for their support early on in the research process. We would also like to thank the people at Oxford Publishing particularly Fiona Briden and Kalaivani K.

Finally, we would both like to thank our families for their and patience through the book writing process.

Contents

List of Figures   xvii
List of Tables   xix

PART I MORAL RENEGOTIATION, LABELING, AND MORAL PANICS

1. Cannabis, Criminology, and Visions of Control   3
   Introduction   3
   Criminology: Crisis, Cannabis, and Imagination   5
   Visions of Cannabis Criminology   8
   Stan Cohen, Criminological Theory, and Illusions of Reform   15
   Deliberative Democracy and Drug Policy   18
   Assumptions, Concepts, and Organization   20
   Conclusion   27

2. Criminalization, Stigma, and Normalization   31
   Introduction   31
   Stigma, Normalization, and Cannabis   32
   Before the Devil's Lettuce   34
   Temperance, Inebriation, and a Godly Society   36
   Cannabis, Stigma, and the Law   43
   The Dynamics of Stigma and Normalization   52
   Conclusion   56

3. Cannabis and the Life Span of Moral Panics   60
   Introduction   60
   Moral Panics and Cannabis   61
   Updating Moral Panics   65
   Conclusion   86

PART II LEGAL RENEGOTIATION, REGULATION, AND RESEARCH

4. Regulatory Models of Cannabis Policy   91
   Introduction   91
   Five Models of Cannabis Regulation   92

Models and Countries: Lessons	99
Conclusion	114

5. Stan Cohen and the Limits of the Cannabis Revolution   119
     Introduction   119
     The Limits of Liberalization   120
     Cohen, Contagion, and Criminological Control   125
     Illusions of Cannabis Reform   127
     Conclusion   145

6. Three Eras of Cannabis Research: An International Review   148
     Introduction   148
     Prohibition and Cannabis Research   149
     Studying Legal Cannabis   160
     Cannabis and Racial Justice   169
     Conclusion   171

PART III CULTURAL RENEGOTIATION AND BARRIERS TO REGULATION

7. Cannabis Policy, Harm Reduction, and Meaningful Decriminalization   177
     Introduction   177
     Categorizing Cannabis Policy   178
     Reducing Harm: Models, Definitions, and Policy Criteria   183
     Cannabis, Tolerance, and Aversion   187
     Regulating Aversion and Meaningful Decriminalization   190
     Conclusion   201

8. Legalization, Polymorphic Governance, and Barriers to Cannabis Policy   205
     Introduction   205
     Regulating Cannabis: From Harm Reduction to Benefit Maximization   206
     Polymorphic Governance, Evidence, and Regulatory Cannabis   209
     Polymorphic Cannabis Policy: Access, Equity, and Tolerance   219
     Barriers to Legal Cannabis: Politics, Competition, and Sales   226
     Conclusion   236

9. Cannabis, Culture, and Pragmatic Criminology   239
     Introduction   239
     Supporting and Building Cannabis Culture   240
     Cannabis and Credible Concerns   247

Cannabis Criminology: Sustaining and Extending Reform 250
Pragmatism and Cannabis Criminology 256
Cannabis Criminology: Insights, Interrogation, and Imagination 263
Conclusion 266

References 269
Index 347

Figures

1.1 Cannabis criminology 11
2.1 Geographic diffusion of cannabis to 1920 34
2.2 Harry J. Anslinger 47
3.1 Moral panic today 66
3.2 Participatory disinformation and January 6, 2021 87
7.1 Spectrum of cannabis liberalization 182
7.2 Possessing cannabis: A conceptual model 183
7.3 Models of cannabis regulation revisited 189
8.1 Cannabis candy 228
8.2 Cannabis packaging as marketing 232
9.1 Adult arrest rate trends of cannabis possession by race between legalization, decriminalization, and no-policy-reform states 253
9.2 Cannabis and prohibition culture jamming 254

Tables

4.1	Netherlands coffee shop guidelines	106
5.1	Countries and cannabis	122
7.1	Decriminalization or legalization of cannabis?	191
8.1	Expected cannabis legislation in 2023	210
8.2	Legalization and regulation of cannabis	216

PART I
MORAL RENEGOTIATION, LABELING, AND MORAL PANICS

1
Cannabis, Criminology, and Visions of Control

Introduction

The legalization of cannabis has been a long time coming. While there is a tendency to consider cannabis prohibition in North American terms, research on cannabis and criminology is international in character and scope (Heidt & Wheeldon, 2022). Once a quiet global revolution (Eastwood et al., 2016), it has expanded as an increasing number of voices demand change. In 2019, the United Nations (UN) called on member states to promote "alternatives to conviction and punishment in appropriate cases, including decriminalizing drug possession for personal use" (UNCEBC 2019). Options range from legalization and regulation in Canada, Uruguay, and a growing number of US states to formal decriminalization in Portugal and informal decriminalization in the Netherlands. Although some jurisdictions in Australia are moving forward with cannabis policy liberalization, countries like the United Kingdom are falling behind. Some reforms have dulled the worst cannabis-based carceral excesses. However, retaining coercive care backed by the threat of criminal charges for merely possessing cannabis is deeply problematic in a liberal democracy.

This book tells three interconnected stories. The first considers the history of cannabis policy, the role of moral panics, and emergent fears about participatory disinformation. As has been observed, few criminologists are aware of, or consider, the impact of historical developments in their own field (Bursik, 2009; Laub, 2004). For criminology and cannabis, the adage applies that those ignorant of history are doomed to repeat the mistakes of the past (Wheeldon et al., 2014). Prohibiting cannabis is inexorably linked to moral assumptions that use the law to uphold one set of cultural values over all others. Drug policy has been influenced by a series of moral panics, which have justified the demonization of drugs, notably cannabis, and the mistreatment of many otherwise law-abiding citizens. Policies that emerged from these panics have had profound and disastrous impacts on communities of color and created perverse political economies.

The second story is about the role of criminology in contemporary cannabis policy. While the influence of criminology on criminal justice practice and policy has waned considerably since 1950, research on the connection between drug use and crime has consistently been used to justify drug (and cannabis) prohibition. Historically, this justification has focused on public safety. The criminalization of cannabis has impacted every arm of the criminal justice system and exported the drug war, undermining human rights worldwide (Braithwaite, 2021). Since the 1980s, public-health models of cannabis regulation appeared, first in the Netherlands (Korf, 2020) and later in Portugal (Stevens, 2011). Nascent models based on medicinal cannabis and consumer cannabis led to the normalization of cannabis in the United States and built on early decriminalization efforts (Dufton, 2017a). Most recently, the notion that cannabis may serve to promote racial justice has gained favor (Mize, 2020). We document the experience of seven countries, including lessons and limits of cannabis regulation. One challenge is that antiquated assumptions around drug use and methodological inaccuracies remain part of criminology's present.

The third story is about how cannabis should be regulated going forward. These suggestions are informed, in part, by the first two stories described above. We consider how misinformation based on moral panics has influenced research and how the body of prohibitionist research has influenced cannabis and other drug policies. We argue that an essential lesson is that reform efforts must contend with moral panic policymaking and the damage done over nearly a century of prohibition. Likewise, we argue the experiences to date, based on international examples of cannabis liberalization, provide a road map based on harm reduction and critical principles such as tolerance, de-emphasizing policing, and voluntary programming. It may be unfathomable that, in 2021, we would allocate limited public dollars to fund policies that are utterly unable to curb drug abuse while causing so much harm to the most vulnerable in society, but many countries continue to do so.

Supporters of cannabis legalization and regulation would do well to acknowledge the irony at the root of legalization. Social movements have forced a reckoning in cannabis policy, but in practice, the sustainability of cannabis legalization may require embracing capitalism, an ideology about which many progressives are deeply suspicious. The need to expand our thinking on the role, nature, and limits of commercial cannabis is linked to lessons from the United States and Canada, where legal recreational cannabis is increasingly accepted. In both countries, significant paradoxes prevail. For example, even as President Joe Biden has done more than other presidents to decriminalize cannabis, meaningful reform remains elusive.[1] There are serious worries by investors and credible concerns by public policy experts that "legal weed" simply cannot win without rethinking how we apply economic thinking to cannabis (Goldstein & Sumner, 2022).

Criminology: Crisis, Cannabis, and Imagination

It is always fashionable to speak of various crises in academia (Hoffman, 2016; Wilson, 2020). As we have previously argued, although all disciplines are, in one way or another, fragmented, the crises in criminology are multifaceted (Wheeldon & Heidt, 2007). On Twitter, some criminologists have begun to voice problems that most prefer to ignore.[2] As Kaplan (2019) notes, criminology suffers from insufficient data, which leads to dubious correlational research based on methodological limitations, which, while pervasive, ensure most published findings are "significant" (Wheeldon et al., 2014). These observations are not new. These problems have been framed as poor explanatory power of criminological theories (Weisburd & Piquero, 2008) and an inability to focus on the processes and causal mechanisms that underlie crime (Wikström, 2008).

The atomistic nature of crime and criminal justice research means criminologists use a piecemeal approach by testing one hypothesis or another, relying on one data set, or focusing on distinct locations. As a result, replicating past findings has proven elusive. This has emerged as a grave concern in psychology, a discipline that has heavily influenced criminology and the criminal justice system (Ioannidis, 2005; Pashler & Wagenmakers, 2012; Simmons et al., 2011). Pridemore and colleagues (2018: 19) suggest that, as a field, criminology has yet to address the potential threats to our evidence base that large-scale and systematic replication attempts pose, and "it is likely we would face challenges similar to those experienced by other disciplines."

In the place of advancing knowledge and reducing harms, research is often driven by governmental assumptions about crime, ensuring that studies supporting the status quo will be more likely to secure funding than those that challenge existing practice and policy (Savelsberg et al., 2004). This is linked to external factors that have played a role in the ideology of crime control, including the rise of neoliberal forms of governance, simplistic notions of individual responsibility, and highly symbolic public discourse about drugs

(Haggerty, 2004). This impacted research on drug use and other criminological phenomena. For example, we document three distinct eras of cannabis research. The difference between findings in each period is profound. Until recently, cannabis prohibition was part of the unquestioned status quo.

As we have argued, criminological researchers working in this area should examine issues using multiple theories (Heidt & Wheeldon, 2015). This idea is not new, revolutionary, or radical. Inspired by Jock Young (2011), this book represents an extended effort to embrace the imagination once more common in criminology; this requires re-envisioning criminological thinking. The history of cannabis prohibition and the questions that have emerged provide a unique lens through which criminology can be viewed. Drug prohibition has influenced many aspects of criminology and continues to inform the study of deviance, crime, and harms inflicted by past and present penal modalities. It has resulted in ingrained stigma and numerous unnecessary contacts between citizens and the criminal justice system. It has created illegal markets and sustained ethnic prejudices and has led to state excesses, including expanding the infrastructure of punishment and control. Despite the high costs of these policies, most studies indicate that prohibition seems to have little effect on cannabis use (Donnelly et al., 1995; Reinarman, 2009; Williams & Bretteville-Jensen, 2014).

Cannabis as Moral-Legal-Cultural Renegotiation

Cannabis liberalization represents a fascinating case study in legal, moral, and cultural renegotiation. Numerous questions are emerging as broad international examples of decriminalization and specific local legalization models increase. We justify our principal focus on cannabis as an object of criminological analysis on several grounds. First, cannabis is the most widely used and extensively sanctioned illegal drug globally. The United Nations Office of Drug Control (UNODC) estimates that approximately 200 million people aged between fifteen and sixty-four used cannabis at least once in 2019 (UNODC, 2021a). Despite decades of evidence suggesting its harm has been widely overstated, cannabis criminalization has impacted every arm of the criminal justice system. Second, this overstatement was based on racial and ethnic animus and served colonial goals internationally throughout the early twentieth century. Prohibition and criminalization were subsequently used to limit the voices and views of people of color and youth in the

1960s by criminalizing protest and demonizing protesters (Marqusee, 2005; Seddon, 2020).

In more recent years, the supposed risks of cannabis have been used to justify police stops, detentions, and searches. Vitiello (2021) has documented how courts in the United States have upheld extreme drug sentences for cannabis-related crimes based on the view that drugs are a national scourge. Moreover, a criminal record has been shown to undermine employment opportunities, limit housing options, and prevent civic and political engagement (Pinard, 2010). If criminology, as a discipline, is to come to grips with the widespread punitive orientation within society, then cannabis reform is low-hanging fruit. Yet, it requires introspection (Maruna et al., 2004; Polizzi, 2010). Neither the punitive character of the justice system nor the racial disparities in policing cannabis are limited to North America (Chen & Einat, 2015; Shiner et al., 2018).

Criminologists worldwide have failed to challenge political leaders, grant funders, media, and moral crusaders who have overstated the social harm of drugs, generally and for people who use cannabis specifically. The retributive character that informed the development of cannabis policy cannot be separated from other work detailing psychological and dynamic dimensions of anxiety, fear, and punishment (Bottoms, 1995; King & Maruna, 2009; Tyler & Boeckmann, 1997; Valier, 2000). It persists partly because of the lack of political power associated with the racial, ethnic, and class characteristics of those most likely to be caught up in the machinations of prohibition-based policies and practices. Just as the overly punitive character of contemporary penal practice has infected therapeutic relationships and correctional programming through coerced treatment models (Spivakovsky et al., 2018), these views have extended into the community and the academy itself.

The reluctance amongst criminologists to challenge cannabis and other drug prohibition can be seen as an example of a broader failure amongst criminologists and within the field. This is not to say that no scholar has ever offered support for depenalization, decriminalization, or even legalization. However, the field has failed to confront how moral panics, racism, and xenophobia shaped drug policies. This has led to inaction in some cases and the justification of prohibition in others. Together, these serve as essential examples of the unconscious embrace of the criminal justice system's focus on punishment, control, and coercive harm, or what has been called criminology's shadow (Maruna et al., 2004). It is often required for those building careers on research grants.

Confronting how structural constraints shape methodological decisions and individual considerations requires a certain kind of introspective and reflective thinking. Acknowledging that prohibiting the consumption of certain substances has always been about controlling those who are different (Miller, 1996) is uncomfortable. So, too, are the consequences. The desire to exert social control of cannabis use has led to a criminal justice system in the United States, for example, in which the financial exploitation of poor, Black, Brown, and politically unconnected populations abound. Focusing on cannabis provides a near-constant reminder that proximity to the most significant power in a liberal democracy to constrain freedom can, and has, overwhelmed the importance of speaking truth to power and protecting fairness within the criminal justice system.

The evidence that billions of dollars have been transferred from subjugated communities to governments and corporations (Page & Soss, 2021: 291–293) is striking. It is past time that the field considers the criminal justice system's role in providing a steady stream of clients to for-profit treatment programs. Mandating "education" programs for those caught using a substance less dangerous than many alcoholic beverages often available in local grocery stores is an example of the long reach of prohibitionist ideas. The strategic submission to drug treatment to avoid a criminal record is not informed consent. Such an approach mocks the values that inform respectful therapeutic relationships. The history of these ideas must be understood if they are to be confronted.

Visions of Cannabis Criminology

After decades of gradual policy liberalization in various jurisdictions, scholars are increasingly focused on regulation (Decorte et al., 2020; Seddon & Floodgate, 2020). As a result, post-prohibition cannabis research programs are emerging. Some are broad. For example, Corva & Meisel (2022) present research through case studies from the United States, Uruguay, Morocco, and the United Kingdom. Newly emerging research areas include governance, public health, markets and society, ecology and the environment, and culture and social change. Others are more specific about program parameters. For example, within criminology, Fischer and colleagues (2021: 58) suggest five areas of particular interest for criminologists operating in jurisdictions where cannabis is legal. These include (i) the deterrent effect of prohibition; (ii) illicit production, markets, and supply in a legalization regime; (iii) use enforcement; (iv) cannabis-impaired driving; and (v) cannabis and crime.

Many of the questions raised by these researchers are essential and must be part of future criminological conversations. However, this book provides an alternative approach to engaging these questions. In general, we remain interested in understanding cannabis and crime based on prohibition's historical deterrent effect. However, the social forces which led to cannabis legalization are increasingly being met by groups and individuals that support the status quo of cannabis prohibition in novel and diverse ways (Heidt & Wheeldon, 2022). A specific concern is how police and other law enforcement trained in the era of the war on drugs adapt to the nascent regime of cannabis legalization. While public perceptions of cannabis use are increasingly liberal, attitudes among law enforcement and police organizations are not. The pushback against efforts to decriminalize and legalize cannabis is worthy of more attention and analysis (Stohr et al., 2020a), especially given the discretion the system affords police.

In many ways, the underlying assumptions of the drug war are still with us. While the war on drugs has been defined in many ways, we like Rodríguez-Gómez & Bermeo's (2020: 20) view. They describe it as follows:

> the violent configuration of prohibitionist and militarized drug policies that mobilize the illicit and lucrative nature of the drug trade . . . [that] connects distant actors, institutions, and regulatory landscapes across the globe.

The continued use of prohibition-era myths to "educate" young people suggests the culture around cannabis within the justice system is unlikely to change overnight.[3] An emerging question is how best to involve those who use and cultivate cannabis to build responsive, responsible, and respectful regulation regimes. Such efforts must make peace with the failures of the past. Seddon & Floodgate (2020: 8) observe:

> The core failure is perhaps the most stark and obvious: very large amounts of money have been spent enforcing prohibitive cannabis laws that have not only failed to reduce or eliminate consumption but have, in fact, coincided with increasing use. Whichever measure or time frame, or place we look at, the picture generally appears similar. For example, in 1961, when the Single Convention was introduced, the global prevalence of cannabis use was relatively low. . . . In 2019, after nearly 60 years of this global prohibition regime, the figure is approaching 200 million.
>
> (UNODC, 2019)

For others, any talk of a failed drug war is silly. The drug war achieved what it set out to do: subrogate people. Some used prohibition to control Black and Brown people and criminalize subcultures associated with jazz, beatniks, hippies, and protesters against the Vietnam War. Later, cannabis justified interfering with skateboard kids, hip-hop musicians, jam bands, and those who listened to them. For some, efforts to frame the drug war in ways that dislodge race and ethnicity cannot be justified. Granderson (2021) argues against accepting the idea that the drug war is a failure resulting from flawed legislation or racial disparities as an unforeseen byproduct. Instead, it was "driven by politics and prejudice" (Granderson, 2021). Christie (2004: 39–40) observes the international character of these policies:

> The war against drugs occurs in the service of high [class] values. With such a purpose one actually goes a long way in the control of those sections of any society usually selected for imprisonment. It is reflected in the prison population. Close to half of the prison population in Norway and Sweden is imprisoned in relation to the sale or use of drugs. By and large they have the same characteristics as those we also had earlier in our prison systems. They are similar to the traditional lower-lower class always found in our prisons. Now they have the connection with drugs as one more attribute.

In one way, the language of failure may make sense. Despite the high costs of policing cannabis use, prohibition has demonstrably *failed* to reduce use (Donnelly et al., 1995; Reinarman, 2009; Williams & Bretteville-Jensen, 2014).

As Levine (2003) has pointed out, drug demonization has benefited politicians, the police, the military, and the media. Likewise, as John Hudak's recent work (2020) explores, the explicitly racist roots of cannabis policy in the United States highlight how various politicians spent much of the twentieth century using cannabis to divide America.[4] It has been used to justify increased policing efforts based on a profound misreading of social disorganization theory (Fagan et al., 2009). Such policies have had no appreciable impact on cannabis use. However, they have long been connected to feelings of race-based alienation (Blau & Blau, 1982). Moreover, they have undermined public faith in the criminal justice system (Zinberg & Robertson, 1972). While racial and ethnic animus is unquestionably part of cannabis policy, it should be noted that cannabis has also been constructed as a threat to demonize other groups deemed undesirable when politically advantageous or expedient.

In our previous work (Wheeldon & Heidt, 2023a), we introduced *Cannabis Criminology*. We focused on cannabis and considered criminological theories, key concepts, and cannabis research. We defined cannabis criminology as an area of criminological study that focuses on how cannabis prohibition has twisted the criminological enterprise in North America and worldwide. Guided by the recognition that research agendas are driven by how cannabis as an issue is constructed, we prioritized a broader description incorporating multiple theories, concepts, and research methods. In addition to the inevitable focus on crime, we presented cannabis criminology as an area of criminology that considers five thematic areas of interest (see Figure 1.1). These include law, society, and social control; police and policing cannabis; race, ethnicity, and criminalization; the economics of cannabis use; and cannabis use and criminal behavior.

The recent history of cannabis legalization provides yet another window through which to view cannabis within criminology. Media has long been used to frame cannabis in negative ways; however, in recent decades, popular media has increasingly normalized cannabis use (Parker, 2005). Television and films portray cannabis use as typical, while celebrities, musicians, popular personalities, and even politicians mock laws against cannabis. By 2019, two-thirds of Americans said that cannabis use should be legal, reflecting a steady increase over the past decade, according to a new Pew Research Center survey (Daniller, 2019). Just as attitudes are shifting, so too is the nature of the backlash. There are still a significant number of personalities in the media who remain committed to demonizing cannabis

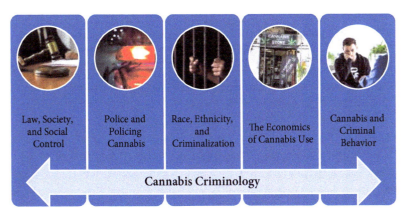

Figure 1.1 Cannabis criminology

and maligning users. Conservative outlets such as FOX, AON, Newsmax, and online media continue to perpetuate cannabis myths and justify prohibitive policies. Even in august publications like the *New Yorker*, pieces have been published in which controversial commentators' extraordinary statements about the risks of cannabis are repeated verbatim by liberal columnists (Gladwell, 2019).

The rise of a new breed of prohibitionists (Heidt & Wheeldon, 2022) suggests another concern. The prohibitionists of the past offered up scholarship rife with conceptual errors, methodological flaws, and practical oversights. However, the "New Prohibitionists" advocate for what has been described as the "treatment-industrial complex" in place of the much-maligned "prison-industrial complex" (Isaacs, 2014). For Boeri (2017: 162–163), the support for treatment is used to quell concerns about drug prohibition and stifle reform by constructing "addiction as a disease . . . legitimized by biomedical science." This is the medical model resurgent. People who use drugs are not rational but "sick" because addiction is a disease; they need help in the form of experts who can treat them.

Anti-legalization groups, such as Smart Approaches to Marijuana (SAM), which have long claimed that cannabis is dangerous and should not be legalized under any circumstances, are re-emerging. In addition, high-profile and even "liberal" commentators, such as Malcolm Gladwell and Patrick Kennedy, have returned to older tropes about cannabis in which the link between cannabis and mental illness is unquestioned:

> These have included theories that combine social and physiological causes in their explanations, such as the gateway effect and amotivational syndrome. The gateway theory suggests that an effect of using cannabis is a progression to more seriously addictive and damaging drugs. Amotivational syndrome suggests that chronic cannabis use induces an indolent and unmotivated state, causing individuals to cease pursuit of their goals, or even stop maintaining their own appearance and health. . . . Neither has been shown to have a basis in evidence.
>
> (Newhart & Dolphin, 2019: 27)

The former *New York Times* journalist and spy fiction author Alex Berenson (2019) has claimed that increased cannabis use will lead to more violent crime. These claims are based on a report from the National Academy of Science, Engineering, and Medicine's (2017) review of cannabis research and the work of a cluster of psychiatric researchers in the United Kingdom, led by Robin Murray (Murray et al., 2017) and Maria Di Forti (Di Forti et al., 2019). In response, Dr Ziva Cooper, Research Director of the University of California Los Angeles's (UCLA's) Cannabis Research Initiative and an investigator of the study cited by Berenson, has stated that the claim that cannabis causes psychosis is wrong and misrepresents her position and that of her colleagues. Others recently published a consensus paper explicitly noting that their work does not prove a causal relationship between cannabis and mental illness (D'Souza et al., 2022). Unfortunately, media outlets continue to seize upon the questionable research of the past, and politicians have used these reports to justify inaction on cannabis reform.

Lenses of Cannabis Liberalization

There are several lenses through which to view cannabis liberalization (Ritter, 2021: 9–11). The traditional view on drugs and drug policy is based on paternalism. This lens assumes the state knows what is best for its citizens and, thus, makes policy based on this privileged view. It is sustained by some doctors, addiction treatment counselors, and others described above as New Prohibitionists (Heidt & Wheeldon, 2021). This outlook can be associated with efforts to frame addiction as something that requires "recovery" through abstinence (Stevens & Zampini, 2018). This flies in the face of a century of reports to, by, and commissioned for governments around the world that advocate little to no cannabis regulation and warn against criminalizing drug use. There may be a role for such a view when people, as a direct result of drug use, are at immediate risk to themselves or others. This almost never applies to cannabis. The continued effort to link cannabis to other illicit drugs represents a danger to people who use cannabis and is an insult to common sense.

When paternalism fails, utilitarianism sometimes emerges. Utilitarianism, in this context, can be understood as drug policy based on what is best for the largest number of people. The trouble is that cannabis prohibition was sustained through its social construction as a danger to individuals and society in general (Newhart & Dolphin, 2019). As we document later in the book, this construction was challenged as people increasingly used cannabis and did not die, go insane, or harm anyone. This occurred first in the 1960s as part of the counterculture, in the 1970s as part of the libertarian revolution, in the 1980s even amidst a conservative backlash, and during the 1990s as part of a mainstream cultural shift (Dufton, 2017a). Indeed, one way to read cannabis reform is that prohibition has been rejected because it is not the best thing for the largest number of people. Indeed, policing and punishing people who use cannabis has been an expensive way to increase cannabis use around the world.

A common means to understand cannabis reform is based on human rights. This view is based on at least three variations. The first is that prohibiting cannabis contravenes autonomy over one's body. In short: people should have the right to consume substances in moderation without the government limiting their ability to do so. This view of rights is an attack on paternalism and has its roots in the consumer empowerment movement (Newhart & Dolphin, 2019). However, it is most often a feature of Western-style liberal democracies, where individual liberty is prioritized. The liberty to consume cannabis is infringed when the state punishes possession, use, or efforts to buy, sell, grow, or transport cannabis. The case for this view of negative liberty, or freedom from intrusion, is strongest among those who find limited evidence for the dangers posed by cannabis use. Indeed, it is often noted that, for decades, the most dangerous part of cannabis was being caught with it (Kaplan, 1970).

The second variation of the human rights argument focuses on the disproportionate harms of cannabis prohibition faced by people of color. These harms exist around the world and are connected to policing, diversion, and imprisonment. As we demonstrate, it is the failure of decriminalization to address racial and ethnic injustice that offers one of the most compelling arguments for legalization. Third and finally, Ritter (2021) associates human rights with the role of people who use drugs in policymaking. She notes the growing recognition of the importance that "people who are directly impacted by drug policies—people who use drugs—. . . have a central position in drug policy formation" (Ritter, 2021: 10). This view of rights can be aligned with a final view of cannabis liberalization, associated with harm reduction.

Harm reduction can be understood in at least four ways. The first is practical and includes policies such as needle syringe programs, overdose prevention centers, and safer supply initiatives such as drug checking. For cannabis policy, this means ensuring that the cannabis provided is what it says it is and is grown and packaged in ways that do not introduce unexpected contaminants. This view of harm reduction can be associated with a second variant, which seeks to reduce the harms that arise from the illicit market. These risks include violence, the subversion of the rule of law, and the corruption associated with criminal networks and drug trafficking syndicates (Ritter, 2021). A specific concern is when otherwise law-abiding people who happen to use cannabis must interact with illegal drug dealers and organized crime groups to obtain cannabis products.

A third view of harm reduction is consistent with human rights concerns about unequal and punitive criminal justice responses to cannabis use. This variant of harm reduction refers to taking steps to confront and attempting to reduce the damage done by the system itself (Quinney, 1970). This approach can be seen alongside efforts to expand restorative justice by employing a variety of programs and practices that focus on resolving conflicts through the active participation of those involved, including victims, offenders, and the broader community. It is explicitly part of the Marijuana Opportunity Reinvestment and Expungement Act (MORE Act) in the United States, designed in part to manage the financial and social reinvestment in communities disproportionately affected by the war on drugs.[5]

Fourth and finally, harm reduction is understood quite literally as a means to diminish the harms associated with some kinds of illicit substances by allowing people to access cannabis. According to this view, the potential benefits of cannabis use to reduce other types of drug use via substitution also amounts to harm reduction. Since illicit substances are unregulated, harm can arise from unknown strength and contents as well as modes of consumption. As we explore, prescribing cannabis as a regulated alternative to other drugs may offer a safer means to reduce associated health and social care costs, not unlike replacing street heroin with methadone or buprenorphine. In the case of cannabis, there is evidence it can lead to some users substituting cannabis for alcohol, cocaine, 3,4-methylenedioxy-methamphetamine (MDMA), and Vicodin (Reiman, 2009) as well as injected drugs, including heroin (Gittins & Sessa, 2020). However, for harm reduction to be embraced, several harmful ideas and methods around drug use must first be "undone" (Szalavitz, 2021). This requires expanding our understanding of cannabis, prohibition, and social control.

Stan Cohen, Criminological Theory, and Illusions of Reform

This book is inspired by Stan Cohen's (1985) seminal work, *Visions of Social Control*. His book began as an effort to determine the extent to which new forms of community intervention that emerged in the late 1970s could be clearly distinguished from the penal institutions they replaced (Cohen, 1979). Although formally less punitive, Cohen argued these new arrangements merely reproduced within the community the same coercive features of the older carceral system. This transference inevitably required additional and more expansive forms of social control. For Cohen (1985: 1), criminology tends to justify the ways in which society responds to behavior and people it regards as deviant, problematic, worrying, threatening, troublesome, or undesirable. These justifications are framed using a variety of terms, from the retributive, such as punishment, deterrence, and segregation, to more sympathetic, such as treatment, prevention, and rehabilitation. These insights helped us to uncover how shifting patterns in cannabis policy suggest reform but may be merely illusory.

The notion that liberalization can result in illusory reform emerged from Cohen's (1979; 1985) critique of community corrections. While anything that disrupts the brutality and other "closely guarded secrets of the penitentiary" is to be lauded, not all reforms are equal. Cohen pointed out that some reforms simply resulted in the same people merely moving their offices, while "doing the same old things they have always done . . . camouflaged as being just ordinary members of the community. . . . This is the real, awful secret of community control" (Cohen, 1985: 75). The illusion of reform is politically useful but conceptually bankrupt. Cohen (1985: 124) concludes:

> the illusion derives, as I will soon show, from the obvious paradox of the state appearing to sponsor a move to disestablish itself. The rhetoric of destructuring is, in fact, used to justify the creation of new structures—a movement from the established closed institutional domains to new territories in the open parts of society.

In this book, we wrestle with three fundamental problems at the intersection of theory and practice, based on the work of Stan Cohen. The first is that policing cannabis is unequal in application and outcome. Based on the public safety imperative, racial disparities in enforcement occur when cannabis is decriminalized (Sheehan et al., 2021) and persist even where cannabis has been legalized (Owusu-Bempah & Luscombe, 2021). The second issue concerns the decriminalization of cannabis and the apparent shift away from the prison-industrial complex and toward the treatment-industrial complex and coercive care (Spivakovsky et al., 2018). Replacing public safety with public-health models of regulation is not an unalloyed good.

The third issue explores the difficulties within jurisdictions that have legalized cannabis to dismantle and disrupt illicit markets. More specifically, emphasizing public-health goals ahead of market conditions complicates legal cannabis as an industry (Wesley & Murray, 2021). The tenets of rational choice theory offer a way to understand how people who use cannabis and those within illicit markets respond to changes in cannabis policy. Although employing rational choice theories to explain cannabis use is not without complications, there may be space for more nuanced applications of economic theories in criminology (Wheeldon & Heidt, 2023b).

We argue these problems stem from the failure to properly frame prohibition as the result of moral panics that have been instigated, perpetuated, and sustained in ways that are difficult to challenge (Ritter, 2021; Szalavitz, 2021). This difficulty comes from a failure to appreciate the intersections between legal, moral, and cultural principles which undergird the criminal justice system. Sustainable solutions require expanding the conversation. They mean confronting the culture of denial of how states, themselves, perpetuate harm (Cohen, 2001). For some, our use of Cohen's ideas alongside an effort to reinvigorate criminology may be perplexing. In 1988, Cohen published work critical of mainstream criminology alongside the new or radical criminology that he helped found.

Rather than suggesting that all forms of criminology be abandoned, Cohen highlighted his opposition to some of the developments in the field. Based on his view of pragmatism, he rejected one-size-fits-all approaches and refused to pledge allegiance to any "master plan" (Ferrell, 1990: 232). Cohen's goal, however, was not to dismantle the criminological enterprise. Instead, he sought to disrupt it and wake criminologists up from what he perceived as dogmatic slumber. This bears some similarity to Young's (2011) call to reinvigorate the criminological imagination. In some ways, these calls have been answered. For example, the American Society of Criminology is the flagship of mainstream conferences in the field. A perusal of the various membership divisions demonstrates that there is a very high level of diversity and critical thought within the field. In 2023, there were special divisions devoted to Convict Criminology, Critical Criminology and Social Justice, Feminist Criminology, People of Color and Crime, and Queer Criminology.

In addition, well-established branches of criminological thought, such as constitutive and cultural criminology (Ferrell et al., 2008; Henry & Milovanovic, 1996), have emerged that challenge the foundations of mainstream criminology and attempt to reconceive the nature of the criminological enterprise. In our first collaboration, we suggested that mainstream criminological theories themselves can be critically repurposed and used to achieve a greater understanding of problems that emerge from policy reform and shape regulations and bureaucracy (Wheeldon & Heidt, 2007). In many cases, this approach can be used to justify further reform of the system and pursue greater diversity and inclusivity. For example, as we will demonstrate later, rational choice theories are helpful in understanding obstacles those attempting to expand legal cannabis markets face. These stem from efforts to impose control and result in overregulation based on the views of a small group of drug policy experts whose personal experience with drugs is quite limited. It is past time to invite more people, including those who use drugs, into policy discussions.

Deliberative Democracy and Drug Policy

A stable and growing evidence base challenges many of the myths propagated by those pursuing cannabis prohibition. An uncomfortable truth to be acknowledged is how ideological beliefs about prohibition often align with anti-immigrant, anti-Black, and anti-youth interests and agendas. As we will explore, the role of morality in policy around inebriating substances, such as opium and alcohol, is a reminder of the maxim that while history may not repeat itself, it often rhymes. For some, the fact that credible research has undermined many of the claims for continued cannabis prohibition is enough to shape future policy. This optimistic account holds that one simply collects the relevant data and presents it to elected leaders, who read it in full and then enact sensible, evidence-based policies. This rarely happens. As we have documented (Wheeldon & Heidt, 2012), criminologists know all too well that policies that tend to reduce crime are often ignored in favor of policies that symbolically uphold simplistic views of law and order.

We argue that if cannabis policy is to move forward, expanding democratic decision-making on drug policy is necessary. Whatever the potential for more participatory approaches that involve an "expansive, organic deliberative process, that allows for messier discussion" (Ritter, 2021: 126), meaningful dialogue requires finding ways to stay grounded. This means contending with how normative preferences and structural positions shape policymaking in irrational and unrepresentative ways (Stevens & Zampini, 2018). One solution is to integrate insights from people who use cannabis in policymaking explicitly. Another is to ensure future policies are based on engagement with the communities in which cannabis reforms are to be implemented. This is especially important given the pragmatic turn within criminology that serves as both a challenge and an opportunity (Wheeldon, 2015). We present a means to understand and connect the work of Jurgen

Habermas and Richard Rorty and make the most of their equitable, inclusive, and transformative views of decision-making based on data, deliberation, and debate.

If Cohen was suspicious of the potential of meaningful reform, Jurgen Habermas is more optimistic. For Habermas, people can reach a consensus, whatever their differences as individuals, cultures, and experiences. Such harmony requires fashioning procedures and processes that allow ego-free compromise and a commitment to moving forward together. Decision-making through good faith exchange and deliberation among actors who are committed to policies for the public good can be achieved through the "forceless force" of conversation (Habermas, 1996: 21). However, if communication can serve as a meaningful means of engaging by replacing coercion with persuasion (Kilanowski, 2021: 9), it is essential to ask who is invited to participate.

Richard Rorty (1994) offers one way to understand how cannabis policy in most countries remains damaging, intrusive, and out of step with public opinion. The success of cannabis reformers is based in part on their ability to reframe prohibitionist ideas and express them in new and powerful ways (Rorty, 1998). This can be connected to culture, media, and music (Heidt & Wheeldon, 2021). Thus, to achieve cannabis reform, Rorty (2006) advises that we

> open ourselves to conversation of all sorts, but perhaps especially to those who expand our sense of human possibility. These include novelists, historians, poets, ethnographers, and philosophers who can help us "reprogram ourselves—to update our moral software."

Cannabis research must, of course, continue. Evidence must be accrued through the replication of studies in different countries and contexts. Local variation must be respected, and research that makes the most of the contributions, insights, and concerns of people who use cannabis and other insiders should become the norm, not the exception. However, evidence alone is not enough. As we present in the chapters to come, liberalizing cannabis policy is likely to be met with updated moral panics, old and new forms of stigma, and resistance from police and others who benefit from existing arrangements.

As an antidote, we revisit what Cohen (1985: 252) called "moral pragmatism." Consistent with a new approach to public criminology, we set out a model of engagement that makes use of visual criminology, embraces irony, and uses social media to challenge misinformation and, when necessary, mock the unconscious moralizing associated with drug mythologies. This requires first cataloging the lessons of international cannabis liberalization and confronting older and otherwise well-meaning scholars who continue to repeat nonsense about cannabis, risk, and punitive drug policies. It means engaging younger scholars, who must chart a course through a maze in which evidence suggests one thing and experts in the field advocate another. To aid these conversations and debates, it is essential to think about how new approaches to data-sharing and online engagement can assist this work.

Assumptions, Concepts, and Organization

There are dangers when attempting to reimagine and rework a topic such as cannabis. Despite the years of research and hundreds of references that underpin this book, keeping up with the growing literature while recognizing past studies was nearly impossible. We predict those well versed in this area are likely to be annoyed as often as they are elated with our efforts. Despite our focus on the global dimensions of cannabis control, there is no doubt we will have missed some scholars, significant research, and essential international developments. Likewise, for those who have spent much of their career working in this area, some may feel that by revisiting older arguments, insights, and examples, we are crashing through an open door, fighting old battles that have *essentially been won*. We respectfully disagree.

Cannabis prohibition remains a costly, foolish, international endeavor that has done incalculable damage to individuals, families, and communities. If so many criminologists, drug researchers, and activists think they have won this battle, then it has been, at best, a pyrrhic victory. Standing by as society forces people to admit consuming cannabis is some sort of weakness or moral failure to avoid the specter of a criminal record is something about which few should be proud. Building a career on research grants designed to perpetuate such techniques is shameful. This sort of denial must not continue.

There are several criminological questions to be addressed. Central to our view is that liberalizing cannabis without carefully thinking through how to disrupt a century of prohibitionist thinking is unlikely to achieve most predefined policy goals. As such, this book is based on several assumptions and a specific view of the criminological imagination and is organized to develop a coherent argument through nonlinear means. Our approach unfolds through three sections, each of which examines aspects of cannabis policy and criminological thought. Throughout the book, key ideas, people, and events are introduced and discussed and then reappear later. This layered approach allows for more detail and nuance and embraces an iterative storytelling style. From cannabis to crime and panics to policymaking, understanding cannabis, its criminalization, and subsequent normalization defy an orderly chronological approach. We argue cannabis legalization and regulation are both inevitable and fraught with peril.

Assumptions

Our approach is based on three problem-defining assumptions. First, stigma remains around cannabis use and feeds into, and is fed by, the prohibitionist tendencies of the past. These harm people who use cannabis, their families, and communities around the world by relying on deeply problematic means to serve moralistic ends. As Ritter (2021) notes, drug policy has historically been shaped by the questions of morality, ideology, and assumptive virtue. The underlying normative and ethical positions about drugs shaped and continue to influence policy in elusive ways. These positions are nurtured by groups within societies whose values and preferences align with those in government. Cannabis policy reflects perhaps the best example of how shifting norms influence governing policy. Yet, mountains of evidence have not succeeded in undoing the decades of damage associated with the drug war. We believe if cannabis liberalization does not consider the persistent power of prohibition, it is unlikely to succeed in reducing the stigma related to cannabis-based contact with the criminal justice system.

Our second assumption builds on the first. Continuing to involve law enforcement in the policing of cannabis leads to racially unequal outcomes and increasingly deadly encounters. It is a waste of resources, a perversion of policing's mission, and erodes public trust and community relations. As we will demonstrate, even where cannabis has been legalized and regulated, police contact for cannabis-related incidents disproportionately impacts people of color. Policing based on drug war tactics appears to increase police brutality and shootings, even as little progress is made in reducing street-level drug activity (Baum, 1996; Tonry, 1994). Recent high-profile police killings of Black men and boys occur within a police culture rooted in "warrior culture," in which aggressive police tactics have been used to further racial divisions and alienate communities (Fagan et al., 2009). Reform means establishing cannabis possession limits and de-emphasizing the role of the police. The challenge of undoing a century of practice means embracing greater accountability around stops, diversions, and arrests.

Third, and finally, diversion is likely to remain a crucial part of decriminalization for both political and practical reasons. While some view forced treatment in lieu of a criminal record as progressive drug reform, this approach to diversion obscures the essential contradictions and hypocrisies at the heart of prohibition. However, there are alternatives to coercive care offered by for-profit treatment programs and entrepreneurial addiction counselors. New and existing community-based organizations can provide those referred for "problem cannabis use" with access to services, resources, and community connections. Based on existing models of community engagement, access to these types of social support can be offered but never mandated.

Such an approach means explicitly abandoning outdated ideas about addiction, crime, and the false promise of prohibition based on the idea that people who use cannabis are "sick" and need to be "treated" (Szalavitz, 2015b; Szasz, 2007; Taylor et al., 2016). Our model is based on the research of psychologists and neuroscientists who specialize in, and have experience with, drug use and addiction (Buadze et al., 2010; Hart, 2017; Ksir & Hart, 2016; Lewis, 2015). Engaging those who need support, manifested through cannabis use that negatively impacts their lives, is consistent with desistance research and life course criminology (Bushway & Uggens, 2021). However, the profoundly unjust practice of continuing to criminalize cannabis and then using the threat of criminal prosecution to coerce treatment must be abandoned. Addiction must be defined and understood in far more nuanced ways.

Beyond these assumptions, another issue looms. This centers on to what extent criminologists are willing to revisit their own assumptions and beliefs about cannabis and consider the consequences of their silence on this issue. The limited dangers represented by cannabis use can no longer justify the political posturing, aggressive policing, and coercive treatment that we have described. Instead, criminologists can support reform by exploring the stigma and shame foisted on people who use drugs and the invisible mechanisms of control that defy normalization. They can continue to document and publicize the failed drug war and its unequal and extrinsic and intrinsic costs. Indeed, the negative consequences associated with these policies extend to police officers themselves. Caught in a web of nonsensical laws and procedures that harm more than they help, a growing chorus of police are demanding support to engage in practices that can tackle serious, violent crime (Law Enforcement Action Partnership n.d.).

Key Concepts

In a book focused on revisiting Stan Cohen's contributions, it is essential to show our work. Some of the concepts we consider are directly derived from Cohen (1985). In this way, we seek to avoid what Cohen (1985: 249) describes as "leaps of fashion [which] are classic examples of what Jacoby terms 'social amnesia.'" As we move from prison to the community and from punishment toward treatment, we seek to recognize the history of these "reforms" and how the past shapes the future in unexpected ways. These include worries about social control, coercion, and the paradoxes which inform efforts to promote reform. Others have built on Cohen's work on social control and pointed us in new directions. For example, in Chapters 2 and 3, we update labeling, stigma, and moral panic, concepts that Cohen previously considered. Their application to our work on cannabis and criminology fits in many ways. It diverges in others.

Some concepts we claim as our own, even as we attempt to locate them in previous work. This includes our focus on differentiating eras of cannabis research and privileging those conducted in jurisdictions where cannabis is legal in Chapter 6. This can avoid the unfortunate conflation of the psychopharmacological risks for people who use cannabis with the risks associated with engaging with illegal markets (Goldstein, 1985). Although we believe our effort to link expanded tolerance and the need to regulate aversion within cannabis policy in Chapter 7 is unique, it can be seen as an extension of the work in chapter 7 of *Visions of Social Control* (Cohen, 1985). Finally, while our application of polymorphic governance to cannabis regulation in Chapter 8 is not wholly new (Aaronson & Rothschild-Elyassi, 2021), we embrace a pragmatic orientation and apply a racial justice lens to explore specific cannabis policy ideas.

While we adapt and update some concepts from his original work, we explicitly engage with several key concepts detailed by Cohen (1985). The first is pragmatism. Cohen (1985: 238) distinguishes this from "technicism: the relative loss of interest in matters of causation, the endless quest for 'what works? [and] the invention of new ways to calibrate pain.'" Instead, Cohen suggests the intellectual's job is to serve as an adversary and to

> provide neither a handbook of practical recommendations on the one hand nor a set of lofty political platitudes on the other. The point is to clarify choices and values. And also to search our own stories for the same type

of hidden agendas, deep structures and domain assumptions we so readily detect in the stories which others tell.

(Cohen 1985: 238)

We align ourselves with this idea, even as we accept the fact that we are unlikely to achieve it consistently.

The second key concept is, to be honest, about how to respond to the failures of the past. When faced with the inevitable disappointments, criminologists and others working to reform systems of social control, reduce human suffering, and protect human rights may seek to clarify their own role. Cohen offers three views (1985: 243):

(1) We were right—we still agree with our original values, preferences and ideologies, but "they" didn't understand us. The problem is implementation: the world is a complicated place and either bureaucratic imperatives or professional self-interest will mess things up.
(2) We blew it—yet again. Benevolent intentions are suspect and the whole business of doing good has to be re-evaluated.
(3) We told you so. This sort of "tinkering" is bound to fail, things are always getting worse and nothing much good can come from this type of society; it is in "the order of things."

While many remain attached to the first view, some may veer toward the second and even land in the third when they read about a British child strip-searched at her school in 2021. Police engaged in an invasive search without parental consent or a responsible adult present, all because a teacher reported: "smelling cannabis" (CHSCP, 2022). In this case, no drugs were found, and the student has since sought therapy for self-harming behavior (CHSCP, 2022). Our hope, despite the many disappointments, is based on a third key concept from Cohen (1985).

By framing the ideological structures and individual choices of those who work within the system as "visions," Cohen (1985: 230) leaves us with

a sample of the images and visions yielded by those contrasting modes of control. First, there is inclusion, with its metaphors of penetration, integration and absolution, its apparatus or bleepers, screens and trackers, its utopia of the invisible controlling city. Then there is exclusion, with its metaphors of banishment, isolation and separation, its apparatus of walls, reservations, and barriers. Its utopia is the visibly purified city.

For Cohen, the history of social control is a choice between exclusion and inclusion. However, this leads to a paradox. While exclusion is merciless and cruel, inclusionary policies can inadvertently lead to the establishment of new forms of exclusion by attempting to normalize people by classifying and problematizing their behavior further.

This paradox animates this book. Instead of dwelling in the pessimistic place that leaves reformers, we seek to build on inclusion by linking it to calls for more expansive approaches to the development of cannabis policies. This includes Cohen's moral pragmatism, Habermasian notions of deliberative democracy, and Rorty's view that the ability to redescribe can open people's eyes and ultimately fashion a more just world (Rorty, 1979: 9). There is power and purpose in confronting past justifications. If different visions of cannabis control can coexist, then we seek the one that maximizes personal liberty, minimizes state intrusions, and provides a means for policy to be based on the views and experiences of those most affected by laws seeking to control cannabis.

Organization of the Book

In addition to framing cannabis, criminology, and social control, Part I of this book examines the history of cannabis policy. The linkages between morality and policymaking are essential to appreciate the moral renegotiation that goes along with legalizing and regulating a substance criminalized for nearly a century. We trace laws against cannabis to prohibitions targeting opium and alcohol that were based on a mixture of local interests and international pressures. No country has embraced cannabis prohibition with the same zeal as the United States, yet in countries like the United Kingdom and Canada, India, South Africa, and Egypt, similar interests emerged. International conventions created a uniform global legal framework to pursue a global drug war (Collins, 2021) and influenced foreign policies pursued as part of the Cold War. While we connect cannabis prohibition to morality, criminalization, labeling, and stigmatization, cannabis liberalization can be connected to normalization. Although the broad movement toward cannabis decriminalization has led to legalization in some jurisdictions, shame associated with using cannabis remains.

Part I of this book concludes by considering the role moral panics have had on research and policy creation. International conventions expanded negative state-based societal attitudes around cannabis and justified punitive national laws worldwide. This ideological zeal continues today. We argue the potential for responsible regulation in the future is hampered by the role of moral panics. We revisit moral panics in sociology and criminology and consider core assumptions, examples, and critiques. We combine this view with an analysis of how a media landscape primed to support and intensify errors can lead to participatory disinformation. Feedback loops allow misinformation to become accepted as fact and provide a means for those advocating prohibition to influence public debate and undermine responsible cannabis regulation (Heidt & Wheeldon, 2021).

Part II re-examines the legal renegotiation that goes along with policy liberalization. We explore cannabis policy based on five regulatory models, including public safety, public health, cannabis as medicine, consumer cannabis, and racial justice. We compare countries and cannabis policies and link existing approaches from Australia, Canada, the Netherlands, Portugal, the United Kingdom, Uruguay, and the United States to these regulatory models. Next, we examine a framework focused on the contagious nature of social control (Cohen, 1985). This refers to formal ways in which the criminal justice system intrudes in the lives of people and the informal mechanisms which expand interference through "wider, stronger and different nets" of social control (Austin & Krisberg, 1981: 165).

Part II concludes by considering three eras of research. Early research was based on structural limitations, problematic assumptions, and inadequate data. While this research fails most methodological tests of reliability and validity, recent research in jurisdictions where cannabis is legal demonstrates that once accepted, findings cannot be replicated. We outline contemporary research from the post-prohibition period to show how emergent research challenges past findings in consistent ways. The era of legal cannabis has opened the door to more nuanced examinations of cannabis through the lens of public safety, public health, medicinal cannabis, consumer cannabis, and racial justice. Under every regulatory model of cannabis, Cohen's concerns (1985) remain relevant.

Part III of the book examines the consequences that moral and legal renegotiation have on societies and further describes the process of cultural renegotiation. This section considers a new model of responsible decriminalization based on the lessons and limits of cannabis control outlined in Part II. We argue for expanding tolerance and regulating aversion. This includes deprioritizing the policing of cannabis and focusing on serious and violent crime, while providing a means to refer those engaging in problem use to community panels and programs. By positioning these measures as voluntary and based on nonjudgmental engagement, we seek to move away from the coercive-treatment models that are often linked to cannabis decriminalization. Finally, we consider how to transition from decriminalization to various models of legalization. The challenge of managing state monopolies in Uruguay, on the one hand, or the messiness of provincial variations in Canada, on the other, demonstrates how models of cannabis liberalization are evolving. We present a "readiness-to-regulate" framework and return to the importance of including the insights and understanding of cannabis insiders.

Our advocacy for expanding community-based services for those for whom cannabis use appears to be related to other social, emotional, or psychological strains is based on support and not coercion. We are deeply skeptical of the value of justice actors attempting to control people's choice of intoxicants by the threat of a criminal record. Framed in this way, we agree that cannabis policy should move away from moralistic policymaking and acknowledge the harms that occur when states interfere with that liberty. However, designing cannabis regulatory regimes without assessing a community's interests, concerns, and fears is unlikely to minimize the harm caused by a century of prohibition.

While the stigma around drug use has been reduced, it has seeped into our collective unconscious in ways that are difficult to untangle. Expanding tolerance, de-emphasizing police, and engaging communities create conditions for assessing a jurisdiction's "readiness to regulate" cannabis. We believe this approach is consistent with Seddon & Floodgate's (2020: 129) observations that

> That question ultimately is how can we design regulation so that we constitute cannabis markets that are not only rights-protecting and justice enhancing but which also promote human flourishing and well-being? The sustainability of those markets, in the context of our planet's finite and depleted resources, should now also become a much higher priority in policy thinking. In the twenty-first century, we need to develop an approach to cannabis regulation that recognizes that we now live in the Anthropocene epoch.

Conclusion

Cannabis prohibition has influenced the criminological enterprise in North America and around the world. The criminalization of cannabis and the demonization of those who use it shaped the laws that govern society to the behavior of police, prosecutors, judges, correctional officers, and others associated with the criminal justice system. Studying cannabis prohibition and control demands, we ask troubling questions about law creation. It highlights a profoundly anti-science orientation that has undermined public policy and driven the development of ever higher cannabis strains and extremely potent cannabis products (e.g., butane hash oil, dab wax, and shatter) with which the public, and even experts and veteran users, have little experience. Ironically, some byzantine regulatory regimes and ill-conceived taxation strategies have preserved, rather than disrupted, black and grey cannabis markets.[6] Indeed, some policies may do as much harm as simply tolerating the unregulated practices of the past.

The proliferation of regulatory experiments extends to reform initiatives in Europe, North and South America, Africa, Australia, and elsewhere (Decorte et al., 2020; Seddon & Floodgate, 2020). Understanding existing approaches and exploring emerging efforts to regulate cannabis requires engaging with the history of prohibition, including the religious, racist, and international dynamics that informed, propelled, and ultimately sustained prohibition. In many ways, current efforts to decriminalize, legalize, and regulate cannabis seek to right the wrongs instituted a century ago. However, before we can envision how best to move toward responsible regulation, we must examine several underexplored concepts central to our view. These include how a history of prohibition informs the stain of stigma around cannabis use and how normalization is complicated by persistent moral panics, research failings, and the expansion of carceral control in communities around the world.

Our road map toward cannabis regulation is based on a responsible research program on cannabis and criminology, drawing on emergent imaginative impulses. This requires engaging with five key ideas. The first is that cannabis and its prohibition have intersected with criminology in a myriad of ways. Part of the goal of this book is to untangle and identify these crossroads. The second idea is that findings from existing cannabis research and studies on adverse outcomes associated with cannabis use need to be drastically reconsidered. Indeed, the problem with much of the existing research on cannabis exists for research on other drugs. These issues are significant when inquiries based on limited methodological frames are used to perpetuate the myths of the past, especially when the consequences of punitive drug policies cannot be separated from both the explicit and unconscious racism present in society.

The third idea is that research would benefit from better acknowledging and incorporating the experiences of people who use drugs and other subcultural insiders. This is not a new idea (Becker, 1963; Copes et al., 2018; 2019; 2021; Greer & Ritter, 2019; 2020; Young, 1971). However, this area deserves much more attention and detailed examples. In addition to efforts to contribute to our understanding of cannabis culture (Sandberg, 2012b), cannabis activists, dispensary owners, cannabis industry workers, craft and medicinal growers, and other insiders can offer essential insights about emergent questions around regulation.

Fourth, we argue that the responsible regulation of cannabis is based on credible research and proven international practices. This might involve pursuing models that prize tolerance, de-emphasize the policing of cannabis, and engage communities to support people who may have problematic use patterns.

Fifth and finally, the justice system has evolved in ways that justify interference and intrusions into the lives of Black and Brown people. Whether this can be attributed to moralistic concerns to protect white people or a desire to criminalize and control nonwhite people is irrelevant. The inevitable moral panics around cannabis liberalization will bring with them both explicit and implicit racial tropes. We argue cannabis researchers and scholars should embrace new approaches to public criminology. These combine the incorporation of visual techniques to information-sharing, the role of irony on the internet, and developing a more strategic understanding of the uses and abuses of social media. This will require reinvigorating the criminological imagination, rethinking scholarship, and providing more pathways for criminologists, who refuse to sit idle as policy is made without the input of those to whom it will apply.

Notes

1. For instance, in 2022, U. President Joe Biden signed an executive order to pardon citizens and lawful permanent residents convicted of simple cannabis possession under federal law and DC statute. However, his administration has failed to push the SAFE Banking Act in Congress, which would allow legal cannabis businesses to access financial support, investment, and protections. See Yakouwitz (2022). Likewise, despite signing the Medical Marijuana and Cannabidiol Research Expansion Act in 2022, Biden has yet to make tangible moves to reschedule cannabis, which remains a Schedule 1 drug under the Controlled Substances Act (CSA). While seemingly arcane, in practice, this means legal cannabis companies

cannot deduct typical businesses expenses on their taxes, file for federal bankruptcy protections, qualify for federal agricultural programs, and qualify for the typical services provided by many banks (Congress of the United States, 2022).
2. See https://www.nytimes.com/2019/08/29/health/marijuana-pregnancy-surgeon-general.html#:~:text=Dr.,risks%20because%20of%20their%20potency.&text=The%20United%20States%20surgeon%20general,women%20and%20their%20developing%20babies.
3. In the United States, some examples of these myths are described in programs including https://www.co.berks.pa.us/Dept/DA/Pages/Marijuana-Diversion-Program.aspx, Center County District Attorney's Office (n.d.), and Oliphant (n.d.). Some programs, like this one in Texas, note the problems of stigma and the limited public safety benefit from prosecuting cannabis possession. Participation in programming is still required (Ogg, n.d.). In the United Kingdom, an overview with a decidedly upbeat view of diversion is given by Transform Drug Policy Foundation (n.d.). In Australia, a useful overview of diversion and the consequences of noncompliance is given by ADF (n.d.).
4. For an overview of this work, see Hudak (2020b).
5. See https://www.congress.gov/bill/117th-congress/house-bill/3617.
6. There is no universally accepted definition of the grey market. In general, black market refers to dealers or suppliers who are associated with gangs and organized crime groups that sell cannabis alongside other drugs. The grey market refers to those who grow cannabis on a smaller, but still illegal, scale, for example, "Mom and Pop" grow ops, growers who divert small amounts to the illegal market. https://www.cbc.ca/news/canada/toronto/joint-ventures-black-market-1.4528840.

2
Criminalization, Stigma, and Normalization

Introduction

Cannabis is one of the most widely used drugs in the world. However, the stigma associated with cannabis use that has existed for nearly a century continues today (Erickson et al., 2010; Rotermann, 2020). Efforts to prohibit the use of cannabis are at least 200 years old. For instance, authorities in the Arab world once regarded the use of hashish as a loathsome habit associated with the Sufis, an economically and socially disadvantaged sector of Muslim society (Beweley-Taylor et al., 2014). Concerns about cannabis re-emerged in the 1890s.[1] However, it wasn't until 1911 that early efforts to prohibit cannabis emerged in the United States. Spurred by racist concerns about Indian immigrants, Black musicians, and Mexican migrants, cannabis prohibition followed efforts to control substances such as opium and alcohol. These efforts were instigated and aided by the moral reform movement, which preached abstinence from all intoxicating substances and played an essential role in defining drug use as a problem, perpetuating ethnic stereotypes and antipathy and creating the infrastructure from which cannabis prohibition was realized.

The criminalization of cannabis has served multiple goals. Early efforts to regulate cannabis involved weaponizing moral reformers' concerns, nativism, and racist attitudes to develop laws and expand informal and formal social control. Prohibition has persisted based on anxieties framed in moral terms (Fisher, 2021) which were used to justify policies that attempted to limit the role of young people, especially Black people, during the civil rights era. Criminalization has been embraced by governments of every political persuasion and was once one of the most widely accepted, reputable, and legitimate government policies of the twentieth century (Levine, 2003). However, the times, they are a-changing.

Beginning with the Netherlands in the 1970s, countries started to chart their own course on cannabis. From Portugal to Canada and Uruguay to Germany, numerous countries and American states have begun a moral-legal renegotiation of the rules and regulations surrounding cannabis use. Understanding this process means revisiting concepts such as stigma, including different types and their interrelationships. It also means investigating the normalization thesis in depth, including research examining the normalization of cannabis among specific groups and subcultures (Parker, 2005; Parker et al., 1998, 2002). In this chapter, we argue these concepts help explain how cannabis was criminalized and why stigma remains, even where cannabis is legal (Reid, 2020). As criminalization has been gradually reversed in practice, policy, and law, new issues have emerged. To confront the future of cannabis liberalization, the roots of morality-based policymaking must be uncovered and interrogated.

Stigma, Normalization, and Cannabis

Cannabis and its use mark the "most consequential case of social construction of the twentieth century" (Newhart & Dolphin, 2019: 241). It was socially constructed as a threat to mental health, the White race, law and order, and social stability. As we argued in Chapter 1, cannabis represents an example of moral, legal, and cultural renegotiation. Cannabis policy touches on identity politics, culture wars, social movements, ecological concerns, and global economies. In criminological terms, cannabis connects ideology, policing, and addiction studies. It may represent a warning to those who embrace simplistic views of evidence-based policymaking. Under the guise of community safety, cannabis has justified criminalizing nonconformists and done significant damage to communities of color based on racial and ethnic blind spots that have only recently re-emerged in the public consciousness. Two broad concepts are essential to the history of cannabis.

The first is stigma. In his classic theory of stigmatization, Goffman (1963) states that stigma is more than just a negative attribute or behavior but rather a process of societal reaction that can spoil a person's identity. First, "normal" members label people as "abnormal." If the "abnormal" person accepts and internalizes the label, it may impact their future behavior. More specifically, labeled individuals may begin to perceive themselves as societal outcasts or outsiders, thus freeing them to engage more fully with their deviant identity

(Lemert, 1951). One type of stigma arises from associations with race, religion, and nation. For example, whether immigrants were Black, Chinese, German, Indian, Irish, Mexican, or German, the prohibition of alcohol, cannabis, and opium all involved criminalizing parts of immigrant cultures (Fisher, 2021). Another type of stigma relevant here focused on character-based shortcomings such as dishonesty and poor self-control, which could be inferred from a history of mental illness, radical political beliefs, or drug addiction.

The second broad concept is normalization. The concept of normalization can be used as an interpretive tool for understanding the growing acceptance of cannabis (Newhart & Dolphin, 2019). The notion of drug use normalization truly emerged in the 1960s. However, references to this concept were made as far back as 1938. For example, sociologist Alfred R. Lindesmith (1938b: 593) argued that theories of drug use "tend to be moralistic rather than scientific" and argued that drug use was associated with cultural milieu, especially the culture of the group to rationalize and situate motivation for drug use (Blackman, 2004). One way to understand this work was through language, cultural norms, and social practices (Lindesmith, 1938a: 264–278). Since 1990, the legalization of cannabis has proceeded along several paths. According to research conducted by Parker and colleagues (1998, 2002), during the 1990s, cannabis and other recreational drugs became normalized amongst adolescents and young people (i.e., fourteen to twenty-two years of age) in Britain and Scotland.

Parker and his colleagues (2002) found considerable support for the five leading indicators of normalization, including increase in availability, increase in accessibility, increased rates of drug-trying, more recent and regular use, and growing social accommodation for "sensible" recreational drug use. Since the original study, Parker (2005) has identified a sixth dimension of normalization known as state response and anti-drug strategies. This dimension refers to changes in state responses that reflect this process. As we explore throughout the book, this includes defining formal distinctions between problematic and non-problematic drug use, encouraging responsible drug use, and replacing scare tactics and inflammatory rhetoric with public health and fact-based prevention strategies. Stigma and normalization have informed cannabis policy and oriented and ordered other historical developments. This process has shaped the criminal justice system over time in profound and sometimes unexpected ways (Dufton, 2017a).

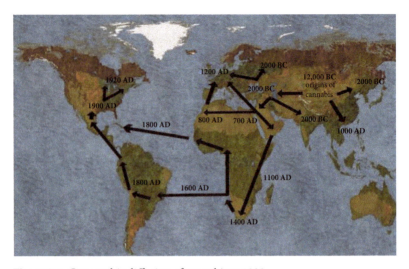

Figure 2.1 Geographic diffusion of cannabis to 1920
Source: Author creation based on Warf (2014).

Before the Devil's Lettuce

Cannabis is a genus of flowering plants in the family Cannabaceae. As nearly every academic exploration of this subject notes, it has been cultivated, traded, and consumed for various reasons and in numerous forms throughout human history (Beweley-Taylor et al., 2014; Booth, 2003; Mills, 2003; Seddon & Floodgate, 2020). Its geographic spread from Asia to the world is linked to its diffusion along early trading routes, later through the slave trade, and finally as part of the modern global economy (see Figure 2.1 for a depiction of this process). The international popularity of cannabis can be understood by the variety of monikers that exist to describe it. These include

> "ma" in China; Arabic "kif"; "bhang, charas, and ganja" in India; and "dagga" in Southern Africa. Likewise, the Sanskrit word khanap gave rise to the "kanab" in Farsi, "kannabis" in Greek, "konopyla" in Russia, "cainb" in Gaelic, German "henf," Dutch "hennep," Swedish "hampa," and English "hemp," although in contemporary usage it has been called pot, grass, and weed.
>
> (Warf, 2014: 417)

As Seddon & Floodgate (2020) note, the origins of cannabis can be traced to Central Asia and the regions known today as Tajikistan, Kyrgyzstan, and the Xinjiang region in Western China (Russo, 2007).

The cannabis plant was used initially as medicine, food, fuel, and fiber. Hemp fibers have been used for millennia to make rope, canvas (from Greek *kannabis*), clothing, paper, shoes, and sails (Booth, 2003). However, as early as 2000 BCE, people cultivated cannabis strains to make the most of their psychoactive effects. David Courtwright (2002) charts a 500-year-long "psychoactive revolution" in which drugs have steadily increased in availability, potency, and popularity. Drug use has long been tied to cultural perceptions, misperceptions, and the politics of moral regulation. Cannabis has long been used for medicine, recreation, religious, and spiritual practices in Asia and the Middle East.

Over several thousand years, cannabis spread from Western China to all corners of the world (Warf, 2014). The first phase developed slowly over millennia. Cannabis spread along early trading routes like the Silk Roads, through various conquests and invasions, and later via migration (Seddon & Floodgate, 2020: 4). In the seventeenth century, Americans grew hemp for rope, sails, and clothing. In 1619, the Virginia Assembly passed legislation requiring every farmer to grow hemp that could be exchanged as legal tender in Pennsylvania, Virginia, and Maryland (Frontline, n.d.). Domestic production occurred throughout the colonies until after the Civil War, when imports and other materials replaced hemp. In the late nineteenth century, cannabis became a popular ingredient in many medicinal products and was sold openly in public pharmacies.[2]

The second phase is associated with the colonial period. Under British rule, medical personnel of that administration began to study the reported therapeutic benefits. For example, *The Bengal Dispensatory and Companion to Pharmacopoeia* (O'Shaughnessy, 1842) reported findings from Indian doctors who recognized the value of cannabis use for opiate withdrawal, appetite stimulation, and analgesia. This book played a significant role in legitimizing cannabis as a treatment option for various illnesses, and cannabis became popular as a medicine in the 1850s and 1860s (Booth, 2003: 75). In addition, several medical journals published articles describing cannabis as a treatment for a broad array of symptoms and illnesses (Hand et al., 2016). As a result, the therapeutic application of cannabis grew in popularity between 1850 and 1900.

In the 1850s, a group of well-known authors and poets including Charles Baudelaire, Alexander Dumas, and Victor Hugo formed the "Club des

Haschichins" ("Club of the Hashish-Eaters") in Paris. The club celebrated recreational cannabis consumption. At the same time, the British and American Pharmacopeia suggested its utility as a sedative and anticonvulsant (Collins, 2020a). Its popularity in North America is often attributed to reports that Queen Victoria's physician, Sir John Russell Reynolds, prescribed it to relieve menstrual cramps (Mills, 2003). Reynolds published an article in *The Lancet* in 1890 which declared that cannabis was "one of the most valuable medicines we possess" (Booth, 2003: 114). In addition, numerous patent medicines produced in Britain and the United States containing cannabis claimed to cure many ailments. As a result, they enjoyed a degree of popularity and enthusiasm from the medical community (Hand et al., 2016).

Starting in the 1900s, several factors caused the early medical use of cannabis to fall from favor. Hand and colleagues (2016: 389) suggest that in North America and Europe, difficulties in determining an exact dosage that would apply to all patients, the inability to inject cannabis directly, and the rise of alternative drugs led to its decline. In addition, its reputation suffered from systematic inaccuracies in documented insane asylum cases in India, Egypt, and other countries, where cannabis use was part of the local culture. The belief that cannabis use could result in "moral insanity" resulted from the bureaucratic necessity of filling in an instigating factor for patients sent to asylums (Rushton, 2018). Staff attributed cannabis use when patients were found unresponsive, incoherent, or otherwise unable to communicate. Moral reformers amplified these concerns by linking moral insanity with ungodly living.

Temperance, Inebriation, and a Godly Society

The criminalization of cannabis cannot be easily separated from the prohibition of other substances. While the temperance movement predates drug prohibition, both were influenced by Protestant calls for a universal standard of sobriety in keeping with their concern for moral reform and the creation of a godly society. Moral criticism of alcohol emerged based on the biblical tradition of preaching against the sin of drunkenness and advocating restraint (Merrill, 1988). Though the Old and New Testaments contain positive depictions of alcohol, the Bible regularly attacks drunkenness, excess, and intemperance. This has informed a recurrent call for moral reform within the Church (Bernard, 1991: 338–342). The first global effort to restrict drugs focused on opium.

Restricting Opium

Before the 1868 Pharmacy Act, which restricted the sale of opium to pharmacists, opium was widely available, typically purchased at the grocer (Seddon, 2007). At the time, opium's uses ranged from toothaches and bruises to coughs and diarrhea. The working class used it as a stimulant before going to work, and mothers found laudanum (a form of opium) useful for quieting babies and escaping reality (Brian, 1994). It was a profitable business for Britain. After Britain captured Calcutta in 1756, the cultivation of poppies for opium was actively encouraged. The East India Company was established for trading and enjoyed a monopoly over business relations with Asia. The British greatly benefited from trade activity in which they exported opium from India to China in exchange for profits and luxury goods (Canadian Drug Policy Coalition, n.d.). More importantly, it allowed the British to offset the cost of imperialism and brought stability to their colonial rule in India (Mccaffery, 2019).

The first modern European law for the regulation of drugs was in the United Kingdom. The UK Pharmacy Act of 1868 was the culmination of efforts to restrict opiate use in the mid-1800s and was based on professional self-interest and class and racial tensions (Ng, 2016). While opium was "respectable" for the middle class to use, its spread to the working class caused concerns about opium abuse contributing to their "degeneracy." Later, public sentiment, driven by xenophobia, associated the drug with Chinese opium dens. In addition to general concerns, specific worries existed about the risk to White women, who might be corrupted and sexually exploited by non-White foreign men (Berridge & Edward, 1987). Mccaffrey (2019: 36–39) suggests the United States began to understand the value of global narcotics control when it acquired the Philippines in 1898 after defeating the Spanish in the Spanish–American War.

As the United States attempted to solidify its hold over the Philippines, Filipino nationalists waged a costly guerilla campaign against US troops. Some suggested the Filipino's unwillingness to succumb to Westernization was because of high levels of opium consumption. American Protestant missionaries worked to convert the population, in part by tackling moral failings associated with opium use. Taylor notes (1967: 309):

> opium consumption in the islands thus offered the United States both a challenge and opportunity to surpass other Western nations with possessions in the Orient in discharging the responsibilities of "White Man's Burden."

Sensationalized news reports of widespread opium use in China led missionaries from North America to move from the Philippines to China to advance their narrative about the evils of opium smoking (Lodwick, 2009: 181). Since opium addicts were inherently untrustworthy, they were banned from church membership. With so many Chinese automatically excluded from the possibility of conversion, missionaries began to campaign against the drug. These crusades took for granted that White Protestant culture was superior to all others. As temperance became aligned with Protestant culture, this specific form of White supremacy helped fuel the oppression of immigrant cultures.

In the United States and Canada, opium prohibition began in the West. Inspired by anti-Chinese sentiment, San Francisco instituted the first known anti-narcotics law in the nation, an ordinance to suppress opium dens. The California state legislature adopted a similar provision in 1881 (Gieringer, 1999). During the 1880s and 1890s, other prohibitions were proposed and were closely tied to fears about Chinese immigration (Bonnie & Whitebread, 1999). Mccaffrey (2019) identifies an underexplored aspect of the anti-Chinese sentiment that drove worries about opium use in the United States. This was related to demographics. More than 90 percent of the Chinese population in the United States, from their arrival in the 1850s until the 1920s, consisted of males. However, women, especially middle-class women, accounted for most opium users (Kandall, 1999). Opium was a key ingredient in patented over-the-counter (OTC) medicines (Bentham, 1998: 65). Drug researchers of the temperance period often noted that "husbands drank alcohol in the saloon, wives took opium at home" (Boyd, 2007: 12).

In the United States, the passage of the 1914 Harrison Narcotics Tax Act regulated opium and restricted its production, importation, and distribution (Dufton, 2017a). The first drug law in Canada was the Opium Act of 1908, which prohibited the production, sale, and importation of opium. It was based on the same anti-Chinese sentiment that existed in the American West and fears about the role of recreational use on White populations. Drug control was born from thinly veiled racist assumptions, American efforts to curb the non-medicinal opium trade in Asia, and the growing influence of the temperance movement in the United States, Canada, and parts of Europe (Mccaffery, 2019). International conventions aimed at limiting the opium trade were seen as the best means to achieve control. Proposed by the United States, the 1909 International Opium Commission took place in Shanghai, China, and centered on controlling the import and export of opium internationally (Wright, 1909).

Anti-Alcohol Activism

Alcohol has a long history and an underappreciated role in human civilization (Forsyth, 2017). Before the Reformation, concerns about alcohol were generally limited. While temperance was undoubtedly seen as a virtue, public drunkenness was tolerated within the boundaries of traditional culture (Hands, 2018). Starting in the 1800s, physicians and moral crusaders persuaded many that alcohol was an addicting, toxic, and dangerously unpredictable stimulant (Levine, 1984). Although Benjamin Rush had published pamphlets identifying alcoholism as a disease decades earlier, it took a state-based mass movement to spread this idea. It ultimately shaped medical practice (Renner, 2019). The largest organization established to advocate temperance was the American Temperance Society, established in 1826.

By the 1830s and 1840s, many societies in the United States began asking people to sign "pledges" promising to abstain from alcohol consumption. Gusfield (1986) links early legislative efforts to prohibit alcohol as a reaction against the drinking practices of the Irish and German immigrants between 1845 and 1855. He argues that temperance reform in this period represented a "symbolic crusade" by Protestants to impose existing cultural values on predominantly Catholic immigrant groups. Indeed, in many states, local laws were passed that attempted to limit the consumption of alcohol.[3] While the American Civil War (1861–1865) weakened the temperance movement, the period from 1880 to 1890 marked the second great prohibition wave. During this period, more state legislatures passed state prohibitionist constitutional amendments than at any other time. Moreover, these efforts had an international dimension. Between 1885 and 1913, fourteen international alcohol conferences served to share information, discuss treatment, and support the spread of temperance. Eventually, these temperance societies began to promote the virtues of "teetotalism" (Edman, 2015).

By the early 1900s, the Anti-Saloon League (ASL) began to gain traction. Members shared principles based on the moral reform movement that inner discipline and self-regulation would maintain social order and improve society. Thus, for moral reformers, the use of any substance that undermined this regulation was suspect. McAllister (2000) argues that temperance reformers worldwide formulated political attitudes towards drugs that were negative enough to blur the distinctions between intoxicants. Indeed, many viewed all intoxicants as equal sources of immorality and social degeneracy (McAllister, 2000: 21). The movement was effective because it was able to marshal a surprising array of groups with diverse interests (Kelly, 2020). At the heart of this movement was a deep irony.

On the one hand, there were the suffragists, the progressives, and the populists. Early feminists such as Susan B. Anthony, Amelia Bloomer, and Elizabeth Cady Stanton embraced prohibition, connecting the campaign to ban alcohol with their own fight for (White) women's rights (Dannenbaum, 1981). They portrayed temperance as a women's issue, citing the havoc drunken, reckless, and violent husbands wreaked upon innocent wives and children. To them, ditching booze was a way to protect the sanctity of the saintly Protestant home (Kelly, 2020). Abolitionists like Frederick Douglass got on board, too. He stated: "if we could but make the world sober, we would have no slavery" because, in his view, "all great reforms go together" (Douglas, 1845: 55).

On the other hand, the movement relied on nativists, whose fervor against alcohol was "couched in anti-Semitic, anti-Catholic, and anti-immigrant sentiment" alongside unapologetic racists, who decided that alcohol was "too dangerous" for Black men to consume (Kelly, 2020). During this period, there was plenty of prejudice to go around. Immigrants from Germany, Ireland, Scandinavia, and Eastern Europe arrived in America only to be denounced for their own established drinking culture. This bigotry often merged with general anti-Semitism as many saloons were owned by Jewish people (Davis, 2012). The American prohibitionist movement celebrated its most significant victory in 1919.

The approval of the Eighteenth Amendment to the US Constitution, the Volstead Act, ushered in federal alcohol prohibition. However, the era of prohibition (1920–1933) was achieved by focusing first on state-based efforts. Although alcohol consumption rose in places like New York and other big cities, saloons closed in small towns in rural America, and consumption patterns shifted away from drinking together and toward drinking alone (Forsyth, 2017). McGirr (2016) charts how the ban built the structure of the federal penal state, fueled the Ku Klux Klan's power, reshaped politics, and served as a dress rehearsal for the much larger and longer-lasting war on drugs. In the short term, it modeled the value of a state-by-state approach to prohibition, which could be leveraged to shape national law. While not a specific focus of this work, it is hard not to see how prohibition fitted into the moralizing urge to discipline the poor and powerless.[4] Even after the 18th Amendment was repealed in 1933 by the 21st Amendment, the influence of the temperance movement in both theoretical and practical terms persisted. The power of state-based prohibition efforts had been proven, and that same social infrastructure could be relied upon to confront the use of other substances. It became a model for the prohibition efforts of the future.

Opium, Alcohol, and Cannabis

As Mills (2003) points out, experienced temperance campaigners linked cannabis to existing temperance and anti-opium efforts in the British Parliament. The connection was first made in 1891 in the British Parliament by Mark Stewart, M.P. for Kirkcudbrightshire in southwestern Scotland.[5] Other critics soon emerged, for example, William Sproston Caine, a Member of Parliament for Scarborough in Yorkshire. Caine was brought up as a Baptist and served as president of the Baptist Total Abstinence Society and the National Temperance Federation. He had experience in attacking the government on alcohol and opium issues based on his travel to India and Egypt. In 1893, he rose in the House of Commons to express his concern about hemp in India.[6] Caine would later describe cannabis as "the most horrible intoxicant the world has yet produced" (Mills, 2003: 86). Opium, alcohol, and cannabis policy are linked based on the role of temperance ideas and their ideological, international, and institutional impacts.

The historical narratives of prohibition overlapped with anti-immigration movements in North America in several significant ways. The prohibition movement viewed immigrants as the primary obstacle to a dry and morally sound nation. Chinese immigrants were first blamed for opium use among White women, and European immigrants were seen as responsible for increasingly permissive attitudes toward alcohol. Perhaps the temperance movement lost the war on alcohol but won the conflict on cannabis by connecting different drugs using similar language (Bonnie & Whitehead, 1970: 970–971). Central here was the connection between temperance, stigma, and propaganda, which linked deeply held religious beliefs with nationalistic and nativist views. By the end of the nineteenth century, the temperance movement had evolved into abolitionism regarding alcohol, along with parallel concerns about Chinese immigration and the "evils" of opium abuse (Renner, 2019).

Missionaries, temperance societies, and conferences looked to early efforts to prohibit opium, and in the United States, the prohibition of cannabis closely followed the repeal of alcohol prohibition. All embraced xenophobia, racism, moral misrepresentation, and a model of social activism that remains relevant. Viewing foreigners in oppositional terms and connecting their cultural practices to immorality is a problematic pattern. Even the language used ("marijuana" instead of "cannabis") was a deliberate effort to appeal to the xenophobia of the time. The exotic-sounding word emphasized the drug's foreignness to White Americans (Halpern, 2018). The ways in which stigma was foisted on people who used cannabis have been remarkably persistent and difficult to dislodge.

Solomon (2020) has argued that failing to recognize these racial antecedents allowed prohibition-era cannabis research to justify policies resulting in adverse outcomes for Black, Indigenous, and Other People of Color (BIPOC). Recent research suggests persistent parallels between race, stigma, and drug use. Lindsay & Vuolo (2021) analyzed 400 articles from the *New York Times* and *Washington Post* and found the public is more likely to support criminalization for Black people while supporting drug treatment for White people. Their findings suggest

> support for medicalized approaches to drug use is more likely to occur for White people and drugs linked to White people, while Black people and drugs associated with Black people continue to be perceived as largely amenable to punitive options.
> (Lindsay & Vuolo 2021: 942)

This propensity for punishment has international dimensions.

Cannabis was included in the preparations for the International Opium Conference in 1911 in The Hague. The Italian delegation raised the issue of international cannabis control over concerns around hashish smuggling in some of its North African colonies (Mills, 2003: 154–156). A letter from the South African delegation to the Committee in November 1923 put cannabis back on the international agenda.[7] In retrospect, criminalizing cannabis served racist and segregationist goals in South Africa.[8] Since "dagga" had long been used by Black South Africans, cannabis could be used to further race-based animus and sustain the populism the White colonial government relied upon (Chanock, 2001: 92–96). When the Egyptian delegation formally proposed widening deliberations to incorporate cannabis, they were supported by Brazil, Greece, South Africa, and Turkey (Seddon, 2020). International cannabis prohibition informed numerous international treaties and conventions in the twentieth century, described as examples of the colonization of drug control.[9]

The long shadow of temperance ideas and their institutional impact deserves perhaps more focused attention. Undoing prohibition (Szalavitz,

2021) cannot be achieved without appreciating how unconscious moralism against inebriation of all kinds was entrenched within key institutions. For example, Benjamin Rush, recognized as an essential figure within the temperance movement, also founded the American Psychiatric Association (APA). As Levine notes (1984), nearly all present-day ideas, such as addiction, substance use disorders, and abstinence-based treatment, can be traced to temperance. To this day, teaching about addiction is minimal in most medical schools, and people who use drugs often encounter negative attitudes from health-care professionals, including medical doctors (Ayu et al., 2022). Stigma against individuals with substance use disorders is embedded within many health-care institutions. This stigma supports "the criminal justice/moral model," which has long guided US drug policy (Renner, 2019: 135).

Cannabis, Stigma, and the Law

The global criminalization of cannabis did not occur all at once. An early example occurred in 1830 in Brazil.[10] In the United States, cannabis regulation began with the Pure Food and Drug Act (1906). It required drug producers to honestly label the contents of their tinctures, including cannabis-based medicines. Cannabis was not part of the first significant drug control conference held in Shanghai in 1909, which focused on regulating the international import and export of opium. While most delegates in 1911 did not support the inclusion of cannabis, these discussions led some countries, including Jamaica, British Guyana, and Trinidad, to pass legislation prohibiting "the cultivation of cannabis and regulated its sale and possession" (Beweley-Taylor et al., 2014: 13–14). During this time, some US states began passing laws against cannabis, "not in response to any public outcry, but as preventative initiatives by drug control authorities to deter future use" (Gieringer, 1999: 263). By the time states sought to control cannabis, it was seen like other intoxicants such as opium and alcohol, in terms of its danger to both physical and moral well-being. This process of criminalization and labeling gave rise to the stigma that has long been associated with cannabis use.

Various stereotypes about people who use cannabis have emerged and evolved during the decades of cannabis prohibition. For example, authority figures characterized users as dangerous and violent during the early years of prohibition. In the 1960s and 1970s, this gave way to societal perceptions of users as lazy, irresponsible, unhealthy, and dirty. A variety of derogatory terms arose to describe users of this drug, such as dope fiend, pothead, stoner, burnout, and druggie; these are still in use.[11] The gateway theory suggests that the effect of using cannabis is a progression to more seriously addictive and damaging drugs (Newhart & Dolphin, 2019: 28). Because of the influence of this questionable theory, many view people who use cannabis as prone to other types of drug use, for example, cocaine, heroin, and methamphetamine. Hathaway, Comeau, and Erickson (2011: 454) point out that despite changing perceptions, drug use is still

> widely seen as a risk to other people and evokes a deeply-rooted sense of cultural anxiety. The use of cannabis in this respect still carries a certain stigma reflecting cultural ambivalence about the use of drugs.

Link and Phelan (2001) have identified four interrelated components of stigma. First, people distinguish between, and label, differences between individuals. Second, they argue that stigma develops because these labels can turn into negative stereotypes that stem from dominant cultural beliefs in society. Third, these negative labels and the stereotypes that emerge from them are used to place people into categories of "normal" and the stigmatized insiders and outsiders, or "Us" and "Them." Fourth, they conclude that once a person has been labeled in a negative way and ostracized, they may experience status loss and discrimination in various aspects of their lives.

The US Congress initially separated drug prohibition from efforts under alcohol prohibition and created a new federal drug prohibition agency. As the first Commissioner of the newly created Federal Bureau of Narcotics (FBN), Harry J. Anslinger accelerated cannabis prohibition on the federal level in the United States. A committed alcohol prohibitionist, Anslinger believed he had a mandate "to pursue any and all violations of drug laws" (Lawson, 2020: 220). Ironically, his focus was initially on other narcotics. Anslinger argued that cannabis control should be handled by individual states rather than the federal government (Musto, 1999: 221–223). Based on the American prohibition of alcohol, Anslinger believed the key to controlling drugs was controlling supplies at the source.

This approach has influenced the development of US drug policy and, by extension, international drug control (Levine, 2003). In preparation for the 1925 Geneva Opium Convention, the United States sought international support to replicate its approach to alcohol to other drugs. Initially, it found little support for its strict approach and stringent controls over the production of drugs. The United States soon found allies by expanding the scope of prohibition (Levine, 2003). In meetings in advance of the 1925 Geneva

Opium Convention, cannabis was identified as a dangerous substance. The criminalization of cannabis proceeded around the world and has shaped criminology in ways that are both obvious and opaque.

Criminalizing Cannabis

In Canada, before the 1920s, cannabis was prescribed by many doctors, and hemp was frequently cultivated for rope and paper making. As Rushton (2018) notes, while cannabis was criminalized in 1923 in the consolidated Opium and Narcotic Drug Act, not a single reference to cannabis can be found in the Sessional Papers or Department of Health reports and records of that time. Hathaway and Erickson (2003) conclude that, based on a review of historical documents from that era, many Members of Parliament had never even heard of cannabis. Despite this lack of knowledge, the Act passed unanimously and without debate in the Canadian House of Commons (Erickson & Oscapella, 1999). Canadian cannabis prohibition, in hindsight, is viewed as a solution in search of a problem. The continued criminalization of cannabis in Canada in the twentieth century can be attributed to international, regional, and socio-political concerns (Fischer et al., 2020a).

One crucial international influence was the 1925 Convention, which included cannabis for the first time. Beweley et al. (2014: 12) note:

> Soon after Egypt had forced cannabis control onto the international agenda, more powerful countries would become entangled in the process of increasing criminalization and seeking tighter international prohibitive measures.

Seddon (2020) argues this convention marked a turning point. Individual countries began to implement national cannabis prohibitions, all of which exceeded the obligations in the Convention, despite the absence of problems related to cannabis use in those countries. This included the United Kingdom's Dangerous Drugs Act (1928), the Dutch Opium Law (1928), and Germany's second Opium Law (1929).

In the United States, efforts to criminalize cannabis began at the state level in 1911 (Campos, 2012). East Indian immigrants of Sikh religion and Punjabi origin (called "Hindoos") were the first popular target of anti-immigrant sentiment after several boatloads of immigrants arrived in San Francisco in 1910. Their arrival sparked an uproar of protest.[12] Some pronounced these new immigrants even more unfit for American civilization than the Chinese (Gieringer, 1999: 53–55).

New laws against cannabis were passed in Massachusetts in 1911, California, Maine, Indiana, and Wyoming in 1913, and Utah and Vermont in 1915. In addition, between 1914 and 1915, New York City and Portland, Oregon, passed local ordinances against cannabis use (Bonnie & Whitebread, 1999).

Campos (2012) argues cannabis use increased during the 1910s due to the prohibition of various other intoxicants at that time. However, by 1931, twenty-nine states had outlawed cannabis. The year Congress repealed alcohol prohibition, "the national focus turned again to California where the light this time shone on cannabis" (Lawson, 2020: 229). Other local and state laws sought to prohibit its use, eventually unifying prohibition through federal legislation. Racial tropes reached their zenith in the 1930s, based in part on a campaign designed to scapegoat, label, stigmatize, and criminalize "dangerous" Mexican immigrants (Tosh, 2019: 333). As Campos (2012) suggests, while Mexican immigrants were certainly targeted based on their supposed cannabis use, numerous non-White groups were identified as "cannabis users." This included Italians, Indians, and Black men and boys, whose behavior was exaggerated, incorrectly associated with cannabis, and used to feed Anslinger's campaign (see Figure 2.2) against the plant throughout the 1930s (Fisher, 2021: 944).

This campaign served institutional and professional goals (Crandall, 2020). During the American prohibition of alcohol, Anslinger served briefly as Assistant Commissioner of the US Bureau of Prohibition. In 1930, he was selected as the first Commissioner of the Federal Bureau of Narcotics (FBN) and remained in his post until 1962. He was instrumental in the development of federal laws and policies in the United States and played an influential role internationally. He shaped international drug policies, participated in several international organizations, and ended his career as US representative to United Nations Narcotics Convention. Harry Anslinger's career corresponded with the end of the prohibition of alcohol and the rise of the prohibition of cannabis. His previous, more relaxed attitude to cannabis lasted only until enforcing the ban on alcohol was no longer an option (Chasin, 2016). Starting in 1934, Anslinger's campaign against cannabis began in earnest (Crandall, 2020: 104).

In 1937, Congress passed the Marijuana Tax Act. The statute restricted possession of the drug to individuals who paid an excise tax for specifically authorized uses. When Congress passed the Marihuana Tax

Figure 2.2 Harry J. Anslinger
Source: Harry J Anslinger "6993340434_b50e0ef591_b" by amandagreer@bellsouth.net is marked with CC PDM 1.0.

Act in 1937, cannabis had already been included in the 1932 Uniform Narcotic Drug Act, and every state had enacted some form of cannabis prohibition. After 1937, possession of cannabis without filing the transfer form and paying the federal tax violated state and federal law (Bonnie & Whitehead, 1970). As Kathleen Frydl (2013) documents, during this period, the United States moved from regulating recreational drugs nationally to criminalizing them. The influence of Harry Anslinger and the FBN on global developments has been documented (Pembleton, 2017). However, beyond strictly American concerns, cannabis and drug control generally are a convenient means to understand the global dimension of criminalization.

Australia is a useful example. The Commonwealth prohibited the importation of cannabis in 1926, following the 1925 Geneva Opium Convention, and enacted controls in the states on unauthorized cannabis use in Victoria with the Poisons Act 1927. Others soon followed: South Australia in 1934, New South Wales in 1935, and Queensland in 1937.[13] While these controls attempted to limit use, criminalizing cannabis can be attributed to the long reach of Anslinger's reefer madness campaign (Cody, 2006). In 1938, the front page of the Australian newspaper *Smith's Weekly* cautioned: "New Drug That Maddens Victims: Warning from America" (Miller, 2019). The article reported that a Mexican drug existed that "drives men and women to the wildest sexual excesses" (Jay, 2001: 7).

In 1940, these warnings were formalized through official channels. The US consul wrote to the Australian government requesting information about state cannabis regulations. Included in the letter was an FBN factsheet on the dangers of cannabis. Based on a detailed memorandum,[14] the FBN alleged widespread habitual use of cannabis and the "alarming influence of addiction to Indian hemp on the development of criminality" (see Manderson, 1993: 125). The Commonwealth agreed to extend the import controls exercised over cannabis, including Indian hemp and its extract and tincture. In 1956, Australia extended these controls and fully prohibited the importation of cannabis into Australia. Tasmania was the last state to criminalize cannabis by enacting the Dangerous Drugs Act in 1959.

From the inception of prohibition to the Second World War, countries around the world agreed to regulate their narcotic production and distribution more carefully. For example, following the Second World War, the United States utilized its position as the leading military and financial power in the world to pressure and coerce first its European allies, then the remainder of the developing world to adopt narcotics prohibition and criminalization policies. This included cannabis. International developments made drug prohibition one of its priorities:

> The broad architecture of modern drug policy was established between 1948 and 1961 under the guidance and recommendations of experts at the World Health Organization (WHO), with a primary goal of controlling opium and coca-based narcotics. In 1961, regulation was formalized at the international level through the Single Convention on Narcotic Drugs, which was amended in 1972 but not since. This policy introduced the concept of drug scheduling.
> (Newhart & Dolphin, 2019: 51)

Since that time, the United States has played a dominant role in drug prohibition by ratcheting up the intensity of international controls. As with many decisions, drug policy was framed through the Cold War and, more specifically, the fear that the spread of communism was an existential threat to American interests (Bullington & Block, 1990: 40). The United Nations Single Convention, adopted in 1961, established the current system of global drug prohibition (Beweley-Taylor, 2001) and consolidated and extended the global prohibition of cannabis (Bayer & Ghodse, 1999: 8–10). Cannabis,

cannabis resin, and extracts and tinctures, were listed under Schedule I, while cannabis and cannabis resin were also listed under Schedule IV. Drugs in Schedules I and IV were under the Convention's "standard regime."[15]

Despite decades of evidence distinguishing cannabis and opium, the regulations were roughly transposed from the core regulatory apparatus limiting the opium and drug manufacturing trades. For example, states that were part of the Convention that allows medical and scientific cannabis and cannabis resin production need to precisely follow the regulatory structures for opium production (Collins, 2020). While the Convention placed no obligation to impose criminal sanctions for possession per se, it does require a Party to implement penal provisions, explicitly connecting cannabis with drugs like heroin and cocaine. As Levine (2003: 147) notes, "In the last 80 years, nearly every political persuasion and type of government has endorsed drug prohibition."

Despite prominent examples of stigma around drug use in general, there has often been pushback. The 1960s marked a shift in the popularity of cannabis in society. White, middle-class youth began to experiment with cannabis as part of their rebellion against, and rejection of, the dominant culture. The counterculture movement influenced the discourse surrounding cannabis, and musicians promoted the drug through their lyrics and their use (Cody, 2006). Seddon and Floodgate (2020: 7) point to an infamous full-page advertisement in *The Times* newspaper in the summer of 1967, signed and paid for by all four Beatles, describing cannabis laws as "immoral in principle, unworkable in practice," that exemplified this new ethos and the growing acceptability of cannabis.

Normalization and Decriminalizing Cannabis

Normalizing cannabis, and its use, emerged during the counterculture of the 1960s based on an apparent increase in the availability of the drug and the growing acceptance of its use. The 1960s was a time of social turbulence in which the "baby boomers," known as the generation born in the decade following the Second World War, challenged their parents' conservative social norms and changed the culture of society (Gerster & Bassett, 1991). During this period, cannabis use became common in communities where it had previously been unknown. White, middle-class youth began using cannabis as an act of rebellion, perhaps because the drug was seen as forbidden, based on its racial and criminal connotations (Marqusee, 2005).

As the teenagers of this era grew up, many viewed drug use as more enjoyable and less dangerous than their government and the media suggested. As the application of cannabis laws became increasingly publicized, from time to time, the public pushed back (Cody, 2006).[16] The Netherlands offered an early alternative to the prevailing view of the dangers of cannabis. Seddon & Floodgate (2020: 43–46) provide an overview. In 1976, the Dutch government decriminalized cannabis use and possession of 5 grams or less. This policy was spurred, in part, by concerns over heroin use by young people and the conclusion that drug policy needed to separate "soft" (e.g., cannabis and some mild psychedelic drugs) and "hard" (e.g., cocaine, heroin, methamphetamine) drugs (Korf, 2020: 286–267). Based on grassroots efforts in the 1970s, Dutch coffee shops formally emerged in the 1980s, whereby the government tolerated the use of a variety of cannabis products, provided that these establishments abided by numerous conditions.

The number of coffee shops across the country expanded rapidly, mainly due to the demand that emerged after easing travel restrictions throughout Europe following the Schengen Agreement. As a result, the Dutch government adopted and adapted the regulatory scheme of the coffee-shop system, granting additional power to local municipalities to impose licensing conditions (Korf, 2020). As a result, Holland, and specifically Amsterdam, benefited from cannabis tourism. Since 1988, the Cannabis Cup has evolved into a globally recognized championship of the best cannabis products in the world.[17] While the Netherlands embraced a more tolerant policy approach to cannabis itself, in the United States, commercial efforts first centered on cannabis paraphernalia (Dufton, 2017a). While state-based cannabis decriminalization grew in the 1970s, reforms stalled following pushback from parent groups and aggressive enforcement practices throughout the 1980s.

Efforts to legalize cannabis re-emerged in the 1990s. California became the first state to authorize the medicinal use of cannabis in 1996. The availability of medical cannabis destigmatized use among a subset of the population and increased supply through diversion to illicit markets (Nussbaum et al., 2015). Introduced above, Parker's groundbreaking research on normalization (Parker, 2005; Parker et al., 2002) led to numerous studies of normalization. Many of these explicitly focused on cannabis. For example, based on interviews with forty-one adults who use cannabis in Canada, Osborne and Fogel (2017) found support for the critical aspects of normalization, including availability/access, drug trying (i.e., experimentation), and rates of use. For example, Haines-Saah and colleagues (2014) analyzed nearly 2,000 Canadian newspaper reports. Their findings suggested that, in media representations,[18] cannabis use was normalized for people who have high levels of power and status in society—they referred to this as "privileged normalization."

Normalization is also a function of recognizing the incongruity between the nature of the "crime" and the consequences of the punishment. Although laws on the books remain highly punitive (Vitiello, 2021),[19] cannabis laws are enforced inconsistently and sometimes not at all. These disparities exist between and among states. For example, in 2020, an estimated 40,000 people were incarcerated in the United States for cannabis offenses, even as the legal cannabis industry was booming.[20]

Normalization can also be seen alongside developments in popular culture. Starting in the 1990s, television and films often portrayed cannabis use as common, mocked its status as a Schedule I drug, and associated smoking pot with subcultures from surfing to hip hop and from skateboarding to jam bands (Heidt & Wheeldon, 2022). Films such as *Dazed and Confused*, *Clerks*, *Friday*, *Half-Baked*, *The Big Lebowski*, and *Harold and Kumar Go to White Castle*, and television programs such as *The Simpsons*, *Roseanne*, *That 70's Show*, *Entourage*, and *Weeds* contributed to normalization. Two areas of emergent interest focus on how the history of cannabis policy might be confronted, understood, and overcome and to what extent cannabis laws based on demonizing users undermined public trust in government. By July 2018, forty-six states and the District of Columbia, and the US territories of Puerto Rico and Guam provide for the legal therapeutic use of cannabis in some form.

The acceptance of the medical potential for cannabis further destigmatized use among a subset of the population and increased the supply of cannabis through diversion to illegal markets (Nussbaum et al., 2015). Reforms designed to decriminalize cannabis in Portugal, Australia, and the United Kingdom soon emerged. Since 2012, nineteen US states have legalized the use and sale of recreational cannabis, with only five still outlawing all cannabis products. In states that have legalized it, regulatory systems have been established to standardize the sale of non-medical (retail) cannabis for people twenty-one years of age and older. Although, in nearly half of all US states, the use of recreational cannabis is legal, possessing cannabis remains a federal crime. While efforts to criminalize, stigmatize, and control its use remain, more nuanced approaches are increasingly replacing these efforts. These shifts, connected to the normalization of cannabis, are underway in the United States and are evident around the world.

A significant milestone occurred in Uruguay in 2013, when it became the first country to legalize the entire cannabis supply chain from production to consumption. The Uruguayan legislation allows up to six cannabis plants to be grown at home and creates provisions for forming cannabis-growing clubs. In addition, a cannabis regulatory institute was established, as was a state-controlled cannabis supply retail network supported through pharmacies (Albrecht, 2014; Pardo, 2014). Demand has far outpaced government-authorized production and access, however. For example, five years after the legislation legalizing cannabis, there were only 13 pharmacies among the more than 1,200 in the country that sells cannabis (Queirolo, 2020). In 2018, Canada became the second country, after Uruguay, to formally legalize the cultivation, possession, and consumption of cannabis and its by-products; provinces and municipalities have allowed dispensaries to open at varying rates.

Europe has emerged as a new site of significant cannabis liberalization. In 2022, Germany legalized and regulated the sale of cannabis to adults through licensed shops; this plan was later scaled back to permitting the sale of cannabis in social clubs only (Sabagh, 2023). This decision followed one taken in late 2021 by Malta, which became the first European Union country to legalize the use and growth of marijuana for recreational purposes. The German and Maltese decisions are likely to be followed by other members of the Union. A referendum in Italy obtained the necessary number of signatures, while Switzerland, Luxembourg, and the Netherlands are discussing the introduction of new drug regulations that move toward formal legalization (Rodriguez, 2021). By 2030, it is estimated that annual sales across the United States will double, reaching nearly $72 billion (GlobeNewswire, 2022). A partial list of new cannabis products includes edibles, drinks, tinctures, creams, toothpaste, sprays, and even body butter. In Canada and the United States, national groups seek reforms that will ensure the cannabis industry is sustainable (NICA, n.d.).

The Dynamics of Stigma and Normalization

Cannabis and its use mark the "most consequential case of social construction of the twentieth century" (Newhart & Dolphin, 2019: 241). It was socially constructed as a threat to mental health, the White race, law and order, and social stability. Cannabis policy touches on identity politics, culture wars, social movements, ecological concerns, and global economies. In criminological terms, cannabis connects ideology, policing, and addiction studies and represents a warning to those who embrace simplistic views of evidence-based policymaking. Under the guise of community safety, cannabis has justified criminalizing nonconformists and done significant damage to communities of color based on racial and ethnic blind spots that have only recently re-emerged in the public consciousness.

These broad findings are also evident when examining cannabis, stigma, and the law. The impact of past cannabis criminalization on future employment and educational opportunities, access to state benefits, and social housing has been recognized (Puras & Hannah, 2017). The view that first emerged in Holland has gained traction. Increasingly, people believe that the prosecution of cannabis offenses does not serve the public interest but instead unnecessarily stigmatizes many young people (Korf, 2020: 287). As Seddon and Floodgate (2020: 70–71) note, there are many public-health benefits associated with acknowledging rather than demonizing cannabis use. Despite the growing normalization, decriminalization, and legalization of cannabis, stigma remains.

Stigma is associated with the use of cannabis in specific circumstances, such as "at work, in the company of children and the elderly, or while driving" (Duff et al., 2012: 281). Reid (2020: 11) suggests that

> claims of normalization may be premature. While stigmas surrounding cannabis appear to have diminished, there is little evidence that such stigmas have entirely disappeared. It is possible that sweeping claims of cannabis normalization may be symptomatic of unchecked social privileges or social distance from cannabis users. Such claims may also be the product of valuing quantitative data over the nuanced accounts uncovered through qualitative investigations.

Qualitative data in this area suggests other important factors.

Hathaway (2004) found that users had specific rules or techniques for managing the stigma associated with cannabis. Some of these included keeping their use hidden from disapproving non-users, adhering to less stigmatizing methods of use (e.g., joints and edibles), and managing the risks that accompany cannabis use and the stigma stemming from being labeled as at risk. These labels can extend to concerns beyond health. In subsequent research (Hathaway et al., 2011), results suggested that while cannabis use has been normalized in the sense of it being more socially and culturally accepted, there were still threats from legal sanctions and stigma associated with its use. The principal concern among participants was informal sanctions imposed by others based on the stigma associated with cannabis use,

This required people who use cannabis to take steps to counter typical cultural assumptions and present themselves as normal.

Indeed, other research also suggests that the stigma remains and that societal normalization of cannabis use has not fully occurred. In fact, there is an increasing tendency in society to medicalize and pathologize drug use (Price et al., 2021). Recent research in Poland considers how people who use cannabis must traverse social worlds, including between more and decidedly less progressive cannabis contexts (Wanke et al., 2022). This work can be connected to other research (Sandberg, 2013). For example, in Jamaica, social concerns about cannabis use have been highly moralized. Negative stigma has significantly influenced the debate on establishing a legal cannabis industry or decriminalizing possession for personal use (Hanson, 2020: 379).

As Hathaway, Comeau, and Erickson (2011) predicted, "Even if raw cannabis were legalized and sold as a commodity like cigarettes or alcohol or coffee, it is unlikely that regulation would transform the social stigma associated with assumptions of abuse or need for treatment" (p. 464). From the research reviewed here, it seems clear that there is a complex relationship between stigma and normalization. At first blush, it may appear that they are mutually exclusive categories: either there is stigma against the activity or it has been normalized. However, these two ideas are best viewed as being on a continuum alongside each other in society. Each will shift in response to various events, and they do not necessarily change at the same time or in tandem with each other.

There is some indication that various government actors can influence stigma and normalization through how they define deviance and crime (Turk, 1966). Young (2011: 121–122) describes early attempts to influence attitudes about cannabis use. One, as noted by Dickson (1968), includes the institutional need to frame the dangers of cannabis through scare stories in response to the declining budgetary appropriation of the FBN following the 1937 Marihuana Tax Act (MTA). For example, in 1938, the first full year of the MTA operation, one of every four federal narcotics convictions was for marihuana violations. This early attempt to change views on cannabis use could be viewed as an attempt to define deviance up. As mentioned by Young, Moynihan (1993) noted that the opposite may occur. Defining deviance down occurred in North America and Europe, arguably since medical cannabis laws came into effect. However, the process has been uneven and inconsistent.

This early panic around cannabis translated into an increased stigma associated with the drug. However, as discussed previously, when White, middle-class youth started to use the drug, attitudes shifted, and this caused a change in the stigma associated with it. More and more people started to view cannabis use as dangerous to mental health and less as a criminal threat (Lempert, 1974). Eventually, cannabis policy and law enforcement practices started to mirror cultural changes and public sentiment, but only for certain groups. Interestingly, despite the normalization of cannabis during the 1990s (Parker, 2005), law enforcement in the United States increasingly focused on low-level cannabis offenses (King & Mauer, 2006). Normalization seems to have occurred; however, it seems to have been a "privileged normalization" that was primarily available to White people, the wealthy, and the politically connected (Haines-Saah et al., 2014).

The existence of privileged normalization will not come as a surprise to those well versed in conflict theory. For example, Turk (1969) observed that the habits and behaviors of the less powerful will be more subject to criminalization and the forces of stigmatization (see also Turk, 1966). Garland (2001: 132) explains how this relates to US federal drug policy in the following passage:

> the American government's "War on Drugs" which has utterly transformed law enforcement in the USA, as well as filling a hugely expanded prison system with disproportionate numbers of poor [B]lacks. . . . Motivated by the politically urgent need to "do something" decisive about crime, in a context where the Federal government mostly lacks jurisdiction (other areas of crime control being the prerogative of states and local authorities) the war on drugs was the American state's attempt to "just say no." Disregarding evidence that the levels of drug use were already in decline, that drug use is not responsive to criminal penalties, that criminalization brings its own pathologies (notably street violence and disrespect for authorities), and that declaring a war on drugs, is, in effect to declare a war against minorities, the US government proceeded to declare such a war, and persist in pursuing it despite every indication of its failure. Why? Because the groups most adversely affected lacked political power and are widely regarded as dangerous and undeserving; because the groups least affected could be assured that something is being done and lawlessness is not tolerated; and because few politicians are willing to oppose a policy when there is so little political advantage to be gained by doing so.

Two types of stigma have fused with each other. More specifically, racist attitudes and stereotypes about poor people came to be connected with other character flaws, such as drug addiction (Goffman, 1963). Efforts to define deviance up generally increase stigma and decrease normalization, while efforts to define deviance down generally decrease stigma and increase normalization. However, these decisions are also made with public opinion in mind. Thus, this process should be viewed as dialectical and reciprocal in nature rather than linear and unbroken.

Conclusion

The effort to control inebriation through policies rooted in moralistic assumptions about right and wrong has led to significant problems and paradoxes. In this chapter, we documented a myriad of international efforts which led to the global war against cannabis, which some suggest is an example of the persistence of colonial thinking and legislation that imposed "oppressive, restrictive, and punitive drug policies" and created systems and structures in Africa, Asia, the Middle East, and the Americas (Daniels et al., 2021: 1). These agreements sought to categorize and control drug use of all kinds, regardless of the danger posed to users, based on narratives on "civilizing" native populations. While the pernicious consequences of early global treaties remain, in recent decades, more tolerant approaches have emerged.

In this chapter, we connected the history of criminalization and decriminalization with sociological concepts like stigma and normalization. Normalization is not just a function of changing patterns of cannabis use, beginning in the 1960s but accelerating in the 1970s and then again in the 1990s. As cannabis became a fixture in US popular culture, liberal attitudes about cannabis began to shape global cannabis culture (Wanke et al., 2022). However, these developments are incomplete. Because laws remain on the books against cannabis even in areas that have decriminalized possession, stigma remains and coexists in a somewhat strange harmony with normalization. As Reid (2020) notes, stigma exists in numerous forms and interacts with normalization and shame in ways that are difficult to parse.

In Chapter 3, we turn to another notion: moral panics. A feature of criminological thought since the 1970s, moral panic research generally focused on how deviance is exaggerated and used by moral guardians to demonize others. While these appear to be key features of cannabis policy, older formulations may not capture the iterative nature of emergent moral panics. Indeed, the sense one gets from reading the history of cannabis prohibition is circular. As Dufton (2017a: 154) notes in her history of cannabis, views on cannabis shift in predictable ways:

> a period of intense hatred of marijuana (the 1930s, the 1950s, the late 1970s into the 1980s) births a moment when the drug suddenly seems all right (the 1960s and early to mid-1970s, the 1990s, today). In both moments, laws change, as does use. Then acceptance births opposition, which births acceptance, and the cycle begins again.

The metaphor of a circular process involving actions and reactions is consistent with recent efforts to understand moral panics: the life cycle. Chapter 3 focuses on the lifespan of cannabis moral panics.

Notes

1. Cannabis was first linked to existing temperance and antiopium efforts in 1891 in the British Parliament by Mark Stewart, M.P. for Kirkcudbrightshire in south-western Scotland. See British Parliament, Hansard's Parliamentary Debates (April 10). Available at: https://api.parliament.uk/historic-hansard/commons/1891/apr/10/the-indian-opium-traffic#S3V0352P0_18910410_HOC_145.
2. For more, see Frontline (n.d.).
3. For examples of state-based approaches, see Encyclopedia.com (2018).
4. For the full description and review, see Berman (2019).
5. Temperance campaigners first linked cannabis to existing temperance and antiopium efforts in 1891 in the British Parliament by Mark Stewart, M.P. for Kirkcudbrightshire in south-western Scotland. See British Parliament, Hansard's Parliamentary Debates (April 10). Available at: https://api.parliament.uk/historic-hansard/commons/1891/apr/10/the-indian-opium-traffic#S3V0352P0_18910410_HOC_145.
6. Caine stated:

   > I beg to ask the Under Secretary of State for India if the Secretary of State for India will instruct the Government of India to create a Commission of Experts to inquire into, and report upon, the cultivation of, and trade in, all preparations of hemp drugs in Bengal, the effect of their consumption upon the social and moral condition of the people, and the desirability of prohibiting its growth and sale.

   See British Parliament, Hansard's Parliamentary Debates (March 2, 1893). Available at: https://api.parliament.uk/historic-hansard/commons/1893/mar/02/hemp-drugs-in-bengal#S4V0009P0_18930302_HOC_146.

7. The South African delegation, which had announced a nationwide ban on the cultivation, sale, possession, and use of cannabis a year earlier, submitted that it was "the most important of all the habit-forming drugs." See National Archive of South Africa (1923).
8. An interesting example is South Africa where, in 1870, cannabis use by Indian immigrants was prohibited, an early case of the prohibition impulse being rooted in racialized discourse. See Seddon (2020: 1568–1569).
9. This refers to the use of drug control by states in Europe and America to advance and sustain the systematic exploitation of people, land and resources and the racialized hierarchies, which were established under colonial control and continue to dominate today (Daniels et al., 2021: 1).
10. Seddon (2020: 1568–1569) states:

    Perhaps the first example was in Brazil in 1830, where a municipal regulation in Rio de Janeiro criminalized the sale and use of cannabis. . . . In Egypt, various prohibitive measures were enacted between the 1860s and 1890s . . . in Greece, a law in 1890 banned cannabis importation, cultivation and consumption. . . . An interesting example is South Africa where, in 1870, cannabis use by Indian immigrants was prohibited . . . an early case of the prohibition impulse being rooted in racialized discourse.

11. It is worth noting that the commonly used term "marijuana" was originally intended as a racial slur and was an attempt to associate Mexicans and Mexican immigrants with the drug (Halpern, 2018).
12. In a prominent letter from 1911, a California pharmacist and later anti-cannabis organizer accused these immigrants as leading to: "demand cannabis indica; they are a very undesirable lot and the habit is growing in California very fast; the fear is now that it is not being confined to the *Hindoos* alone but that they are initiating our whites into this habit" (emphasis added). Cited by Gieringer (1999) based on his review of the Records of US Delegation to the International Opium Commission and Conferences of 1909–1913, Record Group 43, Entry #40, Correspondence between Hamilton Wright and Henry J. Finger (National Archives).
13. See https://parlinfo.aph.gov.au/parlInfo/download/library/prspub/05E30/upload_binary/05/e30.pdf;fileType=application%2Fpdf#search=%22poisons%20act%201934%20south%20australia%22.
14. See reference to this memorandum at UKCIA (n.d.a).
15. See https://www.dea.gov/drug-information/drug-scheduling.
16. Cody (2006: 39) notes:

    Paul McCartney experienced a series of cannabis arrests, but it was the Rolling Stones that were the target of greatest police surveillance in Britain. Mick Jagger and Keith Richards were arrested following a police raid at Richards' home in 1967. The police had received a tip off about the party by a national newspaper wanting a scoop. . . . Initially, both men were handed down prison sentences, Jagger for three months and Richards one year, but these were later successfully appealed. The original sentences created a fury, and a protest was held in Fleet Street and a sit-in in London's Hyde Park. It was argued before the appeal that the sentences Jagger and Richards received did not fit the crime, and they were being used as scapegoats in the media. . . . [It] was evident after the raid that the police had an easy target in rock musicians, who also created great publicity. This led to corruption in the police force, which was later accused of planting evidence and framing stars such as John Lennon and fellow Beatle George Harrison.

17. For more, see High Times (n.d.).
18. It should be noted that the findings of Haines-Saah et al. (2014) focused upon how cannabis use is portrayed in the media. While compatible with Parker's work (1998; 2002; 2005) on normalization, the emphasis in this research is slightly different as they draw more upon Manning's (2006) notion of symbolic framing.
19. Vitiello (2021: 447–448) notes:

> Some states impose severe penalties for drug offenses. Some, like Louisiana, have repeat offender laws that can lead to extremely long sentences. For example, Bernard Noble had prior drug convictions. His conviction for possession of two marijuana cigarettes netted him a sentence of 13 years at hard labor in Louisiana's state prison. . . . Gulf War Veteran Derek Harris faces a true life sentence under Louisiana's habitual offender statute. His last crime was the sale of a small amount of marijuana to an undercover agent. Other Southern states like Mississippi impose long prison terms for marijuana offenses. For example, an African American man received an 8-year prison term for possession of marijuana, allegedly for personal, medical use. Ditto for Alabama, where a man in his 70s received a life sentence for possession of about three pounds of marijuana.

20. Pinning down these statistics is difficult. See Oleck (2020) and Bloom (2021) for some of these issues.

3
Cannabis and the Life Span of Moral Panics

Introduction

Chapter 2 argued that the stigma associated with cannabis use shaped criminalization worldwide. From opium to alcohol, prohibiting substances was a means to ensure moral judgments drove policy. Those with different backgrounds and behaviors were subjected to the strictest means of control. Embedding the moral certainty of the temperance movement within the criminal justice system allowed various stigmas to overlap and led to the criminalization of cannabis worldwide. We also presented the concept of normalization to understand the development in recent decades of efforts to decriminalize, legalize, and regulate cannabis. The tension between the criminalization of cannabis and its increased toleration deserves deeper exploration.

In this chapter, we consider moral panics and cannabis. First, we begin revising the role of Harry J. Anslinger in the co-construction of race, addiction, and insanity. This led to perhaps the first moral panic, which emerged from media-manufactured fears and relied upon techniques and assumptions consistent with early labeling theory. Moral panic research in criminology can be traced to Jock Young's (1971) study of the social meaning of drug-taking and Stanley Cohen's (2002 [1972]) construction of mods and rockers in the United Kingdom. The moral panic thesis gained traction as an example of the constructionist framework. It offered a critical approach to state power rooted in the potential for moral guardians through the media to construct, amplify, and exaggerate deviance. However, various critiques have emerged (Horsley, 2017). We assess these critiques and show how reformulations of the moral panic framework remain relevant. Central to this discussion, we believe, is thinking about the lifespan of moral panics (Bennett, 2018).

In this chapter, we argue the oscillating cycle of cannabis concern, from significant to nonexistent (Dufton, 2017a) suggests moral panics are best seen as a life cycle or lifespan (Klocke & Muschert, 2010). Cannabis moral panics can be associated with racialization, criminalization, popularization, medicalization, and regulation through Klocke and Muschert's (2010) hybrid model of moral panics. By acknowledging how moral panics have lifespans (Bennett, 2018), we document the race-based reefer madness of the 1930s and 1940s up to the panic around schizophrenia and psychosis that has become prominent over the past decade (Alshaarawy & Anthony, 2019; Bernerth & Walker, 2020; Biasutti et al., 2020). Finally, we argue that new moral panics may emerge in the cannabis regulation era. The intersection of information cocoons, moral panics, and participatory disinformation may represent a new chapter in a long-standing effort to prohibit cannabis by exaggerating the dangers associated with using it.

Moral Panics and Cannabis

Cannabis use has long been connected to racial prejudice and concerns about mental illness. Prohibition grew out of various negative stigma and stereotypes attributed to the subcultures with which it was associated. Indeed, stigma is one of the primary tools in creating a moral panic (Cohen, 2002 [1972]). Stigma distorts or magnifies the harm caused by the activity or group in question and amplifies how society panics based on that distortion and the nature of the reaction to address the perceived threat. Theories about moral panics emerge from a perspective based on labeling theory and social constructionism. Imported into the social sciences by symbolic interactionist scholars such as Frank Tannenbaum (1938) and Herbert Blumer (1992 [1969]), Mead's ideas provided much of the philosophical impetus behind the popularization of social constructionism that took hold during the post-war era (Horsley, 2017).

As demonstrated in Chapter 2, cannabis laws were passed based on a nexus of national concerns and international pressures. However, the moral panics that have sustained stigma around use emerged most forcefully when White youth were seen to be threatened by their use of cannabis. Fisher (2021: 933) notes:

> The lawmakers who erected America's earliest drug bans acted first and foremost to protect the morals of their own racial kin. And because the morals of most importance to White lawmakers were those of their own

offspring, they acted fastest and most forcefully when a drug took White youth in its clutches.

During the 1930s, efforts were underway to connect cannabis and insanity in popular culture, specifically in the United States.

One film is often referenced. Directed by Louis Gasnier and produced in 1936, *Reefer Madness* is a morality tale commissioned by a church group to educate parents in the United States about the dangers of cannabis. As Boyd (2010: 12) notes:

> Reefer Madness portrays innocent middle-class white, small-town youth being lured into marijuana addiction, sexual depravity, insanity, and murder. The evil drug that compels them into corruption and crime is marijuana.

The themes of criminality, insanity, violence, and sexual immorality depicted in *Reefer Madness* are also prevalent in several other independent films produced during the same era, including *Assassin of Youth* (1935) and *Marihuana: The Weed with Roots in Hell* (1935). While cannabis propaganda efforts never really disappeared after Congress passed the Marijuana Tax Act (1937), they re-emerged in earnest in the twentieth century through varied national and international drug control initiatives.

In the 1930s, a national propaganda campaign against the "evil weed" was led by Harry J. Anslinger. As introduced in Chapter 2, Anslinger famously associated cannabis with wicked, non-White populations in stark and explicitly racist terms. His "Gore Files" included a collection of horror stories in which offenders were usually racially identifiable, either Black or Hispanic (McWilliams, 1990), and Anslinger used the pejorative term "n-----" in official Federal Bureau of Narcotics correspondence (Fisher, 2021).[1] In addition, Anslinger relied on racist sentiments about Mexicans and African Americans that predominated early in the twentieth century to push the Marihuana Tax Act (Chasin, 2016).

In a famous *American Magazine* article published a few weeks before the Marihuana Tax Act was passed, Anslinger cautioned that cannabis was as "dangerous as a coiled rattlesnake" (Anslinger & Cooper, 1937: 19). The article would be reproduced in publications such as *Reader's Digest* in 1938. It contained a highly descriptive account of how the drug was responsible for the death of an innocent man:

> In Los Angeles, a youth was walking along a downtown street after inhaling a marihuana cigarette. For many addicts, merely a portion of a "reefer" is

enough to induce intoxication. Suddenly, for no reason, he decided that someone had threatened to kill him and that his life at that very moment was in danger. Wildly he looked about him. The only person in sight was an aged bootblack. Drug-crazed nerve centers conjured the innocent old shoe-shiner into a destroying monster. Mad with fright, the addict hurried to his room and got a gun. He killed the old man, and then, later, babbled his grief over what had been wanton, uncontrolled murder. "I thought someone was after me," he said. "That's the only reason I did it. I had never seen the old fellow before. Something just told me to kill him!" That's marihuana!

(Anslinger & Cooper, 1937: 19)

These campaigns succeeded in part because they successfully linked cannabis and sin. Yet, this framing carries with it an internal and inevitable reaction. When evil is dramatized, it may reinforce what is being vilified. This process played an essential role in maintaining cannabis prohibition despite its ineffectiveness, shortcomings, and lack of scientific justification.

Dramatizing Evil

Many trace the origins of social constructivist and labeling theories in criminology to Tannenbaum's (1938) work on the dramatization of evil. He argued that overly aggressive state intervention, especially in the case of youth, "dramatizes evil" and could trigger further criminal behavior. In an observation that would re-emerge in the 1960s, Tannenbaum described the process of making a criminal, which relied upon

tagging, defining, identifying, segregating, describing, emphasising, making conscious and self-conscious; it becomes a way of stimulating, suggesting, emphasising, and evoking the very traits that are complained of.

(Tannenbaum, 1938: 19–20)

Individuals who engage in deviance are singled out for stigmatizing treatment and publicly defined as a criminal. As a result, they are likely to find the ratio of their contacts, also defined as criminals. This change leads to adopting a criminal identity, and a criminal career becomes a natural progression.

During the 1950s, Howard Becker published articles on musicians and subcultures (Becker, 1951) and cannabis use (Becker, 1953, 1955). He drew heavily on the symbolic-interactionist approach developed by earlier members of the Chicago School (Blumer, 1969; Mead, 1934). During the 1960s, cannabis was the subject of learning and subcultural studies. For example, Becker (1963: 147) observed that law and social rules are not formed in a vacuum and are susceptible to *moral entrepreneurs* who seek to reform laws to impose a particular moralistic world view and then try to ensure rules are enforced by deferring to police or agents of social control when they apply laws consistent with this world view.

In his groundbreaking research, Becker (1963: 147) argued that law and social rules are not formed in a vacuum: "Rules are products of someone's initiative, and we can think of people who exhibit such enterprise as *moral entrepreneurs*" (italics in original). He identified two "species" of moral entrepreneurs: the crusaders and the rule enforcers. Crusaders care passionately about their cause, believed they dealt with a dangerous evil in society, and could work as activists or politicians. The reforming crusader is more concerned with ends than means and often relies upon experts of various types, for example, legal, scientific, medical, and psychiatric. Rule enforcers tend to defer to police or agents of social control responsible for enforcing laws and regulations.

In his classic media analysis of youth gangs, *Folk Devils and Moral Panics*, Cohen (2002 [1972]) built on this framework by adding the notion of a moral panic, borrowed from Marshall McLuhan (1964). Cohen described several processes that lead to moral panics (Bennett, 2018). He argued that initially, a condition emerges that presents a threat to societal values and interests. The mass media presents this condition in a stylized and stereotypical fashion, causing high-status and influential people to speak out. Eventually, experts and professionals are recruited to diagnose the problem and propose solutions. These solutions are implemented, and the condition vanishes or breaks down and no longer causes great concern. Cohen (2002 [1972]: 9) suggests:

> Societies appear to be subject, every now and then, to periods of moral panic. A condition, episode, person or group of persons emerges to become defined as a threat to societal values and interests; its nature is presented in a stylized and stereotypical fashion by the mass media; the moral barricades are manned by editors, bishops, politicians, and other right-thinking people; socially accredited experts pronounce their diagnoses and solutions; ways of coping are evolved or (more often) resorted to; the condition then disappears, submerges or deteriorates and becomes more visible. Sometimes the object of the panic is quite novel and at other times it is

something which has been in existence long enough but suddenly appears in the limelight.

For Cohen, outsiders are more broadly defined as *folk devils*, and this concept was applied to the mod and rocker subcultures in the 1950s and 1960s. These folk devils are characterized as "in the gallery of types that society erects to show its members which roles should be avoided, and which should be emulated, these groups have occupied a constant position as folk devils: visible reminders of what we should not be" (Cohen, 2002 [1972]: 2). Goode and Ben-Yehuda (2009 [1994]) went on to further define specific attributes common to all moral panics, distinguishing these from the processes that animated Cohen's (2002 [1972]) work.

First, *concern* about the phenomenon is heightened and circulates in society. Second, increased *hostility* against specific individuals or groups (i.e., folk devils) is associated with the problem in question. Third, there must be a *consensus* or a relatively large number of people and organizations (i.e., moral entrepreneurs) that believe there is a real threat caused by the wrongdoing of some group and its members. Goode and Ben-Yehuda (2009 [1994]: 38) state: "This sentiment must be fairly widespread, although the proportion of the population who feels this way need not be universal or, indeed, even make up a literal majority."

A fourth aspect of a moral panic is *disproportionality*. In many moral panics, there is a perception that the problem is causing more harm than it is and that a large of people are engaging in the behavior. Goode and Ben-Yehuda (2009 [1994]) provide several indicators of disproportionality, including exaggerated figures/stats, fabrication of figures/stats, rumors of inflated harms, tall tales, unequal attention paid to comparable conditions, and a varying level of concern over time. Fifth, *volatility* represents the essence of a moral panic as they are thought to be chaotic and somewhat unpredictable; it may disappear suddenly and then resurface at an unforeseen moment. As Figure 3.1 comically suggests, this might be seen along a spectrum. These concepts are certainly relevant to the criminalization of cannabis.

Updating Moral Panics

The moral panic framework remains one of criminology's most widely used and frequently referenced concepts. It is older than many assume.[2] Horsley (2017) and other critics are convinced that this concept no longer

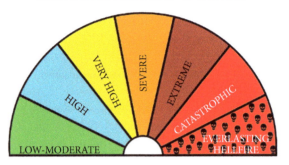

Figure 3.1 Moral panic today
Source: "MORAL PANIC TODAY" by Esperluette is licensed under CC BY 2.0. To view a copy of this license, visit https://creativecommons.org/licenses/by/2.0/?ref=openverse.

helps provide criminology with a viable analytical framework. Others have attempted to wrestle with, revise, and update the central thesis. One useful model by Goode and Ben-Yehuda (2009 [1994]) identifies three types of moral panics. On the most basic level, moral panics may originate amongst the public without aid or support from special interests and elite groups; these are called *grassroots moral panics*. A grassroots moral panic describes a form of collective behavior marked by suddenly increased concern and antagonism in a large segment of society, occurring in reaction to widespread beliefs about a newly perceived threat from moral deviants (Cody, 2006).

The second type of moral panic may be initiated by elites and those in power, such as high-ranking government officials, chief executive officers of powerful corporations, or those with substantial amounts of money. The concept of *Elite-engineered moral panics* was developed at length by Stuart Hall and his associates (Hall et al., 1978). They suggest that small and powerful groups deliberately campaign to generate and sustain fear within society over an issue they often know is not as dangerous as it is made out to be (Goode & Ben-Yehuda 2009 [1994]). According to Cody (2006), sometimes, this is done to divert attention away from the real problems in society which might have the ability to undermine the interests of the elite. Central to the theory is the idea that the elite has influence over other members of society, dominating the media, determining legislation, and shaping the direction of the law.

A third type is *interest-group moral panics*. These emerge after small groups in the middle levels of society initiate moral panics to express or promote their morality or ideological stances and gain material benefits and status, for example, wealth, fame, and notoriety. An interest group can refer to various groups, including professional associations, media entities, religious groups, social movement organizations, educational institutions, or any combination of the above (Goode & Ben-Yehuda, 2009 [1994]). While elite-engineered moral panics assume the media is among the most influential force in shaping public consciousness, interest groups that instigate moral panics are more mercurial (Cody, 2006). Interest-group moral panics often originate in statements by members of the ruling class and are amplified by the media. Specific interest groups can sustain these panics over time. In short, the media is not responsible for creating the news but reproduces dominant interpretations of issues to support interest groups aligned with the state (Schissel, 1997).

There has been a wide range of moral panics about various activities over the past hundred years. In the 1950s, people were concerned that comic books would give rise to violence among young boys. Strict codes were set up to prohibit any type of violent content; however, these were later abandoned in the early 2000s. Since Cohen's pioneering study, several other moral panics have been identified (Critcher, 2003: 1–19). These include panics in Britain concerning muggings (1972–1973) and pedophile activity (1994–2001). In the United States during the 1970s and 1980s, there were widespread moral panics over Satanism, rock, and rap/hip hop music—these concerns culminated in explicit lyrics stickers on cassette tapes and compact discs. In the 1980s and early 1990s, concerns about ritual child abuse appear to have risen to the level of a moral panic. More recently, we have seen moral panics around video games and violence in media.

Drugs have also been a focus of moral panic research. Goode and Ben-Yehuda (2009 [1994]) identify several examples. These include well-used examples such as the "reefer madness" of the 1930s as well as phencyclidine (PCP) in the 1970s, crack cocaine in the 1980s, and ecstasy and methamphetamines in the 1990s and 2000s. These panics can be observed in other places, including the United Kingdom (Critcher, 2003). More recently, one could argue that there have also been moral panics around synthetic drugs such as flakka, bath salts, and fentanyl- and ketamine-laced cannabis.

Critiques of Moral Panic Theory

Despite its popularity and the emergence of several moral panic theories discussed previously, there have been several important critiques of the concept. David and colleagues (2011: 215–228) organized a wide variety of moral panic critiques into what they call "dimensions of dispute." While the breadth and diversity of these viewpoints suggest the continued salience of the moral panic framework, it requires some updating. One focuses on media, distinguishing between older models and current technological advances that make media readily accessible with little parental control. Some changes are about access. For example, downloadable content has replaced tapes and discs. Other changes speak to who can create and share content. Rather than "news" emerging from a corporate-owned network, content can be created by anyone with a cell phone and shared online by those with rudimentary technological skills. As a result, some questioned the effectiveness of this concept. In his exploration of the history of moral panics, Garland (2008: 19) notes:

> the term "moral panic" emerged from late 1960s social reaction theory, especially the concern with the media's role in stereotyping and misrepresenting deviance and the perception that such reporting might contribute to a deviancy amplification spiral.

Garland argues that the power of the concept has been reduced from misapplication and overuse. One objection is the casual use of the term. For example, Jewkes (2004) observes that the media has started to use the term to describe any type of widespread societal concern that appears. Ironically, having seeped into common parlance and the very media it often condemned (Hunt, 1997), moral panic is rarely linked to broader criminological questions and social theory (Rohloff & Wright, 2010).

Other critiques focus on terminology and the failure to interrogate the definition of morality, which is value-laden and appears contextual (Jewkes, 2004). After attempting to explain the events that led to the prohibition of LSD by using moral theory, Cornwell and Linders (2002: 313) came to similar conclusions and noted that

> Still, we argue, by rescuing the notion of moral panic from some of the early problems that accompanied it, specifically with regards to a lack of specificity . . . the concept has been stretched so far beyond the original limits that

the array of social phenomena now fitting within the loosened boundaries no longer resemble each other in any analytically meaningful way. That is, the overlap with adjacent concepts (e.g., moral crusades, social problems, social movements, fads) is now so great that the moral panic concept has lost most of its own conceptual ground.

They go on to note that the distinguishing feature—disproportionality—is laden with ontological and methodological issues that render it useless to any serious analysis.

Hall (2012) goes further. He claims that the term "moral panic" misstates the role of media. Public concern, he stated, is not manufactured to keep deviant behavior in line but whipped up only to be soothed. Although the mass media obviously exaggerates the harm that street crime causes, the purpose is not to cause a "panic" and justify further authoritarian governance. Instead, the news always concludes its reports with solutions to crimes provided by the criminal justice system. This fosters a sentiment of complacency, not panic, and apathy, as opposed to anger. As David and colleagues (2011: 216) point out, this can be observed in the "shifting scope of the term moral panic, particularly its extension to cover themes that might not initially seem primarily moral in character—such as health scares and environmental protection."

We believe that, while valid in some cases, critiques of moral panics center around media overuse and conceptual ambiguities that cannot be uniformly applied to every situation. First, it seems irrational to dismiss an entire body of theory because the media has co-opted the term and muddied the conceptual waters. Second, while Garland (2008) is correct in pointing out the difficulties in assessing disproportionality, since there is no way to measure what a proportionate reaction should be to a specific action, one can examine the history and analyze comparable cases. Analyses comparing countries, states, provinces, and cities or similarities between the harms of illegal and legal drugs offer a means to better understand how to define a proportionate response. When these types of analyses are performed, the findings often suggest that past responses to cannabis use and possession have been highly disproportionate.

A more interesting objection centers on the question of whether people remain merely passive consumers of news. Previous research in this area has perhaps overemphasized the role of consensus and embraced a one-sided perception of the role of the media (Deflem, 2020). For example, Jewkes (2004) disputes the assumption that people are gullible enough to allow themselves to be manipulated by the media and the government again and again. This echoes an earlier critique. Thornton's (1994) study of British club cultures reveals that fanzines, pirate radio, websites, and email distribution lists are among many media outlets regularly used to counter existing moralizing discourses.

McRobbie and Thornton (1995) recognized that mass media had changed profoundly since the concept of moral panic emerged. They argue that "folk devils" are less marginalized than they once were and are castigated by mass media *while being* supported and defended, often at the same time. These observations cast a shadow on the potential of moral panics at exerting social control. Hier (2008: 178) offers some notable examples of this:

> Thornton's (1996) ethnography of youth club cultures in Britain, she found that youth not only reject approving or supportive coverage in the mass media but that they thrive on the legacy of previous folk devils. Parnaby's (2003) investigation of efforts to regulate "squeegee kids" in the City of Toronto, Canada, demonstrates how a plurality of pro-squeegee discourses (e.g., youth poverty) forwarded by anti-poverty activists, city councilors, and journalists was mobilized to resist efforts to outlaw squeegeeing.

Evidence of such activity can be found if one studies the history of cannabis policy and the subcultural reaction to it. This started early on with the emergence of head shops, which sold paraphernalia and cannabis legalization websites. It can also be seen in the more recent presence of legalization campaigns online. Pro-cannabis organizations like the Drug Policy Alliance (DPA) and the National Organization for the Reform of Marijuana Law (NORML) maintain a social media presence.

One of the problems with efforts to rethink moral panic is that they have led to the "deconstruction of traditional models without a reconstruction of alternative modes of explanation" (Hier et al., 2011: 262). Cannabis offers one way to begin to build an updated explanation. Just as stigma and normalization help explain the criminalization and decriminalization of cannabis, the moral panic framework may help frame this history in more specific ways. By applying past critiques, we advance a new formulation. This is based on Garland (2008), who expands on the list of moral panic indicators identified in Goode and Ben-Yehuda's (29009 [1994]) work. This elaboration is intended to reflect elements of Cohen's (2002 [1972]) contributions that Garland believes were overlooked by Goode and Ben-Yehuda (2009 [1994]).

Garland (2008) suggests that two items could be added to the existing list: (i) a moral dimension that involves introspection and soul-searching and (ii) the notion that the behavior (in this case, cannabis use) is symptomatic of a more serious underlying issue. For example, Garland (2008: 15) states:

> a specific group of deviants is singled out for "folk devil" status, in large part, because it possesses characteristics that make it a suitable screen upon which society can project sentiments of guilt and ambivalence. Detailed accounts of this process of denial and projection are developed... [to examine] the societal reaction to AIDS in the early 1980s and... the emergence in the 1890s of the "black beast rapist" folk devil in the American South.

Thus, the underlying cause of the disturbance is the collective concern on the part of some groups in society that their way of life is being threatened. How can we make sense of moral panics, given the fractured state of media and news sources in the United States and the growing lack of consensus on things like democracy, vaccines, racism, and human rights?

One effort is to widen the focus of moral panic studies by examining the relationship between the criminologies of moral panic and moral regulation (Hier et al., 2011). This involves recognizing that moral panics involve a unique political dynamic of "double problematization" involving both the reasons for and implications of sensationalized representations of folk devils *and* simultaneous struggles over the proper regulatory responses to matters of crime and law and order. Thus, broadening the scope of moral panic analyses must extend "beyond the episodic nature of resisting primary definitions" and be seen as "episodes of contestation and negotiation that emerge from and contribute to or reinforce broader processes of moral regulation" (Hier et al., 2011: 260). One possible reply is to think of moral panics in terms of lifespans.

Understanding the Lifespan of Moral Panics

While moral panic theory might be rooted in some vague and fuzzy concepts, this is no reason to dismiss the theory and abandon the entire research program. As noted above, while useful, many of the critiques can be resolved. There have clearly been broad societal overreactions to drug use and many other activities in the past. It is clear to us that it would also be ill advised to argue that there is currently a full-blown moral panic over cannabis legalization. However, as will be demonstrated later, a significant backlash and a possible reinvigoration of the previous moral panic around cannabis is one of many possible outcomes. One view expressed by Bennett (2018: 543) is that "the concept of moral panic is not really adequate to explain the ongoing nature of society's relationship with controversial issues such as psychoactive drugs and their use."

Previous theories of moral panics were static in nature. The notion that moral panics have a beginning, middle, and end is implied in some later writings about moral panic. Unfortunately, this idea is never wholly developed within the theory:

> The fragmentary and the integrated belong together: moral panics have their own internal trajectory—a microphysics of outrage—which, however, is initiated and sustained by wider social and political forces.
> (Cohen, 2002 [1972]: xxxix)

Bennett (2018) argues that these events, while seemingly singular and specific, are, in fact, interrelated and must be seen as such if they are to be properly understood. Thus, moral panics are not static entities but, instead, have different trajectories. This implies the existence of many overlapping waves of moral panic in operation at the same time. If modern moral panics are to be understood, the nature of these trajectories and their complex interrelationships must be further explored.

Klocke and Muschert (2010) have proposed a hybrid model of moral panics that incorporates aspects of both Cohen's (2002 [1972]) process-based model and Goode and Ben-Yehuda's (2009 [1994]) element-based model while also accounting for changes that have occurred in the media since these theories were proposed. This new model attempts to account for the indeterminate and volatile nature of many contemporary moral panics while allowing for the more modern tendency of folk devils to resist while acknowledging the disproportionate distribution of social and institutionalized power. The hybrid model of moral panics takes a more developmental approach and considers the impacts beyond singular volatile media and social lifespan. Instead, moral panic frameworks need to "identify what happens during a moral panic . . . how it happens [and] allow for the possibility of counter-narratives not only from folk devils but also from others engaging in the fragmented mediascape" (Klocke & Muschert, 2010: 301).

Understanding the history and developmental stages of moral panics and cannabis is essential. Cody (2006) identified four key phases in the moral panic around cannabis that serve a useful organizing function: *racialization, criminalization, popularization,* and *medicalization*. These phases can be situated within the hybrid model offered by Klocke and Muschert (2010) to help better understand the development and dissipation of moral panics. Indeed, it seems that the moral panic around cannabis is still alive; however, it has evolved to fit the changing political landscape. Klocke and Muschert's (2010) hybrid model of moral panics identifies three stages, each with several substages, which moral panics progress through during their lifespan: cultivation, operation, and dissipation. *Cultivation* refers to the early stages in which stakeholders and narratives emerge that encourage the growth of moral panics. Critical conditions include conflict among different groups with competing ideologies, rapid social changes, economic or political crises, and increased media attention.

The *operation stage* occurs in response to a troubling event or series of events reported by the media that identify the threat at hand. These events are distorted, predictions about future crime and deviance are made, and dramatic images are connected to the behavior. This also includes a period of magnification of harms that provides explanations as to why the folk devils are a threat to society alongside testimony by "experts" such as police, politicians, community leaders, and other moral entrepreneurs—this reoccurring narrative can be seen in a variety of media, including opinion polls, letters to the editor, protests, web pages, blogs, Facebook posts, and tweets. This stage also includes a period of attempts to regulate behavior that may consist of various approaches, including surveillance, legal mobilization, and implementation of new institutional structures to control the behavior (Klocke & Muschert, 2010).

The final stage identified in the hybrid moral panic model is referred to as *dissipation* and describes what happens as moral panics fade away. In cases where the moral panic has been successful, and the moral entrepreneurs succeed, there may be some sort of institutional, ideological, or social change that emerges to address the problem. In cases where a moral panic fails, there may be a degree of normalization regarding the targeted behavior or group. Eventually, the moral panic may be debunked and dismissed by society; however, even after it has died out, the lasting institutional and societal change caused by it may continue to impact society (Klocke & Muschert, 2010).

Cultivation Stage: Racializing Cannabis Use
As demonstrated in Chapter 1, the first cannabis moral panic was an extension of anti-immigrant sentiment that initially targeted Indian and Chinese

immigrants. Later, these sentiments were applied to Mexican and Black populations in the United States. Differing physical characteristics denoted non-White inferiority, and these attitudes were held against Aboriginals in Australia and West Indian immigrants in Britain. By undermining the cultural tradition of cannabis use by the groups who were the target of these moral panics, legislation was used to control non-White people who were seen as an existential risk to White Anglophone ideals.

This early phase of racialization identified by Cody (2006) fits squarely within the cultivation stage in the hybrid model of moral panics (Klocke & Muschert, 2010). Cannabis and other drugs were targeted during the transition from the "Roaring Twenties" to the Great Depression, and one must keep in mind that these generations were living in the aftermath of the First World War. These are precisely the conditions identified by Klocke and Muschert (2010: 300), including "value conflicts and lifestyle clashes between diverse cultural groups . . . Economic (e.g., recession) and political crises (e.g., war) or other challenges to social hegemony (e.g., social movements, youth, and alternative sub-cultures)." As noted in Chapter 1, various drugs, including cannabis, cocaine, and opium, all became targets of criminalization during this period, and racist depictions were used in varying ways to garner support for criminalization.

The moral panic around opium that resulted can best be understood through the grassroots model. The general public was concerned about the economic threat of Chinese labor, which led to the panic surrounding opium. The cannabis panic then transformed into both an interest-group and an elite-engineered panic in which the media was used to publicize concerns and enact legislation to protect White people from the threat of cannabis.

Operation Stage, Phase One: Criminalization of Cannabis
Canada criminalized cannabis in 1923. The United Kingdom followed suit in September 1928 through an addition to the Dangerous Drugs Act of 1920. A decade later, the US Congress passed the Marijuana Tax Act (1937). In the United States, criminalization was aided by a propaganda campaign that targeted people of color, including Mexican immigrants and Black musicians. This panic simply updated the racialized themes of past moral panics, while offering criminal sanctions to address popular concerns.

While this moral panic emerged from a climate of largely media-manufactured hysteria, the role of elites like Henry J. Anslinger and William Randolph Hearst, who influenced (and controlled) the media, was essential. Hearst was a media mogul and supported the criminalization of cannabis, in part because his own paper-producing companies were being replaced by hemp. Likewise, the DuPont Company's investment in nylon was threatened by hemp products (Norland & Wright, 1984). Through Anslinger's moral crusade and a series of articles published in Hearst's paper, jazz was blamed for "endangering the morals of young people by encouraging the release of animal passions through sensual dancing, boy–girl contact, the sexual content of jazz lyrics and of course the link with drug taking" (Blackman, 2004: 83). Newspapers in other countries like Australia and Britain repeated racist tropes, warned of cannabis-inspired moral degradation, and extended the American-inspired "Reefer Madness" campaign (Booth, 2003).

Klocke and Muschert (2010) explain that the operation stage is initiated by a shocking episode or series of events involving the behavior. There was no one specific event or story that caused societal attitudes to shift favorably toward cannabis prohibition but rather a series of articles telling shocking stories of cannabis was released to the public. Becker (1963) notes that from July 1937 to June 1939, there were seventeen articles in popular magazines about the dangers of cannabis, and many of these directly acknowledged help with facts and figures given by the Federal Bureau of Investigation. These stories often described horrible atrocities committed under the influence of cannabis. For example:

> An entire family was murdered by a youthful [marihuana] addict in Florida. When officers arrived at the home, they found the youth staggering about in a human, slaughterhouse. With an ax, he had killed his father, his mother, two brothers, and a sister. . . . The officers knew him ordinarily as a sane, rather quiet young man; now he was pitifully crazed. . . . The boy said he had been in the habit of smoking something which youthful friends called "muggles," a childish name for marihuana.
> (as cited in Becker, 1963: 142)

These developments are an example of magnification of the problem described by Klocke and Muschert (2010) in their hybrid model of moral panics. This period was characterized by moralization, officiation (e.g., use of experts and officials, in this case, doctors, police, and criminal justice officials), and amplification of the problem. Criminalization also served interest groups such as religious organizations that echoed moral worries associated with the temperance movement. While anti-immigration groups could support the criminalization of non-White culture, criminalization would later serve to disrupt the anti-war left, race and gender equality activists those who embraced noncapitalist social and economic models, and people who sought spiritual inspiration from drug-induced intoxication. Once again, a confluence of interests and organizations could benefit by leaning into the panic over numerous decades.

Operation Stage, Phase Two: Panic over Cannabis Popularization
The 1960s began what has been described as the "popularization" moral panic. The invention of the contraceptive pill altered sexual morality, student activism and feminism were born, and freedom of speech and the rights of the individual were the basis for demonstrations and sit-ins (Booth, 2003). Musicians openly questioned the laws, norms, and practices of their parents' generation, and youth started asking difficult questions about the norms that governed society (Muncie, 2004). The popularization of cannabis use emerged from the youth counterculture in the 1960s, which could be viewed as a forerunner to the later shift in the 1990s to cannabis normalization identified by Parker and colleagues (1998, 2002; Parker, 2005). As cannabis became popular among specific segments of the White middle class, especially college students, Campos (2018) describes the cultural shift by linking it to a famous edited volume.

David Solomon's 1968 edited volume, *The Marijuana Papers*, combined sociological, historical, and botanical essays with literary contributions. Together, these sources established the basic structure of a reformist critique of cannabis prohibition. Campos (2018: 8) argues that Solomon articulated the historical moment of "the Sixties" in a nutshell:

> that benevolent herb whose effects contrasted so sharply with the "psychologically numbing" alcohol of the mainstream; that natural wonder whose persecution was just another injustice blindly accepted by the anesthetized, conformist, and decidedly misguided older generation.

Those who protested America's involvement in the war were associated with cannabis use, but cannabis and other drug use by soldiers was well known.

Southeast Asia was a source of readily available cannabis. It has been estimated that 75 percent of the soldiers sent to Vietnam used it at some point (Brownlee, 2002: 54). Cannabis use by troops in Vietnam served as a way of escaping the horrors of the war and was easy to conceal and carry (Booth, 2003). This fed developments on the ground:

> After social uses of cannabis were popularized in the 1960s and 1970s, the sensational characterizations of earlier in the century became difficult to

maintain. Many more people had tried cannabis or knew people who used it without suffering any dire consequences. Modern claims of harm shifted away from the most outrageous exaggerations but maintained a quality of disproportionality that is characteristic of moral panics.

(Newhart & Dolphin, 2019: 21)

The confluence of Vietnam veterans and popular musicians and bands who used, wrote, and sang about cannabis created a unique moment.

The moral panic that resulted in this period was a reaction to the broader revolution of cultural transformation and youth identity (Duff, 2003). The panic that was created involved demonizing the drug and those who supplied it. For example, language framed cannabis use as the result of "'evil' traffickers who were trapping so many 'children of good families' through the lure of cannabis" (Del Olmo, 1991: 18). Instead of "killer weed," cannabis came to be known as the "drop-out drug" (Newhart & Dolphin, 2019: 21). This brought into focus the institutional complicity in criminalizing young people (Kaplan, 1970). Once again, the interest-group moral panic that attempted to restore the social equilibrium in society served elite interests in maintaining the status quo (Springhall, 1998).

Operation Stage, Phase Three: Medicalization of Cannabis Use
Ironically, medicalization does not refer to the increased use of cannabis for medical conditions. Medicalization, instead, refers to "the increasing attachment of medical labels to behavior regarded as socially or morally undesirable" (Abercrombie et al., 1994: 244). While medicalization emerged in the 1960s, concerns focused on medical cannabis emerged first in 1924, during the Second Opium Conference. Mohamed El Guindy, the delegate from Egypt, now ostensibly independent from Great Britain, proposed the inclusion of cannabis in the Convention. Support came from Brazil, Greece, South Africa, and Turkey (Transnational Institute, n.d.). El Guindy painted a horrific picture of the effects of hashish. As described by Beweley-Taylor, Blickman, and Jelsma (2014: 14), the delegation claimed:

> that a person "under the influence of hashish presents symptoms very similar to those of hysteria"; that the individual's "'intellectual faculties gradually weaken and the whole organism decays"; and that "the proportion of cases of insanity caused by the use of hashish varies from 30 to 60 percent of the total number of cases occurring in Egypt." Cannabis not only led to insanity, according to El Guindy, but was a gateway to other

drugs, and vice versa. If it was not included on the list with opium and cocaine, he predicted, cannabis would replace them and "become a terrible menace to the whole world."

These reports could not be substantiated. In fact, some of the earliest studies into medicinal cannabis use conducted in a mental asylum (Moreau, 1841, 1845) concluded that hashish *calmed* patients, increased their appetites, and helped them sleep (Booth, 2003). Nevertheless, El Guindy's provocative claims caused a stir among the delegates.

While the connections between insanity and cannabis are long-standing, the "medical model" proper emerged as a response to the popularization of cannabis among young people and is based on the idea that modern medicine can cure all social problems by adopting a medical framework to understand problematic behavior and advocating medical intervention to treat this behavior (Conrad et al., 1992).

A significant development during this period was the explicit identification of the cannabis user as "sick" and the growing language based on addiction/dependence stereotypes (Cody, 2006). This could be viewed as a new form of institutional regulation and an attempt to control cannabis use through an appeal to health and medical concerns rather than through punishment or threats posed by aggressive minority users. Klocke and Muschert (2010: 304) elaborate on this process in the passage below:

> Agents of social control and action groups mobilize financial and human resources to take corrective legislative, civic, and law enforcement measures against the new threat. The mobilization of regulatory forces may become institutionalized with the creation of new formal organizations, such as neighborhood crime-watch groups or law enforcement task groups, the passage of new laws or tougher penalties.

Experts also became much more involved during this era, including medical doctors, psychiatrists, and psychological researchers.

As the drug became associated with White, middle-class youth, the explanation of its use changed from being seen as a form of "badness" to one of "sickness" (Conrad et al., 1992). Lempert (1974) has argued that this shift from punitive to medicalized policy was more than likely a product of "moral dissonance" on the part of policymakers and the general public over cannabis laws. Moral dissonance is based on Festinger's (1957) concept of cognitive dissonance, which refers to psychological stress that arises from observing situations where behaviors and beliefs do not match or are incongruent. In this case, moral dissonance arose when the White children of the upper and middle classes started to be labeled as criminals for violating cannabis laws. Lempert (1974: 8) explains further:

> it is interesting to note that the Salem witchcraft mania began with accusations against the three lowest status women in the village and ended after a series of leading citizens were accused; the movement of prohibition drew strength from the *association of drinking* with immigrants and ended at a time when the children and grandchildren of immigrants were achieving considerable wealth and social status; and marihuana was criminalized when it was used largely by Blacks and dance hall musicians, with the movement for decriminalization taking root when the children of the white middle class began to smoke.

The medical discourse includes the addiction/dependence model. Claims of harm are based on the purported adverse effects on the mental health of people who use cannabis. As this discourse became more established, it has become difficult to dislodge. When behaviors or complaints become connected, labeled, and defined as part of a problem, these constructions are legitimized by key institutions and their representatives. When medicalization is completed, it can be difficult to remember that the problem was constructed in any other way. It appears to be a "fact," and its incorporation into medical treatment is now uncontroversial (Newhart & Dolphin, 2019: 31).

The moral panic associated with the medicalization of cannabis built on early claims that the use of the drug would lead to mental illness. Initially, it concentrated on the immediate short-term effects supposedly related to the drug, such as promiscuity and violent crime. Today, it is the risk of damaging, long-term effects that are presented to induce fear (Goode, 2005). The medical moral panic arose from an interest-group perspective, including the medical profession and other anti-cannabis groups. Initially, the panic resulted in segregated sanctions. Cannabis legislation began to differentiate laws between and among users, the corrupted, who might deserve a lesser penalty, and traffickers, who, as the corruptors, deserved greater punishment (White & Habibis, 2005; Young, 1971).

Of course, criminal sanctions are not the only means of exerting social control over people who use cannabis. As introduced in Chapter 2, stigma can occur through a sequential model that defines deviance and integrates it within therapeutic parlance (Conrad et al., 1992). These choices have constrained the pathways for patients, doctors, advocates, and policymakers; perpetuated a moral panic; and limited appropriate medical uses of cannabis.

Dissipation Stage: Normalization, Legalization, and Recirculation
Medicalization implies a contest between deviant cannabis use and legitimate medical use; however, this fails to fully capture the relationships between medical and recreational use. The medicalized moral panic that has been identified around the use of cannabis has paradoxically coexisted with the increasing use of cannabis products to treat specific medical conditions. Our focus on the current developments toward regulation concerns the recreational use of cannabis and the inevitable backlash. This should be distinguished from valuable work examining the regulation of the medical use of cannabis (Newhart & Dolphin, 2019).

It is untenable to argue the current pushback against legalization amounts to a moral panic per se. Cannabis policies are being liberalized at an unprecedented rate, stigma has been reduced, and there is a legitimate sense that full legalization is simply a matter of time. Klocke and Muschert (2010: 304) note that these changes do not necessarily indicate that the moral panic has ended but instead that it has entered a new stage:

> As a MP [(moral panic)] recedes, whether through "success" (the moral threat of the folk devils is mitigated) or "failure" (e.g., MP is revealed as a faulty myth), there are several possibilities of the outcomes of the decline. One possibility is that the normalization of the threat and attempts at regulation become an accepted part of the routines of daily life. Another possibility is that the panic results in longer lasting social or institutional transformation (e.g., new laws), either in support of moral regulation of folk devils, or against it and accepting them as part of a changing democratic culture. The immediacy of a MP may also dissolve if the premises of it are debunked, offending behavior drops off, or another pressing social problem takes its place.

Today, the prohibition-based regimes of the past are increasingly regarded as being intrusive. They needlessly violate privacy, are expensive to maintain, and are inevitably socially divisive. As social norms shift, the cost outweighs any benefit. An excellent example of this shift was the massive outcry following the suspension and non-selection of the top American female sprinter Sha'Carri Richardson after testing positive for cannabis prior to the 2021 Tokyo Olympics (Draper & Macur, 2021). The decision was mercilessly mocked online, connected to Richardson's racial background, and led to allegations of a double standard (Amore, 2021). Physician and cannabis researcher Sue Sisley stated to the Washington post:

> I understand that the Olympics have the ability to sanction players based on conduct and for using performance-enhancing drugs, but there's no evidence that cannabis is performance-enhancing. . . . This seems genuinely unfair that we continue to punish athletes based on a test that should not even be done. Why do the Olympics continue to test for THC at all?
>
> (Kilgore and Maese, 2021)

The World Anti-Doping Agency (WADA) guidelines state that substances are banned if they meet two of three following criteria: (i) the substance is a performance-enhancing drug, (ii) the substance represents an actual or potential risk to health; and (iii) the use of the substance violates the spirit of the sport.[3] WADA has gone to great lengths to justify including cannabis on its list, even commissioning a paper on the subject that argued cannabis fits all of these criteria (Huestis et al., 2011, as cited in Pereira & Yamada, 2021). Ironically, alcohol and tobacco consumption are nowhere to be found on this list, despite having negative impacts on the body and not being in the spirit of athletic competition. At the time this chapter was written, no rules had changed.

This is a stark reminder of the fact that while social norms are changing, the global prohibition regime remains in place. It seems inevitable that regulation will lead to a backlash against the increased use and prevalence of cannabis. If the past is any indication, misleading claims from media sources will build on existing racial, ethnic, or cultural stereotypes. The concern is that any legitimate dangers associated with increased use will be magnified and presented in such a way as to instill a "panic." Even if such instigations do not produce effects identical to the cannabis moral panics of the past, these mini panics, which seem to be a regular feature of Fox News, are likely to capture the public's attention.

In some jurisdictions, these fears may result in legislation that may do more harm than good. For example, Room and colleagues (2010) note that, in some parts of Australia, despite a shift away from total prohibition, some states have experienced an increase in the number of people entangled within the criminal justice system after introducing reforms. As Hamilton (2001: 108–109) observes,

While there is no significant change in the pattern of prevalence of use of cannabis in South Australia, there has been a paradoxical increase in the number of people charged with cannabis offenses.... This increase is viewed as a net-widening effect and is thought to be related to the relative ease of intervention by police under the Controlled Substance Amendment Act.

In Chapter 5, we show how net widening has become a feature of cannabis reform. In addition, it is likely that we will see older ideas about cannabis, addiction, and mental health re-emerge. Claims that increased access will lead to an increase in use among youth have already been made, and there are many emerging concerns about what use will do to developing brains. Older alarmist associations between cannabis and psychosis (Berenson, 2019; Gladwell, 2019) are currently being revisited (D'Souza et al., 2022), and there are concerns about motor vehicle accidents that arise from drivers who use cannabis, emergency room visits for accidental ingestion, and bizarre claims about cannabis products which are close to 100% THC causing new health maladies (Caron, 2022). Cannabis prohibition will not go gently into that good night.

A new and perhaps unexpected worry relates to the environmental costs of producing cannabis to stock nascent business enterprises. While cannabis emerged as an environmental policy matter under prohibition, it intensified after cannabis's medical decriminalization. These concerns may straddle interest groups concerned with the outside role of agribusiness, the use of pesticides, and worries about the use of agricultural land for cannabis instead of food production (Polson, 2019). Consistent with the history of cannabis, there are pervasive myths that surround cannabis production. These usually arise from the deliberately misleading practice of linking issues that have emerged because of illegal, unpermitted growers with new and more regulated cannabis operations (Steinfeld, 2020). Concerns around reclamation, pollution, stewardship, and sustainability have led to a shift in thinking about cannabis production (Polson, 2019: 245). The future will likely involve better specifying how large-scale producers can offset any environmental damage associated with commercial cannabis while ensuring that smaller-scale producers are not regulated out of the market.

Cannabis moral panics have emerged from both genuine public concern and material and status interests from all levels of the social hierarchy (Cody, 2006). Therefore, a moral panic may not have to meet all the criteria for just one of the theories discussed above. Today, rather than a meta-moral panic that captures society collectively, we may be living through an age in which it is normal for numerous moral panics to be in operation simultaneously (see also Klocke & Muschert, 2010). This could be conceptualized as a *multiverse of moral panics*. Each panic emerges from specific media ecosystems and, in turn, influences smaller and smaller groups of people to engage in more and more radical behavior. Whether they originate from elite-driven efforts, interest groups, or the grassroots, concerns that emerge from one source are often picked up by another. While the concept of moral panics surrounding cannabis initially arose when people still trusted network news, the future of this idea requires resituating it within the media ecosystem.

Moral Panics, Information Cocoons, and Participatory Disinformation

Research has begun to show how information spread online is not fully captured by traditional media sources. These include focusing on the rise of conspiracy theories in the United States, key differences between newspaper articles and online interactions through social media (Tangherlini et al., 2020), and the role of online interactions, which fueled an anti-immigrant moral panic in the context of Brexit (Martins, 2021). In both cases, online interactions offered a new means by which to understand how those susceptible to misinformation searched for meaning in ways that reified their sense of belonging and identity. While both Brexit and the January 6 Insurrection are outcomes that are consistent with moral panic concepts, including concern, consensus, hostility, disproportionality, and volatility (Goode & Ben-Yehuda, 2009 [1994]), they went further. The ways in which participatory disinformation fueled not only online sentiment but real-world outcomes deserve more attention.

The ways in which these developments are connected to broad political instability extend beyond criminology. In the United States, Walter (2022) suggests these elements may result in extremists who use, and are used by, social media and engage in scattered yet persistent acts designed to destabilize democratic bodies through extra-political means. In 2021, school boards, hospitals, and vaccine clinics were targeted. It seems likely that the same trends that animated and radicalized these groups will impact how we consider moral panics in the twenty-first century. Panics may come faster and be more intense. While they might be short-lived in duration, their influence has the potential to generate feelings about people, places, and activities that are difficult to dislodge once they are established. If history is any indication, cannabis is an easy target.

To make an informed guess about how moral panics may operate in the future, it is useful to examine how they operated in the past. Without a renewed focus on the quality of the justification for claims presented as true, good, or sound, there may be no way to build bridges between people and, thus, no way to advance pragmatic means to improve lives (Wheeldon, 2015). Creating a problem, defining a scapegoat, and projecting one's fears onto ever smaller segments of the population is the preferred business model for many media conglomerates (Pariser, 2011). It may not be laudable, but it is very profitable. It represents a challenge for post-prohibition cannabis research programs, especially studies focused on cannabis and criminal behavior.

If moral panics represent "episodes of contestation and negotiation that emerge from and contribute to or reinforce broader processes of moral regulation" (Hier et al., 2011: 260), then they may serve simultaneously as risks to rights and justice and opportunities to educate and inform. Yet, to pierce the online bubbles from which these ideas emerge, a new generation of scholars needs to think carefully about engaging in social media and embracing the inherent irony of the internet age. These questions are revisited in Chapter 9. However, combatting prohibition myths by sharing credible research requires that quality analyses be undertaken. In terms of cannabis, reliable research has been difficult to find. While this is changing, undoing the harmful ideas and methods that have shaped policy must be "undone" if responsible approaches are to gain a foothold (Szalavitz, 2021).

Rather than confronting large-scale meta-moral panics that once appeared to capture society's collective fear, contemporary criminologists must contend with numerous moral panics that are operating at the same time (Klocke & Muschert, 2010). This phenomenon appears to be increasing and requires identification and better specification. In the moral panic multiverse, filter bubbles create distinct subcultures in which algorithms isolate people from information and viewpoints that may challenge or conflict with their current views (Pariser, 2011). The problem with these bubbles is myriad. Not only are they used to conceal online commercial imperatives that most fail to understand, but they also create informational cul-de-sacs that tend to foreclose access to other viewpoints and perspectives. Perhaps most worrying is how these bubbles create the impression that individual and narrow self-interest is all that exists.

This is especially true when these "informational cocoons" (Sunstein, 2001) connect individuals with other like-minded people who share their personal political preferences and, perhaps more importantly, antipathies:

> The resulting divisions run along many lines—of race, religion, ethnicity, nationality, wealth, age, political conviction, and more. . . . With the reduced importance of the general interest magazine and newspaper, and the flowering of individual programming design, different groups make fundamentally different choices.
>
> (Sunstein, 2001: 4)

Individual concerns emerge from, or are manufactured within, a specific media ecosystem. These concerns are shared, often quickly, and take on a life of their own. Subcultures emerge that establish a realm that is increasingly difficult to understand unless one inhabits that same informational universe.

In the United Kingdom, one need only consider Brexit and the ways in which specific lies and general untruths permeated both online rhetoric and broadsheet coverage (Lewis, 2019). The racism at the root of the fear of foreigners and migrants was joined with nonsensical tales, easily fact-checked, that drew upon nostalgia, British exceptionalism, and the general lack of understanding about the economic consequences of leaving the European Union. As Dougan and O'Brien (2019: 201–202) note, the *Leave Campaign* employed four tactics categorized as telling lies, selling fantasies, suppressing/abusing the opposition, and blaming scapegoats. Together, these were weaponized and used to encourage people to "take back control." The result, according to MacKenzie & Bhatt (2020: 217), is that

> Brexit's "post-truth" politics poses a serious challenge to the values of truth and trust. . . . The Brexit process, the means by which the U.K. will negotiate its withdrawal from membership of the European Union (E.U.) following the referendum in 2016, has revealed that large sections of mainstream political parties and the mainstream media lack "even a basic degree of knowledge or insight about institutions, relationships," processes and forces (such as those on which the E.U. and universities operate) which are "crucial to national life."

Consider Pizzagate, the QAnon conspiracy, the COVID-19 anti-vaccine movement, or the confluence of conspiracies that led to the January 6 2021 riot and insurrection at the US Capitol. Part of why the 2021 insurrection in the United States remains so difficult to understand was that it was based on assumptions and misinformation that only existed within specific subcultures.

In the Philippines (Ong & Cabañes, 2018), the role of political operators who can use social media to share misinformation, manufacture panics, and weaponize participatory disinformation has been documented. In 2016, this confluence led to the election of Rodrigo Duerte, who launched a bloody war on drugs which led to a "systematic assault on civilians" (Reuters, 2021). Five years later, many similar aspects are evident. On January 6, 2021, elites, including elected political leaders, political pundits, partisan media outlets, and social media influencers, engaged large online audiences generated through disinformation. During and following the 2020 election, Trump supporters repeatedly spread the message that the 2020 election was rigged. This set an expectation of voter fraud and became a "frame" through which events were interpreted.

Audiences adopt these frames and begin to generate false/misleading stories that tend to reinforce the frame. This sometimes occurs intentionally but more often is the result of unconscious assumptions and a sincere misinterpretation of events around them. These audiences are transformed by activists and social media influencers and help amplify these stories, passing the content up to the political elites, who have seen their work read back to them. They then re-share it and claim this as additional evidence from "the people." Participatory disinformation makes for a powerful dynamic. These tight feedback loops between "elites" and their audiences (facilitated by social media) seem to make the system more responsive—and possibly more powerful and unwieldy.[4] Figure 3.2 provides one view of participatory disinformation in the run-up to this repellent event.

Conclusion

Cannabis and its use were socially constructed throughout the twentieth century as a threat to mental health, the White race, law and order, and social stability (Newhart & Dolphin, 2019). It represents an essential example of the social and political power of bad ideas (Schrad, 2010). Moral panics based on race, crime, social unrest, and medical use hold essential lessons for the current backlash against efforts to legalize and regulate recreational cannabis. In this chapter, we reviewed the various theories of moral panic

CONCLUSION 87

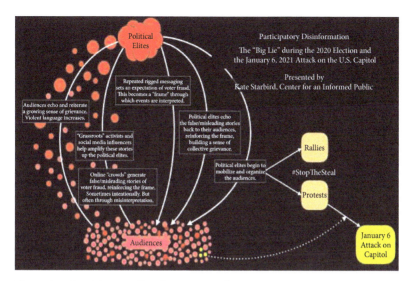

Figure 3.2 Participatory disinformation and January 6, 2021
Source: Katie Starbird, used with permission.

and several critiques (Deflem, 2020; Garland, 2008; Jewkes, 2004; Rohloff & Wright, 2010). To update the concept to fit within the modern media landscape, we propose that this concept be framed based on how the rise of social media allows moral panics to be operating at once and often build on each other in a variety of ways.

While it is helpful to acknowledge that moral panics have a certain lifespan (Klocke & Muschert, 2010), these panics seem to be operating in new and complex ways. They have implications for sustaining and extending cannabis and other drug policy liberalization. As Reid (2020: 4) notes,

> While the stigma surrounding cannabis appears to have diminished, there is little evidence that such stigma has entirely disappeared. Medicalization and legalization certainly help reduce cannabis stigmas, but these transformations in policy do not entirely shift social perceptions on their own . . . the lived experience of a post-prohibition society is not the same as a one where cannabis is normalized. Such policies remove structural sources of stigmas, but since stigmas vary in their source, negative attitudes towards cannabis stem from a combination of overlapping institutional, social, and individual forces.

Even though regulation has followed normalization in some countries, there is still substantial stigma associated with cannabis use. The fallout of decades of demonization remains. A recurrent worry is the mental health concerns around cannabis use. From the reefer madness of the 1940s to the panic around schizophrenia and psychosis that has become prominent over the past decade, we have examined the changing nature of the stigma against, and panic around, cannabis use. These observations are important, especially given the outsized influence of prohibitionist ideas.

Cannabis has long been the subject of misinformation. However, given recent examples in the Philippines, the United States, and the United Kingdom, the combination of misinformation, filter bubbles, and the cyclical and expanding nature of untruth can create alternative universes which take for granted ideas that were never subject to scrutiny. Just as the history of moral panics involved defining and delineating how different groups instigated panics (Cody, 2006), it is increasingly evident that these groups do not operate as mutually exclusive actors. Instead, they interact and build one on top of the other to create an informational ecosystem that is impossible to understand if one is outside of it. When multiple truths, each can be weaponized as part of grievance politics and authoritarian impulses.

Notes

1. "Memorandum from H.J. Anslinger, Commissioner, Bureau of Narcotics, Department of the Treasury, to District Supervisors & Others Concerned" (December 4, 1934).
2. "However, the earliest usage [can be traced] to 1831 and a critique of the French government's habit of enacting military cordons around Cholera-afflicted towns, amplifying the original infection and causing unrest amongst the towns' populations. The basic framework of this argument is not too different from the moral panic theory we know today" (Horsley, 2017: 84).
3. See https://www.wada-ama.org/en/content/what-is-prohibited.
4. For a useful overview which influences this description see Grass (2021).

PART II

LEGAL RENEGOTIATION, REGULATION, AND RESEARCH

4
Regulatory Models of Cannabis Policy

Introduction

Cannabis policy is evolving worldwide (Seddon & Floodgate, 2020). Twenty countries, from Belize to Switzerland, have decriminalized cannabis possession. It has been legalized in Uruguay, Canada, and many US states. Recently, Mexico's Supreme Court ruled that cannabis prohibition was "unconstitutional" (BBC News, 2021). In Europe, legal cannabis will soon be available in Germany and Malta. As part of a coordinated COVID-19 response, most Canadian provinces declared non-medical cannabis retail sales an "essential service" (Canadian Centre on Substance Use and Addiction, 2021). Based on cannabis's relative safety (D'Souza et al., 2022; Eliason & Howse, 2019) and the undeniable damage done by prohibitionist policies, especially to Black, Indigenous, and Other People of Color (BIPOC) around the world (Wheeldon & Heidt, 2023a), change is coming (UNCEBC, 2019).

In 2019, the United Nations (UN) called on member states to promote "alternatives to conviction and punishment in appropriate cases, including decriminalizing drug possession for personal use" (UNCEBC, 2019). The wide variety of cannabis liberalization approaches worldwide requires a conceptual framework to understand regulatory approaches to cannabis. This chapter explores five models that guide contemporary cannabis policy. These include the public safety model (Fischer et al., 2021), the public health model (Wesley & Murray, 2021), the medicinal model (Newhart & Dolphin, 2019), a commercial model (Mahamad et al., 2020), and an emergent racial justice model (Bender, 2016).

These five models serve as a useful starting point to contemplate cannabis policy in North America and around the world. By their nature, monomorphic models of cannabis regulation offer a singular view of cannabis governance. While incomplete, given the range of models which may coexist within a jurisdiction, defining these models provides an essential starting point. Although assessing these models individually, it is possible to focus on fundamental assumptions, operational goals, and practical outcomes, and this chapter tries

Visions of Cannabis Control. Jon Heidt and Johannes Wheeldon, Oxford University Press.
© Jon Heidt and Johannes Wheeldon 2023. DOI: 10.1093/oso/9780198875215.003.0004

to clarify where these models converge and where substantive gaps exist. We consider seven jurisdictions where cannabis policy has been liberalized to describe these models, including Australia, Canada, Portugal, the Netherlands, the United Kingdom, Uruguay, and the United States.

Five Models of Cannabis Regulation

Regulatory frameworks and models guide policies and practices. Assessing regulatory models often proceeds by examining distinct characteristics associated with their assumptions, goals, approaches to legitimacy, and policy instruments (Majone, 1994). These models are often described as competing with other regulatory approaches for governing influence within a jurisdiction (Dunleavy & O'Leary, 1987). Efforts to frame cannabis regulation are emerging (Corva & Meisel, 2021; Seddon & Floodgate, 2020; Wheeldon & Heidt, 2023b). However, two early views on cannabis remain dominant in policy discussions. For example, one vision was to retain prohibition but reduce sanctions, while another was to regulate cannabis like alcohol (Caulkins et al., 2015: 51–52). While these two approaches nominally move beyond solely focusing on the criminal justice system to control cannabis, both fail to consider how social control may evolve, transform, and expand (Cohen, 1985).

Public Safety

Cannabis policy reform remains constrained by the assumption that it is somehow connected to crime. Fischer and colleagues (2021) consider five areas of cannabis-related research based on these concerns. These include the deterrent effect of prohibition; illicit production, markets, and supply in a legalization regime; use enforcement; cannabis-impaired driving; and cannabis and crime. As we have observed elsewhere, the fact that cannabis prohibition has existed for a century means that for most of our lives, simply possessing cannabis meant one was engaging in criminal behavior (Wheeldon & Heidt, 2023b). These assumptions lead to operational goals which view the criminal justice system as the primary and legitimate response to the cannabis threat. Moreover, the enforcement of cannabis prohibitions has long been costly (Kaplan, 1970), racist (Mize, 2020), and based on ideology, not evidence (Ritter, 2021).

In operational terms, public safety models often hold that the criminal justice system is the best way to manage cannabis and the people who use it. Unfortunately, as we have shown, this has allowed groups with access to policymakers to link criminal justice and drug policy to justify their ideological views (Heidt & Wheeldon, 2022). In addition, the selective use of evidence to support the idea that cannabis threatens safety and security allows myths to be accepted as accurate by the people "who have the resources to translate them into political action" (Stevens, 2011: 86).

By introducing stricter public smoking regulations with more severe penalties (Shepherd, 2018), consuming cannabis remains associated with crime. In addition, despite little compelling evidence that cannabis-impaired driving poses dire public safety risks (Brubacher et al., 2019), many US states have added new cannabis-focused driving prohibitions to existing impaired driving laws (Compton, 2017). While mixing cannabis and alcohol represent safety risks on the road, public safety efforts have outpaced the evidence base (Pearlson et al., 2021). Adopting public safety models has a variety of outcomes (Kaplan, 1970).

Seddon & Floodgate (2020: 8–9) summarize how the practical costs of relying on public safety and cannabis prohibition have been high in economic, social, and political terms. These include:

- facilitating a large and untaxed income stream for groups and individuals involved in crime;
- criminalizing millions of young people for behavior that, for most, is short-lived and causes minimal social harms;
- enforcement activities that fall most heavily on marginalized and excluded communities, undermining social justice;
- enforcement being disproportionately targeted at minority ethnic groups, driving racial injustice;
- incentivizing the creation of more potent and more dangerous synthetic cannabinoids.

A comprehensive focus on public safety would include the risks associated with illicit markets, such as exposure to violence, the subversion of the rule of law, and the corruption related to criminal networks and drug-trafficking syndicates (Ritter, 2021). One clear public safety risk is that people who use cannabis are forced to seek dealers who maximize profits by selling various illicit drugs.

Public Health

Public health models assume cannabis use represents a risk to well-being. This assumption can be traced to references to insanity and addiction during early international drug control meetings in the 1920s.[1] This association served political ends and spread through the US-based "Reefer Madness" era of the 1930s (Heidt & Wheeldon, 2022). By 1969, a "global drug prohibition regime" emerged that limited cannabis research and focused solely on the harmful effects of cannabis (Newhart & Dolphin, 2019: 57–65). In the 1990s, the assumption that cannabis led to addiction re-emerged. The Brain Disease Model of Addiction (BDMA), based on early work by Alan Leshner (1997), was connected to the gateway theory of drug use.[2] Until recently, this view served as the primary justification for global drug policy (Volkow & Li, 2005). This approach is based on medicalizing deviance. Framed as progressive penology, it may simply serve as a socially acceptable means to extend social control (Cohen, 1985: 140–141).

Operationally, embracing this model means medicalizing people who use cannabis. Conrad and his colleagues (1992) suggested a five-stage sequential model that reflects the medicalization of cannabis use. It amounts to a deliberate shift from blaming problematic behavior as "badness" to viewing the same behavior as "sickness." This process unfolds through five distinct stages.

1. Definition—The conduct or behavior in question is viewed as morally deviant before the emergence of medical definitions.
2. Prospection—The medical nature of deviance is "discovered" for the first time, and this "discovery" is typically announced in a professional medical journal. It might appear as a new medical or diagnostic term or reports of medical treatment for the conduct or behavior.
3. Claims-making—Various organized interest groups aim to expand the medical territory by accentuating the size and solemnity of the problem, and such interest groups will gain profit if the new medical perspective is adopted. An example would be pharmaceutical companies.
4. Legitimacy—The proponents of the medical deviance designation make a request to the state to recognize the medical viewpoint. They seek powers of definition and management over the problem.
5. Institutionalization—The medical viewpoint is officially part of the medical or legal classification system. It is included as an official diagnosis in the medical manuals, and medical treatment for it is readily available. Moreover, institutions of social and ideological control such as

government, National Institute of Health (NIH), American Psychiatric Association (APA), media, etc., support the new medical perspective financially and intellectually.
(Conrad et al., 1992: 266–271)

In practical terms, viewing cannabis use as a risk to public health is consistent with other strategies to limit behaviors such as gambling or consuming alcohol (Wesley & Murray, 2021). Public health was identified as a focus of the first decriminalized cannabis policy in the Netherlands (Sifaneck & Kaplan, 1995). Today, more than thirty countries have implemented models of drug decriminalization that include public health interventions (Eastwood et al., 2016) and investments in drug treatment (Beweley-Taylor et al., 2014). This treatment is often organized through police-led diversion programs. Diversion programs come in many forms and serve different functions. Most "direct people away from criminal sanctions and towards educative, therapeutic, or social services" (Stevens et al., 2021: 31). Ideally, these programs are based on values such as agency, autonomy, and respect.

Medicinal Cannabis

The medicinal cannabis model assumes some people who use cannabis do so for therapeutic purposes. People have known about the medicinal uses of cannabis for centuries (Booth, 2003; Seddon & Floodgate, 2020). In the 1800s, physicians in Britain and the United States used cannabis as a sedative and anti-convulsant (Collins, 2020a) and as an ingredient in patented medicines (Hand et al., 2016). Medicinal cannabis reappeared in the United States in the 1970s during a brief period of state-based cannabis liberalization (Dufton, 2017a). The view that cannabis could be therapeutic complicates public health models, which describe cannabis as a risk to health and well-being. California became the first state to authorize the medicinal use of cannabis in 1996, following the statewide Proposition 215 in 1996, led by patients. Accepting medicinal cannabis further destigmatized use in California and beyond (Nussbaum et al., 2015).

Operationally, the medicinal cannabis model is quite developed in many US states. Thirty-four states have medical programs currently serving patients, and seventeen states have programs that allow limited access (Mize, 2020: 3). There remains a gap between legal status and availability in Canada (Valleriani et al., 2020),[3] and especially in Europe (Bifulco & Pisanti, 2015).[4]

Substantial evidence supports the use of cannabidiol (CBD) in children with rare seizure disorders. However, there is less clinical evidence for other medical conditions (Zürcher et al., 2022). This is partly due to fifty years of politicized cannabis research focused on uncovering any and every possible adverse outcome associated with consuming cannabis (Newhart & Dolphin, 2019). This is slowly changing. In 2020, the UN strengthened the international imperative for ensuring access to cannabis-based medicines (UN, 2020). In 2022, the US Senate approved a bill that would reverse decades of policy and require the Department of Health and Human Services (HHS) to investigate cannabis health benefits.[5]

Practically, this means engaging with populations that use cannabis and other drugs in new ways and supporting research that can "reflect lived experiences and local knowledges free from rigid discourses about problematic behaviours, harm, and risk" (Kiepeka et al., 2019: 61). Clinical assessments will be aided by improving access to cannabis for research (Schwabe et al., 2019) and techniques to define and describe psychoactive, CBD-elevated strains (CBD dominant and balanced strains) and leveraging genomic markers for strain selection in clinical trials and manufacturing medicines (Jin et al., 2021). As the number of jurisdictions that have liberalized cannabis laws grows as sites for research, new data sets comprised of those who use, prescribe, and have witnessed the impacts of legal and regulated cannabis emerge.

Consumer Cannabis

Cannabis as a consumer good assumes that cannabis is a profitable business and that there is no legitimate reason to constrain responsible consumption by adults (Kaplan, 1970). Consumer cannabis followed cultural shifts in the United States in the 1970s.[6] By 1977, state-based decriminalization efforts meant that cannabis possession warranted little more than a fine for people living in a quarter of the states in the country (Dufton, 2017b). While cannabis remained illegal, a new industry arose. During this period, paraphernalia sales, including sales of pipes, bongs, rolling papers, and drug-oriented magazines and toys generated more than $250 million a year (Dufton, 2017a: 73). In the 1980s, in the Netherlands, coffee-shop culture emerged (Seddon & Floodgate, 2020). Consumer culture has been extended through new cannabis businesses. The global cannabis market has been estimated at $US 20 billion in 2021 and is projected to reach $US 128 billion by 2030 (GlobeNewswire, 2021).

Operationally, consumer cannabis has led to various retail models. In addition to the first and distinctive coffee-shop system in the Netherlands (Seddon & Floodgate, 2020), US states have adopted a commercial enterprise system allowing private, for-profit firms to be licensed to cultivate, process, distribute, and sell cannabis and cannabis products (Seddon & Floodgate, 2020: 19). In Uruguay, despite the 2013 legalization of cannabis, it was not until 2017 that retail sales in pharmacies were authorized, subject to strict conditions (Queirolo, 2020). In Canada, retail cannabis is available through government-operated stores, based on the Liquor Commission model, and the more common private-licensed stores (Heidt, 2021). One area of growing interest is cannabis tourism (Liu & Stronczak, 2022). Once confined to Amsterdam, companies now offer tours in Washington and Colorado (Keul & Eisenhauer, 2019).

In practical terms, consumer cannabis was first explored in a remarkable paper by Sifaneck and Kaplan in 1995. Central to their study was exploring coffee-shop culture. A coffee-shop menu lists the different types of marijuana and hashish. These have changed over time. For example, in 1995, a typical menu included strains such as "Skunk," "Congo," and "Super Thai," along with different hashish varieties from Morocco, Turkey, and Afghanistan (Sifaneck & Kaplan, 1995: 491). Today, popular and widely available cannabis strains include "White Widow," "Super Silver Haze," "Amnesia Haze," "OG Kush," and "Girl Scout Cookies" (Marijuanarates, n.d.); however, proprietary and patented cannabis strains also exist (Roberts, 2019). In addition, some cannabis businesses are developing more specialized strains of cannabis, blending tetrahydrocannabinol (THC) and CBD to encourage creativity, energy, intimacy, or relaxation. For example, one effort to combine nostalgia with environmental sensibilities focuses on "reviving the mellow sensibility of the casual smoke . . . 100% Organic hemp flower and pre-rolled joints serve up a clean buzz without the fuss."[7] New genomic techniques attempt to define and describe THC-dominant, CBD-dominant, and balanced cannabis strains. While these are nominally designed for medical purposes, it is not difficult to imagine how this research will influence new consumer cannabis products (Jin et al., 2021).

Racial Justice

An emergent model assumes cannabis legalization can serve to expand racial justice. As cannabis liberalization has emerged, so too have calls to address the persistent role of racism within cannabis policy (Mize, 2020). Cannabis is associated with the social control of minority groups and is a driver of social and racial injustice (Shiner et al., 2018). As Bender (2016: 690) noted in a review of the early years of cannabis liberalization in the United States, race and cannabis prohibition have been linked from

> the initial criminalization of marijuana rooted in racial stereotypes, the enforcement of that prohibition throughout the twentieth century to the present day by means of racial profiling . . . [and] continues to disproportionately impose serious consequences on racial minorities, while white entrepreneurs and white users enjoy the early fruits of legalization.

Critical race theory (CRT) suggests laws are often structured to maintain White privilege (Delgado & Stefanic, 2012). Specific to cannabis reform, CRT requires considering how race shapes "who benefits and is burdened by reform" (Crawford, 2021: 459).

Operationally, adopting a racial justice model of cannabis regulation involves considering social equity programs, criminal record relief, and community reinvestment (Mize, 2020: 22–28). Federally, in the United States, the Marijuana Opportunity Reinvestment and Expungement Act (MORE Act), if signed into law, would decriminalize cannabis and expunge nonviolent federal marijuana convictions. It would also create the Office of Cannabis Justice to oversee the financial and social reinvestment in communities disproportionately affected by the War on Drugs.[8] Various other approaches are being considered at the state and municipal levels. Adopting a racial justice model of cannabis would "enable those injured by prohibition to benefit from the unique entrepreneurial opportunities offered within the burgeoning cannabis industry" (Mize, 2020: 1).

Practically, acknowledging disparate treatment and the adverse outcomes of living with aggressive policing and ethno-racial profiling is important (Chohlas-Wood et al., 2022; Sewell et al., 2021). It is now clear that, while racial disparities in enforcement occur when cannabis is decriminalized (Sheehan et al., 2021), cannabis legalization may disincentivize pretextual stops and promote other forms of justice reform (Brown, 2022). Legal cannabis raises another practical complication for racial justice models. In the United States, too many states fail to "enable those injured by prohibition to benefit from the unique entrepreneurial opportunities offered within the burgeoning cannabis industry" (Mize, 2020: 1). Most states prevent people with certain criminal convictions from being employed in cannabis establishments (Howell, 2018) or participating in other parts of the cannabis industry.[9]

Models and Countries: Lessons

In 2020, after two years of intense debate, the UN Commission on Narcotic Drugs (CND) voted to remove cannabis from Schedule IV of the 1961 Single Convention on Narcotic Drugs. By doing so, the UN finally acknowledged the therapeutic value of cannabis and strengthened the international imperative for ensuring access to cannabis-based medicines (UN, 2020). Despite this development, cannabis remains in Schedule I of the 1961 Single Convention on Narcotic Drugs and under the same strict controls as heroin and cocaine. Efforts to reform cannabis policy exist on a spectrum and vary broadly in Australia, Canada, Portugal, the Netherlands, the United Kingdom, Uruguay, and the United States.

Australia

The Australian experience defies uniform explanation. In public safety terms, sales of cannabis are still prohibited in Australia, and it remains an offense to ingest cannabis in public. For example, despite allowing police to issue warnings or formal caution for cannabis possession, arrests increased. According to official stats by the Australian Criminal Intelligence Commission, arrests have increased from 57,170 in 2010 to 71,151 in 2019.[10] Consumer arrests (possession) account for the most significant proportion of arrests, accounting for 91 percent of national cannabis arrests in 2018–2019. Although possessing cannabis is still considered a criminal offense, most states and territories treat cannabis possession as a civil offense.

Efforts to move beyond the reliance on public safety began in 1987, when the state of South Australia decriminalized cannabis use, possession (up to 28 grams), and cultivation (up to ten plants) with a new policy known as Cannabis Infringement Notices (CINs), as part of the Cannabis Expiation Notice (CEN) System (Sutton & Hawks, 2005). Public safety models were de-emphasized by moving toward public health models, specifically diversion programs. Diversion expanded to all states and territories following the Council of Australian Governments Illicit Drug Diversion Initiative (IDDI), signed in 1999. Since 2004, diversion programs have expanded (Hughes &

Ritter, 2008). For example, in Western Australia, the Cannabis Intervention Requirement (CIR) issued by police applies to citizens possessing less than ten grams of cannabis. While CIRs may be resolved by completing a Cannabis Intervention Session (CIS), failure to participate can lead to prosecution (Decorte et al., 2020).

Medical models in Australia are still evolving, and market forces are slowly changing regulatory approaches. Medicinal cannabis has been legal in numerous Australian states and territories since April 2016, with terminally ill patients living in Victoria being the first to be granted access to medical cannabis (Seddon & Floodgate, 2020). In 2016, the Narcotic Drug Amendment Act introduced a national licensing scheme for regulating the cultivation and supply of cannabis for medical and scientific purposes (Hughes, 2020). In 2021, the Therapeutic Goods Administration (TGA) changed the classification for products containing small amounts of CBD. Under the new rules, cannabis products in this category are classified as "schedule 3" medicines and can be sold in pharmacies without a prescription (Koehn, 2019). Australia's medicinal cannabis sector is estimated to be worth more than $2 billion, and companies are pursuing low-dose products with hopes they will be available through pharmacies by 2023 (Koehn, 2021).

There is no legal recreational cannabis in Australia; however, there is evidence that many users change their methods of obtaining cannabis to fit within limits provided by decriminalization policies (Barratt et al., 2005). In addition, there are other signs that the growing acceptance of cannabis in Australia is changing the conditions on the ground. For example, recently, the Australian Capital Territory (ACT) took a profound step toward legalization. While it stopped just short of establishing a commercial system and regulated supply of cannabis, it legalized possession. As Seddon and Floodgate explain (2020: 60),

> in January 2020, ACT introduced new regulations permitting the cultivation of up to two cannabis plants per individual (with a maximum of four plants in a household), the possession of up to 50 grams of dried cannabis or 150 grams of fresh cannabis, and the use of cannabis within private accommodation for those aged 18 and older (ACT Government 2020).

Regarding racial justice, Australia faces equity and access issues, especially within cannabis diversion programs. As Hughes and colleagues (2019: 13) explain,

Evaluations have found some groups of people may be excluded or fare less well in drug diversion programs, particularly those residing in rural/regional areas and Aboriginal and Torres Strait Islander people.

Kate Sear provides a recent overview (Lens, 2020). She notes that data from New South Wales suggests significant race-based differences regarding diversion. Between 2013 and 2017, more than 80 percent of Indigenous people were processed through the formal justice system, while just over half of non-Indigenous people faced criminal charges in court. A national study co-authored by well-known drug policy experts uncovered some contextual reasons that represent barriers to diversions, including police trust, admitting a drug offense, and institutional factors that shape who gets diversion and who goes to court (Hughes et al., 2019).

Canada

Before cannabis legalization in Canada in 2018, federal enforcement agencies and provinces deployed significant public safety resources to control the production and distribution of cannabis for many years (Dandurand, 2021). Despite these efforts, cannabis-growing operations were becoming more numerous and increasingly sophisticated. During the 1990s and early 2000s, the cannabis market generated significant profit for criminal groups with little apparent risk and minimum investment (Plecas et al., 2002). Eventually, profits waned as competition from the grey market grew, and other more profitable drugs flooded the market (Langton, 2018). Cannabis continued to be widely available across the country. Further, in many areas such as Vancouver and other cities, penalties for simple possession of most drugs (and particularly cannabis) are not enforced consistently or uniformly applied, and few people were imprisoned for drug use alone. Bill C-45, legalizing cannabis, passed the Senate in March 2018 and became official law on June 19, 2018. One public safety goal was to take the proceeds of cannabis sales "out of the hands of organized crime and other illegal actors" (Wesley & Murray, 2021: 1081).

Canadian cannabis policy was based on the Canadian Drugs and Substances Strategy (CDSS), which promised a comprehensive and collaborative public health approach (Health Canada, 2016). Legal cannabis was first sold in dispensaries starting in October 2018; however, many provinces opened only a handful of dispensaries, most of which were located far away from larger urban areas (Heidt et al., 2018). This slow roll-out is consistent with a public health approach (Wesley & Murray, 2021), as are federal regulations designed to limit advertising and youth access (Haines-Saah & Fischer, 2021). In addition, based on the Canadian approach to federalism, provinces and territories were allowed to set added restrictions around possession limits, minimum age, public use, and personal cultivation (Corva & Meisel, 2022).

Medical cannabis has been federally legal in Canada since 1999 (Bennett, 2021: 192). However, early regulations made access to medical cannabis difficult, limiting its use by patients. The Supreme Court ruled in *R. v Smith* (2015)[11] that all forms of medical cannabis were permissible. The federal government has since determined it must provide reasonable access to a legal source of cannabis for medical purposes (Government of Canada, n.d.a). As a result, there are many accepted conditions for which medical cannabis may be prescribed in Canada,[12] although medical cannabis has been criticized as inaccessible (Valleriani et al., 2020). In Canada, the supply of medical cannabis is controlled by the federal government, which regulates production and distribution through licensed sellers. With Health Canada approval, patients are also allowed to grow their own cannabis or designate someone to grow it for them. Some research suggests some people who consume cannabis do so because of a lack of access to mental health care (Lake et al., 2019). This might also be connected to the relative inaccessibility of legal medicinal cannabis, reported by some surveyed in a study based in the downtown Eastside of Vancouver (Valleriani et al., 2020).

The Canadian experience is remarkable because it represents the world's largest regulated cannabis market, including supply, distribution, and sales. Different provinces have allowed other retail models, including government-operated stores and the more common private-licensed stores. Further, provinces also allowed retail stores to open at different rates (Seddon & Floodgate, 2020). This variation has shaped the way new legal consumers access cannabis. To date, legal cannabis has not significantly disrupted illicit markets in many provinces, and regulations around potency, price, and advertising have limited the potential of the legal market (Heidt, 2021; Wesley & Murray, 2021). This recognition has led to a fascinating experiment in British Columbia (BC), where the government seeks to convince "illegal cannabis growers to begin selling legally in an effort to squeeze out illicit marijuana from the marketplace."[13]

Adopting racial justice models in Canada remains a work in progress. As Owusu-Bempah & Luscombe (2021) demonstrate, even where cannabis has been legalized and regulated, police contact for cannabis-related incidents is racially disproportionate. Racial and ethnic justice in Canada must also contend with the federal and provincial legacy toward Indigenous and First Nations communities. For example, Koutouki and Lofts (2019: 709) argue, "[t]here is potential for Indigenous communities to benefit from cannabis legalization, but also a very real risk that the new legal framework will simply perpetuate existing injustices." This could mean providing a means for Indigenous communities to benefit from the cannabis industry by reforming rules and regulations that limit agricultural development on reserves.[14] It also requires reviewing why the federal government failed to consult Indigenous communities before enacting cannabis legislation, especially regarding how best to share excise taxes (Koutouki & Lofts, 2019).

Portugal

The decriminalization of drug use in Portugal is often misrepresented. Despite the decriminalization of the use, possession, and acquisition of all drugs in 2001, Public Safety models of drug control remain, and criminal penalties are still applied to drug growers, dealers, and traffickers (Hughes et al., 2018). Law 30/2000 significantly changed the legal response to people who use drugs. Possession of over 25 grams of cannabis could result in four to twelve years in prison. However, experts estimated those found guilty would most likely receive between one and seven years in prison for possessing up to 10 kilograms of cannabis (EMCDDA, 2017a). Nevertheless, possessing drugs for personal use is still an administrative violation, and penalties may involve fines or community service (Eastwood et al., 2016).

In public health terms, decriminalization was based on growing concerns regarding the population of heroin users, rates of HIV among people who inject drugs, and open-air drug markets (Laqueur, 2014: 5). Decriminalization was accompanied by significant investments in health and social programs, including prevention, drug treatment, harm reduction, and social reintegration (Beweley-Taylor et al., 2014). Key features include the introduction of a system of referral to their local Commissions for the Dissuasion of Drug Addiction (Comissão para a Dissuasão da Toxicodependência) for individuals stopped in possession of 25 grams or less of cannabis (Hughes & Stevens, 2007). These Commissions serve as administrative bodies established in each of Portugal's regions and are supported by a technical team of health and social experts. The vast majority of those referred to the commissions by the police for cannabis have their cases suspended, meaning they receive no penalty (Murkin, 2014). Through these commissions, referrals to treatment for problem drug use is an option. However, while treatment may be encouraged, it is never required.

Medical cannabis was legalized in 2018, and Portugal's National Medicines Authority, called Infarmed, is the government agency responsible for regulatory oversight. It has complete control of the supply chain, from cultivation to sale. Doctors may prescribe cannabis-based products from pharmacies (Seddon & Floodgate, 2020). Approved uses include chronic pain associated with oncologic diseases, epilepsy and treatment of severe seizure disorders in childhood, multiple sclerosis, nausea and vomiting caused by chemotherapy, and appetite stimulation in the palliative care of patients undergoing oncologic treatment or with AIDS (Portugal News, 2020). In 2020, five companies obtained authorization from Infarmed to grow, import, and export cannabis for medicinal purposes over a total cultivation area of 120 hectares (Kings, 2020; Portugal News 2020).

While medicinal cannabis exists and those possessing 25 grams or less of cannabis are diverted away from the justice system, Portugal has not taken steps to provide for the legal cultivation, distribution, or sale of cannabis. Regarding racial justice, the UN reports that people of African descent in Portugal experience systemic racism (UNHCR, 2020). Although Portugal does not collect data on race among the prison population, it does provide demographic information on gender and citizenship. Overall, foreign nationals are incarcerated for drug offenses at a higher rate than Portuguese nationals. The reverse is true for minor trafficking charges (Sander et al., 2016). While racialized enforcement patterns have been observed, without a legal market, the potential for cannabis to create opportunities for those historically oppressed does not yet exist.

The Netherlands

In public safety terms, cannabis arrests have increased, although these remain very low by international standards. For example, Room and colleagues reported only 19 cannabis arrests per 100 000 in the Netherlands in 2005 (Room et al., 2008: 77). In 2020, there were more than 300.[15] This may be related to policy changes. For example, while the threshold amount for cannabis prosecution had long been set at 5 grams, in 2012, the government revised the Opium Act Directive. Instead of saying, "a police dismissal should follow if a cannabis user is caught with less than 5 grams of cannabis," it now states that "in principle, a police dismissal will follow if a person is carrying less than 5 grams of cannabis."[16] This policy change now allows for the arrest and prosecution of individuals possessing less than 5 grams of cannabis in certain circumstances. However, experts estimate that even if possessing up to 10 kilograms, most people found guilty would be sentenced to less than a year in prison (EMCDDA, 2017b).

A complex form of "de facto" drug decriminalization that allows for limited sales of cannabis exists in the Netherlands (MacCoun, 2011). This policy approach is known as *gedoogbeleid* or "tolerance policy" (Hocker, 2014). The foundation for this drug strategy can be traced to the Opiate Act of 1976 (Brewster, 2017). Dutch policymakers have acknowledged that people will use drugs regardless of the laws and have focused on not alienating and stigmatizing users. Sifaneck & Kaplan (1995) defined two public health goals related to people who use cannabis in the Netherlands. The first, "keeping off," refers to people who use cannabis but do not progress to more risky drug use. Stopping this progression is achieved by limiting the availability of drugs to youth and creating a culture of controlled use and self-regulation through the coffee-shop system (Hamid, 1992). Far more common than "stepping on" was the concept of "stepping off," which refers to the use of cannabis to assist people who use other drugs in the absence of suitable alternative medications (Grinspoon & Bakalar, 1997).

In terms of medical cannabis, the Netherlands has permitted legal access to medical cannabis since 2003. The Office for Medicinal Cannabis (OMC) is responsible for producing and supplying medical cannabis. The OMC has a monopoly on "supplying medicinal cannabis to pharmacies and processes applications for exemptions from the Opium Act relating to cannabis and cannabis resin."[17] Doctors can prescribe cannabis for a range of medical conditions, including symptomatic relief of pain caused by multiple sclerosis (MS) and any other types of chronic pain, nausea and vomiting caused by chemotherapy or radiotherapy, and palliative cancer treatment (Schlag, 2020: 3). Qualifying medical patients can purchase high-quality cannabis at lower prices than can be purchased in the Dutch coffee shops (Seddon & Floodgate, 2020).

The Dutch approach to decriminalization provides the basis for consumer cannabis. The coffee-shop policy, which allows for the sale of cannabis, is intended to reduce the potential that they will encounter harder drugs. However, as noted above, the sale of small quantities is ignored if shops adhere to the "AHOJ-G" criteria outlined in Table 4.1.

Table 4.1 Netherlands coffee shop guidelines

Letter	Meaning
A	No advertising: no more than (very) low-profile signposting of the facility
H	No hard drugs: these may not be sold or held on the premises
O	No nuisance (*Overlast* in Dutch): including traffic and parking, loitering, littering, and noise
J	No sales to underaged customers (*Jeugdigen* in Dutch) and no admittance of underaged customers to coffee shops
G	Transaction size is limited to "personal use," defined as 30g (grams) per person per coffee shop per day

As Grund and Breeksema (2013: 23) note, these include rules and limits on advertising, sales of "hard" drugs, nuisance, the sales to underaged customers, and personal transaction size and stock limits for the coffee shop in grams. As Sifaneck & Kaplan (1995: 494) observed,

> part of the function of the Dutch coffee shop is to provide a safe and appropriate setting for cannabis smoking. Proprietors must make their shops safe (i.e., free of hard drugs, aggression, petty crime, etc.) as well as comfortable and inviting.

For all the benefits of the Netherlands' approach to cannabis, the country continues to wrestle with the role of the coffee shop, the value of separating drug markets, racial justice, and the limits of tolerance.

The United Kingdom

The application of public safety models toward cannabis persists in the United Kingdom (Johnson, 2021). However, this varies by country. In general, criminal justice intrusions based on cannabis possession has declined. For example, prosecutions and cautions, warnings, and notices combined fell dramatically in England and Wales. In 2010, these intrusions totaled more than 140,000. They fell dramatically to 57,120 in 2017 (BBC News, 2019). Between 2011 and 2015, 31 out of 43 England and Wales police forces reported that 126,789 people were charged with cannabis possession while 193,260 (41 percent) received warnings. A further 22 percent were either given cautions or fixed penalty notices (Cockburn, 2016). Between 2016 and 2020, there was a further reduction in prosecutions from 17,019 in 2016 to 14,115 in 2020. In addition, there has been a reduction in those sentenced from 15,771 in 2016 to 11,702 in 2020 and a reduction in the average length of a custodial sentence from 542 months in 2016 to 405 in 2020.[18]

While the punitive language of prohibition remains, there has been a shift away from public safety and toward public health through police-led diversion programs (Spyt et al., 2019). Since 2016, four separate trials have taken place in England and Wales. Three pilots in Avon and Somerset, Durham, and West Midlands Constabularies can be considered "deferred prosecution" schemes. The fourth and most recent is the Drug Diversion Pilot (DDP) implemented by Thames Valley Police. By avoiding the traditional criminal justice system, these programs emphasize providing individuals with an opportunity to avoid receiving a criminal record by attending education and prevention programs. Early reports from police agencies in 2016 suggested nearly 80 percent of those offered the "diversion" scheme as an alternative to prosecution accepted and later completed the drug education course (Daly, 2016).

In the United Kingdom, medical cannabis was legalized in 2018. Access is highly restrictive. As of 2020, fewer than ten NHS prescriptions had been issued (Schlag, 2020). David Nutt (2022) notes most of the estimated 1.4 million patients using cannabis for recognized ailments identified elsewhere are forced into the illicit market, which risks unknown product dose and quality. In the United Kingdom, as of 2020, four conditions have been identified for possible treatment with cannabis in the United Kingdom: chemotherapy-induced nausea and vomiting, multiple sclerosis (MS), and two severe treatment-resistant epilepsies (Schlag, 2020: 2). Despite research suggesting its efficacy and allowing many children to stop taking multiple ineffective epilepsy drugs (Nutt, 2022), access is limited.

While there is no consumer cannabis in the United Kingdom, Gornall (2020) describes a large and growing network of individuals and organizations lobbying for a legal cannabis industry. Developments in Scotland demonstrate one approach. In 2021, Lord Advocate Dorothy Bain announced that police in Scotland could issue a formal warning, called a "recorded police warning," for possessing small amounts of all drugs to address the underlying causes of Scotland's drug death crisis.[19] While the scheme would not extend to drug dealing, and officers retain the discretion to report some instances to prosecutors, this policy amounts to the de facto decriminalization of the possession of small amounts of any drug in Scotland. These developments are essential. However, legal cannabis cannot succeed without changing the culture of prohibition.

Regarding racial justice, the inequality faced by people in different regions of the United Kingdom is often linked to the selective enforcement of drug laws and referrals to diversion schemes.[20] The problem is not improving. In 2018, Black people were sentenced at 11.8 times the rate of White people for the offense of cannabis possession, while government statistics estimate that Black people use the drug at a lower rate than White people (Shiner et al., 2018). Subsequent analysis suggested Black people in 2020 faced 148.4 prosecutions for cannabis possession per 100,000 people compared to 12.2 per 100,000 for White people. In 2021, it was reported that Black people are twelve times more likely to be prosecuted for cannabis possession and amount to 20 percent of those convicted, even though they make up only 5 percent of the population (White, 2021). Lammy (2017) concluded these disparities amounted to institutional racism. In May 2022, London Mayor Sadiq Kahn announced a new London Drugs Commission to review (UK) law, focusing on cannabis and racial justice, in partnership with University College London (Chiswick Herald, 2022).

Uruguay

Unlike every other country explored in this chapter, there has been no penalty for possessing cannabis for personal use in Uruguay since the 1970s. Uruguay decriminalized drugs long before it developed its cannabis policy. Public safety models are still present. Police in Uruguay may arrest a person if they find more than 40 grams. A criminal investigation may be undertaken if a judge determines the cannabis was not for personal use. Police-enforcement practices and judicial processes have led to the incarceration of many people who use drugs. In the immediate years following legalization, some expressed concern about the number of people who use drugs that are caught up in the Uruguayan criminal justice system (Corda, 2015). However, recent data suggest reductions in drug law prosecutions overall, specifically for drug possession (JND, 2020). Early worries about those "placed in pre-trial detention, with the de facto presumption of a cultivation or trafficking offense but no formal charges" (Eastwood et al., 2016: 36) have been qualified. For example, between 2015 and 2020, a dramatic decrease can be observed from 69.2 percent of total prisoners in pretrial detention in 2015 to just over 22 percent in 2020.[21]

In public health terms, a key objective of cannabis policy is to limit the consumption of cannabis (Decorte et al., 2017: 48). There are three ways of acquiring cannabis: growing it yourself or accessing it through cannabis social clubs (CSCs) or through pharmacies. These are mutually exclusive: individuals registered as self-growers cannot become members of CSCs, neither can they register to purchase cannabis at pharmacies. Likewise, individuals cannot belong to more than one CSC at a time. Registered users who want to change how they can acquire cannabis must wait three months for the change to be approved.[22] In addition to growing cannabis on one's own, the government allows cannabis social clubs (CSCs), which are grower collectives permitted to cultivate cannabis and distribute the proceeds to members.

CSCs need to go through a series of steps to be authorized. Clubs are capped at forty-five members. Members must be Uruguayan nationals and at least eighteen years old or older. Belackova and colleagues (2017) suggest that the CSC model can diminish the adverse health risks resulting from cannabis use through educational activities, dissemination of information on reducing mental health risks, and promoting safe smoking practices. Currently, CSCs do not perform any risk reduction tasks (Pardal et al., 2019). There is potential for more robust engagement. Walsh and Ramsey (2016: 6) suggest another goal of the policy was to enable users to access medicinal cannabis.

Those who want to consume legal cannabis must register with the Institute for the Regulation and Control of Cannabis (IRCC). Medical cannabis users are required to present prescriptions, which are valid for thirty days, during which time accessing cannabis through any other legal method is forbidden (Walsh & Ramsey, 2016). Most legal cannabis contains low-potency THC (Seddon & Floodgate, 2020). Higher-potency cannabis has since been introduced into pharmacies, although it is still capped at a moderate 9 percent THC potency (Hudak et al., 2018). Cannabis edibles or other cannabis-infused products often used medially in other countries are not available for sale in pharmacies (Transform, 2017). While Uruguay has arguably the strictest system of legalization in place (Montañés, 2014), implementation has been challenging. Today, legal cannabis cannot meet existing demand in both the medical markets. For example, in 2020, only 11 percent of people who use medical cannabis bought it legally (JND, 2020).

Despite the country legalizing cannabis in 2013, providing consumer cannabis through pharmacies began in 2017. Registered consumers must be Uruguayan and eighteen or older, and the limit is 40 grams per month, with identity and registration confirmed at the point of sale with a fingerprint scanner (The Guardian, 2017). In 2018, the government authorized 16 pharmacies to become cannabis distributors, selling only to the nearly 5,000 cannabis consumers registered with the government. Users can choose between "Alfa 1" and "Beta 1," which have relatively low THC content compared to most legal cannabis in North America. One fascinating development in Uruguay is the emergence of cannabis clubs regulated by law. In 2019, 110 CSCs were operating in full compliance with existing regulations (Pardal et al., 2019). While consumption is allowed in CSC facilities, interviewees declare that while that is a frequent practice, the clubs do not have a policy or rules guiding the consumption on the premises of the CSC (Queirolo et al., 2019). Most consumers choose to take the product home. When consumption in the CSCs happens, it occurs when clubs organize parties or meetings. Of interest is the use of social media to "raise awareness about cannabis consumption in general and the Uruguayan regulation in particular" (Decorte et al., 2017: 46).

Another development is a political shift toward a focus on the economic benefits of cannabis. According to an analysis by the Wilson Center, Uruguay is poised to become a regional cannabis exporter. For example, "producers in Uruguay have a first-mover advantage to gain a niche in export markets and generate revenue and employment for the country" (Iglesias et al., 2019). The irony is that while the government is hoping to expand exports, the provision of cannabis through pharmacies is insufficient to meet existing in-country demand. Despite demand, sales through pharmacies have not exceeded 2 tons per year, even though demand within existing markets is more than 40 metric tons a year (JND, 2019: 127).[23] It is not possible to conclude there is no institutional racism in Uruguay. Reports of discrimination and disparate rates of imprisonment are increasingly common (UNHCR, 2022). This appears to be a specific challenge for the Afro-Uruguayan people living in Montevideo.[24] However, racial justice models do not yet appear to be as relevant to Uruguayan cannabis policies.

The United States

The United States represents the largest and most complex case of cannabis criminalization. In public safety terms, cannabis has been demonized for a century. In terms of the sheer number of cannabis arrests, no country compares to the United States. As Vitiello (2021) notes, many Southern states continue to impose severe penalties for cannabis. In Louisiana, Mississippi, and Alabama, defendants have been sentenced to years in prison for engaging in the same cannabis-related activities, now legal one state over. Punitive laws remain on the books in several American states.[25] In Texas, possession of any amount up to 2 ounces will result in 180 days in prison. In Arkansas, possessing any amount of up to 4 ounces may land you in prison for up to a year. A second offense may result in a prison term of six years. In Florida, possessing more than 25 grams is a felony, punishable by up to five years in prison. In Georgia, possessing more than an ounce of cannabis can net you up to ten years in prison, while possessing 30 grams or more in Mississippi is a felony and penalties range from three to thirty years in prison.

In 2019, police in the United States made 545,602 arrests for cannabis-related violations. Of those arrested for cannabis-related activities, some 92 percent (500,395) were arrested for cannabis possession offenses only.[26] In 2020, police across America made a marijuana-related arrest "every 58 seconds," according to Erik Altieri, the Executive Director of the National Organization for the Reform of Marijuana Laws (NORML) (Earlenbaugh, 2020). While still far too high, this number has fallen over the past decade. In 2010, there were 757,969 arrests, 87 percent for simple possession, according to the FBI's Uniform Crime Report.[27] The reduction in cannabis arrests should be seen alongside declines in federal cannabis prosecutions. The US Sentencing Commission reports that trafficking cases in 2019 significantly declined since states started repealing their cannabis prohibition laws. Federal defendants charged with cannabis-associated crimes decreased by 28 percent (US Supreme Court, 2019). There were just over 2,100 federal marijuana trafficking cases in 2018, compared to nearly 7,000 in 2012. Following the regulated retail operations in Colorado and Washington, cannabis trafficking offenses have decreased by 67.3 percent.[28]

While a growing number of states have legalized cannabis, where cannabis possession has been decriminalized, public health approaches seek to reduce the use of criminal sanctions by directing people toward "educative, therapeutic or social services" (Stevens et al., 2021: 31). When those arrested with small amounts of cannabis can avoid a criminal sanction by participating in a treatment program, it is often described as "voluntary." Cannabis diversion programs exist throughout the country. In Pennsylvania, following the successful completion of the program, those diverted must pay all court costs, and the District Attorney's Office will dismiss the charges. However, if an individual does not wish to participate, the charges will be handled as any other charge (Ogg, 2019). Some programs in Texas note the problems of stigma and the limited public safety benefit of prosecuting cannabis possession. Participation in the Misdemeanor Marijuana Diversion Program (MMDP) is still required to avoid a criminal record (Ogg, 2019). Those arrested must register and complete a "Cognitive Decision Making" class instead of facing traditional arrest and prosecution (Ogg, 2019).

California became the first state to authorize the medicinal use of cannabis in 1996, following the statewide Proposition 215 in 1996, which was led by patients. As Vitiello (2021: 18–19) notes, until the HIV/AIDS crisis, medicinal proponents of cannabis were few and far between. The acceptance of the medical potential for cannabis further destigmatized use among a subset of the population and increased the supply of cannabis through diversion to illegal markets (Nussbaum et al., 2015). Newhart & Dolphin (2019: 25) connect the renewed medical interest in cannabis to a shift in its portrayal by media outlets like CNN. It is also the case that cannabis had been shown to have medical value for children in the literature at that time (Barthwell et al., 2010; Kondrad & Reid, 2013; MacDonald, 2009, Porter & Jacobson, 2013). By July 2018, forty-six states and the District of Columbia, and the US territories of Puerto Rico and Guam provided for the legal therapeutic use of cannabis (Newhart & Dolphin, 2019). Depending on the state, patients may qualify for treatment with medical cannabis if they have a qualifying condition. These include Alzheimer's disease, amyotrophic lateral sclerosis (ALS), HIV/AIDS, Crohn's disease, epilepsy and seizures, glaucoma, multiple sclerosis and muscle spasms, severe and chronic pain, and severe nausea or vomiting caused by cancer treatment.[29]

In 2012, consumer cannabis in the United States emerged in earnest. Colorado and Washington formally legalized recreational cannabis. In Washington, cannabis is regulated through the state Liquor Control Board and is taxed at a rate of 37 percent.[30] Personal cultivation and home-growing are not allowed (Bishop-Henchman & Scarboro, 2016). Colorado created a special agency, the Marijuana Enforcement Division (MED), to regulate cannabis and currently taxes cannabis at a somewhat lower rate of 29 percent (Bishop-Henchman & Scarboro, 2016; Smiley, 2016). Tracking legal recreational cannabis in the United States is a near-impossible feat. Legal recreational cannabis can be purchased in Alaska, Arizona, Colorado, California, Illinois, Maine, Massachusetts, Michigan, Montana, Nevada, New Jersey, New Mexico, Oregon, and Washington. At present, recreational cannabis may be legal but not yet available as a consumer good in Connecticut, Montana, New York, Rhode Island, Vermont, and Virginia. This list will be out of date by the time this book is in print.

Even as the cannabis industry continues to take root state by state, federal prohibition remains. Although some federal cannabis reform has been achieved, President Joe Biden has, to date, refused to legalize cannabis through executive order or instruct his administration to take other steps. This could include rescheduling cannabis through the Department of Health and Human Services (HHS) or requesting a formal assessment of the scientific, medical, and public health implications before submitting that review to the Justice Department, allowing for reclassification under federal law. Instead, as in other countries, the ambivalence toward cannabis has coincided with reduced prosecutions. President Biden told TIME magazine:

> I think the idea of focusing significant resources on interdicting or convicting people for smoking marijuana is a waste of our resources. . . . That's different than [legalization]. Our policy for our Administration is still not legalization.
>
> (Miller, 2014)

While prosecutions are down federally, race remains relevant (Alexander, 2010). These include racially unequal outcomes and increasingly deadly encounters (Baum, 1996; Tonry, 1994).

Black and Brown people continue to be arrested at higher rates than White people (Koch et al., 2016). Sheehan and colleagues (2021) show that arrest rate disparities based on race *increased* following cannabis decriminalization. Only full cannabis legalization can disrupt racial disparities in cannabis enforcement. Reversing a century of punitive cannabis policies means creating opportunities for BIPOC. In 2020, the House of Representatives took an essential step by voting in favor of removing cannabis from the federal Controlled Substances Act. Bills seek to create pathways for BIPOC ownership opportunities in the emerging industry and establish funding sources to reinvest in communities disproportionately affected by the War on Drugs. If passed, a 5 percent tax would be added to retail sales of cannabis to go to the Opportunity Trust Fund (OTF). This rate would increase to 8 percent over three years. The Office of Cannabis Justice would manage the OTF and pursue financial and social reinvestment in communities disproportionately affected by the War on Drugs.[31]

Models of racial justice are also emerging at the state level. In Oregon, Measure 110 decriminalizes simple possession of all illicit drugs. According to a report from the Oregon Criminal Justice Commission (2020), this change will drastically reduce the overrepresentation of racial and ethnic minorities in the criminal justice system; in fact, if previous statistical trends hold true, Indigenous people from Oregon will go from being over-represented to under-represented in the criminal justice system because of these changes. This is an example of an encouraging trend. For example,

> [a] number of US states, in particular New York and Massachusetts, have paved the way for a social and racial justice model of cannabis reform. Release present guiding principles in preparation for the eventual legal regulation of cannabis in the UK. These principles are designed to ensure that the same people who are locked up by punitive drug policies are not locked out of the legal market, and that cannabis reform is an opportunity to repair history.
>
> (Release, n.d.)

Adopting these models may begin the process of reconciliation by recognizing and attempting to rectify the consequences of the political and economic inequalities associated with cannabis prohibition.

Conclusion

This chapter has provided an international overview of cannabis policy liberalization around the world. We argued the range of options requires a conceptual framework to understand regulatory approaches to cannabis. Given the wide variance between policy models and their underlying assumptions, operational goals, and practical outcomes, we considered seven jurisdictions where cannabis policy has been liberalized. We organized developments through the public safety model, the public health model, the medicinal model, a commercial model, and an emergent racial justice model and applied these regulatory models to developments in cannabis policy in Australia, Canada, Portugal, the Netherlands, the United Kingdom, Uruguay, and the US states. In the Canadian province of BC, an example of the changing landscape of cannabis policy is evident. As noted in the introduction, within a span of two years, accessing cannabis moved from a criminal sanction to an essential service (BC Gov News, 2020).

There are several observations that emerge from our international analysis. The public safety model, while rhetorically in retreat, continues to emerge, especially related to racial disparities in cannabis arrests. This is most obvious when comparing disparities in arrest rates in jurisdictions where cannabis is decriminalized versus legalized (Sheehan et al., 2021), even where cannabis has been legalized and regulated. For example, in Canada, police contact for cannabis-related incidents is racially disproportionate (Owusu-Bempah & Luscombe, 2021). However, public health models may simply add and augment public safety approaches rather than replace and reform efforts to police cannabis and the people who use it. Consistent with Cohen (1985), thus far, cannabis reform has expanded the number of people who come under the supervisory gaze of the state by reducing the penalties, on the one hand, but expanding the kinds of intrusions people caught with cannabis face.

Within public health models, there are a variety of approaches (Stevens, 2011: 132–134). The general reallocation of resources from punishment to treatment takes a variety of forms. In the Netherlands, public health means expanded access to cannabis while promoting responsible use through the coffee-shop system (see Figure 4.1) (Sifaneck & Kaplan, 1995). In Portugal, these have been achieved by investments in referrals to voluntary health and social support programs (Beweley-Taylor et al., 2014). In Australia, the United Kingdom, and the United States, the focus appears to be on diversion programs that employ "traditional risk-based rhetoric about cannabis" (Watson et al., 2019: 474). Canada and Uruguay have adopted public health approaches that focus less on diversion programs and more on regulations. In Canada, rules designed to limit advertising and youth access have been successful (Haines-Saah & Fischer, 2021: 192). In Uruguay, required registration, limited access, and low potency are favored public health approaches (Decorte et al., 2017).

Medicinal cannabis, consumer cannabis, and racial justice models appear to be most developed in North America. In the United States, medical cannabis is widely available, as is consumer cannabis, including a growing number of products such as edibles, drinks, tinctures, creams, toothpaste, sprays, and even body butter. National groups are organizing and lobbying to seek reforms that will ensure the cannabis industry is sustainable (NCIA, n.d.). Efforts to consider how cannabis reform can support racial justice and reconciliation, although they remain a work in progress, exist in ways they do not elsewhere. In Canada, access to legal medical cannabis is not assured (Valleriani et al., 2020), and critics argue the overregulation of cannabis means legal cannabis cannot compete on price or potency, neither can it displace the illicit market (Mahamad et al., 2020). Efforts to consider equity in Canada demand legal frameworks and policies to encourage Indigenous communities to benefit from cannabis legalization, should they choose (Koutouki &Lofts, 2019).

Notes

1. See National Archive of South Africa. Draft letter, Prime Minister to Secretary, League of Nations, SAB BTS 2/1/104 L.N. 15/1SA, November 28, 1923.
2. This "theory" suggests that cannabis use results in progression to more seriously addictive and damaging drugs (Newhart & Dolphin, 2019: 28). While it has never been proven, it remains a persistent prohibition myth (Szalavitz, 2021).
3. In Canada, the supply of medical cannabis is controlled by the federal government, which regulates production and distribution. Some research suggests high cost, low quality, and insufficient access limit medical cannabis in some provinces in Canada (Wheeldon & Heidt, 2022), and patients turn to illicit markets to meet their medical needs.
4. In Europe, medical cannabis is less developed. While medical cannabis is available throughout the continent, there is a gap between legal status and availability to patients. Countries such as the United Kingdom, the Netherlands, Poland, and Portugal have established medical cannabis legislation. In Austria, it has been legal to prescribe since 2008, and since 2015, Finland has made medical cannabis available (Seddon & Floodgate, 2020: 53). Germany made it legal for doctors to prescribe medical cannabis in 2017 (Schlag, 2020). Greece and the United Kingdom approved the legalization of cannabis for medical use in 2018. In 2019, legislation was signed to permit a five-year pilot of the Medical Cannabis Access Programme (Seddon & Floodgate, 2020: 54). In other countries, including Sweden, Latvia, Belgium, and Albania, medical cannabis is illegal to buy, or sell, or use. France, Ireland, and Denmark are running trial periods for medical cannabis. However, in Croatia and Finland, just one cannabis medicinal product is available by prescription. For a useful overview, see: https://www.pharmexec.com/view/navigating-the-european-market-for-medical-cannabis.
5. The full Bill is available at: https://www.feinstein.senate.gov/public/_cache/files/f/9/f9877e00-8bac-45c5-b0a4-ad73f36bb296/A790203221D32AE509C4E2DEFEDBE6D6.2022-03-23-10-09-02-uid-575-hen22240.pdf.
6. This included the founding the National Organization for the Reform of Marijuana Laws (NORML) in 1972 and the first issue of *High Times* in 1974.
7. See https://dadgrass.com.
8. See https://www.congress.gov/bill/117th-congress/house-bill/3617. Other provisions of the MORE Act include ending the criminalization of cannabis at the federal level going forward; it would also be retroactive. Cannabis arrests, charges, and convictions would be automatically expunged at no cost to the individual. A 5 percent tax on the retail sales of cannabis would be imposed to go to the Opportunity Trust Fund. The measure was amended to start at 5 percent and increase the tax to 8 percent over three years. The MORE Act would create the Office of Cannabis Justice to oversee the social equity provisions in the law. The bill would ensure the federal government could not discriminate against people because of cannabis

use, including earned benefits or immigrants at risk of deportation. The measure would open the door to research, better banking and tax laws, and would help fuel economic growth as states are looking for financial resources.
9. For instance, until recently, Illinois prevented those with cannabis-related convictions from entering the cannabis industry and denied licenses and loans to those with criminal records, even though this comprised more than 30 percent of adults in Chicago. See Fitz & Armstrong (2022). The authors point to an analysis by Equity and Transformation (EAT) for further detail (EAT, 2019).
10. See https://www.acic.gov.au/sites/default/files/2020-09/Illicit%20Drug%20Data%20Report%202018-19_Internals_V10_Cannabis%20CH_0.pdf.
11. *R. v Smith* (2015), SCC 34, Judgments of the Supreme Court of Canada. Available at: https://scc-csc.lexum.com/scc-csc/scc-csc/en/item/15403/index.do.
12. See https://medicalmarijuana.ca/patients/who-is-eligible-3.
13. See https://www.canadianevergreen.com/news/b-c-pushes-for-black-market-cannabis-to-go-legal-faces-criticism-from-craft-growers/?utm_source=dlvr.it&utm_medium=twitter&fbclid=IwAR2IngKoCDVcmZ3DYbw6O6NAlocvquqL9rz3VXh3Ej6qV50pUEpHoNYRmMw.
14. For a useful overview, see https://policyoptions.irpp.org/magazines/august-2019/canada-must-respect-indigenous-cannabis-laws.
15. In response to a request to the Ministry of Justice and Security, the following statistics for arrests for cannabis possession in the Netherlands since 2016 were provided. In 2016, there were 319 arrests; in 2020, there were 330 (private communication from E. Avdatek, Juridisch adviseur, on October 26, 2021).
16. See https://www.emcdda.europa.eu/node/2583_fi.
17. See https://english.cannabisbureau.nl.
18. Prosecution data is available here: https://www.gov.uk/government/statistics/criminal-justice-system-statistics-quarterly-december-2020. Use the outcomes by offence tool.
19. See https://www.parliament.scot/chamber-and-committees/what-was-said-and-official-reports/official-reports/meeting-of-parliament-22-09-2021?meeting=13315&iob=120787.
20. For instance, in 2021, the Guardian reported that the UK Home Office had refused to publish annual stop-and-search data, and several policy reform organizations suggested that racial inequities were persisting (Townsend, 2021).
21. See https://www.prisonstudies.org/country/uruguay.
22. The procedure for these changes is outlined in article 60 of the following decree: https://www.impo.com.uy/bases/decretos/120-2014.
23. According to *Monitor Cannabis*, demand within existing markets is more than 40 tons a year, which is close to JND's estimate of 44 tons (Marcos Baudean, Private communication 2021).
24. See https://minorityrights.org/minorities/afro-uruguayans.
25. For a useful comparative overview, see https://norml.org/laws.

26. See https://ucr.fbi.gov/crime-in-the-u.s/2019/crime-in-the-u.s.-2019/topic-pages/persons-arrested.
27. See https://ucr.fbi.gov/crime-in-the-u.s/2011/crime-in-the-u.s.-2011.
28. See https://www.ussc.gov/sites/default/files/pdf/research-and-publications/quick-facts/Marijuana_FY20.pdf and https://www.justice.gov/opa/pr/justice-department-issues-memo-marijuana-enforcement.
29. Qualifying conditions include Alzheimer's disease, amyotrophic lateral sclerosis (ALS), HIV/AIDS, Crohn's disease, epilepsy and seizures, glaucoma, multiple sclerosis and muscle spasms, severe and chronic pain, and severe nausea or vomiting caused by cancer treatment. See https://www.mayoclinic.org/healthy-lifestyle/consumer-health/in-depth/medical-marijuana/art-20137855#:~:text=Is%20medical%20marijuana%20available%20as,dronabinol%20(Marinol%2C%20Syndros.
30. See https://dor.wa.gov/taxes-rates/taxes-due-cannabis.
31. See https://www.congress.gov/bill/117th-congress/house-bill/3617.

5
Stan Cohen and the Limits of the Cannabis Revolution

Introduction

Chapter 4 provided an overall optimistic account of cannabis reform. However, rumors of the death of cannabis prohibition have been greatly exaggerated. For example, just days before the US House of Representatives voted to decriminalize cannabis at the federal level, a ninety-one-year-old man was released from a Florida prison after serving twenty-eight years for trafficking cannabis (Andrew, 2020). Nevertheless, the reach of longstanding US-led prohibitionist pressures is still evident (Stevens, 2011). In the past eighty years, nearly every political persuasion and type of government have endorsed prohibition as one of the most "widely accepted, reputable, legitimate government policies of the entire 20th century" (Levine, 2003: 147). Between 1969 and 1989, Denmark and Iceland banned cannabis, Nepal canceled licenses for cannabis shops, and Bangladesh banned sales. In 1992, Lebanon criminalized cannabis possession and use, and Poland criminalized possession in 1997. In Switzerland, a referendum to decriminalize cannabis failed in 2008, and many countries in Eastern Europe retain restrictive cannabis policies.[1] In 2020, just over 50 percent of New Zealanders who voted did not support legalizing cannabis. This was described as a "triumph for fear-mongering."[2]

The United Nations Office on Drugs and Crime (UNODC) reports cannabis enforcement is undertaken in almost all countries worldwide.[3] This control expands and extends even as cannabis liberalization proliferates. Opposition to even modest reform remains obstinate in some countries. In this chapter, we outline some limits of liberalization. We begin with the challenge of how to categorize and conceptualize reform. We seek to create a taxonomy of different regulatory arrangements for dealing with people who possess cannabis, based on previous literature (Stevens et al., 2022). This remains a work in progress. In addition, we consider how to conceive of the harms that result from cannabis-related criminal justice contacts. The Global Drug Policy Index (GDPI, 2021a) serves as the first ever global accountability and evaluation mechanism to describe drug policies and assess the commitment to decriminalization. Paradoxically, despite liberalization, drug policies around the world rely on prohibition, criminalization, and police intervention and intrusion.

To understand this paradox, we apply Stan Cohen's (1985) pessimistic view of efforts to decarcerate, decriminalize, and divert those caught up in the criminal justice system. Cohen (1979) showed how reforms designed to replace carceral tendencies within correctional institutions simply extended such approaches into our communities. Applied to cannabis, we demonstrate how moving from public safety to public health brings new forms of social control, while leaving in place older structures that remain unequal in application and outcome (Owusu-Bempah & Luscombe, 2021; Sheehan et al., 2021). Intrusions by police are exacerbated by laws that make it legal to possess cannabis but illegal to consume it anywhere other than your home (Wheeldon & Heidt, 2023b). The widespread use of drug testing for cannabis in the criminal justice system is deeply problematic, given the tenuous link between cannabis use and crime. Insufficient and improperly administered drug tests lead to rampant false positives and punitive and unwarranted outcomes (Zraick, 2022). It has become part of the background of the criminal justice system.

Another set of concerns relates to the decriminalization of cannabis and the apparent shift from the prison-industrial complex to the treatment-industrial complex and coercive care (Spivakovsky et al., 2018). Too often, cannabis liberalization comes at the cost of expanding paternalistic public health models and abstention-based diversion programs. Finally, the goal of dismantling and disrupting illicit markets has been undermined by administrative difficulties within jurisdictions that have legalized cannabis. Regulations are onerous, marketing efforts are constrained, and consumer-centered approaches are anemic. Emphasizing public health goals ahead of market conditions complicates legal cannabis as an industry and limits the impact on illicit markets (Wesley & Murray, 2021). We consider illusory reform around the world and note how cannabis control is expanding.

The Limits of Liberalization

In Chapter 4, we compared seven countries based on their histories, past approaches to cannabis use, and the impact of recent reforms to better understand cannabis liberalization. While the potential of this approach to bring clarity to this area cannot be doubted (Seddon & Floodgate, 2020), merely mapping the legal terrain is insufficient. Such efforts must consider policies, practices, and the interactions between public safety, public health, and emergent governance approaches (Burris et al., 2020). Despite several worthy efforts to date, creating a clear and precise taxonomy of different regulatory arrangements for dealing with people who are found in possession of cannabis remains a work in progress (Stevens et al., 2022). We will return to the complexities of decriminalization and alternative sanctions in Chapter 7.

Below, we present one approach. We begin by considering how regulatory models for cannabis, including public safety, public health, medicinal cannabis, and consumer cannabis, vary by country. Table 5.1 outlines the seven countries of interest, four classes, and nine key categories of liberalization. We focus here on federal or national law, as opposed to local jurisdictions, including US states, countries within the United Kingdom, or states or territories in Australia. As the racial justice model of cannabis has yet to be embraced in any of the countries considered, it is not reported below. We will return to this model in the chapters to come.

While Table 5.1 offers one view of cannabis liberalization, it also demonstrates the limits of reform. Previous efforts to rank countries deserve more attention. Based on their comparison between Florida, the Czech Republic, and Australia, Belackova and colleagues (2017) struggled to arrive at a clear definition of the country's "punitiveness," given differences between laws on the books, laws in practice, official arrests rates, and sentencing data. Thus, the level of criminal justice intrusion a citizen is likely to face for possessing cannabis, from no criminal sanction to prison, varies. Categorization is difficult. Simplistic indices on drug policy must consider the following:

> the complexity of drug laws, the differences in legal systems, the variance in offense categories, the multitude of parameters that can be taken into account in assessing laws on the books (e.g., minimum and maximum sentences, threshold quantities) and the relevance of different indicators of law enforcement.
>
> (Belackova et al., 2017: 156)

Perhaps more significant than Aristotelian fidelity to unyielding categorization or narrow definitions, reform frameworks demand contemplating how any sanction for the possession of cannabis is likely to be applied to the least advantaged in any jurisdiction.

Table 5.1 Countries and cannabis

Country	Depenalization — Reduced sanction	Decriminalization — Practices	Decriminalization — Policies	Decriminalization — Laws	Medical — Access	Legalization/consumer-centered — Possession	Legalization/consumer-centered — Growing	Legalization/consumer-centered — Buying	Legalization/consumer-centered — Selling
Australia	●								
Canada	●	●	●	●	●	●	●	●	●
Netherlands	●	●	●	●	●				
Portugal	●	●	●	●	●				
United Kingdom	●	●			●				
Uruguay		●	●	●	●	●	●	●	●
United States	●	●			●				

Source: Authors.

This is especially relevant in the United States, given how prohibition specifically targeted Black and Hispanic Americans (Earp et al., 2021). While the depenalization of cannabis remains important where draconian sentences for drug possession exist, focusing on depenalization fails to properly account for how differing approaches to decriminalization perpetuate public safety models. One way to understand this phenomenon is to consider cannabis arrest data. For example, in 2005, there were 269 marijuana possession arrests for every 100,000 citizens in the United States, 206 in the United Kingdom, and just 19 in the Netherlands (Room et al., 2008: 77). Although dated, this comparison remains instructive. It speaks to the need to differentiate models of decriminalization. One foundational problem is summarized in practical terms. The issue is:

> decriminalization, in terms of substantive law and the procedure conditioning its application, does not always achieve the diminution in police authority imagined by proponents. Often this is because the law adopted really amounts to depenalization, imposing a fine and lessening or denying the possibility of incarceration or creation of a criminal record, yet leaving intact police power to execute arrests and carry out searches. It also can be the case that legislative efforts to reclassify possession as noncriminal do not actually limit police authority as a result of broad judicial understandings of what qualifies as an arrestable offense.
> (Logan, 2014: 322)

Consistent with the shift from public safety to public health, there is a worrying trend in which cannabis decriminalization is accompanied by police-led diversion and mandated treatment programs. One potential problem with this arrangement is that diversion programs are connected to other aspects of the justice system, such as police, prosecutors, judges, and increasingly commercial addiction management enterprises. Stoicescu and colleagues (2022: 134) note that the program can be considered compulsory if individuals are denied the "unconditional right to refuse treatment, due process protections, or evidence-based drug treatment." Since failing to complete many diversion programs can result in a criminal conviction, this right of refusal cannot be said to be unconditional. A criminal record has been shown to undermine employment opportunities, limit housing options, and prevent civic and political engagement (Best & Colman, 2019; Pinard, 2010). As we have observed (Wheeldon & Heidt, 2023b), electing to participate in treatment programs to escape the lifetime impacts of a criminal record may be a good decision; it often amounts to a false choice based on coerced consent.

Diversion programs exist along a spectrum and vary. Efforts to identify, classify, and categorize diversion are an important contribution to understanding how diversion has expanded. Stevens and colleagues (2021) argue diversion may be de facto (based on practice) or de jure (based on law). Such an approach, as they note, may occur at various stages of the criminal justice process, for example, pre-arrest, pre-charge/pre-indictment, pre-trial, and pre-sentencing. In many countries, informal diversion based on law enforcement discretion exists. In these cases, police give out-of-court disposals when they encounter citizens possessing small amounts of cannabis, including cannabis warnings or community resolutions. This approach to reform may still foster criminal justice intrusion, shame and stigma, and the perpetuation of systemic racism. As Niamh Eastwood, Executive Director of Release, notes,

> For too long, officers have been using the smell of cannabis as an excuse to target people, mainly people of colour and young people. This is despite [Black people] using drugs at a lower rate and being less likely to be found in possession when searched compared to the white population.
> (Childs, 2020)

Perhaps the need for new descriptors is the failure to document the totality of criminal justice intrusions on citizens possessing cannabis. One recent development consistent with international rights protection is the Global Drug Policy Index (GDPI). The methodology (GDPI, 2021b) document outlines five critical dimensions. Key indicators include the absence of extreme measures, such as the use of the death penalty, torture, militarized police, life sentences, and nonconsensual confinement for treatment. In addition, numerous dimensions of the proportionality of criminal justice responses are included, such as disparities in enforcement, use of imprisonment for nonviolent offenders, arbitrary arrest, decriminalization in practice, policy, law, the existence of administrative sanctions, the nature of diversion programs, and the extent to which nonparticipation in diversion programs are punished criminally. While the index does not include all the seven countries of interest in our analysis and does not focus on cannabis specifically, the report offers valuable insights for cannabis liberalization in the context of drug reform. Numerous call-outs within the text of the report refer to cannabis and the castigatory approaches in Mexico, Norway, Jamaica, and Kyrgyzstan

(GDPI, 2021a). Globally, cannabis remains the most policed, prohibited, and punished drug (UNODC, 2021a). The GDPI (2021a: 34) finds:

> Most countries' drug policies are misaligned with governments' obligations to promote health, human rights and development, and continue to rely on criminalisation, interdiction, forced eradication and police interventions as a form of drug control.

Other findings include the global dominance of drug policies based on repression and punishment, deep inequality between and among countries, and differences in the application of drug policies within the countries examined. The report notes that "Inequality is deeply seated in global drug policies . . . due to the colonial legacy of the 'war on drugs' approach" (GDPIa, 2021: 17). Another important finding is wide disparities between state policies and how they are implemented on the ground. This observation begs the question: is the failure to date one of effort or inevitability? For Cohen (1985: 21), by studying how reforms are implemented, it becomes apparent that "the original design can be systematically, not incidentally, undermined."

Cohen, Contagion, and Criminological Control

One of Stan Cohen's contributions was the combination of the prescient concern that reforms that sound benevolent may be a "monster in disguise, a Trojan horse" (Cohen, 1985: 38) and a detailed example of how systems of control continue to proliferate and penetrate social and cultural life (Cohen, 1979). Stevens (2011: 106) argued that Cohen described bifurcation in crime control policies that have both hard and soft ends. The hard end is there to deter offenders and reassure the public, while the soft end expands—at a lower cost—the number of people who come under the supervisory gaze of the state. Cohen (1985) relies on several metaphors to describe the outward creep of the soft end of social control. One is fishing nets, used to ensnare those labeled deviant. Cohen (1985: 42–43) asks:

> First, there are matters of quantity: size, capacity, scope, reach, density, intensity. Just how wide are the nets being cast? . . . How strong is the mesh, or how large are its holes . . . are the same fish being processed quicker or more new ones being caught? Second . . . just how clearly can the net and the rest of the apparatus be seen? Is it always visible as a net? Or is it sometimes

masked, disguised or camouflaged? Who is operating it? How sure are we about what exactly is being done in all the component parts of the machine? Third, there is the ripple problem. What effect does all this activity—casting the nets, pulling them in, processing the fish—have on the rest of the sea? Do other non-fish objects inadvertently get caught up in the net? Are other patterns disturbed: coral formations, tides, mineral deposits?

In this way, Cohen (1985) builds on work that suggests efforts to curtail the state's authority, such as diversion, decarceration, decriminalization, and due process, ironically contribute to the expansion of state control (Austin & Krisberg, 1981: 165).

Another contribution is Cohen's (1985) fascination with the pervasive use of Orwellian language. For example, he concludes that, despite euphemistic-sounding reforms, policies often result in increasing numbers of people in the system, including those who previously would not have been processed. This is an example of *wider* nets. For example, diversion programs strengthen existing webs and create new nets by formalizing previously informal organizational practices and creating practices where none existed. If expanding nets bring more people into the system, *denser* nets increase overall dominance through various interventions. For example, expanding community control often increases the number of people caught in the system. Diversion programs designed to keep clients away from the criminal justice system must develop screening procedures to differentiate between the wrong clients and the right ones (Cohen, 1985: 171–172). This screening often leads to additional programming by the state or others approved by the state.

This vision of social control deviates from an amorphous conception which can include almost everything from child socialization to incarceration (Cohen, 1985: 2). Cohen's focus is the state's regulation of crime and deviance. While valuable in 1985, social control, as conceived by Cohen, cannot be divorced from those who have extended his work. Ironically, the Cohen-inspired attempt to explain the criminal justice system's evolution and development over the past thirty years may require criminologists to return to broader definitions of social control. Kraska (2006) argues that the role of nongovernmental crime control and punishment phenomena, the rise of paramilitary groups, the treatment industrial complex, and other criminal justice organizations and private companies not typically involved in the state's criminal justice functions must not be ignored. Just as the "War on Drugs" is more problematic than the use of drugs, the growth and power of the justice system may cause as much harm as crime itself (Kraska, 2006: 71).

Cohen's "visions" of control connect Rothman's history of the origins of the asylum in early nineteenth-century America and the optimism and utopian thinking which inspired the focus on behavior modification with Foucault's extraordinary "archaeology" of deviancy control systems. Rothman (Gaylin et al., 1978: 72) asks why well-meaning people acting on behalf of others behave so "harshly, coercively and callously" and allow reforms to be transformed into a caricature to serve the interests of the caretakers and managers. For Foucault (1979), it is not the people but how power itself is dispersed and exercised through techniques of objectification and classification, where it produces domains and rituals of truth. Thus, people are both *subject to* and *agents of* power. Rothman and Foucault demonstrated how the power of the asylum and the prison extended state authority in expected and unexpected ways. Cohen's (1985) contribution is to build on these accounts by revealing that, while promising to be less burdensome, new applications of the old power extend control, expand intervention, and contain within them the potential for these approaches to be replicated, not restricted.

The expansion of social control produces dysfunctions and unanticipated consequences. Since the focus of control has become dispersed and diffused, boundaries between those persons under control (being punished and being treated) and those not under control become blurred. From incarceration, bureaucracy and professions, classification, and evaluation, Cohen (1985) shows that procedures designed to replace the carceral tendencies of control require new procedures to decide who is eligible for non-carceral substitutions, such as diversion, treatment, or social support. This has the effect of increasing dominion applied to everyone. However, control has deepened for a predictable percentage of those caught in the net. Deemed ineligible for carceral alternatives, they are sent to traditional custodial institutions. These observations can be applied to cannabis through the lens of predation, coercion, and regulation.

Illusions of Cannabis Reform

Framing cannabis reforms as illusory derives from what Cohen considers the inherent paradox of a state appearing to sponsor a move to disestablish itself. In fact, "the rhetoric of destructuring is used to justify the creation of new structures" (Cohen, 1985: 124). These new structures of control may emerge when the state has effectively lost control and often refuses to try and police it (O'Brien, 2018). Cannabis use is increasingly ubiquitous in many jurisdictions. It represents an example of deviance that was slowly defined down over several decades. Garland (2001) described a similar situation faced by criminal justice authorities regarding crime more generally. He describes a predicament faced by criminal justice authorities that involved acknowledging the normalcy of high crime rates and the inability of the criminal justice state to control them. One adaptation in practice is known as defining deviance down (Moynihan, 1993). According to Garland (2001: 118), this refers to

> filtering complaints and cases out of the system, or else by lowering the degree to which behaviors are criminalized and penalized. This process occurs at the "shallow" and hence less visible end of the criminal justice.
>
> (Garland, 2001: 117)

As applied to cannabis, Stevens (2011: 11) suggests people who use cannabis may face less formal punishment today but suffer a higher rate of interference through less visible arrangements. For Cohen (1985: 44), these arrangements increase:

(1) ... the total number of deviants getting into the system in the first place and many of these are new deviants who would not have been processed previously (wider nets);
(2) ... the overall intensity of intervention, with old and new deviants being subject to levels of intervention (including traditional institutionalization) which they might not have previously received (denser nets);
(3) new agencies and services [that are] supplementing rather than replacing the original set of control mechanisms (different nets).

Supervised by the state, such efforts include predatory policing, pretextual stops, and the increased use of drug testing, which *widen* the net. Such arrangements may also be farmed out to a range of non-state actors. For example, pathologizing people who use cannabis allows the system to force them to submit to problematic forms of the social "help–control complex" (Lowman et al., 1987: 9). These systems of control are less accountable because, although the state supports them, they may be implemented by private entities.

Reforms may amount to *denser* nets because, rather than serving your sentence in a carceral sense, these programs require people to accept that they were "bad" or "wrong" for using cannabis. This expansion from the mere warehousing of human beings toward more psychologically tricky terrain is worthy of more investigation (Drake, 2012). Finally, cannabis liberalization has led to new forms of control or *different* nets. States have adopted several adaptive strategies to extend authority over legal cannabis (Aaronson & Rothschild-Elyassi, 2021). This involves limiting access to licenses, preventing new products, or pursuing policies that undermine small growers and give advantages to large corporations (Wesley & Murray, 2021).

Police and Predation

The predatory practices of the criminal justice system represent an example of *wider nets*. This results in exploiting the poor, Black, and other politically unconnected populations through fines, fees, forfeitures, prison charges, and bail premiums. Police often receive substantial federal subsidies. In some cases, they can keep property they seize as part of drug arrests. Indeed,

> While drug-related asset forfeitures have expanded police budgets, critics say the flow of money distorts law enforcement—that some cops have become more interested in seizing money than drugs.
> (Burnett, 2020)

Page & Soss (2021) suggest the US criminal justice system has become a financial predator, transferring billions of dollars out of poor communities and into government budgets and private companies. Criminalizing cannabis aided this process (Alexander, 2010).

This predation has led to the over-policing of Black and Brown people and those with less political capital (McDonald, 2021), policing for profit in Alabama (Slate, 2022), and civil asset forfeiture laws by which police and prosecutors can confiscate and keep money and property they suspect is part of a drug crime, even after all charges are dismissed.[4] Anti-narcotics police can legitimately do undercover investigations almost anywhere and target nearly anyone. Government officials have used anti-drug squads to conduct surveillance operations and military raids that they would not otherwise have been able to justify (Baum, 1996; Duke & Gross, 1993; Gray, 1998; McWilliams, 1992). Cannabis laws have also been used to justify police intrusions and interfere with otherwise law-abiding citizens. It is tied to police discretion.

In the United Kingdom, Stevens (2011: 104) notes police retain discretion to arrest anyone found smoking cannabis for further interrogation. Many cannabis arrests are resolved through informal out-of-court clearance, such as a cannabis warning or other community resolution.[5] The Lambeth Cannabis Warning Scheme (LCWS), which ran from 2001 to 2002, offered an example of how such a system might work. Under this scheme, possessing small quantities of cannabis for personal consumption was still a recordable offense but would no longer lead to the individual being arrested. The pilot ran for thirteen months. Adda and colleagues (2014: 1130) concluded:

> We found evidence that the policy caused the police to reallocate effort towards crimes related to the supply of Class-A drugs, as well as reallocating efforts towards non-drug crime: there are significant reductions in five types of non-drug crime, and significant improvements in police effectiveness against such crimes as measured by arrest and clear-up rates.

While the pilot ended on July 31, 2002, the Home Secretary announced that cannabis would be declassified from a Class-B to a Class-C drug in 2004 (Turnbull, 2009).

Many assumed that although it remained an arrestable offense, police would pay less attention to cannabis once it was reclassified and address cannabis use through a combination of warnings and cautions (Lloyd, 2008). In a truly Cohenesque development, discretion overwhelmed efforts to de-emphasize policing cannabis. It led to net-widening, a sharp increase in the number of people caught in the criminal justice net for minor possession offenses, and an intensification of police efforts targeting minor possession offenses (Shiner, 2015). Although cannabis street warnings did not form part of an official criminal record, they are the only on-the-spot warning that counted as sanction detection. Thus, while maintaining the power of arrest, reclassification incentivized officers to target cannabis possession to meet performance targets (Bear, 2014).

One obvious policy example is the use of stop and frisk/stop and search by the police. As discussed in Chapter 4, in the United Kingdom, one is twelve times more likely to be stopped and searched if one happens to be Black than if one is White, even though it is less likely that drugs would be found (White, 2021). Shiner and colleagues (2018: 61) concluded:

> The uneven enforcement of drug laws and selective criminalization of black and minority ethnic communities is a profound source of injustice

that demands redress. It is scarcely believable that ethnic disparities have widened, despite the introduction of recent reforms that were meant to address the problem and that the situation is not being treated as a matter of urgency by government ... specific measures and safeguards are required to tackle entrenched ethnic disparities in drug policing.

The focus on nuisance crimes and drug possession is rooted in a preoccupation with the moral and social control of non-White people. One risk is that these approaches will result in police corruption, further reduced respect for the law, and heighten political cynicism (Zinberg & Robertson, 1972).

In the United States, police surveillance has long been a part of everyday life for African Americans and other minority groups (Kennedy, 1997). In Canada, following cannabis legalization, some municipalities voted in favor of an outright ban on cannabis dispensaries to limit consumption in their communities as of 2021. Some jurisdictions have also introduced stricter public smoking regulations with more severe penalties (Shepherd, 2018). There is evidence that despite legalization, both Black and Indigenous people remain over-represented in arrest statistics in five large cities (Browne, 2022; Owusu-Bempah and Luscombe, 2021).

There is no better way to appreciate the commonplace intrusions that people of color face than research by Geller and Fagan (2010). Based on data from 2.2 million stops and arrests carried out between 2004 and 2008, they identified significant racial disparities in the implementation of cannabis enforcement. They argue that the racial imbalance in cannabis enforcement suggests policing cannabis amounted to a pretext—just an excuse to stop, search, and interfere with non-White people. Although they found no evidence of the success of the policy, they note the high social costs and conclude that "nonwhite New Yorkers bear a racial tax from contemporary policing strategy, a social cost not offset by any substantial observed benefits to public safety" (Geller and Fagan, 2010: 591). Just as Jim Crow responded to emancipation by rolling back many of the newly gained rights of African Americans, "the drug war is again replicating the institutions and repressions of the plantation" (Boyd, 2002: 845).

Confidence in law enforcement suffers when their activities are seen as predatory, assaultive, or fail to adhere to acceptable substantive normative benchmarks (del Pozo, 2022). This damages consensus views in law enforcement and can lead to calls for police reform that are existential instead of incremental (Vitale, 2018). For example, in a federal civil rights lawsuit, a $900,000 settlement was awarded to the "Cartersville 70" because police tactics used in the case were racially motivated. After violating their constitutional rights against search and seizure, this group's members were subjected to invasive strip searches and denied medical services.[6] In addition, they had their privacy violated when their booking photos were illegally shared online (Lockhart, 2019).

The use of strip searches was also a feature of intrusive policing of a fifteen-year-old Black student in the United Kingdom. The shocking search by London Metropolitan Police officers occurred at a Hackney School near London. As we noted in Chapter 1, it occurred after a teacher called the police because they stated the student "smelt of cannabis" (Crew, 2022). According to a review of the incident, the student, who told police she was on her period, was made to bend over, spread her legs, use her hands to spread her buttocks and cough (CHSCP, 2022). An official review found that racism was "likely to have been an influencing factor in the decision to undertake a strip search" (CHSCP, 2022). No cannabis was found. The potential for racism to guide discretion is not limited to the United Kingdom. In the United States, Plunk and colleagues (2019: 763) note that while decriminalization has reduced youth arrests, most states fail to "explicitly describe when youths can be arrested for possession of small amounts of cannabis."

The quest to "find" cannabis is a focus within probation and parole in the United States. New detection and monitoring tools have led to the emergence of urine analysis. It has emerged as a central part of community-based sanctions. Individuals on probation are subject to drug testing regardless of conviction offenses. Positive test results often lead to additional punishment, from probation sanctions and technical violations to revocations, which may result in a period of incarceration for some (Reichert et al., 2020). While common, punitive responses to drug test results run counter to guidelines by the American Society of Addiction Medicine (ASAM) (Jarvis et al., 2017). Drug testing remains a frequent condition of juvenile justice programs, even though it is "not a significant predictor of successfully completing diversion" (Harris & Wylie, 2022: 36). The use of drug testing was described as "embarrassing" and "degrading" by participants in a treatment program (Strike & Rufo, 2010: 303).

Drug testing is a common feature of contemporary justice policy that illustrates the widening net of social control. In the United Kingdom, starting in 2022, anyone testing positive after arrest for "trigger" crimes such as theft, fraud, or drug possession would be required to be assessed for treatment (Riley-Smith, 2021). Those who refuse treatment will face prosecution, with a maximum penalty of up to six months in jail or a £2,500 fine (Riley-Smith, 2021). Drug testing on arrest applies to all forty-three police forces in England and Wales starting in 2022 (Riley-Smith, 2021). Cannabis is central to the carceral control that permeates society. Even random drug testing, once limited to probation orders or conducted within US prisons (Nguyen et al., 2021), has expanded beyond the criminal justice system.

Employers increasingly use drug testing, despite research that cannabis does not significantly impact work productivity (Bernerth & Walker, 2020). For example,

> certain employers are required to test for marijuana under federal law—the federal government classifies marijuana as a dangerous drug akin to heroin—and others want to make sure they don't employ drug users who could threaten workplace safety...
>
> Today most of the nation's largest private-sector companies have some sort of drug testing program.
>
> (Quinton, 2022)

Threats to workplace safety are not associated with consuming cannabis generally (Anderson et al., 2018; Biasutti et al., 2020). However, in many states where cannabis is legal, employers can still fire workers and bar applicants for failing to pass random drug tests (Ricciardi, 2020; Schencker, 2020).

Despite this example of the non-state expansion of cannabis control, the role of public safety and police where cannabis is legal in US states persists. By securing state or local cannabis licenses, operators make themselves vulnerable to potential federal prosecution (Martiroysan, 2017) since federal law considers cannabis a Schedule 1 drug (Hannah & Mallinson, 2018). Local police may attempt to prevent growth and distribution, potentially partnering with federal law enforcement (Polson & Petersen-Rockney, 2019). In addition, landowners leasing land or facilities to cannabis operations can be held liable for criminal activity and their property seized by the federal government. The disconnect between state and federal law increases the risk for local businesses (Karch, 2021), even in states and localities that permit cannabis activities (Fersko, 2018).

Finally, to return to the concept of *wider nets*, as cannabis use has become normalized, its status is changing from a "serious" to a "nuisance" crime. Legalizing cannabis has resulted in increased complaints about cannabis odor. For example, it is illegal to consume marijuana openly and publicly in Colorado. In Denver, adults are permitted to consume marijuana in private or at licensed marijuana hospitality businesses, some of which offer retail sales. However, in 2013, a Denver city ordinance was proposed. It would

> prohibit smoking on private property if it is visible to the public, such as on a front porch or in a car, or if the odor of pot could be detected from a neighboring property... offenders could face a fine of $999 and up to a year in jail.
> (Associated Press, 2007)

While unsuccessful, other nuisance crimes have been identified. State or local cultivation rules do not always address concerns connected to growing cannabis, from the smell of the plants to the sounds of fans used to help them grow (Ryskamp, 2020). Indeed, a 2019 poll found half of Americans thought the smell of cannabis was a problem and a quarter of those polled said they "hated it" (Holden, 2019). Of course, like tobacco smoke, secondhand cannabis smoke presents health risks (ANRF, n.d.). The prevalence of concerns in this research and within the literature suggest cannabis as a nuisance crime speaks to the general failure of regulatory approaches to provide places to consume cannabis. Challenges persist. For example,

> A key regulatory challenge for cannabis-legal states and municipalities is establishing where residents can legally smoke cannabis or consume aerosolized (i.e., vaporized or "vaped") cannabis. Public cannabis consumption often conflicts with state smoke-free air laws that prohibit smoking and federal and state laws.
> (Steinberg et al., 2020: 203)

Control and Coercion

Increasing the *density* of social control has emerged alongside the rise of public health models. While nominally able to disrupt the dependence on the police-punishment complex (Simon, 2007), embracing the medical model may reduce penalties for some, while pathologizing those who use it. Cohen (1985) documented that the growing number of professionals and experts has increased alongside therapy and treatment modalities based on new versions of behaviorism. One result is that "[c]rime and delinquency nets... become blurred in themselves... [and] get tangled up with other welfare, treatment and control nets" (Cohen, 1985: 61). Care and control professionals and their academic auxiliaries help explain how control systems grow. The key here is classification, which is "deeply lodged in the framework of punishment" (Cohen 1985: 194).

One effort has been to define cannabis use disorder (CUD) by expanding on older descriptions of problem cannabis use. Symptoms of CUD, according to the current Diagnostic and Statistical Manual of Mental Disorders (DSM-5), include:

- Use of cannabis for at least a one-year period, with the presence of at least two of the following symptoms, accompanied by significant impairment of functioning and distress:
- Difficulty containing use of cannabis—the drug is used in larger amounts and over a longer period than intended.
- Repeated failed efforts to discontinue or reduce the amount of cannabis that is used.
- An inordinate amount of time is occupied acquiring, using, or recovering from the effects of cannabis.
- Cravings or desires to use cannabis. This can include intrusive thoughts and images, and dreams about cannabis, or olfactory perceptions of the smell of cannabis, due to preoccupation with cannabis.
- Continued use of cannabis despite adverse consequences from its use, such as criminal charges, ultimatums of abandonment from spouse/partner/friends, and poor productivity.
- Other important activities in life, such as work, school, hygiene, and responsibility to family and friends are superseded by the desire to use cannabis.
- Cannabis is used in contexts that are potentially dangerous, such as operating a motor vehicle.
- Use of cannabis continues despite awareness of physical or psychological problems attributed to use—e.g., anergia, amotivation, chronic cough.
- Tolerance to Cannabis, as defined by progressively larger amounts of cannabis are needed to obtain the psychoactive effect experienced when use first commenced, or noticeably reduced effect of use of the same amount of cannabis
- Withdrawal, defined as the typical withdrawal syndrome associated with cannabis, or cannabis or a similar substance is used to prevent withdrawal symptoms.

(American Psychiatric Association, 2013)

The severity of the disorder depends on the number of symptoms. A mild case of CUD involves presenting with two or three symptoms. A moderate case involves four or five symptoms, while a severe case is present when six or more symptoms apply to a cannabis user (American Psychiatric Association, 2013). Consistent with Cohen's (1985) view of expanded control through differentiated categorization, contemporary descriptions of CUD now combine two older stand-alone concepts related to cannabis abuse *and* cannabis dependence (American Psychiatric Association, n.d.; Jutras-Aswad et al., 2019; Porter, 2021).

The most prestigious of America's professional medical associations remain skeptical of cannabis' medicinal uses:

> The federal government has imposed unique barriers to medical research on cannabis and maintains pressure up and down the legal chain from international law to state and local policies . . . this limits the influence of expert medical opinion. . . . Instead, ideology is pitted against science and the will of the public.
>
> (Newhart & Dolphin, 2019: 27)

Expanding professional definitions of "problem cannabis use" has justified increasing drug treatment programs. More than thirty countries implement models of drug decriminalization based on public health interventions (Eastwood et al., 2016). In the context of cannabis, net-widening occurs when formal interventions are given to people who, in the past, would have had their offenses ignored. Framing the use of drug treatment as an *alternative* to imprisonment may sound promising. However, data from England and Wales suggests that court-ordered drug treatment has been used as an "adjunct and not an alternative to imprisonment" (Stevens, 2011: 93).

Focusing attention on diversion programs is crucial because this is the site of two significant challenges to cannabis liberalization (Wheeldon & Heidt, 2023b). The first surrounds discrepancies regarding who gets diverted from the formal criminal justice system. The unequal application of policing cannabis is seen alongside disparities within diversion programs. For example, Sanchez and colleagues (2020) reviewed records from more than 8,000 adult participants in Harris County, Texas' Marijuana Misdemeanor Diversion Program (MMDP). They found differences in the ethnic, gender, and racial characteristics of those directed to a cannabis diversion program. These may be connected to differential and race-based policing patterns.

These findings are not limited to North America. For example, research in Australia suggests that diversion schemes result in net widening and undermine equity and equal access (Abel, 1997; Christie & Ali, 2000; Hughes et al., 2019; Sutton & Hawks, 2005). In the United Kingdom, minority ethnic groups are more likely to receive sentences with higher average severity. A recent report suggests that Black, Asian, and other Minority Ethnic (BAME) children are less likely to get formal out-of-court disposal than other children (Irish Penal Reform Trust, 2021). The focus on diversion disparities must contend with a contradiction. Reducing the number of those sentenced to prison or saddled with a criminal record is important and encouraging. However, tying these reductions to mandated diversion programs reinforces problematic assumptions that cannabis use is risky and potentially harmful.

For Cohen (1985: 51–52), one problem with diversion programs is based on his distinction between *traditional* or *true* diversion and *new* variants. Traditional diversion removes people from the criminal justice system and requires no further treatment, no service, and no follow-up. By contrast, new diversion variants combine the administrative controls associated with screening people with the requirements of any program delivered within the system or by those closely aligned with it. There are two issues worth exploring here. The first is to what extent these programs are voluntary or compulsory. When those arrested with small amounts of cannabis can avoid criminal sanction by participating in a treatment program, it is often described as "voluntary." Although research on how due process protections, coercive care, and cannabis are linked through diversion programs is underdeveloped, these sorts of mandated programs are not without their critics (Ashton, 2008; McSweeney et al., 2007; Price et al., 2021; Spivakovsky et al., 2018; Szasz, 2007). However, the "Cohen complications" are increasingly evident.

One problem is definitional. Programs that include treatment are considered compulsory and not voluntary if individuals are

> denied the unconditional right to refuse treatment; if the process for ordering treatment is conducted without due process protections; or if the conditions of treatment violate human rights, including the denial of evidence-based drug treatment and related health and social support services.
> (Stoicescu et al., 2022: 134)

It is difficult to see how due process protections and the unconditional right to refuse treatment are consistent with programs that threaten criminal prosecution if participants fail to comply with guidelines. This is noted as a specific issue in the United Kingdom (Transform Drug Policy Foundation, n.d.) and in Australia, where those deferred can be removed from the program for failure to comply (Hughes et al., 2019), and non-completion could result in a criminal conviction.

Another problem is based on rights. Forced treatment backed by the threat of criminal prosecution is deeply troubling in ethical, public health, and criminological terms (Stevens, 2012). These programs are not evidence-based, given the lack of clear evidence for the value of coerced programming (Klag et al., 2005; Luciano et al., 2014). Compelled cannabis treatment rarely involves the health and social supports related to success for those who engage in problem substance use. This means focusing on care, treatment, and harm reduction may be replaced by emphasizing control, punishment, and abstinence (Ashton, 2008). Recent research in Scotland demonstrates some problems when diversion embeds health-focused support *"within* criminal sanctions, rather than acting as *alternatives"* (Price et al., 2021: 118, our emphasis).

As described above, the intersections of public health and public safety models of cannabis policy can be observed in the United Kingdom. In a white paper entitled *Swift, Certain, Tough. New Consequences for Drug Possession* (Home Office, 2022), people who are caught using cannabis recreationally will be required to attend and pay for a drug awareness course if it is their first offense. Third-time offenders may be assigned a drug tag to monitor their usage and potentially have their passports and driving licenses confiscated (Morris, 2022). This speaks to a second problem. There may be broader social costs when diversion programs pervert public health by ignoring the values that inform therapeutic relationships, such as agency, autonomy, and respect. Too often, diversion program curricula are designed to scare, shame, and stigmatize participants.[7] Even well-intentioned programs may unconsciously perpetuate stigma by adopting abstinence frames or suggesting people (e.g., the 200 million people in 2019 who used cannabis) are somehow bad, sick, or otherwise wrong.[8]

Accepting this approach obscures the contradictions and hypocrisies at the heart of prohibition. It results in acquiescing to outdated ideas about addiction (Szalavitz, 2021; Taylor et al., 2016) and accepting the "abstinence-focused rhetoric" that focuses on "risk and harm," despite observations that this type of messaging is inconsistent and profoundly unhelpful to educate and inform young people. A review of educational material from Canadian provinces and territories suggests that many continue to promote "messaging that is predominantly infused with traditional risk-based rhetoric about cannabis" (Watson et al., 2019: 474).

The shift toward public health models reproduces many carceral features of the public safety model. However, when drug treatment services are linked with the rhetoric of "tough and effective community sentences" (Home Office, 2021), this approach becomes more likely.[9] The lack of evidence to justify such policies is startling. As noted, 90 percent of people who use drugs do not develop problematic or dependent drug use (Cole, 2022). This number is even smaller for people who use cannabis.[10] While there may be a role for limited compelled treatment in specific circumstances, it is hard to see how that could apply to cannabis. Coercion is a feature in cannabis diversion programs in Pennsylvania (Ogg, 2019) Texas (Ogg, n.d.), the United Kingdom (Transform Drug Policy Foundation, n.d.), and Australia (ADF, n.d.).

Diversion is likely to remain part of cannabis policy. However, viewing mandatory treatment programs in place of a criminal record as progressive reform is hardly the meaningful change many spent decades working toward. Even if there were clear evidence that mandating cannabis programs based on abstentionist frames worked to minimize use, they would remain problematic in moral and ethical terms (Stevens, 2012). Even in Portugal, stigma has not been erased. People who use drugs report facing stigma despite the decriminalization of drug possession and investing in public health, harm reduction, health care, and social reintegration (Beweley-Taylor et al., 2014). Policy reforms have led to increased surveillance of people who use drugs and further invasion of their privacy. People who use drugs face drug testing routinely implemented without informed consent by untrained law enforcement personnel who "pressure, impose, or coerce people who use drugs into decisions or actions," including treatment (INPUD, 2021: 34). The bias toward certain forms of intoxication is obvious. As an organization representing the rights of people who use drugs in Portugal noted that "there are no fines for alcohol drinkers" (INPUD, 2018: 16).

Legalization and Regulation

Cohen (1985: 272) concludes *Visions of Social Control* by noting understanding the "differences between state and market control might well be the crucial theoretical issue for the future." As argued above, cannabis control has been achieved by replacing public safety models with public health.

An emergent concern is how efforts to legalize and regulate cannabis have emphasized public health over more traditional approaches to consumer models related to access, marketing, and advertising. Access can be understood in this context as approaches in Canada that position those licensed to provide legal cannabis to the market not as "sellers" of the previously illicit product but as "protective 'providers' of cannabis in a highly regulated consumer environment" (Wesley & Murray, 2021: 1099). We return to this question in subsequent chapters.

This is consistent but distinct from observations that legal cannabis policies are expanding the state's regulatory role into governance areas previously managed by penal forms of power (Aaronson & Rothschild-Elyassi, 2021). While undeniable, this might be better understood by recognizing how penal forms of power influence public health, and these together influence the desire to control the cannabis market. There are three key aspects here. The first is who can participate in the legal market (Mize, 2020). The second is how the production of legal cannabis is regulated and priced (Mahamad et al., 2020). The third, and final, issue is how legal cannabis is sold. While the legal cannabis market may struggle to compete with illicit markets based on cost and convenience, it is how advertising and marketing have been limited (Wesley & Murray, 2021), undermining consumer education and threatening the sustainability of the legal cannabis market. Marketing cannabis is identifying customer needs and determining how best to meet those needs. By contrast, advertising involves promoting a company, a product, or a service by informing a customer base of how a company or product can meet consumers' needs.

As noted in Chapter 4, states with legalized cannabis have also set strict standards for who can participate in the cannabis industry. Some American states prevent people with certain criminal convictions from being employed in cannabis establishments (Howell, 2018) or participating in other parts of the cannabis industry.[11] These exclusions have a racial dimension (Mize, 2020). Although it is understandable that some jurisdictions may wish to limit those with lengthy criminal histories and connections to organized crime groups, the majority of those involved in the illicit cannabis industry prior to legalization do not fit these criteria (Capler & Boyd, 2016).

In Canada, Bennett (2021) raised another issue. Between 2014 and 2018, policy shifted from allowing consumers and small cannabis operations to grow medical cannabis to one that supported "a supply chain that more closely resembled synthetic pharmaceuticals [so that] large commercial operations were licensed and home grows prohibited" (Bennett (2021: 192).

Following the implementation of the Cannabis Act in 2018, different standards exist for large-scale and micro-producers. Limiting access to licenses, pursuing policies that undermine small growers, or preventing access to new products remain of concern (Raycraft, 2021).

As Kavousi and colleagues (2022) note, in the wake of state legalization in the United States, many local governments began to use land use, police power, and taxation authorities to regulate or ban cannabis activities locally. This may be encouraged by state statutes (Carnevale et al., 2017; Lux, 2019; Payan et al., 2021). Due to the industry's legal uncertainty, lease prices for cannabis dispensaries and cultivation facilities can be up to 75 percent higher than the average for conventional retail spaces (Nemeth & Ross, 2014). This places smaller craft growers at a significant disadvantage. In Canada, questionable regulations have benefitted larger cannabis operations. Slade (2020) has described how federal regulations in Canada require that micro-cultivators have a production facility already in place, making it nearly impossible for many of them to apply. This ensures that the market will be dominated by economic elites and creates significant obstacles for smaller craft growers.[12]

The second issue concerns how legal cannabis is regulated and priced. In the Netherlands, the role of regulation offers some important insights. Since 2000, regulation has increased, and the amount of cannabis allowed for possession in coffee shops has been reduced (Brewster, 2017; Chatwin, 2016). In 2012, two new criteria (B and I) were added to the Netherlands Coffee Shop "AHOJ-G," presented in Chapter 4. Coffee shops need to be small and closed (*Besloten*) and include only residents (*Ingezetenen*) (Grund & Breeksema, 2013: 39). These new rules were meant to reduce the number and size of existing coffee shops and prevent tourists from engaging in cannabis use. Instead of keeping tourists away from cannabis, the new regulations had the unintended consequence of driving locals to illegal cannabis markets (van Ooyen-Houben et al., 2016). In 2021, the mayor of Amsterdam, Femke Halsema, sought to ban foreign tourists from cannabis cafes with the goal of limiting anti-social behavior. Coffee shop proprietors responded that banning tourists from regulated establishments would push them toward the illicit market and "into the hands of ruthless drug gangsters on the streets" (Holligan, 2021).

The relationship between regulations and the illicit market is also a concern in Uruguay. Those in Uruguay who wish to grow or purchase cannabis must register with the government, and many remain opposed to the highly regulated pharmacy system (Cruz et al., 2018). Queirolo (2020) notes that heavy regulations often cause cultivators to fall behind in production, contributing to the shortage of cannabis in pharmacies. This shortage creates a catch-22 in which registered users trying to follow the law are forced to buy from the illicit market. This may explain why many were reluctant to register in the first place. According to surveys by Junta National de Drogas (JND), there are about 259,000 users in Uruguay (JND, 2019). Only approximately 78.000 are registered as legal users. This is just 25 percent of the total population of people who use cannabis. While many eschew registries, according to Marcos Baudean, cultivators are in favor because it protects them from police and prosecution. Baudean (2022: 76) notes:

> . . . the weakness of Uruguayan regulation is the underdevelopment of licensed retail. Currently, a significant portion of the supply remains illegal (mainly unregistered local producers). Traffickers have been displaced as main suppliers because their product is of poor quality.

Regulations impact access. Canada provides some interesting examples.

While the federal government in Canada proposed some regulatory measures, they offered few universal guidelines that provinces or municipalities must follow. Provinces have further stipulated how cannabis will be regulated (e.g., through private licensing and dispensaries or government monopoly through the liquor control board); however, municipalities may place further restrictions on it as they see fit. For example, in Nova Scotia, cannabis is sold through the Nova Scotia Liquor Corporation (NCLS), although not in the same physical location as alcohol. Alberta has proceeded to open private-licensed locations and allowed access rapidly. In contrast, British Columbia has taken a much slower approach despite a well-developed cannabis culture in the province. Unsurprisingly, from October 2018 to June 2019, sales in Alberta were the highest of any province at CA$123.6 million, topping Ontario (a province much larger than Alberta), which brought in CA$121.6 million in cannabis sales (Ward, 2019). Conversely, as discussed, cannabis sales in British Columbia (BC) were among the lowest of any province in Canada, despite BC's cannabis notoriety.

Unfortunately, regulations in Canada have led to high prices and questionable quality. After a year, illicit cannabis markets still seemed to be thriving in Canada, particularly in BC. The National Cannabis Survey conducted by Statistics Canada (2019b) found that over 40 percent of Canadians still obtain their cannabis from illegal sources, that is, black or grey markets. Interestingly, business experts do not seem optimistic about suppressing the black market and predict that illicit sellers will account for approximately 70 percent of all cannabis sales (Williams, 2019). The reasons behind this are varied and complex; however, the approach to regulation plays a vital role as some suggest that there are too many regulations and fees (Fletcher, 2019; Levinson-King, 2019). In general, these costs, high taxes, and competition with the illegal market make it hard to achieve profitability (Schroyer, 2020; Schwab et al., 2019; Wagner et al., 2018). In Canada, since legalization, the cost of illicit cannabis has decreased, while tetrahydrocannabinol (THC) levels were higher when compared to legal cannabis (Mahamad et al., 2020).

The Cannabis Council of Canada (C3) represents more than 700 licensed producers and processors of cannabis. In 2021, the group recommended reducing excise tax and regulatory fees, limiting provincial mark-ups, and better regulating existing online illicit cannabis sales (Raycraft, 2021). While the C3 directly links regulations and sustainability, other issues are also relevant. Questions of cost, convenience, and consumer-centered cannabis are emerging. Licit cannabis in Canada cannot compete in terms of cost or potency. It also cannot rely upon marketing or advertising efforts that could educate consumers about licit alternatives. Described as demarketing, Wesley & Murray (2021: 1080) note:

> Canadian provincial governments . . . chose subdued brand personalities for their cannabis retail agencies, again emphasizing responsible consumption over increased sales . . . lack of attention to displacing the illicit market may have long-term ill effects on public safety.

After reading Cohen (1985), it is difficult to avoid recognizing the connections between public safety, public health, and consumer cannabis and the ways in which control is expanded when they intersect.

Public safety assumptions about cannabis inform public health models, which then shape legal cannabis markets and result in increased public safety concerns. This cycle of cannabis control, described historically by Dufton (2017a: 254) as moments in which "laws change, as does use. Then acceptance births opposition, which births acceptance, and the cycle begins anew," takes on a new meaning. For Cohen (1985: 112),

> The contradictory nature of control ideologies explains much of what happens to policies carried out in their name, and then deposits new ideological residues to be resolved in the next cycle of change.

Uruguay's approach to cannabis suggests another way these modalities of control are linked.

The Institute for the Regulation and Control of Cannabis (IRCCA) keeps records of all registered users in Uruguay to prevent individuals from registering under more than one form of access or in more than one cannabis social club. As in other jurisdictions, all forms of cannabis advertisement, promotion, and sponsorship are strictly prohibited (Rolles & Murkin, 2016). However, unlike US states and Canada, Uruguay was less motivated by the potential for legal cannabis to generate tax revenues. While Uruguayan law stipulates that value-added tax (VAT) is applied to sales of cannabis, it does not specify a percentage and is instead considered in the sale price (Pardo 2014).

Taxes raised through cannabis sales are used to fund the Institute for the Regulation and Control of Cannabis (IRCCA), which is focused on public health, including national campaigns to educate the public about cannabis use (Rolles & Murkin, 2016: 254). In addition to growing in one's own home or accessing cannabis through a pharmacy, Uruguayans may join a cannabis social club (CSC). The law establishes a maximum amount of cannabis per club member (480 grams per member/year). Any surplus yield must be turned over to authorities. The clubs must follow several other requirements:

> clubs must first constitute a nonprofit organization (stating as its sole purpose the cultivation and distribution of cannabis among its members) and complete the mandatory registry with the Registry Office at the Ministry of Education and Culture. . . . Once the Ministry of Education approves the registry, the clubs must register with IRCCA, which will ultimately approve the club opening after inspecting their premises and crop plan . . . CSCs cannot be located within 150 m of education or addiction treatment centres, and they must be at least 1.000 m away from other cannabis clubs' headquarters.
> (Decorte et al., 2017: 45–47)

The first clubs were linked to activism. As regulation advanced, new kinds of clubs appeared. Today, there are CSCs with a clear commercial objective. Pardal et al. (2019) note that truly social CSCs may be losing ground to quasi-dispensary clubs. A relevant issue here is that medical users have sought to join CSCs. Some clubs have sought to accommodate their needs. In some cases, these medical users must present a medical certificate or a prescription from a doctor—but this is not necessarily common practice.

Decorte and colleagues (2017) note an issue for clubs was cannabis quality. The focus on public health is creating market conditions for those who seek to meet the demand for high-potency THC. This creates public safety concerns. For example,

> traffickers are trying to find a way to stay in the cannabis business. There are indicators of this attempt, such as the increasing number of flower buds in police seizures . . . [in addition] most local growers are not registered. For that reason, when they sell their product, they commit a crime. Until March 2020, the police did not consider these producers a target. However, the promise of the new government is greater repression of trafficking at all levels. If the police decide to target local producers and it produces scarcity in illicit cannabis supply, while there is no improvement in the legal supply, who will step in to satisfy demand?
>
> (Baudean, 2022: 76)

While not a focus early on, this seems to be a more significant concern in the years following legalization.

Conclusion

Legal cannabis is available for purchase in an ever-growing number of countries, and a range of political actors have found common cause on an issue that provides economic benefits, confronts paternalistic assumptions, and engages questions of racial justice. However, these reforms have not emancipated citizens from state control. Instead, as we have shown, control has shifted from public safety to public health, maintained by public safety, and from public health to consumer-centered models, constrained both by public health edicts and public safety commands. This is not to say that cannabis liberalization has been a failure. It represents a work in progress. It is a reminder that there are very few examples of the state relinquishing its authority in meaningful rather than performative ways. The United States remains an important example of leadership in some states and federal foot-dragging.

In 2022, US President Joe Biden signed an executive order to pardon citizens and lawful permanent residents convicted of simple cannabis possession under federal law and District of Columbia statute. While Biden has done more than other US presidents to reform cannabis laws, his administration has failed to push the Secure and Fair Enforcement (SAFE) Banking Act in Congress, which would allow legal cannabis businesses to access financial support, investment, and protections (Yacowicz, 2022). Despite a request that the Health and Human Services and the Justice Department review whether cannabis should remain as a Schedule 1 substance under the Controlled Substances Act (Bustillo, 2022), Biden has not yet announced support for specific bills that would expand cannabis research. This piecemeal approach permits the purchase of low-THC cannabis or replaces prison or a criminal record with compulsory prohibition-based programming. Declaring, based on such modest modifications, that cannabis reform is somehow complete amounts to accepting the soft bigotry of low expectations.

Framing the limits of cannabis reform based on Cohen (1985) indicates the ways in which reforms fail to disrupt the broader, systemic influence of a century of prohibition and fifty years of the "War on Drugs." As we have shown, police predation, as well as control and coercion, persist. While not controversial, these adverse outcomes are often framed as a failure of otherwise well-meaning reform. It may be easy in 2022 to cynically mock the assumption that policymakers are good-faith actors seeking to make the best decisions based on sound data, appropriate research designs, and logically connected conclusions. It is not hard to find counter-examples. The idea that some politicians embrace ideology, self-interest, or avarice is inarguable. For Cohen (1985: 32), it is not a matter of a few bad apples spoiling the bunch or the result of "administrative mistakes, lack of funds, [or] prejudiced custodians." Instead, the reason that control persists can be explained by Cohen's effort to connect the work of Rothman and Foucault. Failing to curb the kinds of control that led to calls for justice reform is a feature and not a bug. This applies to cannabis.

Notes

1. For more, see. Retrieved March 30, 2022.
2. For more, see EMCDDA (n.d.).
3. For instance, in the period 2010–2019, sanctions were reported by 151 countries, covering 97 percent of the global population. See UNODC (2021).
4. https://www.wbur.org/news/2021/08/18/civil-forfeiture-police-money-massachusetts-worcester-joseph-early (last accessed June 5, 2022).
5. See Allen & Tunnicliffe (2021) for drug Crime Stats for England and Wales. Retrieved March 30, 2022.
6. See https://www.ajc.com/news/crime/police-to-pay-cartersville-70-members-900k-to-settle-federal-lawsuit/6TOMFPFSZZHRRIDBJMNFQNS4CM.

7. Peter Krykant, Project Lead at Cranstoun and a Trustee at Release in the United Kingdom, notes, "abstinence drug recovery programmes say your [sic] selfish, hopeless & doomed to die if you leave or don't accept their ideology & at the same time say we will love you till you can love yourself": https://twitter.com/PeteKrykant_OPC/status/1499850255633895427?s=20&t=csd5XZAdRjO7Qlbgg7lCNw. In the United Kingdom, an overview with a decidedly upbeat view of diversion can be found at Transform Drug Policy Foundation (n.d.). In Australia, a useful overview of diversion and the possible consequences of noncompliance is given by the Alcohol and Drug Foundation (ADF, n.d.). In the United States, some examples of these myths are described in programs including Ogg (2019), Center County District Attorney's Office (n.d.), and Oliphant (n.d.). Some programs, like the one in Texas (Ogg, 2019), note the problems of stigma and the limited public safety benefit from prosecuting cannabis possession. However, participation in programming is still required.
8. The UNODC reports that more than 200 million people used cannabis in 2019. Cannabis enforcement for use, cultivation, or sale is undertaken in almost all countries worldwide. In the period 2010–2019, sanctions were reported by 151 countries, covering 97 percent of the global population. See UNODC (2021).
9. Beyond the United Kingdom, worries that federal decriminalization of cannabis in the United States will be combined with expanded coercive care is of increasing concern (Lekhtman, 2020).
10. A report by SAMHSA (2020) suggests just over 5 percent of people who use cannabis of twelve years and older may meet the criteria for a CUD (SAMHSA, 2020: 29).
11. For instance, until recently, Illinois prevented those with cannabis-related convictions from entering the cannabis industry and denied licenses and loans to those with criminal records, even though this comprised more than 30 percent of adults in Chicago (Fitz & Armstrong, 2022). The authors also point to EAT (2019).
12. See, e.g. Passifume (2022).

6
Three Eras of Cannabis Research
An International Review

Introduction

Stan Cohen had a mixed view of criminological research. While he considered various approaches as part of his assessment of social control (Cohen, 1985: 44–48), he also was very skeptical of the field of criminology. Although his doubt that modern criminology could disrupt the expansion of control was further developed in later work (Cohen, 1988), the outlines of this view emerged in *Visions of Social Control*. Cohen (1985: 7) argued most criminological studies focused on the shift from carceral to community-based efforts were "of a uniformly low level" and tended to be "evangelical," "fudgy," or "nihilistic." All are built, he argues, to require more research, more funding, and better access. This tends to build up the apparatus of the state, even as studies were designed to explore its abolition. Chapters 4 and 5 suggest concepts like normalization and stigmatization have informed cannabis liberalization and the diffusion, as opposed to the relinquishment of cannabis control. Control applies to the retention of public safety precepts, the extension of public health models, the application of medical and consumer cannabis, and the failure, to date, to adopt governance models that embrace racial justice. In this chapter, we identify and describe three eras of cannabis research. The first era spanned 1961 to 1972. It was marked by increased prohibition-based policies, even as scholars argued that criminalizing cannabis would do more harm than the substance itself, and interest in the pharmacology of cannabinoids (Pertwee, 2006).

From 1973 to 2017, the second era was the longest and most consequential. It followed the emergence of "drug scheduling" and was marked by two crucial developments. First, while some claims of the harms of cannabis were qualified, others were extended. Concerns that cannabis caused violence and crime shifted to worries that it negatively impacted work ethic (i.e., amotivational syndrome)—this, in turn, reorganized political actors involved in drug control (Himmelstein, 1983: 13). Second, this process of medicalization retained public safety bulwarks, while expanding control, by associating cannabis with mental health conditions and a range of related adverse outcomes. The third era, since 2018, is increasingly based on research conducted where cannabis is legal. Findings have qualified many of the claims put forth during the second era. In the post-prohibition period, researchers once cited to justify the criminalization of cannabis have reversed course.

This chapter presents a history of cannabis research by drawing distinctions among three eras. President Richard Nixon declared a war against drug abuse in the first era. Over time, this reoriented public policy and led to costly practices associated with the War on Drugs. In the second era, the view that drug use inevitably led to addiction was linked to drug addiction as a brain disease (Leshner, 1997). As we discussed in Chapter 1, this was seized upon by a group we called the New Prohibitionists (Heidt & Wheeldon, 2022). Using a mix of selective analysis, a misreading of the research, and exaggerated claims, this group and their views find their way into many modern media outlets. Finally, changing the legal status of cannabis has opened the door to more nuanced examinations of stigma and public safety, coercion and public health, the value of medical cannabis, and the complications of consumer cannabis. To avoid the problems of past research, we present cannabis research since 2018 and focus on research from jurisdictions that have legalized cannabis. Studying illicit substances means accepting too many confounding variables associated with users and the studied substance. Referred to as post-prohibition cannabis research (Corva & Meisel, 2022), this refers to how the entanglement of prohibition, decriminalization, racism, legalization, commercial interests, and regulatory models all shape research. We argue emerging research programs designed to consider legal cannabis will allow investigations of greater depth and detail and explore how cannabis legalization impacts people, economies, and communities.

Prohibition and Cannabis Research

Although early efforts to control cannabis occurred more than 200 years ago (Beweley-Taylor et al., 2014), the structural problems with cannabis research resulted from international control efforts. In the 1920s, cannabis became connected to race and ethnicity, and criminalization followed concerns that cannabis led to violence, mental instability, and addiction.[1] As discussed in Chapter 3, during the Second Opium Conference in 1924, Mohamed El

Guindy, the delegate from Egypt, ostensibly independent from Great Britain, proposed the inclusion of cannabis within the Convention. El Guindy had support from Brazil, Greece, South Africa, and Turkey (Transnational Institute, n.d.) and painted a worrying picture of the effects of hashish. International concerns that cannabis led to insanity and addiction informed early international drug control efforts.

In the United States, anti-drug campaigners of this period warned against the encroaching "Marijuana Menace" and linked the use of cannabis with violence, crime, and other socially deviant behaviors. This new plateau of misinformation provided the foundation for the continual escalation of penalties and proliferation of offenses (Bonnie & Whitebread, 1970: 1063). Since non-White people primarily used cannabis, it was quickly linked to "racially inferior" underclass communities (Tosh, 2019), and many Americans were persuaded that cannabis was evil (Vitiello, 2021: 449). The language used ("marijuana" instead of "cannabis") was also a deliberate effort to appeal to the xenophobia of the time. The exotic-sounding word emphasized the drug's foreignness to White Americans (Halperin, 2018). In the United States, cannabis was connected to immigrants, insanity, Mexicans, Black people, crime, anti-war protesters, and hippies. Efforts to study any potential benefits were prevented by a "global drug prohibition regime" (Collins, 2021) that emerged and ensured most research was *designed* to link cannabis with harm (Newhart & Dolphin, 2019).

The First Era: Early Cannabis Prohibition (1961–1972)

In 1961, the broad architecture of modern drug policy was established under the guidance and recommendations of experts at the World Health Organization (WHO), with a primary goal of controlling opium and coca-based narcotics. The Single Convention on Narcotic Drugs of 1961 (Newhart & Dolphin, 2019: 51) was adopted, despite evidence from numerous countries that downplayed cannabis's danger. In 1944, the New York Academy of Medicine issued an extensively researched report known as the *La Guardia Report*. The report concluded that, contrary to popular belief, cannabis did not induce violence, insanity, sex crimes, or lead to addiction or other drug use. Instead, the report concluded that cannabis was less dangerous than other drugs (New York Academy of Medicine, 1944). At the time, Anslinger derided the report as "giddy sociology and medical mumbo-jumbo" (Booth, 2003: 240).

The War on Drugs began as a war on drug abuse. Richard Nixon was elected US President in 1968 on a promise to restore "law and order" to a nation shaken by riots, protests, and assassinations (McArdle, 2018). For Nixon, smoking cannabis meant embracing the lawlessness he thought was sweeping the country. Yet, within the logic of "law and order," disrespect for the law seemed to be the root of many problems. In a 1994 interview with Harper's Magazine, Nixon's counsel and Assistant to the President on Domestic Affairs, John Ehrlichman, confirmed Nixon's intended purpose to use narcotics legislation to target his opponents. In the interview, Ehrlichman stated:

> The Nixon campaign in 1968, and the Nixon White House after that, had two enemies: the antiwar left and black people. You understand what I'm saying? We knew we couldn't make it illegal to be either against the war or black, but by getting the public to associate the hippies with marijuana and blacks with heroin, and then criminalizing both heavily, we could disrupt those communities. We could arrest their leaders, raid their homes, break up their meetings, and vilify them night after night on the evening news. Did we know we were lying about the drugs? Of course, we did.
> (Baum, 2016)

In 1969, the *Wootton Report on Cannabis* was prepared by the Hallucinogens Sub-Committee of the Advisory Committee on Drug Dependence in the United Kingdom, chaired by Lady Wootton. The committee "published two separate reports, prioritizing the cannabis report, which would become widely known as the Wootton Report" (Seddon, 2020: 1572). While the report did not recommend legalization, it concluded penalties for cannabis should be drastically reduced because there was no evidence that it caused "violent crime or aggression, anti-social behaviour, or is producing in otherwise normal people conditions of dependence or psychosis, requiring medical treatment" (UKCIA, n.d.b).

Two reports in the 1970s also challenged cannabis prohibition. In the United States, a report by the *National Commission on Marihuana and Drug Abuse* (1972) commissioned during this time summarized their findings by stating, "criminalization of possession of marihuana for personal use is socially self-defeating as a means of achieving this objective" (US National Commission on Marihuana and Drug Abuse, n.d.). In Canada, a similar report used language reminiscent of cannabis reformers. Seen as a counterpart to the *Wootton Report* and the *La Guardia Report*, the *Le Dain Commission* (1974) suggested:

We must weigh the potential for harm, individual and social, of the conduct in question against the harm, individual and social, which is caused by the application of the criminal law, and ask ourselves whether, on balance, the intervention is justified.

(Le Dain, 1973: 940)

The commission recommended leaving in place offenses for trafficking and cultivating cannabis but repealing the prohibition against simple possession.[2]

Government-commissioned reports in India, Panama, the United Kingdom, the United States, and Canada have repeatedly concluded that cannabis need not be treated like other drugs and that punishments associated with possession or use should be drastically reduced. However, these ideas could not overcome the prohibitionist inertia and the confluence of international regulation and national interests. For example, US scholars interested in cannabis noted that restrictive state and federal laws prevented scientific investigation of cannabis and its uses (Mikuriya, 1969). In the United Kingdom, Jock Young (1971) focused on how people who use drugs embraced the drug subculture, while having their identity mediated and constructed by influential people in society.

The Second Era: The Drug War (1973–2017)

Just as the 1961 Single Convention began the cannabis prohibition internationally, the 1972 amendment introduced the concept of drug scheduling (Newhart & Dolphin, 2019: 51). Schedules are a categorization scheme that involves three domains: (i) accepted medical use, (ii) abuse potential, and (iii) potential for public health harms through risk to safety or risk of dependence (Newhart & Dolphin, 2019: 55). Failing to distinguish between opium, cocaine, and cannabis ensured a common approach to their regulation (Collins, 2021; Mills, 2003; Sinha, 2001). In 2017, the US Committee on the Health Effects of Marijuana of the National Academies of Sciences (the HEMNAS Committee) noted that despite significant changes in state policy and the increasing prevalence of cannabis use, research on cannabis remains limited by restrictive policies and regulations, based on its status as a Schedule I substance (National Library of Medicine, 2017).

Regulatory restraints include a series of review processes that include the National Institute on Drug Abuse (NIDA); the US Food and Drug

Administration (FDA); the US Drug Enforcement Administration (DEA); institutional review boards, offices, or departments in state government; state boards of medical examiners; the researcher's home institution; and potential funders. In addition, more than a dozen letters, applications, approvals, authorizations, and certificates are required to begin research (National Library of Medicine, 2017). In the United Kingdom, drug research requires a special license. For instance, research on cannabis in the United Kingdom requires acquiring a license for eight weeks and costs £5,000. Controlled drugs can only be administered in licensed institutions, of which there are only four in the United Kingdom (Nutt, 2015). Another institutional problem worthy of consideration relates to the complex relationship between funding and research.

Cannabis research that can inform public health care and keep pace with changes in cannabis policy and patterns of use requires funding. The National Institute for Health (NIH) is responsible for funding research across many health domains. However, because cannabis was historically perceived to have only adverse effects, most cannabis research has been conducted under the auspices of NIDA. This research focuses on studying factors related to substance abuse and dependence and the adverse health effects and behavioral consequences associated with the abuse of cannabis. As Newhart & Dolphin (2019: 27) note,

> Scientific discourse has trickled down to set the terms of popular culture discourse in many respects. Topics about physical harm, mental harm, gateway theories, and amotivational effects dominated media and common understandings of cannabis among the public.

Despite the changing status of cannabis, cannabis research continues to be funded by an organization that views it in purely negative terms.

During this era, the research fixated on the prevalence of cannabis use disorder (CUD), a presumed association between crime and violence, and efforts to uncover cannabis-triggered psychosis/schizophrenia. The first relates to CUD. The DSM-V combines two older stand-alone concepts related to cannabis abuse *and* cannabis dependence (Jutras-Aswad et al., 2019; Porter, 2021). Ritter (2021: 21) suggests that "between 10% and 30% of people who consume cannabis will develop a cannabis use disorder." In support of this claim, Ritter (2021) cites two studies (Hasin et al., 2016; Wagner & Anthony, 2002). Wagner and Anthony (2002) focus on the transition from drug use to drug dependence. They present evidence on risk based on the initiation of cannabis, cocaine, and alcohol use and risks for progression from first drug use to the onset of drug dependence.

In studies like this, the analysis works backward from the most severe drugs to the least severe drugs and infers, without any evidence, that one came first (Andresen, 2012). This approach has been used in an analysis of Australian high school students, where the increased frequency of cannabis use led to increased rates of illicit and licit (tobacco) drug uptake (Swift et al., 2012). In France, Mayet and colleagues (2012) found that cannabis use greatly increased the risk of illicit and licit (tobacco and alcohol) uptake. Using survey data from the United States, some research suggests cannabis was a trigger for cocaine uptake (O'Brien et al., 2012).

A more recent study (Hasin et al., 2016) presents nationally representative data on the past-year prevalence rates of cannabis use, CUD, and CUD among adults who used cannabis in the United States between 2001 and 2002 and 2012 and 2013. They conclude cannabis use "doubled over a decade" and "there was a large increase in marijuana use disorders during that time" (Hasin et al., 2016: 1236). There are two interesting findings here. The first is the question of the doubling of cannabis use in a decade, which, the study authors note, contrasts with numerous other studies (Hasin et al., 2016: 1241). The second claim is that while not all people who use cannabis experience problems, "nearly 3 of 10 marijuana users manifested a marijuana use disorder in 2012–2013" (Hasin et al., 2016: 1326).

While the DSM-5 mentions seven conditions attributable to cannabis use (Patel & Marwaha, 2022), cannabis psychosis is not one of them, and diagnostic inaccuracy results from the casual use of psychiatric terminology. Johns (2001: 116–117) summarizes some common methodological failings. He states:

> (a) studies fail to adequately separate organic from functional psychotic reactions to cannabis; (b) they have insufficiently discriminated between psychotic symptoms and syndromes of a psychosis, and (c) they have not balanced the weight of evidence for and against the category of cannabis psychosis.

There is evidence that cannabis use may contribute to psychotic disorders in certain circumstances and among certain people. However, these connections are complex. Drug use, in general, is often associated with other risk factors, such as certain personality types, early-life trauma, and family adversity (Gage et al., 2013). This has not stopped some groups from misrepresenting research or media outlets from reporting these misrepresentations. The failure to take seriously the moralistic pandering associated with:

> members of powerful groups [who] mine the mountains of evidence that have been produced ... selectively, in order to find nuggets of evidence.... Political tactics contribute to this distorted use of knowledge, but a deeper influence is the use of drug policy as a symbolic discourse which ideologically sustains inequalities in the distribution of power, resources and respect.
> (Stevens, 2011: 129)

We have framed this development by focusing on the New Prohibitionists (Heidt & Wheeldon, 2022).

Inter-Era: Reform, Media, and the New Prohibitionists (2012–2017)

In 2012, Colorado and Washington legalized recreational cannabis. In response, Smart Approaches to Marijuana (SAM) was established in January 2013 by former Congressman Patrick Kennedy (D-R I), David Frum, Kevin Sabet, and others.[3] SAM supports increased funding for mental health courts and the treatment of drug dependency (Dobuzinskis, 2013). In 2018, they proposed that they

> Require mandatory assessment of problem drug use by a treatment professional after the first citation; those who are diagnosed with a substance use disorder can be diverted into a treatment track where they receive the appropriate level of care, those who are not problem users can be directed to social services for follow-up and addressing other life factors contributing to drug use.
> (SAM, 2018)

The underlying assumption, according to Paul Armentano, deputy director of the National Organization for the Reform of Marijuana Laws (NORML), is that only people with problems use cannabis (Angeli, 2018). These efforts were built on earlier parent-led opposition to cannabis and the establishment of other anti-cannabis organizations in the United States that followed the brief period of state-led cannabis liberalization in the 1970s (Dufton, 2017a).

The idea that people who use cannabis have "problems" is the result of coordinated efforts to exaggerate and distort research and tends to minimize or ignore research that challenges their assumptions about the dangers of cannabis (Heidt & Wheeldon, 2022). This approach has spanned eras. The New Prohibitionists, like the "Old Prohibitionists" of the past, oppose drug policy reform based on their belief that cannabis use is dangerous. Findings of potential links between cannabis, psychosis, and violent crime have remained of interest among a small group of researchers and received extensive media attention (Berenson, 2019; Gladwell, 2019).

On successive evenings in prime time in June 2022, Fox News host Laura Ingraham linked cannabis to psychosis and psychosis to mass shootings, an increasingly common feature of American society (Ortiz, 2022). Cannabis legalization, she argued, was fueling increased use, adverse mental health outcomes, and gun violence. As we have noted, researchers Murray and Di Forti have long stated that their work does not prove a causal relationship between cannabis and mental illness. However, these claims were used in a highly publicized article in *The New Yorker*. Malcolm Gladwell (2019) argued that cannabis is not as safe as we think and suggested that serious risks are being overlooked amid the hype surrounding the benefits of cannabis legalization. One issue is potency. Gladwell writes,

> Because of recent developments in plant breeding and growing techniques, the typical concentration of THC [tetrahydrocannabinol], the psychoactive ingredient in marijuana, has gone from the low single digits to more than twenty percent—from a swig of near-beer to a tequila shot.
> (Gladwell, 2019)

The fixation on THC concentration was also a feature of a 2022 article in the *New York Times*. Cristina Caron suggests there are cannabis products with THC levels near 100 percent. Embracing the new tradition of the tortured metaphor, she cites Beatriz Carlini, a research scientist at the University of Washington's Addictions, Drug, and Alcohol Institute, who states THC concentrates are "as close to the cannabis plant as strawberries are to frosted strawberry pop tarts" (Caron, 2022). These articles are both uninformed (Heidt & Wheeldon, 2022) and adopt an anti-cannabis bias which furthers stigma (Kavousi et al., 2022). Until recently, research funded exclusively to find harms related to cannabis use supported this stigma (Newhart & Dolphin, 2019).

Findings that link cannabis use and crime are a function of cannabis's legal status (Fischer et al., 2021) and the risks of seeking out an illicit substance (Goldstein, 1985). There is little research in this inter-era period that explores if, how, and why legalization reduces the personal safety risks involved with seeking cannabis illicitly. Instead, based on older eras of cannabis prohibition, the psychopharmacological risks for people who use cannabis were conflated with the risks associated with engaging with illegal markets. Since criminalizing cannabis led to territorial disputes and fears of informants, these policies ensured cannabis was explicitly linked to criminal behavior, including systemic violence.

Concerns about cannabis, psychosis, and schizophrenia appeared in the National Academy of Science, Engineering, and Medicine's (NASEM) study in 2017. They concluded, based on their review, that

> cannabis use is likely to increase the risk of developing schizophrenia, other psychoses, and social anxiety disorders, and to a lesser extent depression.... Heavy cannabis users are more likely to report thoughts of suicide than non-users, and in individuals with bipolar disorder, near-daily cannabis users show increased symptoms of the disorder than non-users.
> (National Academies, 2017)

The authors report that central to this finding is a meta-analysis by a team that included Marta Di Forti and Robin Murray (Marconi et al., 2016). However, the paper reports that a causal link between cannabis and psychosis, or schizophrenia cannot be established. By contrast, they conclude that public health interventions should

> educate people at heightened risk of schizophrenia (e.g., through having a family history of the disorder, or having experienced psychosis-like symptoms) of the potential additional risk of cannabis exposure.
> (Marconi et al., 2016: 1268)

This is very sensible. However, it cannot be used to justify the statement that "cannabis use is likely to increase the risk of developing schizophrenia."

The vast majority of people who use any kind of drug do not develop problematic or dependent drug use (Cole, 2022). In 2020, the Substance Abuse and Mental Health Services Administration (SAMHSA) in the United States reported that just over 5 percent of people aged twelve and older who use cannabis had a CUD (SAMHSA, 2020: 29). While problem drug use is an issue for a small minority of those who use any drug,[4] problem cannabis use appears to be a significant issue for an even smaller percentage of young people with a heightened risk of schizophrenia, estimated at much less than 1 percent of the population (McGrath et al., 2004) and an even smaller number of adolescence between the ages of thirteen and eighteen years (Androutsos, 2012). The NASEM (2017) review fails to make clear that most of the research on the mental health risks of cannabis is limited to those with specific pre-existing mental health conditions, most commonly schizophrenia. However, as we have noted, the New Prohibitionists focus on expanding prohibition via public health and advocating for coercive drug treatment and diversion programs (Heidt &Wheeldon, 2022). These are indistinguishable from other drug policy reformers, who suggest cannabis use leads to addiction (Ritter, 2021).

By the end of the second era of prohibition research, evidence indicated that cannabis legalization was reducing costly burdens on the criminal justice system (McGinty et al., 2016). In the United States, legalization was estimated to save nearly $14 billion annually in enforcement costs, roughly $10.5 billion of which are borne by state and local governments, specifically local law enforcement agencies (Caulkins, 2010; Miron, 2010). Reallocating funds generated by legal cannabis were used to support community health initiatives (Pardo, 2014), increase tax revenue, and spur local economic growth (Johns, 2015). Legalizing cannabis increased safe access to cannabis, and the health benefits of cannabis reported by patients increased (Pacula & Sevigny, 2014). However, moral objections and concerns about community quality of life began to emerge (Johns, 2015).

The Third Era: Post-Prohibition Research (2018–Present)

Near the end of the prohibition era of research, Pacula and Sevigny (2014) suggested cannabis legalization was shown to reduce costs for governments and, therefore, taxpayers. They went on to observe that researchers need "a bit more time and a lot better data" to answer the most important cannabis questions (Pacula & Sevigny, 2014: 209). In hindsight, what was needed was research that was not funded contingent on efforts to establish the harms of cannabis use. Researchers during the War on Drugs era were limited by structural factors such as the legal status of cannabis, drug scheduling, and perceived risk to public health, which all had a direct impact on how cannabis research proceeded. As Newhart and Dolphin (2019: 26–27) noted, past

> scientific research on cannabis has been skewed, because research whose aim is to prove harm has been well funded, but research meant to discount harm or show benefits has been successfully delayed or blocked and has not been eligible for financial support.

Research conducted since cannabis legalization has demonstrated three broad findings. The first is that legal status impacts research. Between 1960 and 2018, up to 80 percent of the psychoactive literature focused on legal substances (Lebrero-Tatay et al., 2022). The converse was also true. Between 2000 and 2018, cannabis research funding by the US National Institute on Drug Abuse (NIDA) focused almost exclusively on cannabis misuse and its negative effects (O'Grady, 2020).[5] Based on their analysis of 956,703 academic publications focused on drug type, country, and legal status, Lebrero-Taty and colleagues (2022) found that restrictive laws and social stigma intended to limit illicit drug use have hindered research on fifteen substances, including cannabis. Bill S. 253, if passed, would reverse decades of policy by requiring the Department of Health and Human Services (HHS) to investigate cannabis health benefits.[6] However, it will be years before this research wends its way through the vagaries of peer review and into journals.

The second finding is that by 2017, five years after the first US states legalized cannabis, reports from Washington (ADAI, 2017), Colorado (Monte et al., 2015), and Uruguay (Walsh & Ramsay, 2016) had documented the benefits of cannabis legalization. Since 2017, this research has increased dramatically alongside calls by the United Nations (UN) to promote "alternatives to conviction and punishment in appropriate cases, including decriminalizing drug possession for personal use" (UNCEBC, 2019). This call can be seen as based, in part, on the United Nations Office of Drug Control's *World Drug Report 2019*, which estimates that 35 million people who use drugs (0.7 percent of the adult population) have drug use disorders (UNDOC, 2019: 1). If the total number of those with a drug use disorder is less than 13 percent, the notion that 30 percent of cannabis users may develop a CUD (Ritter, 2021) defies common sense. Indeed, research since 2017 paints a very different picture from the risk-laden framing of the prohibition eras. In fact, many findings mirror those of expert committees established before and during the first era of cannabis research.

The third finding is the recognition of the need for better research designs, rigorous analysis, and more meaningful efforts to explore cannabis legalization (Kavousi et al., 2022). The best way to explore the role of legal status and changes in crime rates generally is based on natural and quasi-experimental research designs. Different jurisdictions have implemented cannabis policy changes in distinct ways (Mitchell, 2015). As discussed, these approaches were part of past research eras (Becker, 1963; Young, 1971); explored cannabis culture (Sandberg, 2008, 2012a); and documented the failure of criminal sanctions to reduce cannabis use (Nelson, 2021), gender, stigma, and cultural norms in Mexico (Agoff et al., 2021) and the potential for cannabis insiders to predict policy problems within legalized jurisdictions (Heidt, 2021; Heidt et al., 2018).

Studying Legal Cannabis

The call by the UN followed existing efforts to legalize and regulate cannabis in Washington, Colorado, Uruguay, and Canada. By 2019, there were many other examples of liberalized cannabis policies around the world. This number has only increased. The changing legal status of cannabis has allowed researchers to test previous findings. This includes examining how changes in legal status impacted cannabis use, property and violent crime, CUDs, and treatment admissions for schizophrenia. The results do not support past findings. In jurisdictions with legal cannabis, the number of people using cannabis has not significantly increased (Grucza et al., 2018; Hawke & Henderson, 2021; Johnson et al., 2019; Ta et al., 2019). In Canada, where cannabis possession has been fully legalized, although slight increases in some age cohorts have been noted, there is no evidence of large increases in use (Statistics Canada, 2019a). Indeed, the percentage of those reporting daily or near-daily use remains unchanged at 6 percent (Rotermann, 2020).

As discussed, concerns about cannabis, psychosis, and schizophrenia appeared in the National Academy of Science, Engineering, and Medicine's (NASEM) study in 2017. A review of the studies compiled by NASEM (2017) shows that many were funded by the NIH and thus obtained funding by explicitly focusing on adverse outcomes. These studies suffer from numerous methodological problems (Heidt & Wheeldon, 2022). Since liberalization, the long-standing notion that use is a *causal* factor for schizophrenia is not only unsupported (Hamilton & Monaghan, 2019) but also has been turned on its head. People with schizophrenia are more likely to develop a CUD

(Ahmed et al., 2021), not the other way around. In an important consensus paper, many prominent researchers in this area now agree that cannabis use is neither necessary nor sufficient to cause psychosis. Instead, it may be just one of many causal components (D'Souza et al., 2022).

This is not to say that there is no reason to continue to study cannabis and its impact on the people who use it. However, drug status appears to influence cannabis psychosis admissions. In the United Kingdom, Hamilton and colleagues (2014) studied the effect of the reclassification of cannabis between 1999 and 2010. When cannabis was classified as more serious, treatment admissions increased. When cannabis was treated as less serious, admissions declined until 2009, when cannabis was reclassified again. The political nature of cannabis disorders also appears relevant to CUD for young people. Using data from the 2002–2019 National Survey on Drug Use and Health, 43,307 individuals who met past-year DSM-5-proxy CUD criteria were identified. Between 2002 and 2019, Askari and colleagues (2021) report that 6.1 percent of people reported using a CUD treatment. However, treatment use decreased by more than 50 percent during this time. Based on data from 2004 to 2012, researchers found no increase in treatment admissions for problem cannabis use in states with liberal cannabis policies (Mennis & Stahler, 2020; Philbin et al., 2019).

How can one reconcile the stark contrast between claims that up to 30 percent of people who use cannabis will develop a CUD (Ritter, 2021) based on old and problematic research (Hasin et al., 2016; Wagner & Anthony, 2002) and reports by the Substance Abuse and Mental Health Services Administration (SAMHSA, 2020: 29) in 2020? The variance between prohibition-era and post-prohibition cannabis research can be understood based on three issues. First, findings from large-scale quantitative studies were quite common during the cannabis prohibition era (1961–2015). This included observational research based on secondary analysis of large data sets and case–control studies that attempted to draw generalizable inferences based on a very small sample (Ksir & Hart, 2016).

Second, definitional issues in the research were widespread and were often left unacknowledged and unresolved. This resulted in operationalization confusion, especially related to dose and variables such as frequency of use and adverse outcomes (Heidt & Wheeldon, 2022). Third, there appears to be a *modesty deficit* in much of the research as limitations were often downplayed or overlooked (Wheeldon et al., 2014). The role of the legal status of cannabis, the challenges with existing data sets, and research design were rarely considered when reporting findings. Instead, researchers reported alarming results with little context. What is worse, perhaps, is that during this era, meta-analyses became very fashionable. Researchers began analyzing huge groups of bad research studies, contaminating the evidence. In the post-prohibition period, research challenges past findings in consistent ways.

Cannabis, Criminology, and Regulatory Models

In previous work, we started to define and apply what we called *cannabis criminology* (Heidt & Wheeldon, 2022). We argued that cannabis prohibition is an issue that touches on criminology's multiple, and sometimes contradictory, dimensions. Focusing on cannabis provides a creative means to understand racism, media misrepresentations, the War on Drugs, police militarization, legitimacy, mass incarceration, and numerous other issues within the criminological expanse. It is a novel way to meet the need for more imaginative explorations and analyses (Young, 2011). In place of efforts that focus merely on law and order (Fischer et al., 2021), we argued cannabis criminology has numerous dimensions. Building on this idea, we defined five key research areas. These include law, society, and social control; police and policing cannabis; dynamics around race and ethnicity; the economics of cannabis use; and cannabis use and crime (Wheeldon & Heidt, 2023b).

We contextualized each area by focusing on relevant criminological theories, related concepts, and key research. By developing a research program, our goal was to encourage researchers to "flood the zone" and replace the problematic research of the past with a commitment to research that is theoretically informed, relies on credible research designs, and defines the concepts which are to be tested and explored in more defensible ways. While we will return to how to think about responsible cannabis research, in this section, we connect cannabis criminology with regulatory models of governance. While we refer to earlier research, consistent with the goals of this chapter, our focus is on research conducted in the post-prohibition period, which we define as 2018 to the present.

Cannabis Use and Public Safety
In the first era of cannabis research, researchers predicted that harsh laws and punitive policies would harm young Americans by alienating them from society while justifying police intrusions and the deterioration of constitutional values (Kaplan, 1970). In the second era, these concerns were proven prophetic. The legal status of cannabis prioritized uncovering harm, and

researchers made some alarming claims. These include connecting cannabis to increased use of illicit drugs; higher arrest rates; lower socio-economic, social, emotional, and mental health outcomes; and violence (Green et al., 2010; Mayet et al., 2012; O'Brien et al., 2012; Schoeler et al., 2016; Swift et al., 2012). These findings have not been replicated where cannabis is legal. In fact, studies repeatedly suggest that cannabis liberalization policies are associated either with no impact on crime or reductions in crime and public disorder (Callahan et al., 2021; Dragone et al., 2019; Hunt et al., 2018; Lu et al., 2021; Morris, 2018).

In response to what Lu and colleagues (2021: 565) call "weak analytical designs lacking contextualization and appropriate comparisons," more robust research challenges past assumptions that cannabis legalization was associated with increases in crime (Chang & Jacobsen, 2017; Dragone et al., 2019). Using a quasi-experimental multi-group, interrupted time-series design focused on violent and property crimes in Colorado and Washington, Lu and colleagues suggested that cannabis "had minimal to no effect on major crimes in Colorado or Washington" (2021: 565). In Canada, the implementation of the Cannabis Act in Canada (2018) is associated with a *decrease* of 55–65 percent in cannabis-related crimes among male and female youth (Callaghan et al., 2021). For context, in 2020, crime rates in Canada fell by nearly 10 percent, and the crime severity index fell by almost 8 percent (Statistics Canada, 2019a).

This is not to say cannabis liberalization results in no consequences requiring a public safety lens. While there is not much research on the impact of cannabis legalization in Uruguay, one paper reported reductions in robbery rates and no change in homicide rates by examining data between 2008 and 2016 (Jorge, 2020). However, local conditions matter. As discussed in Chapter 4, most Uruguayans who use cannabis have not registered with the state, as required by law. Likewise, "most local growers are not registered. For that reason, when they sell their product, they commit a crime" (Baudean, 2022: 76). Public safety is relevant in terms of how to protect those buying legal cannabis. For example, Hughes and colleagues (2019) found minor increases in all types of crime except murder and auto theft near dispensary areas in Denver, Colorado. They suggest that this may be attributable to more significant foot traffic and larger numbers of people carrying cannabis and cash in these areas because the dispensaries lack access to federal banking.

One clear public safety benefit of cannabis legalization is that it reduces the personal safety risks involved with seeking cannabis illicitly. Osborne and Fogel (2017) note many in their research supported legalization and viewed cannabis prohibition as unjust and perpetuating crime and violence from the drug trade. Young cannabis users in Nevada, where cannabis is legal, report valuing the security associated with a legal purchase. Amroussia and colleagues (2020: 98) conclude that "recreational cannabis legalization has opened a legally, socially, and behaviorally 'safer' alternative to purchase cannabis as compared to the informal black market." While more study is needed (Jorgensen & Harper, 2020), cannabis legalization may improve public safety by increasing police effectiveness (Brown, 2022). Makin and colleagues (2019) suggest that freed from having to enforce cannabis prohibition, police devoted more resources to solving more serious crimes. In Colorado, Brinkman and Mok-Lamme (2019) found that each additional cannabis dispensary leads to a reduction of 17 crimes per month per 1,000 residents, which equates to roughly a 19 percent reduction in the overall average crime rate over the sample period.

Public Health and Social Control
Efforts to recast public safety concerns through public health models are still guided by concerns that cannabis liberalization will lead to an increase in use. In the United States, Johnson and colleagues (2019) found cannabis use in Washington state peaked before cannabis was legalized. Following decriminalization in Massachusetts, Connecticut, Rhode Island, Vermont, and Maryland, there was no increase in youth cannabis consumption rates (Grucza et al., 2018). These findings appear consistent throughout the United States to date (Hall & Lynskey, 2020). Stevens (2019) analyzed survey data from thirty-eight countries from 2001–2002, 2005–2006, and 2009–2010. No significant association emerged between less stringent cannabis policies and increased rates of adolescent cannabis use.

One clear public health benefit is that legal cannabis can establish regulations around its cultivation, sale, and use (Silver et al., 2020; Valdes-Donoso et al., 2019). These regulations may limit toxins such as hydrogen cyanide, pesticides, and other chemicals often found in illicit cannabis operations (Adams, 2019; Ferguson et al., 2019; Thompson, 2018). While legalization can improve the quality, legal sales can also support public health goals. Cannabis tax revenues support public education and public health interventions, including efforts to discourage underage drug use (Carnevale et al., 2017). Some states and localities levy an "impact fee" to help cover municipal costs related to the industry's local operation (Bartlett, 2021). Kavousi and colleagues (2022) note that in California, New Jersey, and Washington, local governments use cannabis tax or fee revenues for public park maintenance, litter clean-up, policing, schools, drug treatment, researching the cannabis industry's impacts, job training, emergency shelters, and general operations, among other purposes (Hodgson, 2021; Rosario, 2021; Santos, 2021).

Another public health benefit is the potential for cannabis to serve as a substitute for opiates (Voelker, 2018). A 2017 survey reported that 41 percent of people stopped or reduced opioid use as a result of cannabis use (Ishida et al., 2019). Recent studies in Vancouver note that cannabis is associated with reduced use of alcohol, cocaine, 3,4-methylenedioxy-methamphetamine (MDMA), and injected drugs, including heroin (Gittins & Sessa, 2020). For example, Reddon and colleagues (2020) conclude that at-least-daily cannabis use was associated with a 16 percent increase in cessation of the injection of opioids. The idea of cannabis use as harm reduction is not new (Lau et al., 2015). In fact, it appeared in one of the first published medical treatises on cannabis (O'Shaughnessy, 1842). Since legalization, research has increased in this area, but questions remain.

Researchers found a significant reduction in Schedule III opioid prescriptions, total doses, and spending in a group of eight states where recreational cannabis was legal (Shi et al., 2019). In 812 counties in US states with legal cannabis, a higher incidence of cannabis dispensaries was correlated with fewer opioid-related deaths (Hsu & Kovacs, 2021). A study in Vancouver suggested those at high risk of overdose reported using cannabis as a harm reduction strategy (Mok et al., 2021). Paul and colleagues (2020) reported that participants explicitly framed cannabis as a form of mental health and substance use treatment. Cannabis was reported to be more effective and "healthier" than psycho-pharmaceuticals and medication-assisted treatments (Lake et al., 2019) and other illicit substances (Reddon et al., 2018, 2021; Socías et al., 2017). In the United States, these public health benefits remain contested based on "interest group lobbying, resident preferences (including political ideology), and political opportunity structures" (Kavousi et al., 2022: 156).

Similar responses to cannabis use are also relevant internationally. However, these appear to vary widely even amongst neighboring countries. For example, Čecho and colleagues (2017) found the shift to decriminalization in the Czech Republic did affect rates of adolescent cannabis use. In countries that embrace repressive cannabis policies, such as Poland, Slovakia, and Hungary, differing responses to drug use emerged. The researchers conclude that religiosity, a factor associated with informal social control, was also crucial in controlling and deterring drug use compared to legislative changes and other associated formal methods such as fines, custodial sentences, and coercive treatment. Recent research in Poland applies the concept of social worlds to connect the boundaries between people who use cannabis and the conservative, punitive, and sometimes regressive anti-cannabis culture (Wanke et al., 2022). For example,

> Polish cannabis users find themselves in an increasingly ambiguous position. They have direct access to the global cannabis culture. It is available via digital channels and in-person experiences of mobility. Yet, they find themselves in a legally and culturally conservative setting lagging behind their European counterparts. These other countries, paradoxically, constitute the basic reference point for cannabis users' social worlds, which are constructed against the backdrop of "insecurity," "lack of control" and "ignorance" and allow them to maintain the "safety" of the setting, "agency" of use and "reflexivity" of knowing (better). Drawing on these three types of boundaries, the cannabis users in Poland maintain the hermeneutic and interactive balance of their social worlds.
>
> (Wanke et al., 2022: 8)

Social worlds are also relevant in Canada. Broad and restrictive regulations disproportionately impacted racial and ethnic minorities, those who use medical cannabis, and the poor (Gagnon et al., 2020). Despite the traditionally tolerant approach to cannabis in most provinces, including by police in British Columbia (Greer et al., 2020), federal legalization has not stopped landlords, and employers emphasized banning cannabis rather than adjusting to the new reality of cannabis legalization. Other forms of stigma persist. For example,

> Parents who use cannabis may be shunned by other parents, students who use cannabis may be forced to complete a rehabilitation program, and workers who use cannabis may be fired. Even if no action is taken, the sentiment often results in heightened scrutiny towards cannabis users where any minor mistake is directly attributed to cannabis intoxication.
>
> (Reid, 2020: 5)

Although the stigma around cannabis use may have been diminished in some ways, further study should consider how other kinds of stigma may influence people with stigmatized identities.

Medical Cannabis and Therapeutic Uses

California became the first state to authorize the medicinal use of cannabis in 1996, following the statewide Proposition 215 in 1996, led by patients. The acceptance of the medical potential for cannabis further destigmatized use among a subset of the population and increased the supply of cannabis through diversion to illegal markets (Nussbaum et al., 2015). Alaska, Oregon, and Washington followed California in 1998. By July 2018, forty-six states and the District of Columbia, and the US territories of Puerto Rico and Guam provided for the legal therapeutic use of cannabis (Newhart & Dolphin, 2019).

As Kavousi and colleagues (2022) note, some states embraced medical cannabis following a 2009 US Department of Justice memo directing US attorneys not to focus federal resources on anti-cannabis enforcement. In some ways, the federal threat of prosecution may be declining (Hannah & Mallinson, 2018; Karch, 2021). The Obama White House discouraged federal prosecution, and Congress adopted an amendment prohibiting federal enforcement of cannabis restrictions in states where medical use is legal and renewed the amendment annually in 2014. Under Trump, despite being expressly provided the authority, prosecution for cannabis crimes declined (Kavousi et al., 2022; Mallinson et al., 2020). In Europe, medical cannabis is less developed. While medical cannabis is available throughout the continent, there is a gap between legal status and availability to patients.[7] This is despite evidence that cannabis can treat medical or health conditions; reduces the use of pharmaceuticals; and rates better on effectiveness, side effects, safety, addictiveness, availability, and cost (Kruger & Kruger, 2019: 31). Recent research, focused on nurses, identified overwhelming support for legalized access to medical cannabis and the importance of overcoming the stereotypes associated with cannabis (Kurtzman et al., 2022).

In public health terms, the opioid crisis may have helped build momentum; opioid overdose deaths appeared lower in states where medical cannabis was legal (Bridgeman & Abazia, 2017); and in 2017, New York and Illinois began explicitly allowing patients to replace opiates with cannabis (Voelker, 2018). Beyond substitution, legalization increases safe access to cannabis and led to increased reports of therapeutic use for those with chronic health conditions who have benefited from using cannabis in its various forms for improving symptoms and their overall quality of life (Erridge, 2020). Findings from some recent studies challenge the accuracy of common "lazy, unfit stoner" stereotypes. Some researchers have found that cannabis users have smaller body-mass indexes (BMIs) when compared to non-users (Alshaarawy &

Anthony, 2019), and many exercise more than non-users (York-Williams et al., 2019). Stigma persists.

In the United Kingdom, access to medical cannabis remains restricted. As of 2020, fewer than ten NHS prescriptions were issued (Schlag, 2020). David Nutt (2022) argues that this amounts to moral failure, requiring patients to access the illicit market. The British Pediatric Neurology Association (BPNA) has refused to recommend that the National Health Service (NHS) allow for prescribing medical cannabis to children with severe treatment-refractory epilepsy. This is despite research suggesting its efficacy and allowing many children to stop taking multiple ineffective epilepsy drugs (Nutt, 2022). When asked why medical cannabis was not being expanded, current chief medical officer, Chris Whitty, linked cannabis legalization to the thalidomide tragedy (PA News Agency, 2019). Connecting cannabis to a drug scandal in which more than 10,000 children were born with a range of severe deformities is a reminder of the long reach of prohibition.

Consumer Cannabis and Constrained Markets

Consumer cannabis has existed in the Netherlands since the 1980s (Korf, 2020) compared to the relatively recent development of the industry in Colorado and Washington since 2012. Breeding cannabis for high psychoactive THC content (McPartland, 2017) has led to new strains described in ways to suggest product variety and distinction based on the common classification of Sativa or Indica and emergent distinctions based on strains that are either THC or cannabidiol (CBD) dominant (Jin et al., 2021). The cannabis industry's economic impact is large and growing worldwide (BDSA, 2021). In Canada, the cannabis market more than doubled in value between 2019 and 2020, increasing to $2.6 billion from $1.2 billion (Coulton, 2022). In 2020, US legal cannabis sales were estimated at $19 billion (Bhattarai, 2021), up from $10.8 billion in 2018 (Murphy, 2019). Consumer cannabis is driven in part by the potential for tax revenues.

While cannabis taxes can fund public services, as described above, cannabis cultivation can bring localities additional revenues. In a survey of Colorado local government officials, many who chose to legalize locally cited the opportunity to gain tax revenue and spur local economic growth (Johns, 2015). Estimates suggest states could earn $10–450 million annually in excise revenues if they legalize cannabis (Boesen, 2021). Washington and Colorado alone were earning at least $12 million per month from the cannabis industry in mid-2016 (Carnevale et al., 2017). In addition to sales taxes, states and localities may levy excise taxes, property, and other special taxes (Kavousi et al.,

2022).[8] Of course, the potential for taxes raises the costs of operating legal cannabis enterprises and reduces competitiveness, given the existence of established illicit markets (Bodwitch et al., 2021; Butsic et al., 2017; Goldstein & Sumner, 2019).[9] Recent research points to labor challenges, environmental difficulties, rule compliance, and cultivation practices (Bodwitch et al., 2021; Wilson et al., 2019). Kavousi and colleagues (2022) argue that larger, well-financed companies are able to withstand these growing pains, and smaller operations tend to struggle (Bodwitch et al., 2019; Goldstein & Sumner, 2019; Mallinson et al., 2020; Schwab et al., 2019).

In the meantime, cannabis tourism is emerging. This may be limited to states with recreational cannabis serving nonresident demand (Long, 2020; Meehan et al., 2020) to more targeted efforts (Liu & Stronczak, 2022). Once confined to Amsterdam, companies now offer tours in Washington and Colorado (Keul & Eisenhauer, 2019). One development is marketing cannabis strains based on unique regions (Crowder, 2020). Craft cannabis growers will need support if they are to expand this commercial area (Bennett, 2021). One challenge is how the inability to advertise cannabis constrains cannabis as a consumer good for large and small cannabis businesses alike (Wesley & Murray, 2021). Even in jurisdictions where advertisement exposure is high, brand awareness for cannabis products is low (Rup et al., 2020). Questions of cost, convenience, and consumer-centered cannabis are emerging (Mahamad et al., 2020). There may be potential for advertising to serve informational goals, a form of education, or a means to initiate dialogue about cannabis. This may be needed because of the long tradition of "abstinence-focused rhetoric" (Watson et al., 2019: 474).

Cannabis and Racial Justice

As we noted in Chapter 4, some states and local governments have made social and racial equity an explicit goal as part of new legal cannabis regimes (Adinoff & Reiman, 2019; Mallinson et al., 2020). This is designed to attempt to address two problems related to social and racial equity. The first is the history of disparate cannabis enforcement (Mize, 2020). The second is based on prospective efforts to expand the diversity in the cannabis industry by addressing barriers to entry, especially for Black and Brown entrepreneurs (Danquah-Brobby, 2017; Rahwanji, 2019). As has long been noted, racial disparities in wealth and discrimination and access to capital make any barrier more prohibitive for disproportionately impacted communities of color (Bender, 2016; Swinburne & Hoke, 2020).

To date, disparities in cannabis enforcement have persisted. In Washington, although arrest rates post-legalization dropped overall, relative racial disparities in arrests increased. Black people were roughly five times more likely than Whites to be arrested (Firth et al., 2020). Stanton and colleagues (2020) found that, despite hopes of decreasing the disproportionate imprisonment of racial and ethnic minorities, legalization did not change the demographics of those incarcerated in Washington county jails (Stanton et al., 2020). These findings are not limited to the Pacific Northwest. In the United States, Black people are nearly four times more likely than White people to be arrested for cannabis violations, despite using cannabis at similar rates (Adinoff & Reiman, 2019). Even after cannabis legalization in Canada, both Black and Indigenous people are over-represented in arrest statistics in four of the five cities examined (Owusu-Bempah & Luscombe, 2021). Recent research focuses on evaluating empirical strategies for identifying unnecessary and discriminatory policing that disproportionately burdens Black individuals without any clear gains in public safety. Such forms of policing "impose greater costs on racial minorities" (Chohlas-Wood et al., 2022: 444).

Sheehan and colleagues (2021) analyzed data between 2000 and 2019 from forty-three US states to compare pre-implementation and post-implementation differences in arrest rates for states with decriminalization, legalization, and no policy changes. While arrests rates decrease when cannabis is decriminalized, Black people are still arrested at twice the rate of White people. These disparities were least pronounced in jurisdictions where cannabis is legal. However, legalization cannot be seen as a magic bullet. These historic disparities have present-day consequences. Individuals with felony convictions for illicit cannabis activities are ineligible for licensing in the licit one (Adinoff & Reiman, 2019; Rahwanji, 2019).

Kavousi and colleagues (2022) point out that this privileges White people without criminal records and disadvantages those disproportionately harmed by drug criminalization (Mallinson et al., 2020; Rahwanji, 2019). Efforts through social equity programs that attempt to increase opportunities for those historically disadvantaged have been criticized (Connley, 2021; Elmahrek, 2020; Reyes, 2021; Schroyer, 2020), but few have been subject to rigorous analysis. One effort by Doonan and colleagues (2022) assessed short-term racial/ethnic and gender diversity across the industry. They found that despite a legislative and regulatory commitment to diversity, this was not apparent in senior positions in this emerging cannabis market. States considering adult-use cannabis markets, and those that have already done so, should monitor participation to identify inequities and adapt initiatives to ensure Black/African American and Latino communities socially and economically benefit from state legalization.

(Doonan et al., 2022: 30)

Conclusion

Three distinct eras of cannabis research produced vastly different results. In the first era, reports by bodies established by states and countries were ignored. Criminalizing cannabis was initially political and served racial injustice (Baum, 2016). Early research establishing the relative harmlessness of cannabis did little to shape national and international policy. By 1972, the War on Drugs and international conventions ensured cannabis research focused on the risks. Throughout the consequential second era, claims of the dangers of cannabis use could not be delinked from the dangers associated with engaging illegal markets. Long prison sentences for people who use cannabis has ruined lives (Vitiello, 2021). In 2012, after the legalization of recreational cannabis in Colorado and Washington, an old approach was reimagined. Like the Old Prohibitionists of the past, the New Prohibitionists warned against the use of cannabis, embellished the harms of cannabis, and found a media ecosystem in which exaggerations of harm were grist to the mill.

Since 2018, although earlier examples certainly exist, cannabis research has focused on research from jurisdictions where cannabis is legal and access is less stigmatized, and while the illicit market persists, it is not the only option for people who use cannabis. The era of legal cannabis has opened the door to more nuanced examinations of cannabis and public safety, public health, the value of medical cannabis, the complications of consumer cannabis, and impediments to racial justice. As we have shown, however, under every regulatory model of cannabis, Cohen's concerns (1985) remain relevant. Racial disparities within public safety models persist (Owusu-Bempah & Luscombe, 2021; Sheehan et al., 2021). In public health terms, the ability to access cannabis to replace the use of other substances remains constrained (Kavousi et al., 2022), and stigma persists for people who use it recreationally (Reid, 2020). Research into medical cannabis remains limited (Jin et al.,

2021), and nonsensical comparisons by medical professionals are common (Nutt, 2022).

No model of cannabis regulation is more constrained than consumer cannabis. This includes how Big Cannabis has been privileged (Bennett, 2021), the inability to legally advertise or market cannabis (Wesley & Murray, 2021), and taxes and fees, which make competing with illicit markets difficult (Mahamad et al., 2020). Today, consumers are limited by old adages, the repetition of poor research, and multilevel stigma, which limits products and restricts access in an attempt to control cannabis use, despite its changed legal status (Reid, 2020). The failure, to date, of models of cannabis regulation focused on racial justice complicates visions of cannabis access that serve to promote other forms of criminal justice reform and reduce disparities in arrest, diversion, incarceration, and other forms of intrusions (Brown, 2022).

Notes

1. See National Archive of South Africa. Draft letter, Prime Minister to Secretary, League of Nations, SAB BTS 2/1/104 L.N. 15/1SA, November 28, 1923.
2. See https://publications.gc.ca/collections/collection_2014/sc-hc/H21-5370-2-1-eng.pdf.
3. See https://ballotpedia.org/Smart_Approaches_to_Marijuana#:~:text=Smart%20 Approaches%20to%20Marijuana%20(SAM)%20was%20established%20in%20 January%202013,initiatives%20in%20Colorado%20and%20Washington.
4. Cole points to a number of sources, including UNODC (2021b: 20), which notes *13 per cent are estimated to suffer from drug use disorders, meaning that their drug use is harmful to the point where they may experience drug dependence and/or require treatment*. This claim has been consistent in the World Drug Reports and other WHO/United Nations reports over the past decade or so. See, e.g. UNODC (2012: 1). The UNODC–WHO 2020 Report (UNODC–WHO, 2021: 20) suggests this number may be much smaller.
5. The empirical realities of funding focused on cannabis harms and its connection to existing research is summarized in O'Grady (2020).
6. The full Bill can be access here: https://www.feinstein.senate.gov/public/_cache/files/f/9/f9877e00-8bac-45c5-b0a4-ad73f36bb296/A790203221D32AE509C4E2DEFEDBE6D6.2022-03-23-10-09-02-uid-575-hen22240.pdf.
7. Countries such as the United Kingdom, the Netherlands, Poland, and Portugal, have established medical cannabis legislation. In Austria, it has been legal to prescribe since 2008, and since 2015, Finland has made medical cannabis available (Seddon & Floodgate, 2020: 53). Germany made it legal for doctors to prescribe medical cannabis in 2017 (Schlag, 2020). Greece and the United Kingdom

approved the legalization of cannabis for medical use in 2018. In 2019, legislation in Greece was signed to permit a five-year pilot of the Medical Cannabis Access Programme (Seddon & Floodgate, 2020: 54). In other countries, including Sweden, Latvia, Belgium, and Albania, medical cannabis is illegal to buy, sell, or use. France, Ireland, and Denmark are running trial periods for medical cannabis. However, in Croatia and Finland, just one cannabis medicinal product is available by prescription. For a useful overview, see Kohut (2021).
8. For instance, Oregon local governments can add a 3 percent tax on top of the state's 17 percent tax (Firth et al., 2020). Illinois cannabis retail is subject to the 6.25 percent normal state sales tax, an additional tax that scales with potency, and potential local taxes up to an additional 3.5 percent (Kavousi et al., 2022). New York's new recreational cannabis tax scheme provides for a 9 percent sales tax, 3 percent local tax, 1 percent county tax, and additional taxes related to THC content. See Syracuse.com (2021).
9. For instance, see Chappell (2019); Daniels (2019).

PART III

CULTURAL RENEGOTIATION AND BARRIERS TO REGULATION

7
Cannabis Policy, Harm Reduction, and Meaningful Decriminalization

Introduction

Possessing cannabis has been decriminalized in many countries and legalized in others, including a growing number of US states (Seddon & Floodgate, 2020). While the number is up to twenty-five countries (TalkingDrugs, n.d.), it will surely increase in future years. Decriminalization maintains a prohibition on production and supply but removes criminal penalties for possessing small quantities of cannabis. Thresholds for personal possession vary, as do the intrusions applied through public safety and public health models. This may include confiscation, fines, screenings, re-education programs, mandatory treatment, or other penalties. Based on the relative safety of cannabis (D'Souza et al., 2022; Eliason & Howse, 2019) and the undeniable damage done by prohibitionist policies, especially to Black, Indigenous, and other People of Color (BIPOC) around the world (Wheeldon & Heidt, 2023a), change is coming (UNCEBC, 2019). While opposition to even modest reform remains obstinate in some countries,[1] cannabis legalization is inevitable. Responsible regulation, however, is not.

In this book, and based on previous work, we have framed cannabis legalization as a case study in legal–moral–cultural renegotiation (Wheeldon & Heidt, 2023b). This chapter focuses on the legal dimension of this broader cultural process. We present three categories of illicit drug policies and adapt them to cannabis by embracing different aspects of the five regulatory models introduced in Chapter 4. In this chapter, we examine efforts to depenalize, decriminalize, and liberalize cannabis policy and offer a means to organize reforms along a linear spectrum from prohibition to legalization. A unique contribution is a visual means to catalog state responses to cannabis possession. By assessing categories of cannabis policy, we note that high levels of criminal justice intrusion in the name of cannabis prohibition persist. Finally, by revisiting existing regulatory models, we consider the nature and impact of cannabis policy-based harms (Wilkins et al., 2022). These include the dangers of public safety, the harms of public health, and the failure to engage questions of race and reconciliation.

Finally, we present a model of meaningful decriminalization based on an assessment of readiness and suggest this model must contend with two profound challenges to cannabis reform, namely, the persistent inequalities associated with policing cannabis and the invisibility of coercive care and control within cannabis diversion programs. We argue meaningful decriminalization requires recognizing how tolerance and aversion have shaped past approaches to cannabis. By expanding tolerance and regulating aversion to cannabis, decriminalization and legalization are more likely to be sustained. Constraining all the concerns which emerge from a careful reading of Stan Cohen (1985) is difficult. Perhaps embracing a harm reduction frame can recast past observations that cannabis reform often amounts to shifting the carceral functions of the public safety model to paternalistic policies associated with public health models.

Categorizing Cannabis Policy

Early attempts to contemplate emergent cannabis policies were connected to other efforts to categorize illicit drug policies. One significant contribution divided regulation into three types:

> (i) legalization—a system in which possession and sale are lawful but subject to regulation and taxation; (ii) criminalization—a system of proscriptions on possession and sale backed by criminal punishment, potentially including incarceration; (iii) depenalization—a hybrid system, in which sale and possession are proscribed, but the prohibition on possession is backed only by such sanctions as fines or mandatory substance abuse treatment, not incarceration.
>
> (Donohue et al., 2011: 3)

Although applied to all drugs, these categories remain relevant when assessing cannabis regulation. However, they may demand a reconsideration, given our work in this book to define five regulatory models that guide current cannabis policies and the changing nature of global cannabis reform.

The first category, legalization, is based on adopting a consumer cannabis framework. It connects libertarian ideas around cannabis and capital with the idea that people should be free to consume what they want, provided they do not harm others. This model would increase access to cannabis and cannabis-related products, usher in a new age of advertising and marketing, and accept that while some problems with cannabis use may emerge, these risks have long been exaggerated. According to this view, public health and public safety complications are outweighed by the cost savings associated with no longer attempting to police cannabis possession (Beckett & Herbert, 2008). In addition, funds raised in jurisdictions that legalize, regulate, and tax cannabis sales can be used to address other priorities (Kavousi et al., 2022). Benefits include disrupting illicit markets, limiting the dangers associated with gangs and organized crime, and avoiding racially and ethnically unequal applications of drug enforcement (Sheehan et al., 2021; Shiner, 2015).

However, to date, legalizing and privatizing cannabis often leads to overregulation, which does not adequately address the lower cost, convenience, and established routines associated with obtaining cannabis access via illicit drug markets (Thies, 2012). Unlike alcohol, advertising is prohibited, and cannabis remains stigmatized. Other challenges are linked to how users and illicit markets respond to changes in cannabis policy.

Rational choice theory offers one means to understanding criminal decision-making (Lilly et al., 2015). These theories suggest we all engage in a cost–benefit analysis before deciding on a proper course of action (Cornish & Clarke, 1986; Felson & Eckert, 2018). These insights can inform laws and regulations and may provide hints at best practices with other illicit drugs. Some calculations on cannabis include cost, quality, ease of access, convenience, and patterns of routine activities. While still in its infancy, given the nature of existing regulations, we call this the "legalize-and-privatize" model.

The second category, criminalization, is based on the oft repeated but empirically questionable associations between cannabis, mental health, and crime. As criminalization has receded, public safety models have been replaced by public health approaches. These approaches are often based on ideas influenced by the brain disease model of addiction (BDMA) and tend to conceptualize all illicit drug use as deviant and pathological with the potential to lead to addiction. These misunderstandings are a persistent feature of cannabis policy and are unlikely to be easily dislodged. As we outlined in Chapter 6, for the tiny number of people with schizophrenia, especially youth, cannabis use represents an increased risk. However, the risk for others has been regularly exaggerated (Berenson, 2019; Sabet, 2021). Prohibiting and limiting cannabis use is furthered by the "Reefer Madness" rhetoric of the past and the adoption of various sanctions, including mandated and coerced "treatment." As we have demonstrated, while the intensity of punishment may have been constrained, the breadth and span of efforts to control people who use cannabis have increased.

As mentioned previously, this view is rooted in public health and assumptions about addiction. Numerous jurisdictions have adopted some measures of decriminalization while retaining the prohibitionist paradigm (Taylor et al., 2016). As discussed in Chapter 2, Gusfield (1986) linked legislative efforts to prohibit alcohol steeped in religious and ideological goals. This is also consistent with recent efforts by a group we call the "New Prohibitionists." Their focus on public health couched in the protection of the children narrative emerges from the explicit acceptance of this model. It is a derivative of the medical model in which cannabis users are sick and in need of protection. When compulsory, these approaches look less like treatment and more like punishment. While some distrust of cannabis liberalization may be based on a good faith misunderstanding of the risks of cannabis, it cannot be divorced from the tendency among this group to deny or ignore the racial inequities that persist under cannabis prohibition (Mize, 2020). As such, we call this the "prohibit-and-punish" model.

Changing attitudes have led to an expansion of the third model. While based on depenalization, this category requires a reconceptualization based on developments in cannabis policy over the past decade. Depenalization as a conceptual category is used differently by different people (Inciardi, 2004; Nolan, 2002; Stevens et al., 2022). In addition, it is sometimes defined in ways that make it indistinguishable from decriminalization (Jesseman & Payer, 2018). As noted in Chapter 5 (Logan, 2014), neither depenalization nor decriminalization necessarily lead to lower levels of criminal justice intrusion. However, due to the diversity in policies and practices that have emerged, it is worth examining how countries with vastly different histories, legal systems, and cultures have pursued several approaches to decriminalizing cannabis (Seddon & Floodgate, 2020).

While decriminalization occurs whenever a country reclassifies cannabis possession from a criminal to a non-criminal offense, there are numerous subcategories. In a recent and laudable effort, Stevens and colleagues (2022) present a taxonomy of alternative sanctions as part of cannabis liberalization. Their scheme contains six alternative measures: depenalization, de facto diversion; de jure diversion, decriminalization with diversion and civil sanctions, decriminalization with civil sanctions, and decriminalization with no sanctions. These six types fall into three classes: depenalization, diversion, and decriminalization. There is value in these legal typologies, and this effort represents a critical contribution to legal epistemology. However, adopting this view as a framework for cannabis reform presents several challenges.

One problem is the wide diversity of examples that fall under this conceptual category. Depenalization is often confused with decriminalization or de facto legalization (Jesseman & Payer, 2018; MacCoun & Reuter, 2001). While some continue to describe reducing sanctions in policy using the term "depenalization"[2] for cannabis, the breadth of depenalization as a concept and category may undermine its pragmatic utility (Wheeldon, 2015). Earp et al. (2021) redefine "decriminalization" as de jure decriminalization to address this confusion. This means that criminal penalties for the personal possession and use of small amounts of illicit drugs would be removed by an act of legislation or judicial decision. One way to understand efforts is by assessing to what extent reforms are de facto, based on practice, as in the United Kingdom and some US states, or de jure, based on law, as in Portugal.

To these established descriptors, we add a fifth category, decriminalization "*in media res*," to account for jurisdictions in which decriminalization practices conform to formally adopted policies, even if cannabis possession is not formally decriminalized in law. The Latin term *in media res*, translated as "in the midst of things," can be understood as an approach to reform moving from de facto to de jure based on established policy. It can refer to countries where formal policies and procedures, as opposed to laws, guide criminal justice actors. Thus, cannabis decriminalization exists as more than de facto but less than de jure. While the Netherlands is one example, other countries are adopting this approach (Seddon & Floodgate, 2020). Spain and Belgium's approach to cannabis social clubs is one example (Pardal, 2022). Figure 7.1 suggests a linear view of cannabis liberalization.

While a helpful starting place, the problems with the simplistic conceptual effort above are myriad. The first issue is that cannabis liberalization is not a one-way street. There are numerous jurisdictions where efforts to decriminalize cannabis have resulted in more citizens in prison, more police involvement, and more anti-cannabis stigma (Belackova et al., 2017). Likewise, countries that retain laws on the books with substantial penalties for cannabis use have seen those responsible for investigating, arresting, charging, and sentencing people use their discretion in ways that sometimes create further issues. In most cases, *de jure decriminalization* is preferable to *de facto decriminalization*, where criminal penalties are suspended depending on local, contingent administrative, or law enforcement practices.

Non-enforcement of the relevant laws or referral of offenders to treatment or education programs is an important marker in comparative cannabis

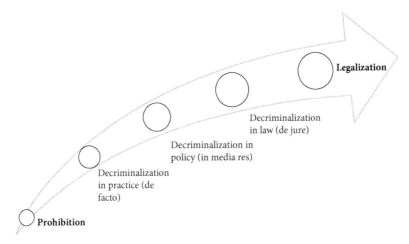

Figure 7.1 Spectrum of cannabis liberalization
Source: Authors.

reform. As Cohen (1985: 109) argues, reforming the state's carceral predilections without defining and considering what the reforms intend to do and how they will be implemented to achieve this results in the "contradictory status assigned to the newer and softer forms of social control." In short, differing expectations are often forced to coexist. A better means to visualize this spectrum is to embrace the notion that cannabis liberalization is a nonlinear project. While the long arc of history may bend toward legalization, there are likely to be missteps, backtracking, and outright errors along the way.

The emphasis on decriminalizing cannabis is conceptually clearer and more reflective of current efforts. Just as *in media res* serves as an "in-between" designation to categorize liberalization, jurisdictions may pursue policies to decriminalize and destigmatize cannabis use as a precursor to legalization. This might include increasing possession threshold limits for arrest and defining problem use for those possessing more than the specified amount of cannabis. In addition to decriminalizing cannabis, this model also promotes destigmatization by de-emphasizing the policing of cannabis while retaining the ability of police to refer problem use to community-based organizations. These organizations can link individuals to resources in their communities but not mandate treatment.

Consistent with Cohen's concerns (1985), the value of this "in-between" designation provides a means to allow for the idea that progression and regression are possible on the road to cannabis legalization. It avoids some of the problems

More		Level of Criminological Intrusion		Less
Lengthy Incarceration	Criminal Record	Court ordered treatment	Police Warning	Valuntary Treatment	Regulated Market
Community Supervision		Diversion		Personal Possession
Criminalization	Depenalization		Administrative Sanctions	Acceptance
Prohibit and Punish		Decriminalize and Destigmatize (Practice; Policy; Law)		Legalize and Regulate

Figure 7.2 Possessing cannabis: A conceptual model
Source: Authors.

associated with categorizing countries as embodying de jure decriminalization, on the one hand, or de facto decriminalization on the other. Many jurisdictions may find themselves in this position in the years to come. Figure 7.2 provides one view of a conceptual model that considers criminological intrusions and three stages of liberalization. These categories include "Prohibit and punish," "Decriminalize and destigmatize," and "Legalize and regulate."

Reducing Harm: Models, Definitions, and Policy Criteria

The history of cannabis policy is a history of harm. Thus, the future of cannabis regulation must consider harm reduction, described as a pragmatic and compassionate set of strategies designed to reduce the harms associated with certain behaviors (Marlatt, 1999). This may include policies, programs, or practices that aim to minimize adverse health, social, and legal impacts associated with certain behaviors often associated with illicit drug use. While it defies efforts to arrive at a standard definition, Harm Reduction International (HRI) provides a helpful clarification. It categorizes harm reduction as

> policies, programs, and practices that aim to minimize negative health, social and legal impacts associated with drug use, drug policies and drug laws. Harm reduction is grounded in justice and human rights—it focuses on positive change and on working with people without judgement, coercion, discrimination, or requiring that they stop using drugs as a precondition of support.
>
> (Harm Reduction International, n.d.)

An incomplete list of harm reduction examples includes clean needle distribution, needle exchange programs, supervised injection sites, naloxone distribution programs, and the provision of safe drug supplies.

Some definitions of harm reduction consider abstinence policies to be consistent with the goals of harm reduction (Lenton & Single, 1998). In the past, David Nutt has suggested that harm reduction and being "tough on drugs" need not be mutually exclusive (Nutt, 2012). We reject this view, especially as applied to cannabis. Abstinence programming tends to proceed by emphasizing risk-based messaging (Watson et al., 2019) that stigmatizes people (Goffman, 1963) while failing to provide them with helpful information (Parker & Egginton, 2002). Alternatively, some research describes harm reduction principles for use in health-care settings broadly applicable within public health. These include humanism, pragmatism, individualism, autonomy, incrementalism, and accountability without termination (Hawk et al., 2017: 70).

Nutt and colleagues (2010: 1559–1560) explored drug harm by examining the physical, psychological, and social harms of using various illicit substances. It was extended by establishing a Europe-wide expert panel to assess drug harm by adapting the methodology (Van Amsterdam et al., 2015) and considering drug policies for regulated licit substances (Nutt et al., 2014). Based on twenty-seven relevant criteria, organized into seven thematically related clusters, drug policy harms have been connected to health and social, political, public, and economic harms and costs associated with crime (Rogeburg et al., 2018: 146). Recent research engaged stakeholder experts to rank cannabis law reform options using these criteria (Wilkins et al., 2022).

By retaining the focus of early work (Nutt et al., 2010) and integrating broader policy criteria (Rogeburg et al., 2018), we reorganize cannabis policy harms based on the relative weighting by drug policy experts (Wilkins et al., 2022). Five key findings included reducing health and social harm, reducing arrests, reducing the illegal market, expanding treatment, and netting tax dollars. These goals can be connected to elements of the five regulatory models introduced in Chapter 4. For example, lowering the number of arrests is related to de-emphasizing the public safety model, expanding treatment is associated with the public health model, and diminishing health harms is connected to regulating cannabis as medicine. Finally, adopting the commercial model is the best way to earn tax and confront the illicit market. Addressing social harms will require adopting key proposals connected to the racial justice model.

Models and Mechanisms of Harm

To understand which models are likely to provide preferred policy outcomes, it may be helpful to consider three of the five models explored to date through the lens of harm reduction. These include public safety, public health, and race and justice.

The Dangers of Public Safety

Continuing to criminalize cannabis will ensure stigma persists, disparate enforcement outcomes are sustained, and intrusions by criminal justice actors endure (Mize, 2020). These have long undermined police–community relations, alienated residents, and undercut legitimacy. This includes the "collateral harms" of cannabis user criminalization (Fischer et al., 2021) and the adverse effects of a criminal record on personal or professional life prospects (Best & Colman, 2019; Kaplan, 1970; Pinard, 2010). A comprehensive focus on public safety would include the risks associated with illicit markets, such as exposure to violence, the subversion of the rule of law, and the corruption related to criminal networks and drug trafficking syndicates (Ritter, 2021). Similarly, most drug dealers maximize profits by taking such a risk by selling a variety of drugs and often make more money from selling harder drugs that are easier to conceal and dispose of, that is, powders and pills. Thus, people who use cannabis are forced to seek out dealers who maximize profits by selling various illicit drugs (Parker & Egginton, 2002: 430).

Even as cannabis liberalization reduces the dependence on the police–punishment complex to control others (Simon, 2007), legalization adds new layers of regulation. The carceral state "continues to cast its shadow over these policy domains" (Aaronson & Rothschild-Elyassi, 2021: 3). Of significant concern is the imposition of procedures that can escalate the severity of sanctions in cases where lenient responses have failed (Braithwaite, 2011). This broadens the array of social control mechanisms that can be used to govern, discipline, and control populations deemed to be "dangerous" or "unruly" (Feeley & Simon 1992), even as it claims to pursue social justice. Central here is how public health models begin to resemble public safety approaches.

The Harms of Public Health

A focus on public health involves focusing on the risks of cannabis through messaging designed to keep people from using cannabis and expanding treatment for "problem use." For a century, people who use cannabis have been routinely characterized in negative and stigmatizing ways

(Newhart & Dolphin, 2019). The public health model tends to rely on inadequate information and risk-based messaging (Parker & Egginton, 2002: 430). These messages do "not resonate with how many youth experience cannabis use" (Watson et al., 2019: 472). Perhaps the most worrying operational implication of adopting a public health model is its justification for coercive cannabis "addiction" treatments, backed by the threat of criminal prosecution.[3] Forcing people to engage in treatment programs may result in associating treatment with coercion, making it less likely that people will seek support when they are ready to engage in any problem.

Beyond the contested value of forced cannabis treatment, it is an example of the carceral creep of the state as it extends its regulatory authority. For McSweeney and colleagues (2007), expanding control using the language of rehabilitation compounds the invasive nature of drug policy. They write:

> On the one hand, the government can ostensibly claim to be fulfilling its duty and obligation to undertake rehabilitative work with criminally involved drug users by introducing measures . . . as an alternative to imprisonment. At the same time, however, measures . . . reduce the role of voluntarism in sentencing and help-seeking processes and further encroach upon notions of proportionality by increasing the intrusiveness of punishment in the name of rehabilitation. These new measures continue a trend whereby community sentences are imposing ever greater restrictions on low-risk offenders, while the stringent enforcement of these penalties is, in itself, contributing to a burgeoning prison population.
> (McSweeney et al., 2007: 482)

The creation of new markets on behalf of for-profit treatment enterprises, which tend to perpetuate prohibition-based assumptions based on a century of misinformation, should be seen alongside suggestions that criminal justice systems can become predatory (Page & Soss, 2021).

Reconciliation and Racial Justice

Framing the harms of cannabis policies designed to alleviate racial injustice is challenging. There are few.[4] As with the medical and commercial models, potential harms will persist if racial issues are ignored. For example, disparate treatment and the adverse outcomes of living with aggressive policing and ethno-racial profiling are severe and widespread (Chohlas-Wood et al., 2022; Sewell et al., 2021). Another harm will occur if states fail to "enable those injured by prohibition to benefit from the unique entrepreneurial opportunities offered within the burgeoning cannabis industry" (Mize, 2020: 1). However, most states prevent people with certain criminal convictions from being employed in cannabis establishments (Howell, 2018) or participating in other parts of the cannabis industry. For example, until recently, Illinois prevented those with cannabis-related convictions from entering the cannabis industry and denied licenses and loans to those with criminal records, even though this comprised more than 30 percent of adults in Chicago (Fitz & Armstrong, 2022).[5]

One of the most consistent findings in the literature over decades is that the adverse effects of criminalizing cannabis disproportionately impact people of color, their families, and their communities. In the United States, the most egregious racial disparities can be seen in the case of Black and Brown people who are forced to endure discriminatory enforcement of drug laws (Alexander, 2010). Unequal arrest and incarceration rates in communities of color are not reflective of the increased prevalence of drug use (Heidt & Wheeldon, 2015). As Solomon (2020: 5) notes,

> To move forward, we need to understand our own history and the false premise on which we have based this misguided policy. We need to treat the cannabis policy started in 1937 the same way we treat segregated schools, miscegenation, and other race-based policy. Our inquiry needs to start with an acknowledgment of the history of racial discrimination in our drug policy and move toward serious evidence-based research. If we fail to do so, we will remain the willing victims of our own racist history.

Until recently, cannabis research has failed to confront the role of assumptions about race, cannabis, and justice (Solomon, 2020). Thinking about tolerance, aversion, and cannabis policy is one starting point.

Cannabis, Tolerance, and Aversion

As we argued in Chapter 2, cannabis prohibition emerged from colonial and neocolonial arrangements that have guided international institutions for decades (Daniels et al., 2021). Cannabis policy was built on successful efforts to prohibit and criminalize opium and was based on intolerance, xenophobia, racism, and a commitment to (im)moral misrepresentations (Gusfield, 1986). Given how the intolerance of cannabis and cannabis use has been encoded in numerous countries and communities, cannabis policies must acknowledge the harms of the War on Drugs. Introduced in Chapter 4, one antidote to ever-expanding control is based on the Netherlands policy of *gedoogbeleid* or "tolerance policy" (Brewster, 2017).

Brown (2006: 19) defines tolerance as: "respect for human difference or for opinions and practices [that] differ from one's own."[6] However, tolerance is not a panacea. She notes that tolerance emerged in early modern Europe to defuse violent religious divergence and reduce persecution. Tolerance provides a conceptual means to decrease conflict across cultural, racial, and ethnic divides. However, it also includes dark and troubling undercurrents. She writes:

> Despite its pacific demeanor, tolerance is an internally unharmonious term, blending goodness, capaciousness, and conciliation with discomfort, judgment, and aversion. Like patience, tolerance is necessitated by something one would prefer did not exist. It involves managing the presence of the undesirable, the tasteless, the faulty—even the revolting, repugnant, or vile. In this activity of management, tolerance does not offer resolution or transcendence, but only a strategy for coping. There is no Aufhebung in the operation of tolerance, no purity and no redemption. As compensation, tolerance anoints the bearer with virtue, with standing for a principled act of permitting one's principles to be affronted; it provides a gracious way of allowing one's tastes to be violated. It offers a robe of modest superiority in exchange for yielding.
>
> (Brown, 2006: 25)

The concern here is not that tolerance as a value is depraved but rather tolerance, like other political concepts, appears good in performative ways while allowing all "objects of tolerance are marked as deviant, marginal, or undesirable by virtue of being tolerated" (Brown, 2006: 14).

Since dislike, disapproval, and regulation lurk at the heart of tolerance, Brown (2006: 24) argues, "tolerance reiterates the depoliticization . . . depicting itself as a norm-free tool of liberal governance, a mere means for securing freedom of conscience." To tolerate is not to affirm but to conditionally allow what is unwanted. Thus, tolerance as an attitudinal orientation means little when compared to actual policies intended to reduce human suffering and promote the fulsome engagement of people once stigmatized and marginalized. While this is a pessimistic account, we read Brown (2006) as a reminder that reform requires regulating aversion alongside any effort to promote tolerance. Practically, expanding tolerance for cannabis use can address immediate harms connected to disparate policing and stigmatization. This includes rejecting justifying pretextual stops based on police suspicion of cannabis possession, usually amounting to reporting the mere smell of cannabis near a suspect.[7]

Of course, this requires confronting racial disparities in criminal justice contacts that persist when cannabis is decriminalized (Sheehan et al., 2021) and remains even in jurisdictions where cannabis has been legalized (Owusu-Bempah & Luscombe, 2021). In this way, prioritizing the freedom of people who use cannabis means considering rights protection, rights fulfillment, and disrupting the tendency for carceral coercion to expand from prisons to the community (Cohen, 1985). Juxtaposing tolerance and aversion in this way represents a novel way to consider two standard models of cannabis regulation. Figure 7.3 provides one way to visualize this. If tolerance is at the root of commercial cannabis, aversion is the basis for those who seek to prohibit and punish cannabis. The best way to constrain this potential expansion is to ensure clear and comprehensive remedies are available when policies that harm cannabis users persist. Adopting such an approach requires regulating aversion to cannabis by pursuing policies designed not only to decriminalize but also to destigmatize cannabis and cannabis use.

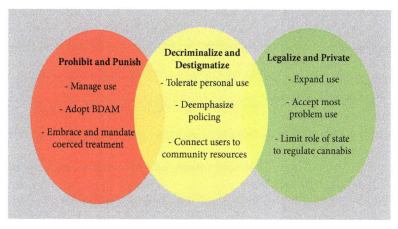

Figure 7.3 Models of cannabis regulation revisited
Source: Authors.

Regulating Aversion and Meaningful Decriminalization

Designed to lead to legal and regulatory models of cannabis that can overcome the ideological barriers that limit cannabis reform, our approach to meaningful decriminalization attempts to address some of the concerns expressed by Cohen (1985). As discussed above, the Netherlands provides the best example of tolerance in cannabis policy. It means not only that people abide by the unpopular choices of others but also that laws and policies are designed to allow for leniency (Brewster, 2017). By contrast, for Brown (2006), aversion, dislike, or loathing is held in check by tolerance. Like the proverbial Dutch boy, Hans Brinker, who saved his village by putting his finger in the dyke, tolerance holds back the hate and revulsion we feel for those who make different choices than we would.[8] However, these barriers must first be identified if Cohen's (1985) concerns about ever-expanding social control can be mitigated. They include the persistent, pernicious, unproven association between cannabis and addiction. This leads to stigma and aversion and represents a challenge to efforts to reform the policing of cannabis.

On the other hand, inconsistent enforcement of cannabis laws on the books may indicate that policy revision is required (Government of Canada, 2019; Hyshka, 2009: 520). This may suggest that the law has become outdated and is no longer taken seriously by law enforcement officials or the public. Specifying the preferred approach to cannabis regulation means revisiting the models of reform presented above. Perhaps more importantly, it requires asking some fundamental questions (Oldfield et al., 2021). In addition to focusing on the type of legal regime or whether the provisions are limited or comprehensive, questions should focus on how users will access and consume cannabis and what reasonable limitations will guide their use. Additional questions refer to how they will receive support for problem use and what remedies they may rely upon should state actors intrude upon their freedom to access and consume cannabis. Table 7.1 lists key questions for jurisdictions considering decriminalization or legalization and some possible responses organized by category.

The answers to these questions suggest what model of cannabis liberalization should be pursued in a jurisdiction. Some replies would suggest support for a thin form of decriminalization. For example, provisions might make cannabis legal to grow, consume at home, and possess in small quantities but remain illegal in other cases. This form of decriminalization would provide no access to support for those who requested it and no specific mechanisms

Table 7.1 Decriminalization or legalization of cannabis?

Category	Key question	Possible replies
Legal provisions	Under what legal regime will liberalization operate?	No change in the law; decriminalize possession; limited medical cannabis law; limited recreational cannabis law
Supply	What forms of cannabis will be available?	Low tetrahydrocannabinol only; flower; edibles; resin; any/all
Quality	How will the state ensure the safety of supply?	It won't; free drug testing; regulations for suppliers; product tracking
Access	How will consumers access cannabis?	Buy from anyone; buy from a regulated store; grow on their own; grow as part of growing cooperatives/social clubs; online/mail order
Consumption	How will users consume cannabis?	Only at home; anywhere except where prohibited; in social clubs/lounges/coffee houses; everywhere
Limits	What reasonable limitations should consumers expect?	Possession limits (flower); possession limits (plants); possession limits (edibles); possession limits (resin); prohibition against driving; limitations associated with employment
Support	How will users access support for problem use?	Private; publicly funded, doctor referred; diversion program referred; compulsory
Remedies	What remedies can users rely upon for infringements?	Complaint; review board; right to sue (privately funded); right to sue (publicly funded)

Source: Authors.

to avoid state overreach or provide remedies should overreach occur. By contrast, other responses could suggest a thick form of legalization, including provisions for a regulated supply of cannabis and easy-to-access licenses to sell cannabis in retail stores and online. Under such a system, it would be legal to grow, buy, and possess cannabis, and consumption may be restricted to certain places, including lounges, social clubs, and designated smoking areas. While we turn to legalization in Chapter 8, it may be useful to consider what policies are consistent with a "decriminalize-and-destigmatize" model of cannabis reform.

We link key findings of policy harms based on their analysis of expert views on cannabis liberalization (Wilkins et al., 2022) and critical criminological concepts, including stigma, enforcement, and interventions. Stigma refers to how cannabis users are labeled, stereotyped, othered, and discriminated against (Link & Phelan, 2001). As Reid (2020) notes, stigma exists in numerous forms and interacts with normalization and shame in ways that are difficult to parse. We use the term "enforcement" to refer to formal efforts to police cannabis, such as arrests and investigatory stops premised on suspicion of cannabis possession. Finally, intervention refers to cannabis diversion programs, especially those that adopt coercive treatment modalities, as described above.

Policing Cannabis: Threshold Limits and Remedies for Overreach

The importance of cannabis policies designed to constrain public safety by addressing racial disparities can no longer be ignored (Wheeldon & Heidt, 2023b). This variant of harm reduction, described by some as "reducing arrests" (Wilkins et al., 2022), requires taking steps to confront and reduce the damage done by the justice system itself (Quinney, 1970). Too often, racial disparities in cannabis enforcement fuel predatory features of criminal justice (Page & Soss, 2021). Brown (2022) suggests cannabis legalization will disincentivize pretextual stops. In terms of de-emphasizing the policing of cannabis, jurisdictions may legalize cannabis or demand police not arrest people for possession.

Another option is to leave laws in place and "attempt to reshape officer attitudes and beliefs" (del Pozo et al., 2021: para 2). However, little has changed in the decade-and-a-half since senior policing scholars concluded that understanding how police change their behavior remains a mystery (Mastrofski, 2004). A recent study sought to understand what influences police to make discretionary referrals to treatment and harm reduction resources rather than arrest on less serious charges (del Pozo et al., 2021: para 27). Based on a survey of 259 police officers, the authors concluded:

> The results of this study suggest respondents believe they have considerable discretion over the drug laws they enforce, the arrests they make, and the items they confiscate. They report using this discretion in different ways for different reasons, distinguishing between their intentions to confiscate

contraband or to charge a person for possessing it. Decriminalizing drug and syringe possession would stop police from making arrests for those acts, but the laws that govern the risk and criminal behaviors associated with substance use disorder would remain in effect, and police would continue to have discretion in enforcing them.

Consistent with worries that reforms in name only change little on the ground, these limits should specify the conditions in which police could justifiably interfere with citizens for cannabis-based offenses and provide remedies for unjustly detained or arrested citizens. For those possessing more than the threshold amount, *unless cannabis possession is directly associated with a crime*, police-led diversion to a community-based panel or committee should be preferred. Such an approach offers a means to overcome a significant challenge related to state-centric definitions of problem cannabis use or the practice of requiring police to fulfill roles associated with social workers or addictions counselors (del Pozo et al., 2021). The best means to address cannabis arrests is not to make them in the first place.

In many US states and the United Kingdom, possessing *any* amount of cannabis is grounds for detention and may lead to arrest. Expanding threshold limits in law would reduce the number of people of color targeted by police. One policy would be to expand threshold limits for cannabis possession. This would drastically reduce the number of people of color targeted by police. While defining personal use to detailing cannabis threshold limits may be subject to vigorous debate, it can proceed based on the experience in other countries and states and with the input of cannabis users in a specific jurisdiction. For example, in Canada and most US states that have legalized cannabis, one can possess up to roughly 1 ounce of cannabis for personal consumption, with a few exceptions.[9] In Portugal, possession of up to 25 grams for personal consumption is decriminalized. Defining threshold limits in law would formalize other efforts currently under review. Although threshold limits remain a relic of prohibition, expanding limits complicates past police practices that justified pretextual stops based on police suspicion of possession.

It could also reduce departmental incentives to conduct pretextual stops targeting those "deemed suspicious," whereby establishing probable cause is based on smelling (or claiming to smell) cannabis. Police forces in New York, Oregon, and Colorado (Brown, 2022: 8–9) have reduced these practices, and this approach has the potential to lead to other reforms. For those possessing more than the threshold amount, *unless cannabis possession is directly associated with a crime*, police-led diversion to a community-based panel or committee should be preferred. Such an approach offers a means to overcome a significant challenge related to state-centric definitions of problem drug use. It can allow police to move away from the past practice of trying to fulfill roles associated with social workers or addiction counselors.

For police, communicating the benefits of such a policy is important. Police officers are some of the best collectors, purveyors, and distributors of intelligence about problem drug use (Russell & Keefe, 2015). However, we must encourage police to explicitly change their mission regarding drugs if we are to make the most of law enforcement's potential in post-prohibition judications. Changing the role of police could be tied to reinvesting public dollars in policing after the devastating consequences of the past few years. Instead of abolishing the police, the public should demand that we defund the War on Drugs and direct investments to combat felony crime and violence in communities worldwide. These could be combined with investments in responses that allow police to better address violence and other felonies.[10]

The role of middle management and sergeants is essential to instill and maintain police accountability (del Pozo et al., 2022; Walker & Katz, 2018). For law enforcement personnel who refuse to adapt, the administrative obligations on individual officers should be increased, creating additional layers of accountability, and the legal basis by which cannabis charges might be overturned at trial. For departments that cannot control their officers, cities and states could require citizen oversight boards with a specific mandate to monitor net widening and issue public reports naming individual officers who continue the over-policing of cannabis. While questions remain about how to establish, structure, staff, manage, and train the police and civilians who staff these units, this does not mean that reforming internal affairs/professional standards or external civilian oversight bodies as accountability mechanisms are unimportant or ineffective (USAID, 2020).

A final means to transform the culture around policing cannabis is to make it easier for citizens to sue police departments for false arrests, discrimination, or harassment. In many jurisdictions, police are typically immune from the financial impacts of these payouts. One means to regulate aversion is to reduce the standard for qualified immunity and restructure civilian payouts by moving them from taxpayer money to police department insurance policies (Ray, 2020a). This is a suggestion that has been a political nonstarter for years. This may be changing. For example, New York state lawmakers have proposed that individual police officers carry liability insurance (Ray, 2020a). In the US state of Virginia, efforts are underway to change the smell of cannabis from a primary offense to a secondary offense. This would mean state police in Virginia could not stop someone because they reported smelling cannabis (Pope, 2020). In addition, in 2020, the Independent Office of Police Complaints (IOPC) upheld the complaint of a Black male cyclist who was stopped and searched in Euston, London, stating police officers should not stop and search people because they smell of drugs.

While police reform is difficult, it is not impossible. In 2021, the Milwaukee Fire and Police Commission removed the use of no-knock search warrants from its standard operating procedures (Bentley, 2021). Banning no-knock search warrants has been a policy that activists, both locally and nationally, have been calling for since the death of Breonna Taylor, killed in her home by police in Louisville in 2020. In addition to banning police officers from seeking and executing no-knock search warrants, the commission expanded whistleblower protections and clarified that officers have an affirmative duty to report serious acts of misconduct and protect the reporting officers from retaliation. They also adopted a new discipline matrix, which lays out a uniform system of disciplining officers for various violations.

In 2022, President Biden signed an executive order outlining several policy reforms. The order directs all federal law enforcement agencies to adopt policies banning chokeholds and carotid restraints, adopt body camera policies, and limit the use of no-knock warrants to certain circumstances (Ciaramella, 2022). The order follows months of protest in 2020 in which an onslaught of images of the killing of unarmed Black people by police, including (but not limited to) Rayshard Brooks, Daniel Prude, George Floyd, and Breonna Taylor, forced many Americans to confront the racial injustices which animated the criminal justice system (Wheeldon & Heidt, 2023a). In addition, it adopts updated use-of-force standards that encourage de-escalation and direct the Attorney General to establish a "National Law Enforcement Accountability Database" to track police misconduct, based on the recognition that "police cannot fulfill their role to keep communities safe without public trust and confidence in law enforcement and the criminal justice system" (The White House, 2022).

Defining and Diverting Problem Drug Use
While rare, problem cannabis use does exist. Although it is generally tied to various other social, emotional, and psychological problems, there are situations in which people may be in possession of more than the proscribed amount. In these circumstances, a determination must be made about whether the person in question might benefit from being connected to local

resources or whether the possession of more than the threshold limit requires further intervention. In this regard, the discretion afforded to police to divert those possessing cannabis to various education or treatment programs is curious. Police are untrained and ill equipped to assess cannabis use or differentiate between occasional, chronic, or problem use. Excesses in criminal sentencing and incarceration are a function of the over-policing of cannabis. It is best seen as an outgrowth of an approach to policing designed to address middle- and upper-class White people's fear of crime and disorder (Simon, 2007).

Diversion programs are often presented as a progressive reform, which, while technically accurate, is a view that suffers from the soft bigotry of low expectations. Many diversion programs, of course, threaten prosecution if participants fail to comply with guidelines. In addition, the unconscious approval of coercive cannabis treatment is problematic (Ashton, 2008; Price et al., 2021; Spivakovsky et al., 2018; Stevens, 2012; Szasz, 2007) and based on exaggerated claims (Heidt & Wheeldon, 2022). As we explained in Chapter 6, influential researchers continue to cite old and methodologically suspect research that asserts up to 30 percent of people who try cannabis will develop a cannabis use disorder (Hasin et al., 2016; Wagner & Anthony, 2002). These findings have not been replicated (SAMHSA, 2020: 29). Askari and colleagues (2021) report that between 2002 and 2019, 6.1 percent of people reported using any cannabis use disorder (CUD) treatment.

Despite these findings, jurisdictions where cannabis has been decriminalized often invest in treatment programs, which exaggerate risks and are now constrained by administrative inertia (Price et al., 2021). One might reasonably wonder where are the increased cases of cannabis use disorder in states like Colorado and Washington or countries like Canada or Uruguay. As outlined in Chapter 6, the evidence for cannabis acting as a causal factor for many mental health disorders, including schizophrenia, has not been established (Hamilton & Monaghan, 2019). Recently, even those who have for decades been funded to uncover the harms of cannabis use now concede cannabis's relative safety and have belatedly admitted it is neither necessary nor sufficient to cause psychosis (D'Souza et al., 2022).

The uncomfortable and unethical blending of public safety goals through public health policies is pernicious (Newhart & Dolphin, 2019). It escalates and expands moral injury by increasing the influence of health-care providers, private treatment professionals, and mercurial addiction counselors (Aaronson & Rothschild-Elyassi, 2021; Gagnon et al., 2020). Critics might worry about the role of cannabis diversion schemes in providing a constant supply of clients to be treated (Isaacs, 2014) through predatory justice practices (Page & Soss, 2021).[11] Using the language of care and treatment to emphasize control and abstinence (Ashton, 2008) harms the credibility of legitimate drug education and treatment programs. As was pointed out fifty years ago, this undermines trust and may limit the potential that people will seek out treatment in the future (Kaplan, 1970).

Rethinking the role of diversion assumes the expanding practice of decriminalizing cannabis by expanding and escalating diversion programs is a problem. Coercing people who use cannabis to avoid a criminal record by participating in abstinence-based and stigma-laden programs proceeds from the idea that any cannabis use is hazardous. However, these diversion programs also suffer from institutional and systemic racism and the adverse carceral impacts that undermine civil rights and democratic values (Roberts, 2017). Inequalities within diversion programs persist. In one recent example, Sanchez and colleagues (2020) found ethnic, gender, and racial disparities among those obliged to attend a cannabis diversion program in Texas. Moving beyond the current practice of embedding support "*within* criminal sanctions, rather than acting as *alternatives*" (Price et al., 2021: 118, our emphasis), we are inherently skeptical of the role of police-led diversion for cannabis possession. Our concern, expressed throughout the book, is that while diversion creates the potential for decriminalizing cannabis possession, it does so by doubling down on stigma. In criminological terms, our worry is also based on the recognition that past efforts have merely shifted control from one set of correctional agencies to community-based agencies that adopt carceral assumptions and punitive priorities (Cohen, 1985). This extension of the medical model is deeply unethical (Stevens, 2012) and an example of the propensity and persistence of prohibitionist policies. However, engaging police and creating off-ramps for cannabis possession beyond the threshold limit but not directly connected to a crime requires creating credible alternatives.

Law and Society: Cannabis, Addiction, and Stigma

Developing alternatives to existing cannabis diversion programs means addressing a fundamental assumption that runs through drug policy of all kinds (Hart, 2017). Is it reasonable to say drugs cause addiction if most drug users never develop substance use disorders (Cole, 2022)? The international consensus, represented by a decade of reports by the United

Nations, is that problem drug use is an issue for a small minority of those who use any drug.[12] While this might have led to the de-escalation of efforts to associate cannabis use with addiction risks, it has not. As presented in Chapter 6, the political nature of cannabis disorders is clear. As cannabis has been decriminalized and legalized, CUDs have remained constant (Askari et al., 2021; SAMHSA, 2020: 29), while CUD treatment admissions are decreasing (Mennis & Stahler, 2020; Mennis et al., 2021; Philbin et al., 2019). For cannabis, the largest risk is for the small number of youth with pre-existing risk factors associated with schizophrenia (D'Souza et al., 2022). Cannabis use has never been shown to be a *causal* factor for schizophrenia (Hamilton & Monaghan, 2019).

Lewis (2015) has challenged the BDMA model and standard views of addiction by incorporating neuroscientific research alongside insights from people who use drugs and who describe themselves as having confronted addiction. He concludes that addiction is a learning phenomenon and that viewing addiction as a disease is harmful and counterproductive for those struggling with problem substance use. Likewise, Hart (2017) argues this demands a rethinking of addiction. Rather than focusing on the substance's specific properties, addiction is best seen as a pre-existing personal vulnerability based on social, economic, psychological, or circumstantial factors. These dynamics precede the drugs themselves, which can lead to addiction. This is consistent with Johann Hari's work (2015) and suggests addiction is born of social factors and psychological deficits, not drugs.

The power of stigmatizing drugs and exaggerating addiction has shaped the treatment philosophy in the United States and increasingly around the world. It is based on the twelve steps of Alcoholics Anonymous, which is a culturally prominent but psychologically problematic means to address problem drug use (Szalavitz, 2021). This approach requires people with addiction to accept they have a disease and engage in recovery based on surrendering to a "higher power," moral inventory, making amends for wrongs done and attending meetings.[13] Even as the *Diagnostic and Statistical Manual of Mental Disorders* used by psychiatric professionals no longer labels addiction as "dependence," the misdiagnosis of addictive disorders is common. This can lead to a cascade of negative outcomes, including stigma, discontinuation of needed medications, undue scrutiny of both patients and physicians, and criminal consequences (Szalavitz et al., 2021).

Research demonstrates that when patients are described as "abusing" substances instead of suffering from a "disorder," clinicians are more likely to recommend punitive approaches (Kelly et al., 2010; Kelly & Westerhoff,

2010; Van Boekel et al., 2013). Applied to cannabis, this view of addiction justifies a range of problematic policies, including over-policing, limiting cannabis sales, restricting the cannabis industry, and continuing to apply public safety-informed approaches to those who use cannabis. As discussed in Chapter 5, while pathologizing people who use cannabis allows the system to force people into programs they do not choose (Lowman et al., 1987), the role of stigmatizing language also impedes reform. A shift from paternalistic and coercive public health models to approaches based on autonomy, agency, and respect, values that serve as the basis of therapeutic relationships is required (Price et al., 2021). Essential here is providing support that is voluntary, evidence-based, and can be refused without criminal justice consequences (Stoicescu et al., 2022: 134).

Connecting Voluntary Services

As Heidt (2021) observed, the attempt to control behavior in ways that reduce freedom and constrain individuals is unlikely to be the basis of sustained change. Nevertheless, it persists because of our collective desire to control the uncontrollable. This sentiment is captured in a passage from the novel, *A Clockwork Orange* (Burgess, 1962: 95):

> It may not be nice to be good, little [Prisoner] 6655321. It may be horrible to be good. And when I say that to you, I realize how self-contradictory that sounds. I know I shall have many sleepless nights about this. What does God want? Does God want goodness or the choice of goodness? Is a man who chooses the bad perhaps in some way better than a man who has the good imposed upon him? Deep and hard questions, little [Prisoner] 6655321.

The mistakes of the past need not be relied upon to determine the future. While creating community-based alternatives that are credible, consistent, and effective are complex, models do exist. These exemplars focus on engaging trained volunteers, are rooted in relationship building, and proceed in ways that are based on mutual respect.

In this sense, diversion programs can be used to stabilize and support those referred by conveying the ethical message of acceptance. Kathy Fox's work (2012, 2013, 2014) on Community Justice Centers (CJCs) and the role of communities in Vermont in supporting those in conflict with the law reveals some important lessons. The value of CJC-based programming includes mitigating exclusion and isolation, embracing destigmatization, and creating relationships based on mutual respect and shared obligation. This can be achieved

> through the actions of community members who communicate a sense of shared moral space, and a genuine sense of belonging... [volunteers] create normative and ordinary relationships of mutual obligation and respect, and aid in the de-labeling process focusing on the other attributes of offenders beyond their criminality.
>
> (Fox, 2015: 82)

Replacing coerced treatment models in use by numerous diversion programs with a "nonjudgmental" approach focused on care, treatment, and harm reduction requires a paradigm shift (Ali & Stevens, 2022) and requires a commitment to variation to meet local needs and evaluative approaches that consider how voluntary and community-based role can be assessed in meaningful ways (Tanguay et al., 2022). When diversion amounts to the supervised connection to existing resources and practices designed to offer community support when requested, it serves as an authentic alternative to the expansion of the punitive character of the criminal justice system. It affirms, rather than demeans, and offers access to voluntary treatment based on consent and respect. Used in this way, diversion programs can provide access to support and services for those whose cannabis use is linked to other social, emotional, or psychological challenges.

While creating community-based alternatives that are credible, consistent, and effective is complex, models do exist that show potential and promise. For example, in Portugal, replacing penal sanctions with referrals to Commissions for the Dissuasion of Drug Addiction allow people who use drugs to be treated by a technical team of health and social experts. However, as the name applies, it assumes anyone who uses any drug is at risk for addiction. While the role of experts is essential, in some cases, community volunteers may play a more important function (Fox, 2012). This is consistent with calls for restorative justice to empower communities to stand up to the harms of a century of cannabis prohibition (Hudak, 2021).

Most cannabis users do not, and never will, need high levels of community and social support. However, harnessing the vital role of the community when use becomes problematic can be protective against the punitive character of the traditional system. Ensuring these supports are based on choice, consent, and respect affirms community-based connections and ethical treatments. However, the most important conceptual change here is reducing stigma by viewing cannabis use as something that may not necessarily signify issues requiring criminal justice interventions. Just as a community member might reasonably worry about someone smoking more than a pack of cigarettes a day or consistently consuming more than three alcoholic drinks daily, someone who uses cannabis in ways that interfere with other aspects of their lives might also lead others to worry. This worry need not require formal intrusion in the form of compulsory drug treatment. Instead, it might trigger meetings where community members signal their concerns, offer their support, and inform people of existing services. As jurisdictions pursue cannabis reform, it may be useful to start slowly and formalize the approaches that work best to reduce stigma and change the culture at the root of prohibitive cannabis policies.

Conclusion

This chapter presented policies consistent with a model of meaningful cannabis decriminalization that creates the conditions under which a legalized regulated model is more likely to succeed. We reviewed established categories of cannabis reform based both on existing models and a novel construction of decriminalization. While legalization has increased since 2012, the role of criminalization has shifted from pursuing criminal punishments to mandatory substance abuse treatment. This blurring of modes of control allows for increasing intrusiveness in the name of rehabilitation while allowing some to suggest the War on Drugs is over. Increasingly, cannabis decriminalization is married with police-led "diversion" provisions where a criminal charge/sentence is suspended or reduced in favor of alternative interventions. While criminal punishment remains on hold if they comply with the alternative measures, these requirements may be numerous, extensive, and onerous (Fischer et al., 2021). These developments are consistent with Cohen's (1985) worry that decriminalization can contribute to the expansion of state control.

Given these concerns, we focused on revisiting existing regulatory models and assessed cannabis policy-based harm. Although these harms apply to a variety of efforts to regulate cannabis, including prohibition and legalization, we focused on policies consistent with decriminalization. By considering models of cannabis regulation through the concepts of tolerance and aversion, we presented a model of meaningful decriminalization designed to destigmatize cannabis and people who use it. Specifically, we argue increasing threshold limits, providing remedies for over-policing, and reframing the mission of police offer one means to reduce a host of harms connected to public safety and public health models of cannabis regulation. This could de-emphasize the policing of cannabis, encourage prosecutors to decline to pursue cannabis possession cases even after an arrest has been made, and begin to shift from mandated programs toward voluntary and community-based models of reform.

This shift means diversion programs amount to increased access to existing voluntary treatment options. In this way, diversion programs can provide access to support and services for those whose cannabis use is linked to other social, emotional, or psychological challenges. While most cannabis users do not, and never will, need such support, in harm reduction terms, harnessing the vital role of the community when use becomes problematic can be protective against the punitive character of the criminal justice system. Ensuring these supports are based on choice, consent, and respect affirms community-based connections and ethical treatments, returning agency to individuals who may need support because they can be freely declined.

Such an approach leaves the door open to subsequent treatment when individuals are ready to bring their best selves to confront the traumas that may have led to their problem use. Focusing on harm reduction as a conceptual lodestar can inform the wide variety of efforts to decriminalize cannabis. Changes based first on tolerance, diversion, and support may lead some jurisdictions to embrace legalization. In these cases, a different set of questions may emerge. Recalibrating public health to focus on reducing harm and benefit maximization requires blending governance approaches and reimagining cannabis culture. In Chapter 8, we turn to how new approaches to legalization and regulation might proceed.

Notes

1. For instance, In the United Kingdom, recent pronouncements by both Conservative Prime Minister Boris Johnson and Opposition leader Keir Starmer suggest cannabis policy will remain punitive and steeped in prohibition myths. The obstinance to cannabis reform allows profound criminological harms to continue, especially for Black Britons, who have faced disproportionate criminal justice intrusions for decades. In May 2022, London Mayor Sadiq Kahn announced a new London Drugs Commission to review (UK) law, with a focus on cannabis and racial justice, in partnership with University College London. Labour MPs, including those in the Shadow government, angrily warned it would

hurt their electoral chances in the next election. When the United Kingdom eventually emerges from its racially retrograde, bipartisan, anti-science slumber, it will have several international options to consider.

On Keir Starmer, see https://twitter.com/LBC/status/1483006601850236932?s=20&t=pLnXvctq8lVQn-BS9qJ8pg. For racial disparities in the United Kingdom, see White (2021). For more on Sadiq Kahn's commission, see Low (2022). The Labour backlash was reported at Waugh (2022).

2. Stevens and colleagues (2019: 3) define depenalization as reducing the use of existing criminal sanctions by state actors. Defining depenalization as a major class within cannabis liberalization is out of place with current practices in 2021 and risks further confusing an already vexing area of study. Depenalization is said to occur when possessing cannabis remains a criminal offense but the punishment for the offense is reduced. One example is the shift in possession of cannabis from a felony to a misdemeanor that has occurred in many US states, sometimes called "defelonization." However, depenalization may occur without legislative changes. In these cases, existing criminal sanctions are no longer enforced in specific circumstances. The difficulty is how many unlike examples this definition captures. For example, while post-conviction or post-sentence diversion measures such as US drug courts (Nolan, 2002) and California's Proposition 36 (Inciardi, 2004) may reduce sentence severity for those found possessing cannabis, the penalties associated with a criminal conviction remain (Stevens et al., 2019). While the punishment for possessing cannabis may literally be reduced in such cases, it is hard to see how such approaches could be considered the same in the same category as a national policy (as in the Netherlands), premised on a blanket refusal to pursue arrest or prosecution for possessing small amounts of cannabis.

3. This was first reported by Riley-Smith (2021). For more recent coverage, see Grierson (2021).

4. One might be the potential for "whitelash," defined as the resistance to racial equality by White people (Bonilla-Silva, 2020). This pales in comparison to the harms from the persistence of racially disproportionate policing. For example, Chohlas-Wood et al. (2022) show that Black and Hispanic individuals detained under New York and Chicago's stop-and-frisk programs were frisked more often than comparably risky White individuals and faced policing tactics that were both unnecessary and discriminatory.

5. The authors point to the analysis by Equity and Transformation (EAT, 2019).

6. Brown points to the Museum of Tolerance online teachers' guide, "Definitions," under "Define: Vocabulary and Concepts." See https://www.museumoftolerance.com/assets/documents/teacher-guide.pdf.

7. See, e.g. in the US state of Virginia, where efforts are underway to change the smell of cannabis from a primary offense to a secondary offense. This would mean state police in Virginia could not stop someone because they reported smelling

cannabis (Pope, 2020). In 2020, the Independent Office of Police Complaints (IOPC) upheld the complaint of a Black male cyclist who was stopped and searched in Euston, London, stating police officers should not stop and search people because they smell of drugs (Childs, 2020).
8. Mary Mapes Dodge created this character and Hans Brinker is and is not based on any actual Dutch folk heroes. Since the book's publication in 1865, the Little Dutch Boy has become part of American pop culture, even though most Dutch people have never heard about him (Hoitink, 2017).
9. A few states allow people to possess considerably more cannabis for personal use. For example, New Mexico and Washington, DC allow up to 2 ounces, while New Yorkers are allowed to possess up to 3 ounces.
10. See https://twitter.com/aodespair/status/1456666960247263243?s=11.
11. In the United States, a troubling example connecting cannabis, racism, predation, and diversion involves a cannabis diversion program operated by the Maricopa County Attorney's Office (MACO). In Arizona, possession of any amount of marijuana can be charged as a felony. To avoid criminal prosecution, defendants in Maricopa County are offered a diversion program where they are required to pay $950 and $15–17 per test for drug and alcohol testing up to three times a week. In 2016, it was reported that $1.6 million was collected from diversion fees and that three-quarters of defendants referred to the program were sent on cannabis charges in Arizona (FFJC, 2019). A year later, an individual stopped in Maricopa County, Arizona, faced up to two years in prison and a maximum fine of $150,000 if she refused to consent to enroll in a marijuana diversion program. Completing the $950 program would allow her to avoid prosecution for the high crime of possessing a small amount of cannabis (Dewan, 2018).
12. Cole points to a number of sources: UNODC (2021b: 20), which notes *13 per cent, are estimated to suffer from drug use disorders, meaning that their drug use is harmful to the point where they may experience drug dependence and/or require treatment.* This claim has been consistent in the World Drug Reports and other WHO/United Nations reports over the past decade or so, e.g. UNODC (2012); UNODC–WHO (2021: 20) suggests this number may be much smaller.
13. For an overview of programs, see Department of Health and Human Services (2020).

8
Legalization, Polymorphic Governance, and Barriers to Cannabis Policy

Introduction

In Chapter 7, we argued that the reliance on public safety and public health models of cannabis regulation can no longer be justified, given the high costs and severe social consequences. In response, we presented a model of meaningful decriminalization designed to de-emphasize public safety models and re-calibrate public health models to avoid expanding social control in the name of cannabis policy reform. Informed by Cohen (1985) and linked to harm reduction, this model requires regulation aversion (Brown, 2006) and constraining the broad stigma that persists regarding cannabis (Reid, 2020). While decriminalization represents legal renegotiation, legalizing cannabis involves moral reflection. Emphasizing the legal aspects of moral-legal renegotiation risks ignoring the moral questions that have long been associated with cannabis. One question surrounds how to frame the benefits of cannabis.

As a sign of the changing social status of cannabis, a substance once criminalized and punished was suddenly deemed indispensable. For example, as part of a coordinated COVID-19 response, most Canadian provinces declared non-medical cannabis retail sales an "essential service" (Canadian Centre on Substance Use and Addiction, 2021). While Canada represents an important model of legal regulation, others exist (Transform Drug Policy Foundation, 2021: 37–45). In addition to legitimating and regulating cannabis production and supply, approaches to legal regulation vary in how people can access cannabis. For example, access may be limited to government retail stores, as occurs in some provinces in Canada, or by allowing a mix of regulated access, including pharmacies, social clubs, or home growing, as in Uruguay. The United States provides the most robust role for a regulated commercial market. While still constrained in numerous ways, many fear that a less regulated legal market may emerge based on self-regulation, as opposed to one monitored by the state.

In this chapter, we combine elements of unitary monomorphic regulatory models by applying the concept of polymorphic cannabis regulation. As a result of this approach, we extend a model of consumer cannabis by linking assumptions and aspects of medical and commercial models. Central to this model is ensuring that a racial equity lens informs retail cannabis. This approach represents a profound reimaging of existing models of legal cannabis. It may also mean embracing advertising and marketing that promote cannabis products *while* rooting such approaches in messaging that promotes responsible cannabis. While we are not the first to consider cannabis and polymorphic regulation (Aaronson & Rothschild-Elyassi, 2021), our effort combines regulatory models in novel ways and offers a conceptual framework to guide policies and practices.

We revisit the two common visions of cannabis policy and outline specific policy reforms consistent with the polymorphic frameworks outlined in Chapter 7. Consistent with Cohen's (1985) concerns, we forecast resistance to cannabis legalization, outline potential regulatory barriers, and begin to consider possible responses to the inevitable pushback. These can be based on existing law. Identifying ideological and moral aversion toward cannabis is a necessary first step in any process designed to confront this outlook. To begin to consider this question, we reflect on how to regulate aversion and present a means to assess readiness for reform in various jurisdictions.

Regulating Cannabis: From Harm Reduction to Benefit Maximization

As discussed in Chapter 2, cannabis has been cultivated, traded, and consumed for various reasons and in numerous forms throughout human history (Beweley-Taylor et al., 2014; Booth, 2003; Mills, 2003; Seddon & Floodgate, 2020). As efforts to legalize and regulate cannabis increase around the world, Seddon and Floodgate (2020) consider several questions as part of their effort to understand cannabis regulation. They ask: how do we balance creating a potentially lucrative legal cannabis industry with protecting public health? How do we hardwire social and racial justice into our reform initiatives? How do we build a cannabis trade that is environmentally sustainable? Our effort in this book is to frame regulatory approaches around explicitly acknowledging the damage done by criminalizing cannabis, which has led to calls to view cannabis policy as harm reduction (Nadelmann & LaSalle, 2017).

As we explored in some detail in Chapter 7, the various forms of decriminalization have not reduced a range of harms. While tolerance offers one means to suspend antagonistic reactions to cannabis use, it may be insufficient. In the Netherlands, tolerance refers to leniency regarding cannabis possession for police and prosecutors. For example,

> Dutch tolerance makes it possible to differentiate between dangerous and less dangerous forms of questionable behavior and to focus less on moral judgments. Tolerance has not impeded efforts against organized crime, nor has it much influenced levels of drug abuse . . . [and] are more effective than those in other Western countries.
>
> (Buruma, 2007: 73)

Embracing tolerance means conceding that people will use drugs regardless of the laws and requires taking steps to focus on not alienating and stigmatizing users (Buruma, 2007). Tolerance, however, is not acceptance. Meaningful decriminalization in many jurisdictions may require efforts to regulate aversion.

Confronting the aversion at the root of many drug policies is part of harm reduction. While decriminalizing the use of cannabis can reduce harms associated with public safety models of regulation, legalization represents the ultimate form of harm reduction. Indeed, legalization "eliminates the many negative consequences of cannabis criminalization for consumers" (Nadelmann & LaSalle, 2017: 4). However, the concept of "harm reduction" alone may not be suitable for justifications seeking to expand legal cannabis to maximize the health benefits of medical cannabis. As early as 1998, some suggested the failure to catalog the benefits of cannabis was a "missed opportunity" (Grinspoon & Bakalar, 1998). Increasingly, cannabis policy is being reframed as a means to "maximize benefits," not just "reduce" harms.[1]

Research indicates that cannabis is far less dangerous and addictive than currently legal substances like alcohol and tobacco and safer than many over-the-counter or prescription pharmaceuticals (Grotenhermen & Russo, 2002). In Canada, a Senate Special Committee on Illegal Drugs recognized that limiting medical access unduly restricted the availability of a substance that, when used, could result in health benefits (Nolan, 2002). This recognition suggested the government had legal and ethical responsibilities that extended "beyond simply reducing the perceived individual and social harms of cannabis use: the federal government has to initiate policies that maximize the personal and public health potential" (Lucas, 2009: 300). This requires reframing drugs from substances that represent risk toward a metaphor of drugs as "tools" (Tupper, 2007: 302).

This shift helps justify governance strategies that move beyond policies based on reducing potential harms, such as decriminalization, and toward systems that seek "benefit maximization" which represents "the other side of the harm reduction coin" (Tupper, 2007: 301). As applied to cannabis, Lucas (2012: 131) notes:

> If we are to ever benefit from drug policies based on science, reason and compassion, national governments will need to abandon the misinformation that underscores drug prohibition, and to start promoting and supporting research into cannabis and cannabinoids as both a relatively safe and effective medicine in the treatment of chronic pain and other serious medical conditions, and as a potential "exit drug" for problematic substance use.

As explored in Chapter 4, Sifaneck & Kaplan (1995) found cannabis served to curtail other kinds of drug use. However, its potential as medicine, at least in clinical terms, is less established.

In North America, medical cannabis is widely available. While in Canada, some describe the relative inaccessibility of cannabis through the legal medical and non-medical systems (Valleriani et al., 2020), thirty-four US states have medical programs currently serving patients (Mize, 2020: 3). Although medical cannabis is available in Europe, there is a gap between legal status and availability to patients. This ranges from more established access in Austria, Finland, Germany, the Netherlands, and Portugal (Seddon & Floodgate, 2020), to less in Denmark, France, Greece, Ireland, and the United Kingdom. In other countries, trial periods and pilot projects making medical cannabis more accessible are underway. However, they remain constrained. For some, the failure to provide access to medical cannabis increasingly appears to be an "ethical issue" (Nutt, 2022).

The focus on medical cannabis as benefit maximization is important. However, cannabis offers some benefits as a recreational intoxicant. Whether to relieve stress, promote creativity, increase intimacy, or enhance a range of experiences, there are various anecdotal benefits associated with the responsible use of cannabis (Cornwell, 2021). While these have not been the focus of sustained research based on benefit maximization, it is worth considering how this is likely to change in jurisdictions where cannabis is legal. These jurisdictions are wrestling with how to develop responsible approaches to regulation. For example,

> Designing a cannabis policy involves unavoidable trade-offs between the goals of minimizing the harmful effects and maximizing the benefits of cannabis use, while minimizing any harm that arises from our efforts to regulate cannabis use, whether that is by criminalizing personal use and cannabis supply or by legalizing its production and sale.
>
> (Hall & Pacula, 2003: 285–286)

Two decades later, these questions remain central. The United States remains a central battleground. In 2023, a series of laws, old and new, may reappear in the United States, as outlined in Table 8.1. The number of laws under consideration is striking.

Other cannabis-based legislation may also be considered in 2023. Some examples include the Capital Lending and Investment for Marijuana Businesses (CLIMB) Act, the Veterans Equal Access Act, the GRAM Act, Common Sense Cannabis Reform for Veterans, the Small Businesses and Medical Professionals Act, the Small and Homestead Independent Producers (SHIP) Act, the VA Medicinal Cannabis Research Act, and the Homegrown Act. Additionally, the passage of the Medical Marijuana and Cannabidiol Research Expansion Act is expected (Weiss & Morel, 2023). However, future cannabis policy must contend with multiple seemingly competing objectives.

Polymorphic Governance, Evidence, and Regulatory Cannabis

This book's five monomorphic visions of cannabis control are connected to existing cannabis policies. However, no country or jurisdiction relies on just one regulatory model to guide cannabis policy. The regulatory state has been a focus of research for regulation and governance scholarship since the 1990s (Aaronson & Rothschild-Elyassi, 2021; Braithwaite, 2000; Levi-Faur, 2014; Majone, 1997). In recent decades, some argue the welfare state, governed by Keynesian techniques of demand management, has shifted to a new form of the regulatory state based on a risk society. In criminology, Kevin Haggerty (2004) considered the consequences of new social forces and mentalities on the influence of criminological expertise. These forces, including

Table 8.1 Expected cannabis legislation in 2023

Name	Previous sponsor(s)	Focus
Cannabis Administration and Opportunity Act (CAOA)	Chuck Schumer (D-NY) Ron Wyden (D-OR) Cory Booker (D-NJ)	Decriminalizes cannabis by removing the drug from the Controlled Substances Act (CSA); reduces barriers to research, restorative justice, equity, taxation and regulation, and industry practices
States Reform Act (SRA)	Nancy Mace's (R-SC)	Federally decriminalize cannabis by deferring to state powers over prohibition and commercial regulation
The Marijuana Opportunity Reinvestment and Expungement (MORE) Act	Rep. Jerry Nadler (D-NY),	Decriminalizes cannabis by removing the drug from the Controlled Substances Act and eliminating criminal penalties for anyone who manufactures, distributes, or possesses cannabis
Harnessing Opportunities by Pursuing Expungement (Hope) Act	Dave Joyce (R-OH) Alexandria Ocasio-Cortez (D-NY)	Assists states with expunging cannabis offenses by reducing the financial and administrative burden of such efforts through federal grants
Secure and Fair Enforcement (SAFE) Banking Act.	Ed Perlmutter (D-CO)	Allows financial institutions to provide traditional banking services to cannabis businesses in states that have legalized cannabis, allowing businesses to access lines of credit, loans, and other sorts of investments

Source: Authors.

"the neo-liberal combination of market competition, privatized institutions and decentered, and increasingly divisive media ecosystems, shape regulatory governance" (Braithwaite, 2000: 222).

Although of relevance to policing and control of crime, this focus has been recently refined based on the need to better define and describe, in scholarly terms, the state's essence to combat the fragmentation that has happened as a result of competing research paradigms (Aaronson & Rothschild-Elyassi,

2021). In the United States, some scholars suggest "[T]he very multiplicity of labels suggests their limitations. . . . These scattered subsystems can only gesture at the background system that comprises governance in its entirety" (Orren & Skowronek, 2017: 9). This may be because assessing state regulatory models often proceeds by examining distinct characteristics associated with their assumptions, goals, approaches to legitimacy, and policy instruments (Majone, 1994). These models are often described as competing with other regulatory approaches for governing influence within a jurisdiction (Dunleavy & O'Leary, 1987).

Cannabis is a substance that lends itself to what has been called a "blended model of regulation" (Aaronson & Rothschild-Elyassi, 2021). As Chapter 7 demonstrates, constraining public safety models requires extending policies that address racial disparities associated with controlling cannabis *and* investing in and incentivizing other approaches to criminal justice reforms (Brown, 2022). In addition, recalibrating public health models mean embracing harm reduction by acknowledging the moral injury associated with mandated cannabis treatment, coerced diversion programming, and abstentionist messaging. Understanding how this approach to blending principles from unitary governance models is assisted by theoretical work (Levi-Faur, 2014; Scott, 2014) that expresses polymorphic governance with reference to chemical properties. For example, a substance is polymorphic if it "crystallizes in two or more different forms" (Mann, 1993: 75).

While these crystalline forms differ physically, they are otherwise the same. Far from being singular and centralized, modern states are polymorphous power networks in which different morphs of the state interact in ways that both "complement and counteract one another" (Aaronson & Rothschild-Elyassi, 2021: 6). Polymorphic governance allows different forms of authority to ascend, depending on the circumstances. Although adopting this approach usefully frames the complex interactions within nascent efforts to regulate cannabis,[2] it complicates the bureaucratic need to define policies in ways that can be communicated, implemented, or assessed. Moreover, critics of such an approach might reasonably fear that the state could use this formulation to justify any policy by reconfiguring justifications as needed to benefit one political calculation or another. If cannabis policy exists as an area of polymorphic governance, what is to be done when tensions emerge and multiple morphs strive for influence? Regulatory governance requires considering some fundamental principles.

In 2020, the International Drug Policy Consortium (IDPC) published twenty principles that serve as recommendations to guide the responsible legal regulation of cannabis. The IDPC serves as a global network of 192 nongovernmental organizations (NGOs); focuses on issues related to drug production, trafficking, and use; and is committed to "evidence-based policies that are effective at reducing drug-related harm" (IDPC, n.d.). The principles it outlines are consistent with many of the abovementioned concerns but are organized based on five key governance considerations. These include protecting the health and rights of those who use cannabis, advancing social justice, promoting robust and sustainable supply chains and business models, removing punishments for cannabis use, and adopting a gender-sensitive approach to redress the previous exclusion of women (IDPC, 2020). In addition, the report states:

> new regulatory frameworks should include mechanisms for collecting, analysing and disseminating comprehensive data on drug markets and drug use, as legal regulation is an ongoing iterative process that responds to the evolution of the market, and to lessons learnt.
> (IDPC, 2020)

The IDPC notes that more than fifty countries have adopted regulatory frameworks for medical cannabis and that a growing number of jurisdictions have regulated recreational cannabis use. As more legal frameworks are established, reformers need to consider to what extent they advance social justice, inclusion, and human rights. Of interest is how the report echoes and further specifies the concerns expressed in this book. Something of a paradox is emerging. On the one hand, social reformers who seek drug prohibition may need to embrace the rationality of the market if they are to minimize the irrationality at the root of prohibition. On the other hand, relying on the market to secure cannabis liberalization will not be enough. One concern is the potential role of Big Cannabis. For example, the report notes that

> Because Canada has been the first large-scale market to regulate cannabis for both medical and non-medical uses, Canadian corporations have positioned themselves as lead global investors, intervening in medical and non-medical markets as diverse as Colombia, France, Mexico, or the United States (USA). In Latin America, Canadian companies have been estimated to control over 70% of both the Colombian and the Uruguayan markets.
> (IDPC, 2020)

Another concern surrounds social justice. As we have discussed in some detail, prohibitionist drug policies have adversely affected communities around the globe. While regulating cannabis through a legal framework offers a means to normalize cannabis use, it may also provide a means to make amends for the harms caused by decades of repressive drug policies. The IDCP report details various reparative measures that can be applied to support those who suffered under cannabis prohibition. Restitution measures include prison release through amnesties, expunging criminal records, and investments in community reintegration projects to begin the process of meaningful redress. This includes providing opportunities for historically disadvantaged populations to participate in the growing cannabis industry.

This report can be seen alongside other recent efforts to consider cannabis regulation. For example, Decorte et al. (2020: 5) provide a series of "case studies of cannabis policy reforms and the experiences of scholars from the alcohol and tobacco research fields to inform this unfolding process of cannabis reform." A central feature of that book is the effort to explore the range of "middle-ground" options that suggest some lessons to guide cannabis reform. Corva & Meisel's (2021) collection offers another international exploration by focusing on the United States, Uruguay, Morocco, and the United Kingdom. By organizing their book to focus on research programs in areas as diverse as governance, public health, markets and society, ecology and the environment, and culture and social change, they invite "researchers to a landscape of entanglement . . . [and] . . . social issues entangled in policies and practices of legalization" (Corva & Meisel, 2021: 16). Another contribution by Fischer, Daldegan-Bueno, and Reuter (2021: 58) suggests five research areas of particular interest for criminologists, including deterrence, illicit markets, use enforcement, impaired driving, and crime.

Based on a literature review relating to outcomes of cannabis regulatory change, Oldfield et al. (2021) found five themes that emerged across the breadth of the literature. These included: normalization, economics, health, community, and gatekeeping. However, they conclude the amount of commentary and opinion about the effect of cannabis regulation has created too much "white noise" within the field. At the same time, they call for collecting pre- and post-implementation data to guide research and policy development when cannabis laws change. Our review indicates a different problem. Despite the increasing interest in understanding cannabis legalization, too few criminologists have provided specific models based on research compiled to date. Such an approach is not for the faint of heart. It requires summarizing existing research, reviewing existing models, and attempting to identify likely limitations. Of immediate interest is how to present existing evidence to guide future policy.

From Decriminalization to Legal Regulation

Decriminalization designed to destigmatize cannabis and constrain the contagious carceral impulse of the state makes the legalization and regulation of cannabis more likely to reduce harm and maximize benefits. However, future approaches are likely to build on past work (Hall & Pacula, 2003; Hyshka, 2009; Lenton, 2004) and contemporary thinking on how best to document existing evidence around cannabis liberalization (Sevigny et al., 2021). However, like decriminalization, we believe responsible regulation must be based on readiness indicators. These indicators can assess whether cannabis legalization is feasible and what approach is likely to sustain public support and meet the needs of different jurisdictions. As we have noted, cannabis is a case study in legal–moral renegotiation. To succeed, legal changes need the support of the public. Establishing an acceptable regulatory framework may be difficult if the public is not supportive. Access to the product could be hampered or delayed (e.g., dispensaries may not be allowed in some municipalities), allowing the illicit market to benefit from increased demand.

While it is helpful to have the support and some input from the police to ensure consistent enforcement of the proposed changes and forewarning of unintended consequences, in many cases, law enforcement already supports change. Not enforcing cannabis laws consistently has long been an approach by individual officers who realize this is not an efficient use of police resources. Operationally, however, a focus on cannabis remains entrenched. Until recently, the Byrne Formula Grant Program required law enforcement agencies in the United States to specify the number of overall drug warrants, drug arrests, and drug seizures when applying for federal grants (Balko, 2013). Prioritizing drug crimes over other investigations often meant focusing on cannabis. It tended to justify unequal and problematic policing practices—specifically against communities of color. Involving the police in drug reform is necessary. However, over-reliance on law enforcement has negative consequences for policy reform. Other voices must be heard and taken seriously by policymakers.

Finally, as implied above, it is also important to have the support and input of people who use drugs and drug activist groups when changing the system (Hyshka, 2009; Lenton, 2004). This is somewhat obvious—if people who use drugs do not support the system, they will continue to support illicit markets. Insight from these groups is often overlooked or minimized. However, an emerging area of research seeks to use lived experiences and practical knowledge of people who use drugs to inform policy (see, e.g., Jansons, 2020;

Lancaster et al., 2014, 2015; Tutenges et al., 2015). Pursuing legal regulation leads to another set of questions (Oldfield et al., 2021). As we demonstrated in Chapter 6, past research on cannabis is not reliable. Based on poor definitions, limited designs, and assumptions, older research continues to be cited and furthers stigma-laden views about cannabis and the people who use it.

In place of poorly designed correlational studies, efforts to decriminalize and legalize cannabis have created natural experiments which lend themselves to better study designs, focused data collection, and more detailed analysis strategies. This has allowed not only for comparisons between and among states but also for analysis before and after legalization. For example, more recent case–control studies, time series analysis, and generalized linear spline models focused on time-varying effect modification have produced findings that challenge past conclusions. In addition, policymakers can rely on post-prohibition cannabis research as they consider how best to define and regulate cannabis markets, including the type of laws needed, issues around commercial supply, retail licenses, caregiver provisions, product provisions, issues surrounding advertising/marketing, and economic/financial concerns. Table 8.2 suggests some of these issues, questions, and options.

The answers to these questions will lead to various policies and priorities. We have summarized our reading of international cannabis research and analysis to further assist policymakers. While we emphasize research conducted in jurisdictions where cannabis is legal and findings that appear consistently, important nuance emerges from qualitative and ethnographic research. The number of qualitative researchers engaging people who use cannabis, the costs of criminalization, and the complexity of liberalization are increasing. Studies in Canada (Heidt & Wheeldon, 2022), Norway (Sandberg, 2008, 2013), Sweden (Feltmann et al., 2021), Nigeria (Nelson, 2021), Mexico (Agoff et al., 2021), and Poland (Wanke et al., 2022) offer profound insights.

Eleven Evidence-Based Edicts for Cannabis Policymakers

Below, we present eleven edicts that can guide policymakers as they engage in cannabis liberalization. These can be divided into things to embrace, including the realities of race and the need to engage police, and things to avoid, such as local bans, over-regulation, and demarketing. Together, these provide a clear path forward that can assist jurisdictions considering cannabis liberalization to avoid past mistakes and plan for the challenges to come.

Table 8.2 *Legalization and regulation of cannabis*

Category	Key question	Possible replies
Legal provisions	Under what legal regime will regulation operate?	No regulation of cannabis; comprehensive medical cannabis law; comprehensive recreational cannabis law (including medical)
Economic/ financial	How will taxes and banking regulations be adjusted?	Minimal changes; changes so consistent with alcohol/tobacco; new and specific provisions designed for cannabis as new market
Commercial supply	What sort of restrictions will be placed on commercial operations that supply cannabis?	None; will require registration and annual licensing; will require workplace safety rules; will implement pesticide and fertilizer controls; will establish cannabis waste regulations
Commercial production	What sort of restrictions will be placed on commercial production?	None; labeling/packaging; testing requirements; product tracking; some of the above; all of the above
Commercial retail	What sort of restrictions will be placed on commercial retail?	None; limit sales; limit number of dispensaries/retail outlets; create zoning/density restrictions; allow cannabis cafes; allow delivery services; allow order services
Caregiver provisions	How can caregivers access cannabis for others?	No requirements; create registry/ identification cards; require specific caregiver qualifications; some of the above; all of the above
Marketing/ advertising	What advertising and product display regulations will apply to cannabis?	No advertising or display; limited advertising and displays; consistent with alcohol/tobacco; no limitations

Source: Authors.

1. **Recognize the racism.**
   One of the most consistent findings in the literature over decades is that criminalizing cannabis adversely affects people of color, their families, and their communities. Moreover, well-meaning efforts to de-emphasize drug enforcement tend to benefit only those with less pigment in their skin. While some may be tempted to imagine this

is merely a perverse example of American exceptionalism, even fully legalizing the sale and use of regulated cannabis in Canada has not, to date, resulted in race-neutral policing.

2. **Adopt a duty of care.**
Consistent with point 1 above, cannabis researchers in this area owe a duty of care to ensure their research does not further the racist policies of the past. We define the duty of care in cannabis research as requiring researchers to define research terms in meaningful and consistent ways, adopt research designs appropriate to the area of study, and—most importantly—present research limitations clearly and honestly. This means prioritizing research conducted in jurisdictions where cannabis is legal or decriminalized.

3. **Seek insights from people who use drugs and other insiders.**
Drug policy has historically been developed without seeking out or incorporating the experiences of people who use drugs and other insiders. This must change. Policy must be based on the views of those who use drugs and have lived and learned from their experiences in the drug culture. People with a history of drug use tend to understand local dynamics and have expertise that must be carefully considered as part of any responsible effort to reform drug policies. Including the views of those who rely on the grey and black markets in developing the legal market is more likely to undermine illicit markets.

4. **Allow limited home-growing and pilot cannabis lounges.**
Several jurisdictions around the world allow citizens to grow cannabis at home legally. This includes Colorado, where cannabis sales are legal, and allowing homegrown cannabis might be a risk to the legal market. Trying to control non-commercial home growing is foolish and impossible to enforce. In a similar vein, public consumption will likely be lessened if cannabis lounges and/or cafes are available. Efforts to study programs of this nature should be pursued.

5. **Engage police and define diversion.**
The development of police-led diversion programs offering a means to blunt the tip of the spear of cannabis enforcement is encouraging. Police contact for cannabis possession perpetuates systematic racism, stokes stigma, and wastes limited public safety resources. However, diversion programs that compel treatment by the threat of criminal prosecution for non-participation are unethical and criminologically intrusive. Diversion programs should be reviewed to ensure they are

voluntary and that coercive and stigma-laden administrative sanctions do not replace existing criminal sanctions.

6. **Avoid local bans.**
Local bans on cannabis dispensaries or retail outlets present several challenges and unintended consequences. First, closing dispensaries that are currently operating will be costly, and they may not shut down immediately without consistent and repeated law enforcement intervention. Evidence suggests that closing dispensaries may increase crime in a neighborhood in some cases. Illicit markets will flourish in these areas, and cannabis will continue to be sold alongside other, more dangerous drugs.

7. **Prevent over-regulation.**
After a century of cannabis prohibition, it is no surprise that early legalization efforts are likely to be slow and attempt to build public support by overcompensating through regulation. Evidence to date suggests this approach, while politically palatable, is likely to lead to less accessible, lower potency products available at higher prices. Existing users are unlikely to experiment with legal cannabis under those circumstances. This approach will likely result in less tax revenue while keeping illicit markets in place and requiring continued or even more resources directed to law enforcement.

8. **Cannabis is not alcohol (or cigarettes).**
Despite significant differences between cannabis, alcohol, and tobacco, policymakers often try to superimpose policies from existing approaches to managing alcohol and tobacco to control and regulate cannabis. Differences between and among these substances must be considered. This involves appreciating variances in use, patterns, adverse outcomes, and relevant history of differing substances. Appreciating how regulations should vary must be tied to involving users in policymaking and recognizing their insights before attempting to regulate cannabis.

9. **Discourage corporate capture.**
While cannabis is likely to be big business in the years to come, allowing large corporations to dominate cannabis markets will complicate efforts to confront illicit markets and may lead to a backlash around environmental and labor concerns. Protecting craft growers and local markets as part of cannabis supply and cultivation investments is more likely to produce cannabis markets that can better cater to cannabis users. This is essential if the illicit markets are to be displaced.

10. **Rethink marketing.**
    Various jurisdictions embrace differing regulations on advertising for alcohol, tobacco, and cannabis. For example, in Canada, the largest legal cannabis market globally, most advertising for cannabis products contravenes the Act. This may be misguided. Existing users with a consistent and high-quality supply of cannabis are unlikely to participate in legal markets. That means for the legal market to thrive, it must appeal to potential customers migrating from the illicit market. In addition to cannabis with high levels of tetrahydrocannabinol (THC) and the often-misunderstood Indica/Sativa distinction, there may be a role for cannabis advertising that combines public health messaging with information about new products, strains, and activities that cannabis may enhance.
11. **One size does not fit all.**
    Legalization is the best way to minimize the harms associated with criminalization, ensure safe access, and minimize the dangers of illicit markets. However, the political realities in different countries, states, and regions may mean that meaningful decriminalization is the most practical immediate step forward. Reform could include increasing possession threshold limits in law, expanding police warnings for non-problem users in policy, and ensuring diversion programs offer resources and community support rather than attempting to impose treatment via the threat of prison.

Polymorphic Cannabis Policy: Access, Equity, and Tolerance

In Chapter 5, we applied Cohen's (1985) discussion of nets of social control to cannabis. We argued widening the nets of cannabis control involves predatory policing, pretextual stops, and the increased use of drug testing. This increases the depth by expanding systems of control implemented by private entities. For example, *denser* nets refer to how compulsory treatment programs expand moral injury by requiring people to accept, or at least feign, that they were "bad" or "wrong" for using cannabis. In Chapter 7, it emerged that blending unitary models of cannabis governance could be used to justify how to constrain the tendency for social control to spread as part of cannabis liberalization. While our model of meaningful decriminalization attempts to address the most pernicious elements of public safety and public health models, legal regulation requires a different calculus. To guide legalization, we present a polymorphic governance model that combines medical, commercial, and racial justice models of cannabis regulation.

Cannabis as Therapy and Medicine

From the medical model, we adopt both harm reduction and benefit maximization. It assumes that separating medical and recreational cannabis emerged from specific historical developments in the United States and serves no purpose other than to create regulatory hurdles and market segmentation. Establishing clinical evidence for the use of cannabis is still emerging (Zürcher et al., 2022), partly due to decades of limiting research and funding studies designed to uncover harm (Newhart & Dolphin, 2019). In the future, medical cannabis will likely be part of mainstream medicine (Nutt, 2022) instead of a stigma-laden alternative. This will allow an evidence-based approach that can "shape policies and practices regarding medical cannabis, thereby reducing harm and maximizing benefits to individuals and society" (Kruger & Kruger, 2019: 31).

In harm reduction terms, cannabis appears to be a replacement substance for people who inject drugs. In 1942, Dr William Brooke O'Shaughnessy reported the value of cannabis use for opiate withdrawal. According to this view, the potential benefits of cannabis use to reduce other types of drug use via substitution amounts to opportunities to expand harm reduction. The idea of cannabis use as harm reduction is not new (Lau et al., 2015; O'Shaughnessy, 1842). Sifaneck & Kaplan (1995: 500) describe this process as one in which "cannabis served as a means of breaking the cycle of hard-drug use and addiction." Some studies note that using cannabis is associated with reduced consumption of alcohol, cocaine, 3,4-methylenedioxy-methamphetamine (MDMA), and Vicodin (Reiman, 2009), as well as injected drugs, including heroin (Gittins & Sessa, 2020).[3] Accessing medical cannabis in the United States often requires a "medical cannabis identification card," which may be available to patients younger than twenty-one.

While medical cannabis programs vary, typically, cards are issued to individuals with verified medical conditions, allowing registered patients to access cannabis at a lower cost, pay lower taxes, and legally purchase products with higher THC potency limits, higher quantity restrictions, and legal access for minors (The Spokesman Review, 2020). However, legislative inconsistencies, insufficient clarity, and resultant challenges regarding medical cannabis mean wide variance in "prescription, possession, education, and research-related policies for health care stakeholders across the United States" (Perlman et al., 2021: 2671). What is clear is that in states where cannabis has been legalized, there is decreasing enrollment in medical cannabis programs, particularly for males (Okey et al., 2022). In addition, as medical users melt into recreational users, maintaining medical access absent clear guidance from physicians expands use for eighteen-year-olds since access to recreational cannabis requires one to reach the age of twenty-one (Silbaugh, 2021).

In terms of benefit maximization, cannabis has long been used as medicine (Courtwright, 2002). The therapeutic application of cannabis grew in popularity between 1850 and 1900. The British and American Pharmacopeia suggested its utility as a sedative and anticonvulsant (Collins, 2020a). Although interest in medical cannabis re-emerged in the 1990s, it was often limited to cannabidiol (CBD) strains (Newhart & Dolphin, 2019: 25). Enhanced access to cannabis for research (Schwabe et al., 2019) will improve research on cannabis-based medicines[4] based on genomic techniques to define and assess the medicinal value of different cannabis strains (Jin et al., 2021). Observations about the limited clinical evidence for the use of medical cannabis (Zürcher et al., 2022) must be qualified by the fact that clinical research is focused on researcher-designated outcomes of interest. Research focused on people who use cannabis has documented numerous medical benefits (Newhart & Dolphin, 2019).

In 2020, the United Nations (UN) strengthened the international imperative for ensuring access to cannabis-based medicines (UN, 2020). In 2022, the US Senate approved a bill that would reverse decades of policy and practice by requiring the Department of Health and Human Services (HHS) to investigate cannabis health benefits.[5] This research will be aided by improving access to cannabis for research (Schwabe et al., 2019) and techniques to define and describe psychoactive, CBD-elevated strains (CBD-dominant and balanced strains) and leveraging genomic markers for strain selection in clinical trials and manufacturing products and medicines (Jin et al., 2021).

Cannabis as Consumer Good

Expanding commercial cannabis assumes there is no compelling public health or safety justification to limit adults' responsible use of cannabis. This focus on public health to the exclusion of creating markets complicates efforts to disrupt illicit cannabis markets. Privatizing the supply and distribution of cannabis and limiting the role of state actors to regulating various aspects of cannabis sales and use avoids the paradox that arises when governments mandated to promote public health are in the business of providing substances like alcohol, tobacco, or cannabis, which may have adverse health impacts (Wesley & Murray, 2021: 1099). Expanding consumer cannabis involves both harm reduction and benefit maximization.

In harm reduction terms, legalizing and privatizing can serve to undermine illicit markets. Legal regulation of cannabis could improve the consistency and quality of cannabis products, limit toxins, and provide a more predictable experience by testing THC/CBD content. Commercial cannabis offers a means to create competition for how to think about cannabis. This may ultimately challenge the long-standing and profoundly problematic monopoly on prohibitionist policymaking (Heidt & Wheeldon, 2022). Harm reduction also considers constraining the desire by states to control cannabis through aggressive regulation, allowing illicit sellers to retain control over the market. Ironically, the overregulation of cannabis results in an illegal market that has remained resilient in many areas of Canada (Mahamad et al., 2020).

In terms of benefit maximization, harnessing the power of commercial markets will create new products. By 2030, it is estimated that annual sales across the United States will double, reaching nearly $72 billion (GlobeNewswire, 2022). A partial list of new cannabis products includes edibles, drinks, tinctures, creams, toothpaste, sprays, and even body butter. This will normalize the use of cannabis and require promoting responsible regulation and policies that focus on law-abiding people, productive citizens, and responsible parents who happen to use cannabis therapeutically or as a source of amusement, relaxation, and pleasure. Engaging with this group may mean rethinking marketing, advertising, and brand awareness (Rup et al., 2020). People who use cannabis in Europe prefer to buy cannabis in a regulated or legal market (Skliamis & Korf, 2022), but the infrastructure to access cannabis remains shambolic, leading to differentiated normalization within the cannabis retail market.

A pressing problem for governing legal commercial cannabis is the role of larger companies and multi-state operators (MSOs) that are lobbying for licensing rules that may create or serve to maintain oligopolies. Unless confronted, this will undermine policies for small cannabis businesses, subvert social equity approaches, and threaten to expand market capture and control as the excesses of the public health and safety models recede. While this risk has been noted in Canada and Uruguay, it is of increasing concern as efforts in the United States to legalize cannabis federally are increasing. Fears about the potential for monopolistic practices of corporate interests have led to some concrete proposals "to promote the growth of a diverse and competitive market, centering consumers and public health while building on effective equity programs already at work in state markets" (Title, 2022: 1).

Proposals include ensuring provisions for homegrown cannabis. This allows that the supply of cannabis for personal use is not limited to the whims of large corporations. Title (2022: 8–12) also outlines a series of measures based on existing antitrust laws created to limit monopolistic practices that threaten the public good. These include prohibiting vertical integration (i.e., prohibiting one corporation from controlling all levels of the supply chain), limiting the market share any one person or entity may control, and protecting and extending incentives for states to license small or disadvantaged businesses. Recent allegations that some large cannabis companies in the United States stole trade secrets, engaged in fraud, and relied on coercive business practices (Danko, 2022; Marin, 2022) make other proposals appear prescient. Reviewing mergers to constrain companies that have engaged in predatory and anticompetitive tactics in state marijuana markets and, importantly, disqualifying corporations from the cannabis industry if they have engaged in corporate crimes, defrauded the public, or caused significant public health damage requires expanding the regulatory state. Title (2022) suggests this would be overseen by a multi-agency task force to enforce anti-monopoly limits.

A final suggestion concerns the threat to the industry, represented by interstate commerce. Rob Mikos (2021) has argued that limiting industry consolidation and boosting minority participation in the cannabis market requires recognizing the challenge posed by interstate commercial cannabis, especially for state regulators. One solution is the Small and Homestead Independent Producers (SHIP) Act (Huffman, 2022), which would allow small cannabis businesses the ability to ship and sell products directly to consumers within and across state lines before larger industrial players are legally able to do so. Another approach would be for Congress to explicitly authorize states to delay or ban interstate commerce (Title, 2022). This staggered approach would allow stakeholders time to gather data and information to proactively regulate the industry before states are required to allow interstate commerce.

Another consideration is how to promote responsible use. There are two immediate concerns. The first is to what extent more liberal approaches to advertising can serve informational goals and move away from messaging that relies on "abstinence-focused rhetoric and/or focus solely on individual-level risk and harm" (Watson et al., 2019: 472). The second is whether marketing that embraces cannabis as part of leisure lifestyles can promote less risky cannabis use. Beyond advertising and marketing, cultural approaches should be explored based on Holland's coffee-shop system, including connecting cannabis to art, poetry, music, pro-social engagement, and responsible use (Sifaneck & Kaplan, 1995). Interest in cannabis cafes and lounges has been expressed in San Francisco and Los Angeles (Kovacevich, 2019), and Massachusetts (Adams, 2022). Two cannabis lounges are operating in Clarke County, Arizona (Torres-Cortez, 2022), and in December of 2022, the New Jersey Cannabis Regulatory Commission proposed rules for cannabis lounges that are soon to open (National Law Review, 2023). In general, however, they remain rare.

Cannabis as Racial Justice

An under-explored area is how to expand commercial cannabis *while* challenging the legacy of cannabis-related racism. While the potential for commercial cannabis to undermine any larger initiative based on equity and racial and social justice certainly exists, other approaches based on a polymorphic governance strategy may be worth exploring. In harm reduction terms, commercial cannabis might also be the best means to address the persistent racial inequities that exist within current drug policies. In terms of harm reduction, legalization is the best means to reducing racially disparate cannabis arrests (Sheehan et al., 2021). Jurisdictions that are serious about confronting race, ethnicity, and cannabis must find new ways to sustain commercial cannabis while expanding access for those historically punished and excluded from business opportunities. White people continue to dominate the legal cannabis marketplace, "a process made easier by their relative reprieve from the war on drugs that has disproportionately devested Black and Latino communities" (Reid, 2021: 16). This amounts to harm.

In terms of benefit maximization, bold thinking is required and may follow the increasing documentation of the failure to make good on the promise of racial justice in the cannabis industry. Our solution to expand commercial cannabis through an equity lens is to privilege Black and Brown-owned businesses by allowing them to sell higher-potency cannabis products, formerly identified as "medical cannabis," to anyone. Based on the provisions of the SHIP act, supporting small Black and Brown-owned cannabis businesses to sell directly to consumers would provide an opportunity for minority-owned cannabis businesses to gain market presence and establish a brand, vibe, and marketing strategy in the short term. Another idea is to promote partnerships that would allow minority-owned cannabis dispensaries early access to proprietary strains developed by craft growers. These are consistent with "reefer reparations" (Mize, 2020: 34) and commercial cannabis. However, numerous questions remain.

This proposal must be seen alongside other federal efforts in the United States and examples to establish a social and racial justice model of cannabis reform in various states (Cannabis Control Commission, n.d.; Oregon State Legislature, 2021; Start Smart New York, n.d.). Massachusetts was the first state to explicitly include a participation-related equity directive in enabling adult-use cannabis legislation. To meet this statutory requirement, the regulatory commission created, and continues to develop and modify, regulations and programs aiming to produce equitable participation in the cannabis industry (Donnan et al., 2022). At least four California cities—Los Angeles, Oakland, Sacramento, and San Francisco—have created "equity programs" via municipal regulations (Mize, 2020: 26–27). Kavousi and colleagues (2022) note that Los Angeles offers special equity permits intended to ensure that sales licenses go to businesses owned by people from communities harmed by drug criminalization and enforcement (Elmahrek, 2020; Reyes, 2021). In New York, half of the adult-use licenses are pledged to applicants meeting social or economic equity criteria. Such applicants can access low or noninterest loans, reduced or waived fees, legal advice, job training, licensing, compliance, and technical assistance (Adinoff & Reiman, 2019).

Unfortunately, to date, these approaches have not been a resounding success. They appear to require more oversight and targeted support by state entities, which often regulate independent businesses rather than explicitly support some businesses over others. For example, entrepreneurs who could benefit from social equity policies often report financial and logistical difficulties in navigating the bureaucracy of cannabis dispensary licensing and regulation (Gerber, 2022). Other challenges have emerged from the applicants themselves. For example, in Los Angeles, social equity licenses cannot be awarded to those with previous out-of-state cannabis convictions (City of Los Angeles Department of Cannabis Regulation, n.d.). In Illinois, a preference for veteran-owned businesses as part of cannabis licenses has led to charges that some social equity programs are unconstitutional (Malyshev & Ganley, 2021). In addition to constitutional concerns, legal cannabis faces obstacles related to the economic and political dynamics associated with establishing a regulated system.

Barriers to Legal Cannabis: Politics, Competition, and Sales

Further cannabis legalization is almost certain to trigger a backlash, perhaps like the parent-based pushback to cannabis decriminalization in the 1970s and 1980s (Dufton, 2017a). This overreaction provided cover for the expansion of the War on Drugs and other related moral panics that may rise to the top of public consciousness. In Chapter 5, we explained how penal forms of power are connected to public safety and influence public health and how these together influence the desire to control the cannabis market. For Cohen (1985), this transference amounts to the creation of new forms of control or *different* nets. States have adopted several adaptive strategies to extend authority over legal cannabis (Aaronson & Rothschild-Elyassi, 2021). This involves limiting access to licenses, preventing new products, or pursuing policies that undermine small growers and give advantages to large corporations (Wesley & Murray, 2021).

Just as our model of meaningful decriminalization requires engaging with Cohen's concern, so too does thinking about our polymorphic model of cannabis regulation. Our model expands on who can participate in the legal market, even as numerous laws and policies serve as barriers to this kind of regulatory reform (Mize, 2020). Likewise, we considered how increasing access to existing medical cannabis products could influence the recreational cannabis markets, creating a different kind of competition within legal markets and with the potential to disrupt illicit markets (Mahamad et al., 2020). A final question concerns cost and convenience. Illicit markets may persist where over-regulation undermines commercial calculations, but limitations on advertising and marketing also must be considered (Wesley & Murray, 2021). These restrictions may undermine consumer education and threaten the sustainability of the legal cannabis market. Together, these represent political, economic, and legal barriers.

Political Barriers

The politics of cannabis is very much in flux. This is a result of competing interests related to ideological concerns and aversion, democratic impulses, and the potential for cannabis taxes to support public services. A common concern as cannabis is legalized is that the market will suffer from "corporate capture," which refers to the domination of a market by large corporations to the exclusion of small operators. These larger corporate actors may exert undue influence over domestic and international markets by virtue of their size, power, and access to decision-makers and public institutions. For example, the organization Transform Drug Policy Foundation (2021: 292) suggests when the legalization of recreational cannabis followed legalized medical cannabis, existing businesses enjoyed an advantage. This approach may weaken regulatory powers through lobbying, funding politicians or political parties, funding of think tanks, civil society organizations and academia, research, membership of government committees or task forces, and movement of staff between corporate and regulatory roles.

This influence ascribed to corporate cannabis is, in fact, the very kind of influence exerted in reverse by the prohibitions of the past and their more recent incarnations (Heidt & Wheeldon, 2022). Lobbying allowed cannabis prohibition to remain in place long after the costs of criminalization far outweighed any benefits. Organizations such as Parents Opposed to Pot, Take Back America, Campaign, Drug-Free America Foundation, Partnership for a Drug-Free World, and Smart Approaches to Marijuana (SAM) have attempted to influence political leaders and state policy and shape media portrayals of cannabis. For example, SAM founder Kevin A. Sabet has advised three US presidential administrations on drug policy, including the Clinton (2000) and George W. Bush (2002–2003) administrations, and served as President Barack Obama's drug control director until 2011. As discussed in Chapter 6, SAM was founded in 2012 in response to the democratic decision by residents in Colorado and Washington to legalize recreational cannabis.

One potential problem with commercial cannabis is how it treats cannabis packaging. Some "candy" in Figure 8.1 is marked with a CA for California and "medicated." While these products include warnings, they are far too similar in appearance to non-cannabis candy such as Skittles, Sour Patch Kids, and Sweet Tarts. There is something of the anarchic approach here to culture jamming, defined as an approach designed to "play with the branded images and icons of consumer culture" (Center for Communication and Civic Engagement, n.d.). It may be politically dangerous. It is a reminder

228 LEGALIZATION, POLYMORPHIC GOVERNANCE, AND BARRIERS

Figure 8.1 Cannabis candy
Source: Authors.

of the adage that history doesn't repeat itself, but it often rhymes. Dufton (2017a: 72) described the rise of the anti-cannabis parents' movement, which was driven by smokable frisbees, bongs shaped like spaceships that were sold openly, often in corner shops and music stores. With little to no regulation or oversight, products appeared to be directly targeted at children. In 1978, a *New York Times* article reported:

> Like babes in Toyland, three boys from 11 to 14 and a 13-year-old girl went on a buying spree recently in "head shops" around the metropolitan area. They came back with $300 worth of drug-culture paraphernalia that included a "buzz bomb," a "Power Hitter," several "bongs," a baby bottle fitted with both a nipple and a hashish pipe.
>
> (Johnston, 1978)

As we have documented throughout this book, the alliance of anti-cannabis politicians, organizations, and individuals shaped international policy. Cannabis that looks like candy feeds into fears about youth access, uncontrolled capitalism, and public health risks. Predicting all the cannabis moral panics to come is not easy. Recognizing the political dangers of adverse reactions to the prevalence of highly potent cannabis designed to look like candy is common sense. One immediate solution would be for cannabis operators to adopt a code of conduct to limit the sales of products that look like candy and support suppliers committed to reducing adverse environmental impacts. Lessons from more than twenty years of cannabis production in California suggest that environmental issues should not be ignored (Silvaggio, 2021).

Political barriers cannot be divorced from political divisions and aversion. In the United States, this includes racial discord. As we have documented, the prohibitionist project has been disastrous for Black people. As Tonry (1994: 27) points out, the policies adopted by the architects of the War on Drugs "were foreordained disproportionately to affect disadvantaged black Americans." The influence of corporate cannabis has thus far limited the equitable development of the cannabis industry, especially for Black and Brown people (Mize, 2020). Kavousi and colleagues (2022: 156) argue that

> Scholars should continue investigating whether cannabis legalization improves racial and social equity or entrenches inequalities. Under what conditions are those who purchase legal cannabis more or less demographically or socioeconomically similar to those who use the illicit market? Where are dispensaries located, and what populations do they serve versus exclude? Who are the growers and distributors, are particular groups over or underrepresented, and what does this mean for who benefits from cannabis-fueled economic growth?

Research can identify where race remains relevant, but the politics of racial reconciliation remains a work in progress.

Cannabis and Economic Barriers

An emergent limitation area for legalization and regulation is the development of responsible regulation regimes in economics and cannabis use. Central here is understanding the role of illicit markets and the impact of drug prohibition. Illicit markets have developed through decades of the War on Drugs (Robinson & Scherlen, 2014). While decriminalization does little to disrupt illicit markets, to date, legal regimes in Uruguay and Canada have shown only marginal successes. This is because legalization and regulation have focused on public health first and access second. Regulations around potency, price, and advertising have limited the potential of the legal market. In Canada, this has led to efforts in British Columbia (BC) to entice illegal growers to join the legal cannabis marketplace (Canadian Evergreen, n.d.).

In BC, the effort to bring illicit market growers onto the legal retail market has focused on the Central Kootenay region by assisting new producers in navigating the byzantine regulatory federal process, understanding market development, and considering security and licensing. To succeed, however, encouraging illicit cannabis suppliers to enter the legal market requires thinking about some controversial conversations. The first is that sustaining the legal market requires listening to groups like the Cannabis Council of Canada (C3), which represents more than 700 licensed producers and processors of cannabis. In 2021, the group recommended reducing excise tax and regulatory fees, limiting provincial mark-ups, and better regulating existing online illicit cannabis sales (Raycraft, 2021).

In the United States, some proposals center on the role of interstate commerce to support smaller cannabis companies and limit the role of "Big Cannabis" (Title, 2022). This means recognizing how the Dormant Commerce Clause (DCC) was formed and the judicial interpretations of the US Constitution's Interstate Commerce Clause that generally prohibits states from imposing barriers to the free movement of goods, persons, and capital (Lawrence, 2022). For example,

> The economics of the Dormant Commerce Clause are tremendously beneficial for the nation as a whole, because it promises a large, national market for producers and encourages greater specialization reflective of the comparative advantages of persons or geographic areas. Indeed, it was the states' imposition of trade barriers and their resulting inefficiencies that inspired the American founders to abandon the original form of American government guided by the Articles of Confederation. The Commerce Clause thus became a central focus of the nation's new (and current) governing document.
>
> (Berke et al., 2022: 8)

One emergent area of interest in the economic regulation of cannabis is whether cannabis companies bring lawsuits against the states arguing that—federal prohibition notwithstanding—the current state restrictions on interstate trade in cannabis violate the DCC (Title, 2022). Economic regulation that can support legal cannabis is relevant in another way.

Combating the illicit market means attracting consumers from the illicit markets. If the legal market emphasizes public health concerns over access, it is unlikely to be able to compete on cost or quality. Ironically, the emphasis on public health, combined with lack of access, also creates a situation in which cannabis consumers are motivated to interact with illicit markets, resulting in more public issues and other complex problems, for example, the temptation to do other, more dangerous illicit drugs and opportunities to become involved in the criminal subculture. Policymakers may need to rethink and critically assess their views on consumer education, awareness, and marketing. The worry about glorifying cannabis might require that education include public health messages alongside more traditional advertising efforts. Requiring cannabis businesses to devote a certain percentage of advertising to public service announcements (PSAs) may be part of the future. Warning people of the possible dangers of using a legal substance is sensible. However, this approach to messaging risks prioritizing public health over all other messages.

Increasing competition by abandoning distinctions between medical and non-medical cannabis would signal that use is a part of society and need not be associated with shame or stigma. It follows research suggesting "no significant differences between those who used medically versus recreationally in race, education, past year depression and prevalence of cannabis use disorders" (Lin et al., 2016: 99). Distinctions between medical and commercial cannabis are not evidence-based (Jin et al., 2021). For example, medical cannabis users have not suffered from access to cannabis products with higher THC content. Absent evidence of harm after nearly thirty years of access to medical cannabis, maintaining a recreational/medicinal distinction creates barriers in retail cannabis that are a vestige of prohibition-era policies. As discussed, this approach could offer one means to overcome the economic obstacles that complicate the desire to sustain legal cannabis markets.

Another effort involves identifying new markets. This is essential if legal cannabis markets are to be sustained and replace illicit markets and the hazards associated with unregulated cannabis commerce. Developing and providing more specialized strains of cannabis with more balanced THC content is one direction for advertising. This might involve high-THC strains advertised for creativity, energy, or relaxation. Another is to consider who is using cannabis and why. The opposite of high-THC strains would be *Dad Grass*. As a company, it embraces nostalgia and newer sensibilities around how cannabis is grown. For example,

> reviving the mellow sensibility of the casual smoke. Our 100% Organic hemp flower and pre-rolled joints serve up a clean buzz without the fuss. Our special collections of merch and apparel pay tribute to the timeless staples of dad style. Past, present, and future. Like your dad's stash, we keep things easy and dependable, never fancy or complicated.[6]

This, of course, is not actual cannabis but rather federally legal CBD-rich hemp flower that contains less than 0.3 percent THC. In other words, these joints might possibly relax the user when ingested, but they will not provide a traditional cannabis high. This should be seen alongside other quasi-marketing efforts. *Miss Grass* sells mini pre-rolls marked in color-coded packaging (see Figure 8.2). "Fast Times" is presented as appropriate for "Bloom + Play" and described as "Sativa dominant. Terpene rich." By contrast, "Quiet Times" is reportedly better to "Anchor + Restore" and is described as "Indica dominant. Terpene rich."[7]

Figure 8.2 Cannabis packaging as marketing
Source: Authors.

Other marketing strategies are emerging, and new consumer groups are in the process of being identified.[8] Several streams have emerged. First, some companies have focused on consumers who are health-conscious and concerned about the environment. For example, the website of Good Brands Cannabis Company characterizes its products as follows:

Good Practices: Our state-of-the-art greenhouse helps us harness the quality and control of an indoor cultivation and the complete terpene profile of an outdoor, sun-nurtured grow.
Good Health: We produce sustainable, pesticide-free, pure cannabis, flowered to the peak of perfection just the way nature intended.
Good Times: With our clean, responsibly grown cannabis, we help you live naturally and enjoy good vibes only.[9]

Marley Natural is another prominent example of a cannabis company that attempts to appeal to this consumer group. Their mission statement reads:

Marley Natural™ is a premium product line crafted with awareness, authenticity, and a genuine respect for nature's nourishing benefits. Our cannabis products and accessories are all responsibly sourced and integrity driven. Each of our offerings is a direct reflection of the Marley ethos that integrates nature's goodness with a belief in the positive potential of herb. As agents of change, we promote positivity, connectivity, and personal transformation. And as believers in progress, we offer an exceptional lifestyle line that is inspired by Jamaica's vibrant energy. We are proud to be the official Bob Marley cannabis brand.[10]

Another marketing strategy consists of appealing to those interested in fashion, music, and art. For example, there are several musical celebrities (e.g., Willie Nelson and Snoop Dogg) who have long been associated with cannabis and have started their own companies based on personal branding.[11] Founded by Shavo Odadjian of the band System of a Down, 22Red is another example of a cannabis company that is reliant on musical branding. Their website reads: "We are a premium lifestyle brand that is focused on cannabis, fashion, music, and wellness." Sport-based cannabis companies have also begun to emerge in recent years.[12] A prominent example here is Highsman Cannabis, run by former National Football League and Canadian Football League player Ricky Williams:

Highsman is a mentality that is defined by an appreciation for greatness, and it comes to life as the official cannabis lifestyle brand of entrepreneur, thought leader and one of the most electric NFL running backs of the century, Ricky Williams. Once scrutinized by sports pundits and fans alike for using cannabis to "take care of his body," the formerly infamous #34 is flipping the script with his new line of personally curated cannabis products, apparel, and accessories—all provoking the Highsman mentality through deliberate Sparks of Greatness.[13]

Former heavyweight champion boxer Mike Tyson has also started his own line of cannabis products—TYSON 2.0—that capitalizes on his sports fame while linking cannabis to wellness:

It started with the undisputed heavyweight champ using cannabis to reach new heights. When Mike was in his prime, he used cannabis to relax his body and focus his mind. It was always a tool close by that aided him in reaching the heights he did in his amazing boxing career. In Mike's words, "Cannabis has always played an important role in my life. Cannabis has changed me for the good both mentally and physically, and I want to share that gift with others who are also seeking relief."[14]

It remains to be seen whether tying cannabis to sports will be a successful marketing strategy.

As far back as 2019, there were references to companies that could become "the Amazon of cannabis" (Gham, 2019). An open question is how companies can adapt to online commerce. This will require managing regulations in which buying or selling cannabis may be legal but sending or receiving it may not be. Online companies providing cannabis exist in Canada and the United States. Even when they are closed and owners prosecuted for operating outside the legal market (CBC News, 2021), new companies emerge to replace those that are closed. There is an irony that even in jurisdictions with legal cannabis, the old whack-a-mole approach to policing cannabis persists.

Legal Barriers: Cannabis, Crime, and Criminal Justice

One research area that is likely to remain central is the question of cannabis and crime. The fact that cannabis prohibition has existed for a century means that for most of our lives, one was engaging in criminal behavior by simply possessing cannabis. As discussed in Chapter 6, while the poor research of the past connecting cannabis and crime has fallen apart as more examples and better designs have emerged, the central paradox is that it is the state that has created criminals out of otherwise law-abiding people. This is an ethical issue, as identified by Milton Friedman in 1991:

> it's a moral problem that the government is going around killing ten thousand people. It's a moral problem that the government is making into criminals—people, who may be doing something you and I don't approve of, but who are doing something that hurts nobody else.
>
> (Perry, 2015)

For many, cannabis use remains deviant, dangerous, and undesirable. It continues to be associated with criminality and criminal behavior. The most important immediate question for serious scholars related to cannabis and crime is impaired driving.

In a recent review on driving and cannabis, Pearlson and colleagues (2021) advocate expanding public health campaigns and public service, applied elsewhere and possibly adapted to address the dangers associated with driving after mixing cannabis and alcohol. In addition, the effects of cannabis vary between individuals when compared to alcohol because of individual variation in tolerance level, smoking technique, and devices and differences in absorption levels of THC. Different substances present different types of risks for drivers (Sewell et al., 2009). In public safety terms, of immediate interest is assessing the value of current tests to determine blood THC levels and gauge impairment through roadside sobriety tests. The accuracy, replicability, and utility for law enforcement of these tests is an area which criminologists may wish to investigate in the future.

In Canada, Uber and Mothers Against Drunk Driving (MADD) developed the "Don't Drive High" campaign in response to Canada's nationwide legalization of cannabis (MADD Canada, n.d.). It consisted of print ads, billboards, and video ads. The campaign included 40,000 $5 Uber discounts through the website (Draaisma, 2018). Ten thousand Canadians are reported to have redeemed these Uber coupons, presumably to use to offset the cost of calling an Uber instead of driving impaired (Media Jel, n.d.). This campaign appears to have influenced a website devoted to warning Canadians about cannabis and the risks of impaired driving. These include legal provisions, links to research, personal testimonials, and videos. The message is clear:

There's a lot going on around you when you drive. You need to be totally focused so that if a split-second—and potentially life-saving—decision needs to be made, you're ready for it. Drugs affect your ability to react and increase the chance of a crash. Don't get behind the wheel or get in a car with an impaired driver—it's just not worth the risk.

(Government of Canada, n.d.b)

New regulatory environments create new forms of crime related to cannabis. This includes possessing more cannabis than the threshold limit, growing and possessing non-legal cannabis, and consuming cannabis in public. Of specific interest is to what extent police will use the potential for nonlegal cannabis possession to justify stops, investigations, and possible arrests. This, perhaps, is easier when considering regulatory actions against illicit growing operations. However, it quickly leads to some strange possibilities. Will police require people who possess cannabis to *prove* that their cannabis is legal? How consistently and rigorously will this be enforced? Will it lead to the creation of criminal records for otherwise law-abiding citizens?

Conclusion

This chapter considered the potential for benefit maximization to guide legal and regulated cannabis. While decriminalization, discussed in Chapter 7, is an example of legal renegotiation, in this chapter, we explored how moral questions complicate efforts to move toward cannabis legalization. These include questions of harm reduction and benefit maximization. It also means recognizing how the role of prohibitionist ideas continues to influence cannabis policy. We applied Cohen's (1985) concerns about illusory reform. Some policies that undergird legal and regulatory cannabis sustain illicit markets, perpetuate racial disparities in the cannabis industry, and further stigma by maintaining regulations steeped in paternalistic views. These are absent compelling evidence and are not based on any sound framework.

Some critics of commercial cannabis retain an ideological aversion to profit-seeking in this area. Indeed, there are other models to consider (Pardal, 2022). More work is needed to consider the benefits of commercial models, especially if they can create the political constituencies required to stand against the adverse influence of the New Prohibitionists (Heidt & Wheeldon, 2022). This worry guides our focus on linking racial justice with medical and commercial cannabis. This polymorphic model of cannabis governance is designed to expand consumer and medical cannabis, compete with illicit markets, and offer a pragmatic means to engage questions of racial equity. Based on our discussion of the limits of reform, inspired by Stan Cohen, we connected resistance to cannabis legalization to aversion and outlined potential regulatory barriers and possible responses to the inevitable pushback to cannabis reform. Legal reforms will not be sustained without engaging the moral and ideological dimensions to cannabis aversion and taking meaningful steps to right the racial wrongs of cannabis prohibition.

In Chapter 9, we consider how to sustain cannabis liberalization and work toward responsible regulation. Essential here is how to confront stigma, expand access, and re-orient research and, specifically, how research is communicated. A central theme of this book is how the history of cannabis, including its control, prohibition, criminalization, and nascent legalization provides a case study in moral, legal, and cultural renegotiation. Such moments provide an opportunity to reconsider the role of deliberative democracy and may point to how other substances, once vilified, are accommodated, normalized, and decriminalized in ways that lead to other efforts designed to reduce human suffering. This requires reconciling tensions between commerce and control, liberty and safety, and justice and fairness.

Notes

1. See Weed Out Misinformation (n.d.) for a justification and useful discussion of this approach in the Canadian context.
2. For instance, policies may seek to limit use by youth by adopting its public health morph, *while* seeking to reduce illicit cannabis markets in the interests of public safety. Other policy approaches may seek to promote legal and regulated commercial cannabis *and* try to ensure retail licenses favor Black, Indigenous, and People of Color applicants or others previously incarcerated as part of the War on Cannabis. This approach to blended or polymorphic governance requires understanding how multiple forms of power of control exits within one regulatory space.
3. According to some research, increasing access to retail cannabis is associated with an estimated 17 percent reduction in all opioid-related mortality rates (Hsu & Kovacs, 2021).
4. This is true internationally: see UN (2020) and, in the US, see https://www.feinstein.senate.gov/public/_cache/files/f/9/f9877e00-8bac-45c5-b0a4-ad73f36bb296/A790203221D32AE509C4E2DEFEDBE6D6.2022-03-23-10-09-02-uid-575-hen22240.pdf.

5. The full Bill can be accessed here: https://www.feinstein.senate.gov/public/_cache/files/f/9/f9877e00-8bac-45c5-b0a4-ad73f36bb296/A790203221D32AE509C4E2DEFEDBE6D6.2022-03-23-10-09-02-uid-575-hen22240.pdf.
6. See https://dadgrass.com.
7. See https://missgrass.com.
8. Because of the regulations and restrictions around marketing and advertising, these examples apply primarily to the United States rather than Canada.
9. See https://goodbrandsco.com.
10. See https://www.marleynatural.com.
11. See https://williesreserve.com; https://www.pentagram.com/work/leafs-by-snoop-1.
12. See https://sportscannabis.ca.
13. See https://www.highsman.com/about.
14. See https://tyson20.com/about.

9
Cannabis, Culture, and Pragmatic Criminology

Introduction

Even after decades of drug reform, prohibitionist tendencies and coercive paradigms based on moral assumptions about the value of abstinence persist (Bowers & Abrahamson, 2020). This movement exists within the criminal justice system and uses the implicit and sometimes explicit threat of punishment to compel "treatment." As discussed in previous chapters, the New Prohibitionists have embraced this thinking to justify their efforts to slow cannabis policy reform. Even some drug court advocates, well placed to extol the value of more meaningful community-based support, refuse to back reforms that can reduce the adverse consequences of cannabis prohibition (Bowers & Abrahamson, 2020). As Dufton (2017a: 254) notes,

> It has happened time and again. A period of intense hatred of marijuana (the 1930s, the 1950s, the late 1970s into the 1980s) births a moment when the drug suddenly seems all right (the 1960s and early to mid-1970s, the 1990s, today). In both moments, laws change, as does use. Then acceptance births opposition, which births acceptance, and the cycle begins anew.

Within the wheel of tolerance and aversion, it is difficult to assess where exactly in the cycle we are at any given moment.

Toleration refers to accepting the reality of cannabis use and the legitimate desire to limit its use's most dangerous aspects. When tolerance fails, regulating aversion is required to reduce the harm that results when animus guides policy (Brown, 2006). Building on the legal renegotiation at the root of decriminalization as outlined in Chapter 7, Chapter 8 outlined some moral questions which underlie the acceptance of commercial cannabis. Consistent with a polymorphic model of legal and regulated cannabis, we proposed policies that would expand commercial cannabis, increase access to medical cannabis, and create opportunities for Black and Brown minority-owned cannabis businesses to compete in markets in which large companies have established dominance and appear to be cementing their advantage.

This chapter outlines one means by which the legalization of cannabis can be sustained. It requires understanding the role of cultural renegotiation as part of cannabis liberalization. We consider how to sustain and extend cannabis reform by outlining three levels of stigma (Reid, 2020) and explore the challenges of linking medical and recreational cannabis. In addition, we attempt to reimagine how criminologists study cannabis and crime and consider why building community capacity to support cannabis users deemed "at risk" is worthy of more attention. Supporting and building cannabis culture means people opposed to cannabis use must consider how they can accommodate cannabis. At the same time, people who use cannabis or benefit from its legal status need to consider which concerns about the growing use of cannabis are credible.

As argued throughout the book, cannabis liberalization is a case study in policy renegotiation. Such moments provide an opportunity to reconsider the role of deliberative democracy. They may point to a process by which other substances, once vilified, can be accommodated, normalized, and decriminalized. This means building cannabis culture in ways that can ensure reasonable regulation but do not sustain illicit markets. It means destigmatizing cannabis and people who use it by developing a responsible approach to cannabis regulation. Such an approach would expand tolerance, regulate aversion, and promote cannabis in mindful, sensible, and rights-affirming ways. The question of how those who disagree on drug policy can find common ground is difficult. It is made more so by commercial media models that rely on participatory disinformation and neo-prohibitionist notions as part of their business plan.

Supporting and Building Cannabis Culture

The need to support and build cannabis culture stems from a firmly rooted puritanical impulse to stigmatize all intoxication (Reid, 2021). Thus, despite decriminalization and legalization worldwide, institutions, organizations, and groups still stigmatize cannabis. In addition, anti-cannabis ideologies appear to have crystallized among some segments of older age cohorts, hampering the ability of those who seek medical cannabis to access and engage in cannabis culture. This stigma persists for those seeking recreational cannabis as people are unfamiliar with scientifically established facts on cannabis, and those who use it "face an uphill battle in dislodging ingrained cultural stereotypes about cannabis and cannabis users" (Reid, 2021: 16). Tackling societal ignorance requires shifting the culture on cannabis.

One idea is that cannabis culture has remained stable based on its association with the hippie and bohemian cultures of the 1960s and 1970s. Sandberg (2012a: 64) defined cannabis culture as a

> collection of rituals, symbols and stories to which all users must relate. These different elements of cannabis culture are linked, and they are embedded in values such as "natural," "organic," "authentic," and "oppositional."

By contrast, research in Poland found people who use cannabis set themselves apart from this history and the "cannabis cultures in the West" (Wanke et al., 2022: 4). As we have argued, cannabis culture is being shaped by commercial interests. Whether it is new cannabis products or packaging designed to serve marketing and advertising goals in jurisdictions where advertising is prohibited, cannabis culture may be transforming. Describing these transformations is a work in progress. It can build on organizational efforts to define macro, meso, and micro levels and is designed to capture the peculiarities and intersections between structural, social, and individual stigma and shame (Reid, 2020: 4–8).

Stigma: Macro, Legal, Institutional

The macro-level involves structural, legal, and institutionalized procedures that oppress and control. For example, our model assumes that police can be compelled to de-emphasize cannabis. As we have demonstrated, this often precedes drug policy reform. The problems run deep, however. After the murder of George Floyd in 2020 and calls for defunding police departments, the challenges (Lum et al., 2021) and adverse consequences (Piza & Connealy, 2022) became apparent. Yet, it served as a reminder that funding can be used as a political tool, which can be wielded when required. There is a view that, in an increasing number of jurisdictions, police are operating outside of the political system. As Brown (2022) notes, cannabis reform represents one means to start to change the culture of policing.

Since questions about cannabis and crime are likely to continue, a different set of questions focused on individual and population-level associations between cannabis and crime may be relevant. Indeed, variations in legal cannabis allow for comparisons between and among cannabis markets before legalization, cannabis arrest rates before legalization, and when legalization was implemented. Other questions concern the type of regulations put in place, the level of observance, and, notably, the nature of cannabis enforcement. Of interest for jurisdictions that legalize cannabis is how this impacts illicit cannabis markets and whether cannabis-based enforcement practices persist. While we have itemized the benefits of de-emphasizing policing cannabis, the potential for better resourcing, a defensible mission, and reduced workload does not appear to engender change in many departments.

Promoting police accountability in the United States and challenging a long history of structural racism, police brutality, and the lack of accountability has devastated public trust (Ray, 2020a). It may be tempting to view financial sanctions, lawsuits, or civilian pay-outs as a possible means to ensure police improve their conduct. There is, however, little evidence of their effectiveness (Schwartz, 2016). Other suggestions for increased accountability include requiring that police provide their name, badge number, and a card with instructions for filing a complaint to the civilian oversight structure as part of every cannabis-involved investigation. A policy designed to regulate aversion would require cannabis-involved cases to proceed to criminal charges only when they meet high standards, including detailed documentation of every investigative stage and additional approvals from a named superior. Research can help identify where barriers to police reform remain.

In 2020, police officers in Washington, where cannabis has been legal since 2012, expressed numerous concerns. These include worries about youth access and use, prosecutorial behavior, and managing nuisance calls about cannabis use in public (Stohr et al., 2020a). While cannabis and serious crime do not appear to be related, there is an open question about cannabis-impaired driving, especially given the risks associated with the co-consumption of cannabis and alcohol (Brubacher et al., 2019; Lira et al., 202; Pearlson et al., 2021). As Kraska (2021, personal communication) notes,

> Changing the role of police from enforcers/punishers to conduits for social services might be underestimating the long history of how the police—an institution structurally mandated to use violence as their core function—will likely find a way to contort this well-intended pivot into the same militaristic march they seem predisposed toward . . . in the U.S. the police have tended to distort well-intended reforms into perverse practices—something academics, in particular, have not reckoned.[1]

This view, while pessimistic, comes from someone who has studied the police for decades. Therefore, it should not be easily dismissed.

There is some evidence that the legal status of medical cannabis, as distinct from traditional medicine, stigmatizes its use and reduces patient comfort, even when cannabis is shown to have a therapeutic value for those seeking it. Reid (2021: 16) notes patients "spent significant amounts of time educating others on the wide variety of cannabis medicines . . . even though cannabis patients say their medicine makes them feel 'normal' as opposed to 'high.'" Staton and colleagues (2022: 6) report patients feeling stigmatized for even asking doctors for medical cannabis. Other participants described how doctors might not express negative views toward cannabis use but simply did not recommend or discuss it with them. Instead, they would offer pharmaceuticals, including opioids. As clinical research continues, medical access may shift. In the meantime, as we have argued, allowing minority-owned cannabis outlets to sell products currently designated as medical cannabis, higher in tetrahydrocannabinol (THC) and therefore desirable to those unable to access the medical marketplace, is a practical way to strengthen the retail cannabis industry and diversify ownership.

Stigma: Meso, Social, and Organizations

Social stigmas work on the meso level. These describe how organizations and groups endorse cultural messages that disadvantage stigmatized people (Reid, 2020). This type of stigma involves how group norms tend to influence individuals based on how they are communicated, including "epithets, shunning, ostracism, discrimination, and violence" (Reid, 2020: 5). Crucial here is how cannabis use is viewed as related to social role expectations. For example, parents who use may be alienated from other non-using parents, and workers who use may be fired from their jobs or forced into treatment programs against their will (Reid, 2020: 5). This operates in at least two ways. One question is to what extent the justice system, adjacent justice agencies, and treatment facilities can move away from coercive care as a central strategy.

As discussed in Chapter 8, this requires reframing language about drugs and people who use drugs. This use of stigmatizing terms can negatively impact the quality of care for those who use drugs and alcohol. It has long been known and recently become the subject of specific guidance. The American Society of Addiction Medicine (ASAM)'s Journal of Addiction Medicine, the

International Society of Addiction Journal Editors (ISAJE), and even the US Office of National Drug Control Policy has recognized the need to be more precise (Saitz et al., 2020). For example, research demonstrates that when patients are described as "abusing" substances instead of suffering from a "disorder," clinicians are more likely to recommend punitive approaches (Kelly & Westerhoff, 2010; Kelly et al., 2010; Van Boekel et al., 2013). The quest for less stigmatizing and more clinically accurate language means referring to "use" rather than "abuse," a person with "substance use disorder" rather than an "addict," and "cannabis as medicine" rather than "medical marijuana" (see Saitz et al., 2020; Wogen & Restrepo, 2020).

Clinicians and scientists should avoid terms like "abuser" and "addict" because they are not clearly defined, vague, and generally inaccurate. Because of the far reach of drug prohibition, even the term "drug user" has acquired negative connotations and should be avoided. These loaded terms can stigmatize and undermine the quality of care for patients. The stigma attached to drug use presents public health burdens and is present within corporations, the judicial system, government, professional groups (including health care), schools and universities, and social service agencies (Wogen & Restrepo, 2020: 57). One approach is to associate this language with predatory justice practices, including using this language as a justification for compelling people to attend cannabis programs to avoid a criminal record. The financial interest associated with some of these programs, especially when the cost is a burden for the person diverted, will be a significant challenge. For example, we have urged researchers to track how much public cannabis revenue is directed to police versus social equity programs in jurisdictions where cannabis is legalized (Wheeldon & Heidt, 2023b).

Another approach considers to what extent community-based organizations can be empowered to play new roles and replace aspects of the criminal justice system. There is a paradox here. Our modern lives seem to leave little room for volunteering and engaging in our own communities, yet people feel ever more disconnected from the structures that constrain their lives. There is more to be said about how community organizations can be encouraged to serve as a nonjudgmental vehicle to connect people seeking services with agencies and organizations that have the mandate to serve them. As Cohen (1985) recognized, the carceral creep that seeps into situations where people occupy positions by which they can judge others must always be a concern.

This type of moralizing is not averted simply because they occur in settings outside the prison walls. This is connected to what Pavlich (2005) has called a perversion of restorative justice. This is more than the observation that the greater integration of restorative ideas within the traditional justice system will lead to its co-optation. Instead, it refers to how replacing the formal system with more informal controls can shift accountability in uncomfortable ways (Cohen, 1985). In the case of restorative justice, these perversions have allowed the term "restorative" to serve as a useful moniker to describe programs that may or may not embrace the principles associated with their success (Burford, 2018).

Stigma: Micro, Individual, and Internalizations

Reid (2020) notes that micro stigmas shape individual decisions, how they may be influenced by the judgment of others, and how this is internalized. These are perhaps best seen as anticipatory and preventative decisions taken to avoid suspicions that one uses cannabis. For example, some people who use cannabis refrain from commenting on cannabis-related issues when they arise in everyday conversations to avoid behavior that might be seen as deviant and to avoid being labeled "pothead" or "stoner." Such strategies can result in anxiety and may compromise and undermine intimate relationships. Of interest is how these stigmas and levels interact. We agree with Reid (2020: 11), who argues:

> Significantly more attention should be placed on the dimensions of cultural and social accommodations in the normalization hypothesis. Furthermore, future research on cannabis stigmas should strive to incorporate and empower the most vulnerable in the community. Doing this will not only protect against making privileged claims to normalization, but it may also serve to identify meaningful strategies to further normalize the plant in society.

One way normalization is limited is the failure to treat cannabis markets like other markets in terms of regulation. For a growing number of people, this approach amounts to paternalism and foolishly perpetuates the state's problematic history of punishing possession, use, or efforts to buy, sell, grow, or transport cannabis. Engaging with this group may mean rethinking marketing, advertising, and brand awareness (Rup et al., 2020). It certainly means thinking about cannabis culture in broader terms. As Sifaneck & Kaplan (1995: 494) observed, part of the function of the Dutch coffee shop is to provide ... activities such as table games, pool, billiards, and table soccer. Cannabis smoking is usually not the sole reason why people patronize coffee shops. The coffee shop serves as an environment for recreation, listening to music, and socializing.

Evidence is emerging that people who use cannabis in Europe prefer to buy in a regulated or legal market (Skliamis & Korf, 2022). The opportunities to do so are still rare.

Another way to create social spaces for cannabis is to consider online options. In terms of normalization, we have set up a Facebook group, *Cannabis, Criminology, and Culture*, to provide a place to share information, design memes, and provide a means to discuss how cannabis has been shaped by criminology and what the future may hold. We credit Chris McCormick (2021) and his work creating, developing, and maintaining the *Visual and Cultural Criminology* Facebook page for this idea. Populated by lawyers, cannabis researchers, academics, artists, musicians, poets, and parents from around the world, this group serves as a space for people who consume cannabis therapeutically or as a source of amusement, relaxation, and pleasure to reflect on the nature of cannabis culture.

To confront individual stigmas, we need to undo what we think we know about drugs (Szalavitz, 2021), especially cannabis. The United Nations Office of Drug Control (UNODC) reports more than 200 million people used cannabis in 2019.[2] Many among this group are law-abiding, productive citizens, who volunteer in their communities and who view consuming cannabis as a recreational activity. A central challenge is the apparent lack of examples of people who responsibly use cannabis and have attained success. Bill Hicks routinely mocked this idea:

> I think drugs have done some good things for us. I really do. And if you don't believe drugs have done good things for us, do me a favor. Go home tonight. Take all your albums, all your tapes, and all your CDs and burn them. 'Cause, you know what, the musicians that made all that great music that's enhanced your lives throughout the years were real fucking high on drugs. The Beatles were so fucking high they let Ringo sing a few tunes.[3]

Even contemporary well-known, well-off, and indisputably successful people feel constrained by the judgment of others about cannabis. For example, Seth Rogan has observed:

> I smoke weed all day and every day and have for 20 years.... For me, it's like glasses or shoes. It's something I need to navigate my life, ... People have tried to make me feel shame about it over the years or have tried to make me seem like I'm weak or stupid for integrating it so completely into my life, but I'm almost 40 now, I'm married, I have a good job, and I have just found that none of the stigmas I was told to be true are true.[4]

It is worth thinking about the consequences associated with discovering your government, teachers, health professionals, and parents deliberately misled you about the relative risks of cannabis or other drugs.

This may be generational. In 2021, a story on "CannaMoms," or mothers that microdose—which refers to the use of small amounts of cannabis—often in lieu of wine or other pharmaceuticals, to manage the stress of parenting, captured our attention. Mom's reported small amounts of cannabis alleviated postpartum depression and allowed them to be more creative with their children. For example,

> generational attitudes are beginning to shift across the board—some of her students even report their grandparents using cannabis . . . this generational easing has occurred at precisely the right time to serve the burgeoning cannamom movement . . . younger generations are less judgmental, so, since the cannamom demographic is slightly younger views of millennials and Gen Zers will help shake off some stigma.
>
> (Staniforth, 2021)

This does not mean that there are no credible concerns about cannabis and its place in society.

Cannabis and Credible Concerns

In the interest of honest engagement and reflexivity (Wheeldon et al., 2014), we feel compelled to consider credible concerns that challenge the views expressed in this book. Such an effort centers on to what extent we are willing to revisit our assumptions and beliefs about cannabis. We have argued throughout the book that the limited dangers represented by cannabis use can no longer (and never did) justify adopting a public safety focus which has led to aggressive law enforcement tactics, disparate racial outcomes, and needless human suffering. Likewise, feigned efforts to replace public safety with public health have led to paternalistic policies, coercive treatment, and stigmatizing encounters with authority figures, medical professionals, and others. However, despite these profound costs, there are legitimate concerns with our vision of cannabis control. These deserve to be identified.

The first caveat that we accept is that there is a misperception that cannabis is a cure-all or panacea. Some hold that it is medicine suitable for all afflictions and nourishes and nurtures those who consume it. It's not, and it isn't. However, the observation that it isn't suitable for everyone all the time has been taken to mean it is good for no one ever. This has done profound harm to people, communities, and societies. Policymakers must be able to hold two divergent thoughts in their heads at the same time. In general, inhaling burning plant matter into one's lungs is never a good idea; at the same time, there may be benefits to using cannabis responsibly.

Smoking allows THC, cannabidiol (CBD), and other terpenes to be absorbed into the blood, leading to a more efficient high. Ingesting edibles is clearly better in terms of respiratory health. However, eating cannabis means the psychoactive compounds reach the bloodstream through the liver, changing the experience and perception of the "high." Some products, such as water pipes (or "bongs") reduce the temperature of the smoke, making it less irritating to the lungs. However, this can be deceiving and does not eliminate toxins in tobacco smoke or protect the lungs in any meaningful way (Santos-Longhurst, 2019). Others suggest vaping cannabis flower (as opposed to concentrates) is a healthier way to ingest cannabis compared to smoking it; however, we are still not certain of the long term effects of vaping. Although, again, inhaling partially dampened fire into the organs that help us breathe is, by definition, risky (Santos-Longhurst, 2020).

Another legitimate concern is that the regular use of significant amounts of cannabis by youth may represent a danger to their physical and mental health, depending on their frequency and patterns of use. It should come as no surprise that these dangers increase as the age of the person consuming cannabis decreases. In Canada, legalization *has* impacted youth in one clear way. As Wang & Post (2019) document, unintentional cannabis ingestion rose in children, increasing child cannabis-related Emergency Department (ED) visits in Alberta. While these events are unfortunate and horrifying for parents, in most cases, no long-term damage has been reported. It is connected to an additional worry: the THC arms race. This appears to be based on the myth that more THC content is the key to an enjoyable cannabis high. As a result, the market has shifted toward high-THC strains and products. This oversimplifies the nature of cannabis ingestion and misrepresents the connection between THC and CBD, as well as the interactions with other terpenes. It is the interaction between these, combined with the set, setting, and other internal and external factors, that influence the experience.

The quest for high-THC cannabis has led to dabbing, which involves inhaling waxy cannabis preparations consisting of highly concentrated THC through a vaporizer or similar device. It has also led cannabis suppliers to focus on high THC as a selling point in their flower or pre-rolled joints. However, it may be helpful to remind those concerned about high levels of THC that "The more THC in a joint, the less the user needs to smoke to get the same effect—making them more healthy, not less" (Boyd & Carter, 2014: 100). However, cannabis insiders and industry experts have stated repeatedly that higher THC levels do not necessarily lead to a better cannabis high.[5] More research should try to uncover the interactions that result in feelings of euphoria, introspection, reflection, and fun associated with consuming cannabis and how this relates to levels of THC, CBD, and other chemicals in cannabis.

Perhaps the biggest worry is failing to appreciate the catalytic effects of mixing alcohol and cannabis. Although we explored alcohol and cannabis in our discussion on driving and motor vehicle safety, the interactions of these substances when used together are also a concern. In general, there is limited research to help guide policy. However, it does seem likely that while people respond differently, combining cannabis and alcohol often increases the effects of both drugs (Dubois et al., 2015; Hartman & Huestis, 2013). Reactions include sedation, alterations in judgment, perceptual effects that include time distortions, and physical effects such as slowed reflexes and decreased motor coordination that can present serious risks when driving or operating heavy machinery (Sewell et al., 2009; Ramaekers et al., 2000). Since they affect different parts of the brain, their combination, particularly at high doses, can lead to situations that place people who simultaneously use alcohol and cannabis at risk (Stevens et al., 2021).

More work is required to update existing public health programs to present an honest picture of known health consequences of cannabis use based on sound and up-to-date scientific evidence. The harmful effects should not be exaggerated or invented (see, e.g., Westoll, 2018). The benefits of using cannabis so publicized in the media should be tempered with more information about responsible ways to use cannabis. In addition, it would be helpful if educational programs about drug use included lessons on the effects of stigma and strategies for reducing stigma around drug use. This could be helpful in the transition from cannabis prohibition and perhaps even in addressing the ongoing opiate overdose crisis that is currently devastating Canada and the United States. This is especially relevant given the potential for cannabis to serve as a replacement for injected drugs and reports that US overdose deaths have risen especially rapidly among Black and American Indian residents (Ingraham, 2022).

Cannabis Criminology: Sustaining and Extending Reform

Sustaining and extending cannabis reform requires engaging with criminology's history.
For Cohen (1985: 85), this means recognizing that

> every one of the major patterns I have described ... expansion, dispersal, invisibility, penetration—is indeed continuous with those original transformations. The prison remains—a stubborn continuous presence, seemingly impervious to all attacks—and in its shadow lies "community control."

This observation is relevant when we examine the reluctance amongst criminologists to challenge cannabis and other drug prohibition. This is not to say that no scholar has ever supported or advised depenalization, decriminalization, or even legalization. However, the field has failed to confront the ways moral panics, racism, and xenophobia shaped drug policies. Too many criminologists have often relied upon incomplete data, poor methods, and deeply problematic analyses when researching drug use (Ritter, 2021). It must be confronted if cannabis culture can emerge in ways that constrain the unconscious embrace of the criminal justice system's focus on punishment, control, and coercive harm (Maruna et al., 2004).

It is past time for the field to consider the criminal justice system's role in providing a steady stream of clients to for-profit treatment programs. Mandating "re-education" programs for those caught using a substance less dangerous than many alcoholic beverages often available in local grocery stores is an example of the long reach of prohibitionist ideas. The strategic submission to drug treatment to avoid a criminal record is not informed consent. Such an approach mocks the values that inform respectful therapeutic relationships. The history of these ideas must be understood if they are to be confronted. The tendency to view hard-won reforms as stable has been challenged in recent years. From reproductive health, the right to vote and holding public officials to account, every generation is obliged to fight to sustain the world their parents left them. This applies to cannabis. While our generation grew up under prohibition and the War on Drugs, our children will face the influence of "New Prohibitionists," who remain influential even as most of their claims cannot be substantiated (Heidt & Wheeldon, 2022).

Focusing on cannabis provides a near-constant reminder that proximity to the most significant power in a liberal democracy to constrain freedom can, and has, overwhelmed the importance of speaking truth to power and protecting fairness within the criminal justice system. It requires acknowledging that billions of dollars have been transferred from subjugated communities to governments and corporations (Page & Soss, 2021: 291–293), and that we continue to document how police benefit from civil forfeiture laws. The potential for this kind of introspective and reflective thinking requires documenting how prohibiting the consumption of certain substances has always been about controlling those who are different (Miller, 1996).

Cannabis and Criminology

In recent work, we explored the prohibition, decriminalization, and liberalization of cannabis policy through the lens of criminological and sociological theory, essential concepts, and cannabis research by focusing on five thematic areas, including law, society, and social control; police and policing cannabis; race, ethnicity, and criminalization; the economics of cannabis use; and cannabis use and criminal behavior (Wheeldon & Heidt, 2023b). By linking critical areas in past and contemporary cannabis research to criminological and sociological theories, including key concepts, emergent concerns, and new directions, we set out an ambitious research program to explore several themes we detail in this book. However, while we rely on existing theories and approaches to guide this research, we argue it is essential that we look to new kinds of data. This means making more of criminology's multi-disciplinary potential.

As we document in Chapter 6, canonical work in this area was completed using qualitative methods (Becker, 1963; Young, 1971). As Becker notes, reflecting on that work, "Instead of talking about drug abuse, I talked about drug *use*" (Gopnik, 2015). We believe more studies are needed that focus on the importance of qualitative research (Jacques, 2014) and engage people who use drugs as an essential source of data. There have been various recent efforts to incorporate people who use drugs within criminological research (Copes et al., 2021; Greer & Ritter, 2020a; Heidt & Wheeldon, 2022).

Prioritizing those who use cannabis and other insiders requires rethinking the problematic and exclusionary methodologies of the past. Translating this research in ways that meet the needs of policymakers is also essential.

Translational Criminology

Translational criminology refers to a movement designed to improve collaboration between academics and criminal justice practitioners. The concept is borrowed from the field of medicine; its goal is to translate research into best practices by improving the communication between researchers and policymakers. The cost(s) of cannabis prohibition is perhaps the best way to understand the challenges inherent in translational criminology. Understanding the "translational process" is essential. For example,

> This translational process can often involve competing ideologies, fear, public pressure, media scrutiny, bureaucratic resistance, and other influences. As a result, how and under what specific mechanisms research is acquired, interpreted, and effectively employed by policymakers and criminal justice practitioners remains unclear. The growing mandate for evidence-based policies and practices makes it imperative to identify and understand the specific mechanisms of knowledge translation within criminal justice.
> (Pesta et al., 2016: iii)

This is especially important for cannabis policy.

There is no lack of evidence for how the social harms of cannabis prohibition vastly outweighed any social benefit. Recently, National Institute on Drug Abuse (NIDA) Director Nora Volkow has acknowledged the errors of the past, the benefits of cannabis regulation, and the need to shift from a punitive approach to drugs to a strategy focused on public health (Peters, 2020). According to one view, what is required are new approaches to data presentation. Burruss and Lu (2022: 264) connect the goals of translational criminology to data visualization, which can "be useful for researchers to both communicate research to practitioners and make that research useful for organizational purposes." Challenging punitive prohibitionist policies that emerge from political contexts may require more than mere translation. Prohibitionist ideas persist despite evidence that legal drugs such as tobacco and alcohol are associated with more significant public and long-term health problems than many illicit drugs (NIH, 2007).

CANNABIS CRIMINOLOGY: SUSTAINING AND EXTENDING REFORM 253

Introduced in Chapter 6, Sheehan and colleagues (2021) compared pre-implementation and post-implementation differences in arrest rates in US states. By focusing on decriminalization, legalization, and no policy changes, their findings highlight in clear ways some contemporary problems around policing cannabis and racial inequality. The idiom that "a picture is worth a thousand words" seems especially relevant to Figure 9.1.

Beyond presenting data, there also may be a role for images that embrace the critical impulse at the heart of some visual criminologies (Wheeldon, 2021). One form of political communication "presents a variety of interesting communication strategies that play with the branded images and icons of consumer culture to make consumers aware of surrounding problems and diverse cultural experiences that warrant their attention" (Center for Communication and Civic Engagement, n.d.). One example is the work of *Adbusters*, an organization comprised of an "international collective of artists, designers, writers, musicians, poets, punks, philosophers, and wild hearts [who have] been smashing ads, fighting corruption and speaking truth to power."[6] From critiquing consumer culture and mocking advisements for alcohol and cigarettes, prohibition culture jamming is a form of political communication that "play[s] with the branded images and icons of consumer culture" (Center for Communication and Civic Engagement, n.d.)

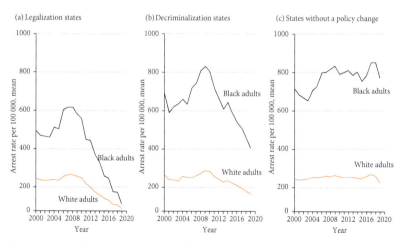

Figure 9.1 Adult arrest rate trends of cannabis possession by race between legalization, decriminalization, and no-policy-reform states
Source: Sheehan et al. (2021: 4).

and combines visually arresting images and ironic text which mimics traditional advertising while mocking the message.

An example, in the same vein as some Ad Council ads of the past, includes the omnipresent "Just Say No" narrative of the 1980s. Figure 9.2 has been shared on social media and debunked every year since its creation (Sadeghi, 2020). While difficult to read, the bottom left near the Ad Council logo states, "If you or someone you know is addicted to marijuana, call Domino's, rent a tape, and enjoy" and includes a phone number for Domino's Pizza. This approach is designed to mock the War on Drugs messages of the past by deliberately exaggerating the risks of smoking cannabis.

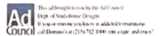

Figure 9.2 Cannabis and prohibition culture jamming
Source: Created as parody by Studiohouse Designs, LLC. Used with permission.

Whatever the value of better "translating" research in ways policymakers can appreciate, understand, and use, broader societal forces complicate the direct implementation of research into policy. Another approach is to create a constituency for reform by focusing on the public at large. Simply sharing this research has been notoriously unsuccessful in shifting policy. Cannabis research focused on issues related to criminology should continue. However, approaches to communicating the results of this research must be updated. While our focus is on cannabis policy, it may have value in other areas in which research is critical of existing practices, and researchers struggle to engage decision-makers or are uncomfortable challenging pervasive myths. Presenting evidence in practical ways is essential. When research suggests politically unpalatable policies, it is crucial to be able to build a constituency to seek credible analysis. This can challenge the prohibitionist tendencies allowing older, limited, and structurally unsound studies that continue to be cited in media reports warning of addiction in ways that are reminiscent of the "Reefer Madness" propaganda of old (LaMotte, 2022).

Updating Public Criminology

As introduced in Chapter 7, the future of cannabis research needs to consider the damage of a century of cannabis prohibition. Those interested in cannabis and crime have an obligation to avoid exploiting this area to serve mercantile careerist concerns (Wheeldon et al., 2014). The danger here is that research that fails to take seriously the past problems of prohibition and the current risks inherent in what we have defined as the moral panic multiverse is likely to sustain, justify, and promote failed punitive approaches. Given these dangers, we argue researchers in this must adopt a "duty of care" when conducting research focused on drugs and people who use them. The Social Care Institute of the United Kingdom defines a duty of care as a legal obligation to

- always act in the best interest of individuals and others
- not act or fail to act in a way that results in harm
- act within your competence and not take on anything you do not believe you can safely do.

(SCIE, n.d.)

While a research duty of care is not a legal obligation, this can be understood as researchers taking personal responsibility for the damage their flawed research might do. It can be defined as a duty to look after vulnerable individuals and communities and protect them from harm that would likely result from poor research.

We are not suggesting that criminologists never engage in cannabis-based research and they do not need to avoid publishing research findings that indicate the danger of cannabis use or the value of one sort of regulation or another. By contrast, we define a duty of care in cannabis research as requiring researchers to take care to explain research terms in meaningful and consistent ways, adopt research designs that are appropriate to the area of study, and—most importantly——present research limitations clearly and honestly. Finally, it should involve cautioning readers that structural racism in the criminal justice system and many other related social institutions may lead to adverse consequences that are likely to impact people of color disproportionately. One solution is for criminologists who engage in drug research to examine the experiences of people who use drugs and others involved with drug subcultures. Lastly, researchers should also consider participatory, inclusive, and creative research approaches rather than the abstracted and exclusionary research designs of the past.

Pragmatism and Cannabis Criminology

The contribution of Alex Stevens to drug reform cannot be overstated. In this book, we borrowed from his view that any drug reform proposal must be assessed according to its ability to reduce inequality, recognize the need for international reform, and be based on evidence (Stevens, 2011). Shifts in cannabis policy have been driven by a revolution, including legal reform, moral reconsideration, and the emergence of cannabis culture through normalization. Change has been further supported by the growing awareness of the harms of cannabis prohibition. As we have taken pains to make clear throughout the book, it is essential to recognize the racial consequences of the drug war alongside inconvenient findings suggesting that depenalization, decriminalization, and even legalization tend to benefit White people over all others. As part of this evaluative scheme, we argue drug reformers should consider to what extent drug reforms are criminologically pragmatic (Wheeldon, 2015).

Noted drug policy scholars (Ritter, 2021; Stevens & Zampini, 2018) are interested in offering a philosophical basis for expanding how to think about regulation, democracy, and inclusive processes. One candidate is pragmatism. Pragmatism was interpreted by Sir Leon Radzinowicz (1966: 101) to mean that criminologists' ought to treat "each problem as it arises and in its particular context, instead of approaching them all on the basis of some single general principle." For some, this has meant reducing pragmatism's philosophical pedigree to mere "practical criminal justice suggestions drawn from conservative theories of criminology" (Wheeldon, 2015: 396). Indeed, it is common to view pragmatism as a convenient philosophic means to justify "correctionalism" and a focus on practical (as opposed to critical) criminal justice policies (Cohen, 1974). As others have noted, theories of crime control that offer administratively useful categories of crime are often used to justify policies that view punishment as the best means to correct behavior (Haggerty, 2004).

In other work, pragmatism in criminology focused on the need to create the conditions by which truth claims can be subjected to more rigorous scrutiny (Wheeldon, 2015). This approach seeks to justify new approaches to criminological thinking by expanding how we think about crime, harm, and social control (Heidt & Wheeldon, 2015). Going forward, we seek to associate the study of cannabis within criminology with a willingness to move between the universal and the local and consider both international lessons and jurisdiction-specific realities. This means seeking common ground by considering cannabis insiders and those who work within systems that embrace prohibition while privileging those who have been harmed by the cannabis policies of the past.

Reforms which fail to consider how the system currently operates and how it might respond to proposed reforms are unlikely to succeed. This is what has been called the theory/practice problem—in which the role of human agency in undertaking action can neither be presumed nor ignored (Wheeldon, 2015). Our emphasis on tolerance of drug use serves as an overarching theme from which specific proposals emerge. However, as we have shown, meaningful reform requires regulating aversion. Ultimately, jurisdictions must consider a host of factors before embarking on cannabis liberalization. Some may choose to pivot from one approach to another. Efforts must also be made to understand the costs and consequences of adopting one model over another. Few will succeed without engaging the local market and consumers of cannabis. The sort of pragmatism presumed by what we call our "readiness-to-regulate" framework presented in Chapters 7 and 8 extends to other parts of our approach to cannabis reform.

Doubt and Consensus Building: Stan Cohen, Jürgen Habermas, and Richard Rorty

The need to consider how pragmatism might apply to cannabis and criminology relates to the long shadow of carceral control. Cohen's efforts to bring sociology back into criminology sought to challenge the ways in which social and psychological processes created labels for difference and proceeded to affix them, with damaging results. This resulted in dehumanized definitions and complicated the work of criminal justice agencies. One example was his work defining moral panics, which he described as an issue constructed as a threat to societal values. While these may disappear, sometimes

> the panic passes over and is forgotten, except in folklore and collective memory; at other times, it has more serious and long-lasting repercussions and might produce such changes as those in legal and social policy or even in the way society conceives itself.
> (Cohen, 2002 [1972]: 9)

His identification of threats to the social order and the ways in which these go on to shape public policy informed his later work.

As we have documented, our focus on Cohen centers on his view of the malignant impact of social control on social and cultural life (Cohen, 1979) and within an ever-expanding justice system (Cohen, 1985). By 1988, Cohen was describing "three voracious gods" that faced scholars working at the intersection of criminal justice and public policy. These include

> first, an overriding obligation to honest intellectual enquiry itself (however sceptical, provisional, irrelevant and unrealistic); second, a political commitment to social justice, and third (and potentially conflicting with both), the pressing and immediate demands for short-term humanitarian help.
> (Cohen, 1988: 122)

Cohen concludes that the only way to discharge these competing duties was to embrace doubt. This includes doubt that socially constructed labels were correct, doubt that progressive rhetoric would lead to meaningful reform, and in later years, doubt that states would, on their own, protect the rights of their citizens (Cohen, 2001). To his work on doubt, Cohen added worries about our tendency to deny the harms visited upon non-conforming citizens, often in our name. Indeed, this later work focused on state crimes, including murder, torture, imprisonment, and coercion but also on what Moon (2013: 194) described as Cohen's concern with the passivity and complicity of bystanders, witnesses, and the human rights apparatus itself. The denial of our own responsibility has increasingly obvious and dire consequences.

Perhaps every generation worries that democracy is in crisis and that we are merely a disaster, a bad-faith actor, or a stolen election away from fascism. Of course, 2022 marks just one year since an attempted coup d'état in the United States. In the United Kingdom, the consequences of Brexit have become increasingly apparent, as Britain has the dubious distinction of being "the first country in the history of the world to impose economic sanctions on itself."[7] Democracy and the assumptions that underpin it appear under near-constant attacks, from fake news to the assault on science and the weaponization of the basic egalitarian decency at the root of the human rights project. The role of participatory disinformation, discussed in Chapter 3, is relevant to these concerns. Recent pronouncements that democracy is on the retreat globally are shocking, but they somehow still feel insufficient (Economist Intelligence Unit, 2020). If just 6 percent of the world's population lives under a "full democracy," it may not make sense to continue to assess countries based on principles nearly no one is embracing. In place of a *democracy index*, perhaps it makes sense to evaluate countries based on their *affinity with authoritarianism*.

Moral Pragmatism and Cannabis Policy

Cohen concludes *Visions of Social Control* (1985: 252–253) by presenting *moral pragmatism*, which he argues is essential to evaluating community control and other such forms of regulation. This means combining the moral imperative to seek reform of the social structures which allow inequity to persist and pursue justice to ensure fairness for the collective good. Unlike simplistic accounts of pragmatism, for Cohen, these values must not be twisted by utilitarian calculations or strategic considerations but exist as essential in and of themselves, given their importance to human needs. Cohen's (1985: 253) pragmatism is thus ontological and epistemological. It "stands against all forms of premature theoretical and political closure, all quests for cognitive certainty which rule out certain solutions as being conceptually impure or politically inadmissible" (Cohen, 1985: 253).

Policy proposals must be evaluated based on how well they adhere to the values of doing good and doing justice and to what extent they can counter the ways in which existing control systems fulfill other social functions, prioritize utilitarian goals over egalitarian objectives, and benefit from deeply rooted inequities that exist within nearly all social systems. This means accepting the role of adversarial nihilist and, when required, questioning the purpose of liberal reforms, which can end up being co-opted by the system, often in unintended ways. As we have argued, in the context of cannabis, this means expanding tolerance and regulating the aversion which persists based on ideological views and a century of messaging about the dangers of cannabis and the people who use it. However, lurking within Cohen's view of pragmatism is a common problem. How can we define policy goals in ways that consider how well-intentioned reforms result in threats to civil liberties, the extension of state power, and disguised coercion?

This window into Cohen's (1985) criminological concerns about the complexity of constraining state power remains prophetic regarding cannabis liberalization. A partial reply might be understood by considering insights from Jürgen Habermas and Richard Rorty. Each provides a different account of participatory approaches to democratic engagement. While Habermas is more optimistic, Rorty's description appears more prescient. Efforts to imagine a more robust role for democratic principles in social institutions are at least a century old (Dewey, 1916). Ritter cites Habermas (2006) and Herman & Chomsky (2002), among others, to present the potential for novel forms of meaningful democratic engagement on drug policy.

Deliberative Democracy and Drug Policy Revisited
For Habermas (2006), the authoritarian impulse at the heart of modern societies is, in part, a function of existing democratic processes, which have failed to live up to egalitarian ideals and expectations. However, he argues that people can reach a consensus, whatever their differences, by engaging "the old promise" of a community of free and equal members, guiding their conduct through collective common reason, which can be redeemed.[8] Such harmony requires fashioning procedures and processes, allowing for ego-free compromise and a commitment to moving forward together. This is consistent with Cohen's view of morality within moral pragmatism and Habermas's focus on inclusion and equality. As Ritter suspects, Habermas would likely endorse her call for "deliberative and discursive democratic practices, alongside broader participatory processes" to guide drug policy (Ritter, 2021: 120).

This is consistent with the need for democracy to be "reconceived under the conditions of complex societies" (Habermas, 1996: 7). One part of Habermas's project is based on his assumption that the world is a site for progress and cooperative achievement. What is needed, he argues, is a commitment to processes that can construct a future that is better than the present. This not only involves making good policy but also includes the methods by which it can be made. For Habermas, the *deliberative ideal* requires reflexivity: minimizing conflict, ensuring impartiality, and reciprocity. These procedurally suitable decisions allow for outcomes that are more inclusive and equitable, less selfish, and mercurial (Habermas, 2006). Such an approach could lead to more "participatory" or "discursive" democracy as part of more "expansive, organic deliberative processes" around drug policy reform (Ritter, 2021: 126).

Ritter does not mention Richard Rorty. However, her interest in citizens' juries represents a pragmatic example, in Rortarian terms, given their practical potential to ensure participatory policy-based processes. According to Ritter (2021: 130), the citizens' jury model provides opportunities for the voices of everyday people, enabled through the provision of "balanced" and "neutral" information to engage with one another. Through structured dialogue, they provide a deliberated and informed consensus view of the public policy issue at hand. Important in Ritter's description is the role of "everyday people." Rorty would support such practices if they ensured a central role for those impacted by the policy in question—in this case, people who use drugs.

Reframed in this way, drug experience becomes significant to a body attempting to create rules and structures to govern these substances. This sort of inclusion might constrain the outsized role of New Prohibitionists, agents from corporate cannabis, or the for-profit treatment industry. However, Rorty might worry that this sort of commitment is a mere social convention that exists only at the "nicer end of the spectrum of western culture, such as in university seminar rooms and as part of scientific debate" (Kim, 2014: 110). He routinely mocked assumptive epistemic certainty and warned of the lethal self-confidence that results from the veiled insistence that one set of purposes is naturally worthier than any other. Rather than focus on some international consensus, cannabis reform may be more likely to succeed when it proceeds jurisdiction by jurisdiction and when we resist the folly of using old language to describe new problems (Rorty, 1979).

Rorty's subsequent focus on the potential for private spheres (1989) to supplement the public process is based on his view that these spheres provide new ways to describe, define, and express philosophical ideas and create the vocabulary needed to translate them into political action.

Applied to criminology (Wheeldon, 2015), Rorty's interest in creating new vocabularies can be seen as consistent with some constitutive criminologists who have advanced critical explorations of crime through "replacement discourses" to challenge inaccurate and sensationalized portrayals of crime in the media (Arrigo & Milovanovic, 2009; Henry & Milovanovic, 1996). This suggests drug policy has changed because activists have been about to redescribe drug prohibition as damaging, intrusive, and out of step with public opinion. By redescribing the injustices of cannabis prohibition, they are "dreaming up new words in which to express alternative possibilities" (Rorty, 1995: 441).

In drug policy, the ascendence of correctionalist thinking might be seen alongside the development that mandating people who use drugs to treatment programs and coercing participation by the threat of a criminal record is now seen as a praiseworthy example of criminal justice reform. The prohibitionist project is now so ingrained that just about any effort to replace the prison as primary means of control is accepted as progress. While this is perhaps consistent with one view of harm reduction, it highlights the challenges associated with reimagining liberty. For a generation who grew up in an era of mass incarceration (Alexander, 2010), the culture of social control (Garland, 2001), and the growing militarization of domestic law enforcement (Balko, 2014), the predation and intrusions of the criminal justice system are now part of the fabric of their world view. As new markets have emerged which have changed the political calculation associated with prohibition, new kinds of pressure have required innovative possibilities for social practice that were unimaginable a decade ago. As we have argued in this book, it means identifying not just legal barriers but social and cultural obstacles as well.

If Cohen reminds drug reform advocates of the dangers of euphemistic but unaccountable reform, Habermas is more hopeful about the potential to bring people together to find shared solutions to communal problems. While such efforts ought not to be abandoned, it is Rorty's view that appears to have been most successful. Instead of trying to get behind the appearance of reality to find the context transcending truth, reform is a result of inventing a new language that can "persuade people to act differently than in the past" (Rorty, 1994: 231) by abandoning the existing justificatory context for cannabis prohibition. Whether one is focused on outlining the limits of reform, working toward a broad democratic consensus, or seeking to redescribe the past in pragmatic and socially valuable ways, establishing a credible view of evidence compiled to date is essential.

Cannabis Criminology: Insights, Interrogation, and Imagination

In Chapter 1, we argued that framing criminology through the lens of cannabis is one means for those in our field to engage their imagination (Young, 2011). From the history of cannabis control to the theories which animate our discipline, criminology and cannabis are connected. Reframing cannabis prohibition as an example of the predation of the criminal justice system facilitates novel ways to understand the criminalization of subcultures. It brings into stark relief the notion that even as decriminalization deprives prisons of inmates, it creates new "patients" to be treated by for-profit enterprises and mercurial specialists.

Cannabis is also a fascinating way to consider moral panics and policymaking, normalization, and social change. It may offer another way to conceive of public criminology, or criminologies if one prefers. Perhaps most importantly, cannabis is a means to understand the importance of who is consulted during the policymaking process. To date, too few have incorporated other voices that may be important to understanding the finer aspects of cannabis legalization and regulation. The voices of people who use drugs and those involved in the cannabis industry seem to have been ignored or drowned out by others during the process of policy formation around cannabis. For example, many of the problems that we see now with legalization in Canada could have been easily predicted by people more familiar with the existing subculture (Heidt, 2021).

The value of cannabis to embrace the criminological imagination means seeking novel constructions instead of solely replicating past studies. It means staying open to the possibility, however unlikely, that you may not know what you think you do. For Young (2011: 180–181), there are

> two criminologies: one grants meaning to crime and deviance, one that takes it away; one which uses an optic which envisages the wide spectrum of human experience: the crime and law-abiding, the deviant and supposedly normal—the whole round of human life, the other a lens that can only focus on the negative, the predatory, the supposedly pathological; one which encompasses a world of creativity and is an agent of *verstehen*, one which is fixated on the scientific and the nomothetic; one who vista is emotion: it is a criminology of excitement, anxiety, panic, and frequently boredom, another whose actors are miserable creatures of rational choice and determinacy, either a passionless foreground or a mechanistic background;

one that is the voice of those below and the investigator of the powerful, the other which echoes the white noise of the criminal justice system; one which seeks to reclaim criminology for sociology, the other which sets up a "crime science" divorced from the great modernist tradition of Marx, Weber, Durkheim, and Simmel. One is the criminology of the imagination; the other frowns on such exuberance and resolutely proclaims the mundane nature of the everyday world. One carefully patrols its borders, shutting out the philosophical, the overly theoretical as too reflective, and carefully excluding war, genocide, state crime, crimes against the environment, and so on, as outside of its "scientific focus," while the other views such boundaries as there are to be crossed and there are to be learnt from, and constantly expands the lens of criminology.

To this passage, we respond there is room for both criminologies within the study of cannabis. But they must be inverted. Regarding cannabis, it is the system that has been "negative, the predatory ... pathological" (Young, 2011: 180) and has used "mechanistic" punishment to respond to the "criminology of... panic" while ignoring the "scientific" and the "rational" (Young, 2011: 180). Perhaps the criminology of the imagination should look to the "mundane nature of the everyday world" and recognize the War on Drugs as a "state crime" (Young, 2011: 181) that demands an armistice.

This sort of imaginative approach can be used to reframe people who use cannabis and other drugs as market insiders (Sandberg, 2012a, 2012b). Not unlike computer hackers who are hired to improve network security at fortune 500 companies, privileging the views of cannabis insiders can result in drafting intelligent policies and regulations for cannabis by better understanding the thought process of people who are involved in the cannabis trade. Surveying insiders to develop policy is not the only cultural shift we are witnessing. Consider reports from the Federal Bureau of Investigation (FBI) and, at the same time, concerns about how the employment policy was limiting hire dates to 2014 (Levinson, 2014). In recent years, modifications have been approved. To attract young tech-savvy applicants, the FBI has loosened its employment policy to ensure those who used cannabis in the past may not be limited from working for the FBI.[9]

We seek to link our work on cannabis criminology, meaningful decriminalization, and responsible regulation within a vision of criminology that is constantly expanding, questioning, and demanding that the exercise of state authority is minimal, justified, and serves the goals of freedom from violence and security from the state. Such an approach shows how political philosophers offer a means to expand conversations, involve those previously ignored, and are rooted in realities, even if they are uncomfortable. This means taking seriously the role of stigma, judgment, and moralizing in policymaking. It requires acknowledging that moral panics may come more quickly and can spread faster than ever before. Drug researchers need to think carefully about how their work may be used to prop up prohibition and take some responsibility for the harm that may result. Policymakers should consider international models, note lessons, and avoid missteps. This approach must consider the potential for the power of the state to escape the confines of polite conversation and refocus good faith efforts in ways that objectify, classify, and tame reform and reformers. By reproducing authority while claiming to abandon and renounce past injustices that resulted, illusions of reform often replace the real thing.

This book has sought to apply Stan Cohen's contributions to sociology and criminology to cannabis reform. Our central concern was how state power extends, expands, and replicates forms of control (Cohen, 1985). Kim (2014) notes that Habermas's defense of traditional philosophy and the value of some sort of international moral basis for collective action still resonates with many. However, there are problems for those who hold on to such notions. The history of cannabis prohibition is one in which rational, impartial, inclusive, and egalitarian approaches have been largely absent and certainly not influential. This is not because there was a lack of international conventions and conferences or because those critical of existing drug policy were not invited to present their ideas. Instead, these ideas could not overcome the prohibitionist inertia and the confluence of international regulation and national interests (Collins, 2021).

Confronting these barriers means gathering data in jurisdictions considering how best to regulate cannabis is essential. This data provides a starting point for policymakers. More importantly, it stipulates boundaries around which to organize efforts to expand participatory and democratic processes in the creation and nascent reform of drug policy. The readiness to regulate framework offers one means to gather local data to create a basis from which to deliberate. It cannot overcome every concern expressed by Habermas about the corrupting character of money or power in such conversations, neither can it address Rorty's doubt that such an effort would provide an objective truth from which to proceed to policy. It could, however, establish some contingent truths for Rorty while ensuring a means to validate these truths through more meaningful Habermasian deliberation. Prioritizing those who use cannabis and other subcultural insiders requires rethinking the problematic and exclusionary methodologies of the past (Jacques, 2014). Incorporating these voices may be crucial to understanding the finer aspects of cannabis legalization and regulation. It may be the best way to apply the contributions of Stan Cohen to the future of cannabis policy.

Conclusion

This book began by outlining three assumptions. The first concerned stigma. There is a tendency among some academic treatments of cannabis to treat the moralizing around drug use as a persistent feature of society, which should be presumed, but not necessarily challenged (Ritter, 2021; Stevens, 2011). It certainly is the case that more than a century of evidence challenging the principles of prohibition has not succeeded in changing drug policy generally. However, in the case of cannabis, morality, ideology, and assumptive virtue associated with abstinence can be challenged and, indeed, overcome. For example, an overwhelming proportion of US adults (91 percent) say either that cannabis should be legal for medical and recreational use (60 percent) or that it should be legal for medical use only (31 percent) (Van Green, 2022). Yet, public opinion and empirical evidence may never entirely overcome the power of prohibitionist assumptions.

The second assumption was that confronting stigma requires understanding how tolerance can be expanded and how aversion can be regulated. Expanding tolerance in policymaking means embracing a rights-based approach against unjustified intrusions by the criminal justice system, abandoning the policing of cannabis use and the practices by which police departments financially benefit from its legal status. In our view, continuing to prohibit and police cannabis use will lead to racially unequal outcomes and increasingly deadly encounters. It wastes resources and erodes public trust and community relations. It also encourages coercive programming, whether in prison or in the community. The authoritarian streak associated with compelling people to engage in treatment sends a powerful and pernicious message that the agency and autonomy of private citizens are less important than the interests of those who hold power. Regulating this tendency is essential, and cannabis reform offers a practical means to do so (Brown, 2022).

Compulsory treatment is inconsistent with the principles associated with liberal democracies and represents a powerful example of how well-meaning people have come to delude themselves that rehabilitation can occur through force (Cohen, 1985). The worrying trend by which cannabis decriminalization is being married with police-led diversion to mandated treatment programs cannot be ignored. This requires revisiting decarceration and the belief that the existence of community-based alternatives that replace incarceration means the war on cannabis has been won. We argued that the view held by a worrying number of drug reformers that forced treatment in lieu of a criminal record is a progressive drug reform is problematic. If decriminalization is combined with increased referrals for "problem cannabis use" to private enterprises, which operate based on the strategic subservience to the nonsense of probation conditions, reformers may win the battle and lose the war.

Our view is that community models of engagement offer a better means to connect those seeking assistance to community-based social supports in ways that are presented but never required. Adopting this view may be relevant to other kinds of drug reform. Indeed, supervised injection sites operate based on this model. By providing a safer place to use drugs, they also connect people and resources. They have been shown to reduce overdose deaths and HIV and hepatitis-C transmissions and increase treatment outcomes for those infected, while offering a means for people ready to change existing drug use patterns. These benefits occur in both sanctioned (Levengood et al., 2021) and unsanctioned (Suen et al., 2022) supervised injection sites. Such an approach means updating our understanding of addiction. It cannot succeed if we continue to view people who use drugs, including those who consume cannabis, as "sick" and needing to be "treated." The profoundly unjust practice of continuing to criminalize drug use and then using the threat of criminal prosecution to coerce treatment must be abandoned.

International examples and an ever-growing evidence base demonstrate that cannabis prohibition has done dramatic harm to citizens worldwide and that moving on from prohibition is associated with a variety of public health benefits and improvements. Cannabis policies must be carefully designed and implemented in ways that reduce, rather than extend, harm. This may require reconsidering the role of criminologists and other scholars. Engaging more participatory approaches based on the optimism of Jürgen Habermas, the qualified hope of Richard Rorty, and the prescient warnings of Stanley Cohen requires doubling down on the impulse at the heart of criminology to understand new perspectives, telling stories of those who are not like us, and ensuring quantitative efforts to define generalizable "facts" are not accepted without assessing these findings in the light of qualitative nuance, ethnographic evidence, and insights and contestations from people who use cannabis, rather than those who seek to prohibit it.

Notes

1. Peter Kraska (personal communication, December 2021).
2. The UNODC reports that cannabis enforcement for use, cultivation, or sale is undertaken in almost all countries worldwide. In the period 2010–2019, sanctions were reported by 151 countries, covering 97 percent of the global population. See UNODC (2021a).
3. See https://www.dead-frog.com/comedians/jokes/bill-hicks.
4. See https://www.celebstoner.com/news/celebstoner-news/2020/10/25/seth-rogen-weed-like-shoes-glasses.
5. See, e.g., Roberts (2020) and https://essencevegas.com/blog/does-more-thc-mean-stronger-effects; see also Timber Cannabis Co. (n.d.).
6. See https://www.adbusters.org/about-us.
7. See https://twitter.com/LBC/status/1434855754469675010?s=20&t=Gsfkn2DmjGoBqbrV5FNPpA.
8. For a detailed and useful overview, see Stanford Encyclopedia of Philosophy (2007).
9. In the past, any cannabis use would have disqualified applicants. Now, cannabis use before eighteen would not automatically disqualify applicants. Applicants should not have consumed cannabis in the past year to be considered (FBI Jobs, n.d.).

References

Aachen, P. (2016). "New Marijuana Law Clears Way for Recreational, Medical Sales in Same Place." (March 30) *Portland Tribune*. Available at: https://pamplinmedia.com/pt/9-news/300048-177791-new-marijuana-law-clears-way-for-recreational-medical-sales-in-same-place.

Aaronson, E. & Rothschild-Elyassi, G. (2021). "The Symbiotic Tensions of the Regulatory–Carceral State: The Case of Cannabis Legalization." *Regulation & Governance* 15: S23–S39. https://doi.org/10.1111/rego.12394.

Abastillas, M., Michael, I., & Smith, T. (2020). "Howard Becker: An Intellectual Appreciation." *Silicon Valley Sociological Review* 18(1): 44–59. Available at: https://scholarcommons.scu.edu/svsr/vol18/iss1/8.

Abel, S. (1997). "Cannabis Policy in Australia and New Zealand." *Drug and Alcohol Review* 16(4): 421–428. https://doi.org/10.1080/09595239700186821.

Abercrombie, N., Hill, S., & Turner, B.S. (1994). *The Penguin Dictionary of Sociology*. London: Penguin Books.

ACDD (Advisory Committee on Drug Dependence) (1968). "Report on Cannabis by the Advisory Committee on Drug Dependence." (The Wootton Report). Home Office. Available at: https://www.ukcia.org/research/wootton/index.php.

Acker, L. (2020a). "Oregon Becomes First State to Legalize Psychedelic Mushrooms." (November 3) *Oregon Live*. Available at: https://www.oregonlive.com/politics/2020/11/oregon-becomes-first-state-to-legalize-psychedelic-mushrooms.html.

Acker, L. (2020b). "Oregon Legalizes Magic Mushrooms: 5 Things to Know." (November 4) *The Oregonian*. Available at: https://www.oregonlive.com/politics/2020/11/oregon-legalizes-magic-mushrooms-5-things-to-know.html.

Ackerman, M.S. & Lutters, W.G. (1996). "An Introduction to the Chicago School of Sociology." *Interval Research Propriety* 2(6): 1–25. Available at: https://www.academia.edu/7042690/An_Introduction_to_the_Chicago_School_of_Sociology._Lutters_Ackerman.

ACLU (American Civil Liberties Union) (2020). "A Tale of Two Countries: Racially Targeted Arrests in the Era of Marijuana Reform." ACLU Research Report. Available at: https://www.aclu.org/sites/default/files/field_document/marijuanareport_03232021.pdf.

ADAI (2017). *Marijuana Research Report. Biennial 2015–2017*. Alcohol & Drug Abuse Institute, University of Washington. Available at: https://adai.uw.edu/pubs/pdf/marijuanaresearchreport20152017.pdf.

Adams, D. (2022). "Marijuana Lounges Could Finally Come to Massachusetts, But Some Doubt They're Viable." (February 7) *Boston Globe*. Available at: https://www.bostonglobe.com/2022/02/07/marijuana/marijuana-lounges-could-finally-come-massachusetts-some-doubt-theyre-viable.

Adams, M. (2019). "Two Reasons to Legalize Marijuana: Embalming Fluid and Fentanyl-Laced Pot on Black Market." (April 18) *Forbes*. Available at: https://www.

forbes.com/sites/mikeadams/2019/04/18/two-reasons-to-legalize-marijuanaembalming-fluid-and-fentanyl-laced-pot-on-black-market.

Adda, J., McConnell, B., & Rasul, I. (2014). "Crime and the Depenalization of Cannabis Possession: Evidence from a Policing Experiment." *Journal of Political Economy* 122(5): 1130–1202. https://doi.org/10.1086/67693.

ADF (Alcohol and Drug Foundation) (n.d.). "Drug Decriminalisation in Detail." Available at: https://adf.org.au/talking-about-drugs/law/decriminalisation/decriminalisation-detail.

Adinoff, B. & Reiman, A. (2019). "Implementing Social Justice in the Transition from Illicit to Licit Cannabis." *American Journal of Drug and Alcohol Abuse* 45(6): 673–688.

Adler, P.A. & Adler, P. (1987). *Membership Roles in Field Research*. Newbury Park, CA: Sage.

Agoff, C., Fondevila, G., & Sandberg, S. (2021). "Cultural Stigmatization and Police Corruption: Cannabis, Gender, and Legalization in Mexico." *Drugs: Education, Prevention and Policy* 29(4): 373–381. https://doi.org/10.1080/09687637.2021.2004089.

Ahmed, S., Roth, R.M., Stanciu, C.N., & Brunette, M.F. (2021). "The Impact of THC and CBD in Schizophrenia: A Systematic Review." *Frontiers in Psychiatry* 12: 694394. https://doi.org/10.3389/fpsyt.2021.694394.

Akers, R.L. & Cochran, J.K. (1985). "Adolescent Marijuana Use: A Test of Three Theories of Deviant Behavior." *Deviant Behavior*, 6(4): 323–346.

Alberti, S., King, J., Hales, J., & Swan, A. (2004). "Court Diversion Program Evaluation: Overview Report: Final Report." Turning Point Alcohol and Drug Centre Inc. and Health Outcomes International Pty Ltd.

Albrecht, L. (2014). "Uruguay's Drug Policy Reform: At the Cutting Edge of Alternative Policy." *Journal of Peace and Conflict Studies* 1(1): 39–49.

Alchian, A. & Allen, W. (1967). *Exchange and Production*. 2nd edn. Belmont, CA: Wadsworth.

Alexander, M. (2010). *The New Jim Crow: Mass Incarceration in the Age of Colorblindness*. New York, NY: The New Press.

Alford, C. (2014). *How Medical Marijuana Laws Affect Crime Rates*. Charlottesville, VA: Mimeo, University of Virginia.

Ali, R. & Stevens, M. (2022) "Moving Toward Voluntary Community-Based Treatment for Drug Use and Dependence." *Health and Human Rights Journal* 24(1): 183–187.

Allcott, H. & Gentzkow, M. (2017). "Social Media and Fake News in the 2016 Election." *Journal of Economic Perspectives* 31(2): 211–236.

Allen, G. & Tunnicliffe, R. (2021). "Drug Crime Statistics for England and Wales." (December 23) House of Commons Library. Available at: https://researchbriefings.files.parliament.uk/documents/CBP-9039/CBP-9039.pdf.

Allentuck, S. & Bowman, K.M. (1942). "The Psychiatric Aspects of Marihuana Intoxication." *American Journal of Psychiatry* 99: 248–251.

Alshaarawy, O. & Anthony, J.C. (2019). "Cannabis Use among Women of Reproductive Age in the United States: 2002–2017." *Addictive Behaviors* https://doi.org/10.1016/j.addbeh.2019.106082.

Allspach, A. (2010). "Landscapes of (Neo-)Liberal Control: The Transcarceral Spaces of Federally Sentenced Women in Canada." *Gender, Place and Culture* 17(6): 705–723.

American Medical Association (1945). "Editorial: The Marijuana Problem." *Journal of the American Nutraceutical Association*, 127: 1129.

American Psychiatric Association (n.d.). "Diagnostic and Statistical Manual of Mental Disorders (DSM-5-TR)." Available at: https://www.psychiatry.org/psychiatrists/practice/dsm.

American Psychiatric Association (2013). *Diagnostic and Statistical Manual of Mental Disorders*. 5th edn. Washington, DC: American Psychiatric Association.

Amore, S. (2021). "People Think Sha'Carri Richardson's Suspension for Pot Is 'Absolutely Insane'." (July 1) *The Wrap*. Available at: https://www.thewrap.com/people-think-shacarri-richardsons-olympic-suspension-for-pot-is-absolutely-insane.

Amroussia, N., Watanabe, M., & Pearson, J. (2020). "Seeking Safety: A Focus Group Study of Young Adults' Cannabis Related Attitudes and Behavior in a State with Legalized Recreational Cannabis." *Harm Reduction Journal* 17(1): 92–99. https://doi.org/10.1186/s12954-020-00442-8.

Andresen, M.A. (2012). "Nipping It at the Boob: The Gateway Properties of Mother's Milk." *The Science Creative Quarterly*. Available at: https://www.scq.ubc.ca/nipping-it-at-the-boobthe-gateway-properties-of-mothers-milk/.

Anderson, D.M., Rees, D.I., Tekin, E. (2018). "Medical Marijuana Laws and Workplace Fatalities in the United States." *International Journal of Drug Policy* 60: 33–39. doi: 10.1016/j.drugpo.2018.07.008. Epub 2018 August 6. PMID: 30092547.

Andrew, S. (2020). "A Florida Man Who Spent 31 Years in Prison for a Nonviolent Marijuana Crime Has Been Released." (December 9) *CNN*. Available at: https://www.cnn.com/2020/12/09/us/richard-delisi-released-from-prison-trnd/index.html.

Androutsos, C. (2012). "Schizophrenia in Children and Adolescents: Relevance and Differentiation from Adult Schizophrenia." *Psychiatriki* 1: 82–93. Greek, Modern. PMID: 22796977.

Angeli, T. (2018). "Anti-Marijuana Group Wants Mandatory Assessment for Consumers." (October 23) Schedule 6 Foundation. Available at: https://www.marijuanamoment.net/anti-marijuana-group-wants-mandatory-assessment-for-consumers.

ANRF (American Nonsmokers' Rights Foundation) (n.d.). "Secondhand Marijuana Smoke: Factsheet." Available at: https://no-smoke.org/secondhand-marijuana-smoke-fact-sheet.

Anslinger, H. & Cooper, R. (1937). "Marijuana, Assassin of Youth." *American Magazine* 124(1): 19.

Anslinger, H.J. (1943). "The Psychiatric Aspects of Marihuana Intoxication." *Journal of the American Medical Association* 121(3): 212–213.

Arnone, D., Barrick, T., Chengappa, S., Mackay, C., Clark, C., & Abou-Saleh, M. (2008). "Corpus Callosum Damage in Heavy Marijuana Use: Preliminary Evidence from Diffusion Tensor Tractography and Tract-Based Spatial Statistics." *NeuroImage* 41(3): 1067–10744.

Arrigo, B. & Milovanovic, D. (2009). *Revolution in Penology: Rethinking the Society of Captives*. New York, NY: Rowman & Littlefield.

Ashton, M. (2008). "The New Abstentionists." *Drug Scope* 1(1): 1–25.

Askari, M.S., Keyes, K.M., & Mauro, P.M. (2021). "Cannabis Use Disorder Treatment Use and Perceived Treatment Need in the United States: Time Trends and Age Differences between 2002–2019." *Drug and Alcohol Dependence* 229(Pt A): 109154. https://doi.org/10.1016/j.drugalcdep.2021.109154.

Associated Press (2007). "Reports: Air Force Assistant to Replace Bzdelik." (April 16) *Denver Post*. Available at: https://www.denverpost.com/2013/10/10/denver-floats-new-rules-that-could-make-even-the-odor-of-pot-a-crime/reports.

Associated Press (2021). "New Washington State Law Makes Drug Possession a Misdemeanor." (May 13) *US News*. Available at: https://www.usnews.com/news/politics/articles/2021-05-13/new-washington-state-law-makes-drug-possession-a-misdemeanor.

August, Karen. 2013. "Women in the Marijuana Industry." *Humboldt Journal of Social Relations* 35: 89–103.

Austin, J. & Krisberg, B. (1981). "NCCD Research Review: Wider, Stronger, and Different Nets: The Dialectics of Criminal Justice Reform." *Journal of Research in Crime and Delinquency* 18(1): 165–196. https://doi.org/10.1177/002242778018 00110.

Aydelotte, J.D., Brown, L.H., Luftman, K.M., Mardock, A.L., Teixeira, P., Coopwood, B., & Brown, C. (2017). "Crash Fatality Rates after Recreational Marijuana Legalization in Washington and Colorado." *American Journal of Public Health* 107(8): 1329–1331. https://doi.org/10.2105/AJPH.2017.303848.

Ayu, A.P., van der Ven, M., Suryani, E., Puspadewi, N., Joewana, S., Rukmini, E., de Jong, C., & Schellekens, A. (2022). "Improving Medical Students' Attitude toward Patients with Substance Use Problems through Addiction Medicine Education." *Substance Abuse* 43(1): 47–55. https://doi.org/10.1080/08897077.2020.1732512.

Baker, J. & Goh, D. (2004). *The Cannabis Cautioning Scheme Three Years On: An Implementation and Outcome Evaluation*. Sydney: NSW Bureau of Crime Statistics and Research.

Balko, R. (2013). "How Did America's Police Become a Military Force on the Streets?" *ABA Journal*. Available at: https://www.abajournal.com/magazine/article/how_did_americas_police_become_a_military_force_on_the_streets/?utm_source=feedburner&utm_medium=feed&utm_campaign=ABA+Journal+Magazine+Stories.

Balko R. (2014). *Rise of the Warrior Cop: The Militarization of America's Police Forces*. New York, NY: Public Affairs.

Ballard, J. (2020). "Lack of Legal Cannabis in B.C.'s 'Access Deserts' Is Helping Illicit Market Thrive, Retailers Say." (December 16) *CBC News*. Available at: https://www.cbc.ca/news/canada/british-columbia/cannabis-desert-12-municipalities-bc-south-coast-1.5842993.

Banerjee, A., Chattopadhyay, R., Duflo, E., Keniston, D., and Singh, N. (2021). "Improving Police Performance in Rajasthan, India: Experimental Evidence on Incentives, Managerial Autonomy, and Training." *American Economic Journal: Economic Policy* 13(1): 36–66.

Barak, G. (1988). "Newsmaking Criminology: Reflections on the Media, Intellectuals, and Crime." *Justice Quarterly* 5(4): 565–587.

Barak, G. (2007). "Doing Newsmaking Criminology from within the Academy." *Theoretical Criminology* 11: 191–207.

Barratt, M.J., Chanteloup, F., Lenton, S., & Marsh, A. (2005). "Cannabis Law Reform in Western Australia: An Opportunity to Test Theories of Marginal Deterrence and Legitimacy." *Drug and Alcohol Review* 24(4): 321–330. https://doi.org/10.1080/09595230500263863.

Barthwell, A.G., Baxter, L.E., Cermak, T., DuPont, R., Kraus, M.L., & Levounis, P. (2010). "The Role of the Physician in 'Medical Marijuana.'" https://www.asam.org/docs/default-source/public-policy-statements/1role_of_phys_in_med_mj_9-10.pdf?sfvrsn= c2a16bb3.

Bartlett, J. (2021). "Smokescreen." (May 11) *The Boston Business Journal.* Available at: https://www.bizjournals.com/boston/ news/2021/05/11/smokescreen-a-lack-of-transparency-in-the-money-c.html.

Barzel, Y. (1976). "An Alternative Approach to the Analysis of Taxation." *Journal of Political Economy* 84(6): 1177–1197.

Batten, G.H.M. (1892). "The Opium Question." *Journal of the Royal Society of Arts* 40: 444–994.

Battistella, G., Fornari, E., Annoni, J.M., Chtioui, H., Dao, K., Fabritius, M., Favrat, B., Mall, J.F., Maeder, P., & Giroud, C. (2014). "Long-Term Effects of Cannabis on Brain Structure." *Neuropsychopharmacology: Official Publication of the American College of Neuropsychopharmacology* 39(9): 2041–2048. https://doi.org/10.1038/npp.2014.67.

Baum, D. (1996). *Smoke and Mirrors: The War on Drugs and the Politics of Failure.* New York, NY: Little Brown.

Baum, D. (2016). "Legalize It: How to Win the War on Drugs." (April) *Harper's Magazine.* Available at: https://harpers.org/archive/2016/04/legalize-it-all.

Baudean, M. (2017). "Baseline for the Evaluation and Monitoring of Recreational Cannabis Regulation in Uruguay." *Monitor Cannabis.* Available at: https://web.archive.org/web/20200304060346/http://monitorcannabis.uy/informe-sobre-el-objetivo-aplicacion-de-la-justicia-de-la-regulacion-del-cannabis-recreativo-en-uruguay-linea-de-base.

Baudean, M. (2022). "Five Years of Cannabis Regulation: What Can We Learn from the Uruguayan Experience?" In D. Corva & J.S. Meisel (eds), *The Routledge Handbook of Post-Prohibition Cannabis Research.* London: Routledge (pp. 63–80).

Bayer, I. & Ghodse, H. (1999). "Evolution of International Drug Control, 1945–1995." *Bulletin on Narcotics* LI(1 and 2), Occasional papers. Available at: https://www.unodc.org/unodc/en/data-and-analysis/bulletin/bulletin_1999-01-01_1_page003.html.

BBC News (2019). "420: Seven Charts on How Cannabis Use Has Changed." (April 20) *BBC News.* Available at: https://www.bbc.com/news/uk-47950785.

BBC News (2021). "Mexico Marijuana: Top Judge Decriminalizes Recreational Use of Cannabis." (June 29) *BBC News.* Available at: https://www.bbc.com/news/world-latin-america-57645016.

BC Gov News (2020). "Province Takes Unprecedented Steps to Support COVID-19 Response." *BC Gov News*. Available at: https://news.gov.bc.ca/releases/2020PSSG0 020-000568https://news.gov.bc.ca/releases/2020PSSG0020-000568.

BDSA (Business and Defense Services Administration) (2021). "BDSA Reports Global Cannabis Sales Exceeded $21 Billion in 2020; Forecasts $55.9 Billion by 2026." (March 2) *Intrado GlobeNewswire*. Available at: https://www.globenewsw ire.com/news-release/2021/03/02/2185408/0/en/BDSAReports-Global-Canna bis-Sales-Exceeded-21-Billion-in-2020-Forecasts-55-9-Billion-by-2026.html.

Bear, D. (2014). "Acting Out, Adapting, or Standing Firm? Drugs Policing in a London Borough." PhD thesis. London: London School of Economics.

Becker, H.S. (1951). "The Professional Dance Musician and His Audience." *American Journal of Sociology* 57: 136–144.

Becker, H.S. (1953). "Becoming a Marihuana User." *American Journal of Sociology* 59(3): 235–242.

Becker, H.S. (1955). "Marijuana Use and the Social Context." *Social Problems* 3(1): 354.

Becker, H.S. (1963). *Outsiders: Studies in the Sociology of Deviance*. New York, NY: Free Press.

Becker, H.S. (1999). "The Chicago School, So-Called." *Qualitative Sociology* 122: 3–12.

Beckett, K. & Herbert, S. (2008). "The Consequences and Costs of Marijuana Prohibition." (December 8) American Civil Liberties Union of Washington, Seattle, WA. Available at: https://www.aclu-wa.org/docs/consequences-and-costs-marijuana-prohibition.

Beirne, P. (1983). "Cultural Relativism and Comparative Criminology." *Contemporary Crises* 7: 371–391.

Belackova, V., Ritter, A., Shanahan, M., & Hughes, C.E. (2017). "Assessing the Concordance between Illicit Drug Laws on the Books and Drug Law Enforcement: Comparison of Three States on the Continuum from 'Decriminalised' to 'Punitive.'" *International Journal on Drug Policy* 41: 148–157.

Beletsky, L. & Davis, C.S. (2017). "Today's Fentanyl Crisis: Prohibition's Iron." *Law Revisited. International Journal of Drug Policy* 46(August): 156–159.

Bell, D. (1992). *Faces at the Bottom of the Well: The Permanence of Racism*. New York, NY: Basic Books.

Bell, D. (1995). "Who's Afraid of Critical Race Theory?" *University of Illinois Law Review* 4: 893–910.

Bender, S.W. (2016). "The Colors of Cannabis: Race and Marihuana." *University of California Davis Law Review* 50: 689–706.

Bennett, C. (2018). "Drugs, Moral Panics and the Dispositive." *Journal of Sociology* 54(4): 538–556.

Bennett, E. (2021). "Consumer Activism, Sustainable Supply Chains, and the Cannabis Market." In D. Corva & J. Meisel (eds), The Routledge Handbook of Interdisciplinary Cannabis Research. London: Routledge (pp. 192–200).

Bennett, J.S. (1974). "Le Dain Commission of Inquiry into the Non-Medical Use of Drugs Tables: Fourth and Final Report." *Canadian Medical Association Journal* 110(1): 105–108.

Benson, M. (2019). "Brexit and the Classed Politics of Bordering: The British in France and European Belongings." *Sociology* 54(3): 501–517. https://doi.org/10.1177/0038038519885300.

Bentham, M. (1998). *The Politics of Drug Control*. London: Macmillan.

Bentley, D. (2021). "In the First Meeting since Norman's Swearing-In, the Fire and Police Commission Bans the Use of No-Knock Search Warrants." *Milwaukee Journal Sentinel*. Available at: https://www.jsonline.com/story/news/2021/11/18/fire-and-police-commission-bans-use-no-knock-search-warrants/8676548002.

Berenson, A. (2019). *Tell Your Children: The Truth about Marijuana, Mental Illness, and Violence*. New York, NY: Free Press.

Berger, P. & Luckmann, T. (1966). *The Social Construction of Reality*. Garden City, NY: Doubleday.

Berke, J., Title, S., Bloomberg, S., Lawrence, G., & Smith, A. (2022). "Regulating Cannabis Interstate Commerce: Perspectives on How the Federal Government Should Respond." *Ohio State Legal Studies Research Paper* 722: 1–11. https://papers.ssrn.com/sol3/papers.cfm?abstract_id=4188089.

Berman, D. (2019). "100 Years since Prohibition: Legacy for the War on Drugs." (October 3) *Marijuana Law, Policy & Reform*. Available at: https://lawprofessors.typepad.com/marijuana_law/2019/10/100-years-since-prohibition-legacy-for-the-war-on-drugs.html.

Bernard, J. (1991). "From Fasting to Abstinence: The Origins of the American Temperance Movement." In S. Barrows & R. Room (eds), *Drinking: Behavior and Belief in Modem History*. Berkeley, CA: University of California Press (pp. 337–353).

Bernard, T.J. & Snipes, J.B. (1996). "Theoretical Integration in Criminology." *Crime and Justice: A Review of Research* 20: 301–348.

Bernerth, J.B. & Walker, H.J. (2020). "Altered States or Much to Do about Nothing? A Study of When Cannabis Is Used in Relation to the Impact It Has on Performance." *Group & Organization Management* 45(4): 459–478.

Berridge, V. (1977). "Opium and the Historical Perspective." *Lancet* 2: 78–80.

Berridge, V. & Edward, G. (1987). *Opium and the People: Opiate Use in Nineteenth Century England*. New Haven, CT: Conn, Yale University Press.

Best, D. & Colman, C. (eds) (2019). *Strengths-based Approaches to Crime and Substance Use: From Drugs and Crime to Desistance and Recovery*. Abingdon: Routledge.

Best, D., Beckwith, M., Haslam, C., Haslam, S.A., Jetten, J., Mawson, E., & Lubman, D.I. (2016). "Overcoming Alcohol and Other Drug Addiction as a Process of Social Identity Transition: The Social Identity Model of Recovery (SIMOR)." *Addiction Research & Theory* 24(2): 111–123. https://doi.org/10.3109/16066359.2015.1075980.

Best, J. (2001). *Damned Lies and Statistics: Untangling Numbers from the Media, Politicians, and Activists*. Berkeley, CA: University of California Press.

Beweley-Taylor, D. (2001). *The United States and International Drug Control, 1909–1997*. London: Continuum International Publishing Group.

Beweley-Taylor, D., Blickman, T., & Jelsma, M. (2014). *The Rise and Decline of Cannabis Prohibition—The History of Cannabis in the UN Drug Control System and Options for Reform.* Amsterdam/Swansea: Global Drug Policy Observatory/Transnational Institute.

Bhattarai, A. (2021). "Greener Pastures: Marijuana Jobs Are Becoming a Refuge for Retail and Restaurant Workers." (September 24) Washington Post. Available at: https://www.washingtonpost.com/business/2021/09/24/marijuana-dispensaries-jobs.

Biasutti W.R., Leffers, K.S.H., & Callaghan, R.C. (2020). "Systematic Review of Cannabis Use and Risk of Occupational Injury." *Substance Use & Misuse* 55(11): 1733–1745. https://doi.org/10.1080/10826084.2020.1759643. Epub 2020 May 22. PMID: 32441179.

Bidwell, L.C., Ellingson, J.M., & Karoly, H.C. (2020). "Association of Naturalistic Administration of Cannabis Flower and Concentrates with Intoxication and Impairment." *Journal of the American Medical Association Psychiatry* 77(8): 787–796.

Bifulco, M. & Pisanti, S. (2015). "Medicinal Use of Cannabis in Europe." *EMBO Reports* 16: 130–132. https://doi.org/10.15252/embr.201439742.

Bishop-Henchman, J. & Scarboro, M. (2016). "Marijuana Legalization and Taxes: Lessons for Other States from Colorado and Washington." Special Report No. 321. Washington, DC: Tax Foundation. Available at: https://taxfoundation.org/marijuana-taxes-lessons-colorado-washington/.

Black, D.J. (1976). *The Behavior of Law*. New York, NY: Academic Press.

Black, D.J. (1984). *Towards a General Theory of Social Control*. New York, NY: Academic Press.

Blackman, S.J. (2004). *Chilling Out: The Cultural Politics of Substance Consumption, Youth and Drug Policy*. Maidenhead/New York, NY: Open University Press/McGraw-Hill.

Blau, J.R. & Blau, P.M. (1982). "The Cost of Inequality: Metropolitan Structure and Violent Crime." *American Sociological Review* 47: 114–129.

Blocker, J.S., Jr (1989). *American Temperance Movements: Cycles of Reform*. Boston, MA: Twayne Publishers.

Bloom, S. (2021). "40,000-Plus Cannabis Prisoners in the U.S., LPP Confirms." (March 17) *Celebstoners*. Available at: https://www.celebstoner.com/news/marijuana-news/2021/03/17/forty-thousand-american-cannabis-prisoners.

Blumer, H. (1992 [1969]). *Symbolic Interactionism: Perspective and Method*. Englewood Cliffs, NJ: Prentice Hall.

Blumstein, A. (1982). "On the Racial Disproportionality of United States' Prison Populations." *Journal of Criminal Law and Criminology* 73(3): 1259–1281.

Blumstein, A., Cohen, J., & Farrington, D.P. (1988). "Criminal Career Research: It's Value for Criminology." *Criminology* 26: 1–35.

Blumstein, A. & Wallman, J. (2006). "The Crime Drop and Beyond." *Annual Review of Law and Social Science* 2(1): 125–146.

Bodwitch, H., Carah, J., Daane, K., Getz, C., Grantham, T., Hickey, G., & Wilson, H. (2019). "Growers Say Cannabis Legalization Excludes Small Growers, Supports Illicit Markets, Undermines Local Economies." *California Agriculture* 73(3): 177–184. https://doi.org/10.3733/ca.2019a0018.

Bodwitch, H., Polson, M., Biber, E., Hickey, G.M., & Butsic, V. (2021). "Why Comply? Farmer Motivations and Barriers in Cannabis Agriculture." *Journal of Rural Studies* 86: 155–170. https://doi.org/10.1016/j.jrurs tud.2021.05.006.

Boehnke, K.F., Litinas, E., Worthing, B., Conine, L., & Kruger, D.J. (2021). "Communication Between Healthcare Providers and Medical Cannabis Patients Regarding Referral and Medication Substitution." *Journal of Cannabis Research* 3(1): 1–9.

Boeri, M. (2017). *Hurt: Chronicles of the Drug War Generation*. Berkeley, CA: University of California Press.

Boesen, U. (2021). "Potential Recreational Marijuana Excise Tax Revenue by State." (January 13) Tax Foundation. Available at: https://taxfoundation.org/recreational-marijuana-tax-revenue-by-state.

Boidi, M.F., Queirolo, R., & Cruz, J.M. (2016). "Cannabis Consumption Patterns among Frequent Consumers in Uruguay." *International Journal on Drug Policy* 34: 34–40. https://doi.org/10.1016/j.drugpo.2016.05.008.

Bonilla-Silva, E. (2020). *Protecting Whiteness: Whitelash and the Rejection of Racial Equality*. Seattle, WA: University of Washington Press.

Bonnie, R.J. & Whitebread, C.H. (1970). "The Forbidden Fruit and the Tree of Knowledge: An Inquiry into the Legal History of American Marijuana Prohibition." *Virginia Law Review* 56(6): 971–1203.

Bonnie, R.J. & Whitebread, C.H. (1999). *The Marijuana Conviction: A History of Marijuana Prohibition in the United States*. New York, NY: Lindesmith Publishing.

Booth, M. (1999). *Opium: A History*. New York, NY: St Martin's Press.

Booth, M. (2003). *Cannabis: A History*. New York, NY: St Martin's Press.

Borodovsky, J.T. & Budney, A.J. (2018). "Cannabis Regulatory Science: Risk–Benefit Considerations for Mental Disorders." *International Review of Psychiatry* 30(3): 183–202. https://doi.org/10.1080/09540261.2018.1454406.

Bottoms, A.E. (1995). "The Philosophy and Politics of Punishment and Sentencing." In C. Clarkson & R. Morgan (eds), *The Politics of Sentencing Reform*. Oxford, UK: Clarendon Press (pp. 17–49).

Bowers, J. & Abrahamson, D. (2020). "Kicking the Habit: The Opioid Crisis and America's Addiction to Prohibition." (June 29) Cato Institute. Available at: https://www.cato.org/policy-analysis/kicking-habit-opioid-crisis-americas-addiction-prohibition.

Boyd, G. (2002). "Collateral Damage in the War on Drugs." *Villanova Law Review* 47: 839–845.

Boyd, S. (2010). "Reefer Madness and Beyond. Popular Culture, Crime and Social Control." Sociology of Crime, law, and deviance series. Bingley, UK: *Emerald Insights* 14: 3–24.

Boyd, S.C. (2007). *Hooked: Drug War Films in Britain, Canada, and the United States*. Toronto, ON: University of Toronto Press.

Boyd, S.C. (2017). *Busted: An Illustrated History of Drug Prohibition in Canada*. Halifax: Fernwood.

Boyd, S.C. & Carter, C.I. (2014). *Killer Weed: Marijuana Grow Ops, Media*, and. Justice. Toronto, ON: University of Toronto Press.

Braakmann, N. & Jones, S. (2014). "Cannabis Depenalisation, Drug Consumption and Crime—Evidence from the 2004 Cannabis Declassification in the UK." *Social Science & Medicine* 115: 29–37. https://doi.org/10.1016/j.socscimed.2014.06.003.

Brake, M. (1985). *Comparative Youth Culture: The Sociology of Youth Cultures and Youth Subcultures in America, Britain, and Canada*. London: Routledge & Kegan Paul.

Braithwaite, J. (2000). "The New Regulatory State and the Transformation of Criminology." *British Journal of Criminology* 40(2): 222–238.

Braithwaite, J. (2011). "The Essence of Responsive Regulation." *University of British Columbia Law Review* 44(3): 475–520.

Braithwaite, J. (2021). "Glimmers of Cosmopolitan Criminology." *International Criminology* 1: 5–12.

Brantingham, P.J. & Brantingham, P.L. (1981). *Environmental Criminology*. Beverly Hills, CA: Sage.

Brecher, E. (1972). *Licit and Illicit Drugs: The Consumers Union Report on Narcotics, Stimulants, Depressants, Inhalants, Hallucinogens, and Marijuana—Including Caffeine, Nicotine, and Alcohol*. Boston, MA: Little, Brown and Company.

Brewster D. (2017). "Culture(s) of Control: Political Dynamics in Cannabis Policy in England & Wales and the Netherlands." *European Journal of Criminology* 14(5): 566–585.

Brian J. (1994). "Opium and Infant-Sedation in 19th Century England." *Health Visit* 67(5): 165–166.

Bridgeman, M.B. & Abazia, D. (2017). "Medicinal Cannabis: History, Pharmacology, and Implications for the Acute Care Setting." *Pharmacy and Therapeutics* 42(3): 180–188.

Brinkman, J. & Mok-Lamme, D. (2019). "Not in My Backyard? Not So Fast. The Effect of Marijuana Legalization on Neighborhood Crime." *Regional Science and Urban Economics* 78: 103–460. https://doi.org/10.1016/j.regsciurbeco.2019.103460.

Brooks-Russell, A., Ma, M., Levinson, A.H., Kattari, L., Kirchner, T., Anderson Goodell, E.M., & Johnson, R.M. (2019). "Adolescent Marijuana Use, Marijuana-Related Perceptions, and Use of Other Substances before and after Initiation of Retail Marijuana Sales in Colorado (2013–2015)." *Prevention Science* 20(2): 185–193. https://doi.org/10.1007/s11121-018-0933-2. PMID: 30043198; PMCID: PMC8086773.

Brown, D. (2020). "B.C.'s Grey Market Is Thriving." (August 6) *StrattCann: For the Cannabis Community*. Available at: https://stratcann.com/2020/08/28/bcs-grey-market-is-thriving.

Brown, M. (2022). "Decriminalization as Police Reform." Ohio State Legal Studies Research Paper No. 683. http://dx.doi.org/10.2139/ssrn.4032811.

Brown, W. (2006). *Regulating Aversion: Tolerance in the Age of Identity and Empire*. Princeton, NJ: Princeton University Press.

Browne, R. (2022). "Exclusive Data Shows Canadian Cops Target More Black and Indigenous Folks for Drug Arrests." (April 19) *Vice*. Available at: https://www.vice.com/en/article/akvpe4/race-drug-arrests-canada.

Brownlee, Nick (2002) *This Is Cannabis*. London: Sanctuary Publishing Limited.

Brubacher, J.R., Chan, H., Erdelyi, S., Macdonald, S., Asbridge, M., Mann, R.E., Eppler, J., Lund, A., MacPherson, A., Martz, W., Schreiber, W.E., Brant, R., & Purssell, R.A. (2019). "Cannabis Use as a Risk Factor for Causing Motor Vehicle Crashes: A Prospective Study." *Addiction* 114(9): 1616–1626. https://doi.org/10.1111/add.14663. Epub 2019 July 3. PMID: 31106494; PMCID: PMC6771478.

Brumback, T., Castro, N., Jacobus, J., & Tapert, S. (2016). "Effects of Marijuana Use on Brain Structure and Function: Neuroimaging Findings from a Neurodevelopmental Perspective." *International Review of Neurobiology* 129: 33–65. https://doi.org/10.1016/bs.irn.2016.06.004.

Buadze, A., Stohler, R., Schulze, B., Schaub, M., & Liebrenz, M. (2010). "Do Patients Think Cannabis Causes Schizophrenia?: A Qualitative Study on the Causal Beliefs of Cannabis Using Patients with Schizophrenia." *Harm Reduction Journal* 7: 22. doi: 10.1186/1477-7517-7-22. PMID: 20920183; PMCID: PMC2954921.

Bullington, B. & Block, A.A. (1990). "A Trojan Horse: Anti-Communism and the War on Drugs." *Contemporary Crisis* 14(1): 39–55.

Burford, G. (2018). "Keeping Complexity Alive: Restorative and Responsive Approaches to Culture Change." *International Journal of Restorative Justice* 1(3): 356–371.

Burgess, A. (1962). *A Clockwork Orange*. New York, NY: W.W. Norton.

Burgess, E.W. (1925). "The Growth of a City: An Introduction to a Research Project." In R. Park, E.W. Burgess, & R.D. McKenzie (eds), *The City*. Chicago, IL: University of Chicago Press (pp. 71–78).

Burnett, J. (2020). "Seized Drug Assets Pad Police Budgets." (June 16) *National Public Radio*. Available at: https://www.npr.org/templates/story/story.php?storyId=91490480.

Burris, S., Cloud, L.K., & Penn, M. (2020). "The Growing Field of Legal Epidemiology." *Journal of Public Health Management Practice* 25: S4–S9. https://doi.org/10.1097/PHH.0000000000001133. PMID: 32004217.

Burruss, G.W. & Lu, Y. (2022). "The Value of Data Visualization for Translational Criminology." In J.S. Wheeldon (ed.), *Visual Criminology: From History and Methods to Critique and Policy Translation*. London: Routledge (pp. 251–279).

Bursik, R. (2009). "The Dead Sea Scrolls and Criminological Knowledge: 2008 Presidential Address to the American Society of Criminology." *Criminology* 47(1): 516.

Buruma, Y. (2007). "Dutch Tolerance: On Drugs, Prostitution, and Euthanasia." *Crime and Justice* 35(1): 73–113.

Bushway, S. and Uggen, C. (2021). "Fostering Desistance." *Contexts* 20(4): 34–39. https://doi.org/10.1177/15365042211058123.

Bustillo, X. (2022). "Biden to Pardon Simple Federal Marijuana Possession Convictions." (October 6) *National Public Radio*. Available at: https://www.npr.org/2022/10/06/1127302410/biden-pardon-marijuana-possession-convictions.

Butler, P. (2017). "Police in America: Ensuring Accountability and Mitigating Racial Bias." *Northwestern Journal of Law & Social Policy* 11: 385–401.

Butsic, V., Schwab, B., Baumann, M., & Brenner, J. (2017). "Inside the Emerald Triangle: Modeling the Placement and Size of Cannabis Production in Humboldt

County, CA USA." *Ecological Economics* 142: 70–80. https://doi.org/10.1016/j.ecolecon.2017.06.013.
Cabral, T.S. (2017). "The 15th Anniversary of the Portuguese Drug Policy: Its History, Its Success and Its Future." *Drug Science, Policy and Law* 3: 1–5. https://doi.org/10.1177/2050324516683640.
Cahill, N. (2021). "California Inches Toward Decriminalizing Psychedelics." (April 6) *Courthouse News*. Available at: https://www.courthousenews.com/california-inches-toward-decriminalizing-psychedelics.
Calabria, B., Degenhardt, L., Hall, W., & Lynskey, M. (2010). "Does Cannabis Use Increase the Risk of Death? Systematic Review of Epidemiological Evidence on Adverse Effects of Cannabis Use." *Drug and Alcohol Review* 29: 318–330.
Callaghan, R.C., Vander Heiden, J., Sanches, M., Asbridge, M., Hathaway, A., & Kish, S.J. (2021). "Impacts of Canada's Cannabis Legalization on Police-Reported Crime among Youth: Early Evidence." *Addiction* 116: 3454–3462. https://doi.org/10.1111/add.15535.
Callahan, S., Bruner, D.M., & Giguerre, C. (2021). "Smoke and Fears: The Effects of Marijuana on Prohibition and Crime." Boone, NC: Appalachian State University Working Papers.
Campbell, A.W. (2018). "The Temperance Movement." Virginia Commonwealth University. Available at: https://socialwelfare.library.vcu.edu/religious/the-temperance-movement.
Campos, I. (2012). *Home Grown: Marijuana and the Origins of Mexico's War on Drugs*. Chapel Hill, NC: University of North Carolina Press.
Campos, I. (2018). "Mexicans and the Origins of Marijuana Prohibition in the United States: A Reassessment." *Social History of Alcohol and Drugs*: 32: 6–37.
Camrose, V. (1947). *British Newspapers and their Controllers*. London: William Ewert Berry.
Canadian Centre on Substance Use and Addiction (2021). "Cannabis Retail during COVID-19." Available at: https://www.ccsa.ca/sites/default/files/2021-01/CCSA-COVID-19-Cannabis-Retail-Policy-Brief-2021-en.pdf.
Canadian Drug Policy Coalition (n.d.). "History of Drug Policy in Canada." Available at: https://drugpolicy.ca/about/history.
Canadian Evergreen (n.d.). "BC Pushes for Black Market Cannabis to Go Legal." Available at: https://vancouversun.com/business/local-business/b-c-pushes-for-black-market-cannabis-to-go-legal-faces-criticism-from-craft-growers#:~:text=In%20B.C.%2C%20the%20effort%20to,growers%20with%20marketing%20development%20and.
Canadian Press (2021). "Drug Decriminalization: Vancouver Sends Preliminary Application to Health Canada." (March 3). *CTV News*. Available at: https://bc.ctvnews.ca/drug-decriminalization-vancouver-sends-preliminary-application-to-health-canada-1.5331851#:~:text=VANCOUVER%20%2D%2DFollowing%20its%20request,substance%20use%20and%20saving%20lives.
Cannabis Control Commission (n.d.). "Equity Programs." Available at: https://masscannabiscontrol.com/equity/socialequityprogram/.
Caron, C. (2022). "Psychosis, Addiction, Chronic Vomiting: As Weed Becomes More Potent, Teens Are Getting Sick." (June 23) *New York Times*. Available at: https://www.nytimes.com/2022/06/23/well/mind/teens-thc-cannabis.html.

Capers, I.B. (2014). "Critical Race Theory and Criminal Justice." *Ohio State Journal of Criminal Law* 12(1): 1–5.

Capler, R., Boyd, N., & MacPherson, D. (2016). "Organized Crime in the Cannabis Market: Evidence and Implications." *Canadian Drug Policy Coalition*. Available at: https://drugpolicy.ca/wp-content/uploads/2016/11/CDPC_Submission_Cannabis-and-Organized-Crime_Aug9-2016_Full-Final.pdf.

Carnevale, J., Kagan, R., Murphy, P., & Esrick, J. (2017). "A Practical Framework for Regulating For-Profit Recreational Marijuana in US States." *International Journal of Drug Policy* 42: 71–85.

Carrabine, E., Lee, M., & South, N. (2000). "Social Wrongs and Human Rights in Late Modern Britain: Social Exclusion, Crime Control, and Prospects for a Public Criminology." *Social Justice* 27(2): 193–211.

Carrington, K. Sozzo, M., and Hogg, R. (2016). "Southern Criminology." *British Journal of Criminology* 56: 1–20.

Carstairs, C. (1999). "Deporting 'Ah Sin' to Save the White Race: Moral Panic, Racialization, and the Extension of Canadian Drug Laws in the 1920s." *Canadian Bulletin of Medical History* 16(1): 65–88.

Carstairs, C. (2018). "How Pot-Smoking Became Illegal." Available at: https://theconversation.com/how-pot-smoking-becameillegal-in-canada-92499.

Caulkins, J.P. (2010). *Estimated Cost of Production for Legalized Cannabis*. Santa Monica, CA: RAND Corporation. Available at: https://www.rand.org/pubs/working_papers/WR764.html.

Caulkins, J.P., Kilmer, B., Kleiman, M.A.R., MacCoun, R.J., Midgette, G., et al. (2015). *Considering Marijuana Legalization: Insights for Vermont and Other Jurisdictions*. Santa Monica, CA: RAND Corp.

Cazentre, D. (2021). "New York's Marijuana Tax May Not Be the Highest. But It May Be the Most Complex. (May 17) *Syracuse.com*. Available at: https://www.syracuse.com/marijuana/2021/05/new-yorks-marijuana-tax-might-not-bethe-nations-highest-but-it-may-be-the-most-complex.html.

CBC News (2021). "$13M in Drugs Seized from The ChronFather, a Calgary Online Dispensary." (December 14) *CBC News*. Available at: https://www.cbc.ca/news/canada/calgary/calgary-police-drug-seizure-chron-father-13-million-cannabis-mushrooms-1.6285808.

Čecho, R., Baška, T., Švihrová, V., & Hudečková, H. (2017). "Legislative Norms to Control Cannabis Use in the Light of Its Prevalence in Czech Republic, Poland, Slovakia, and Hungary." *Central European Journal of Public Health* 25(4): 261–265. https://doi.org/10.21101/cejph.a5019.

Center County District Attorney's Office (n.d.). "Misdemeanor Marijuana Diversion Program." Available at: https://www.centrecountypa.gov/DocumentCenter/View/17132/Description-of-Misdemeanor-Marijuana-Diversion-Program.

Center for Communication and Civic Engagement (n.d.). "Culture Jamming." Available at: https://depts.washington.edu/ccce/polcommcampaigns/CultureJamming.htm.

Chang, T.Y., & Jacobson, M. (2017). "Going to Pot? The Impact of Dispensary Closures on Crime." *Journal of Urban Economics* 100. 120–136.

Chanock, M. (2001). *The Making of South African Legal Culture 1902–1936: Fear, Favour and Prejudice*. Cambridge, UK: Cambridge University Press.

Chappell, B. (2019). "California Says Its Cannabis Revenue Has Fallen Short of Estimates, Despite Gains." (August 23) *National Public Radio*. Available at: https://www.npr.org/2019/08/23/753791322/california-says-its-cannabis-revenue-has-fallen-short-of-estimates-despite-gains.

Chasin, A. (2016). *Assassin of Youth: A Kaleidoscopic History of Harry J. Anslinger's War on Drugs*. Chicago, IL: The University of Chicago Press.

Chatwin, C. (2016). "Mixed Messages from Europe on Drug Policy Reform: The Cases of Sweden and the Netherlands." *Journal of Drug Policy Analysis* 11(1): 1–12. https://doi.org/10.1515/jdpa2015-0009.

Chen, G. & Einat, T. (2015). "The Relationship between Criminology Studies and Punitive Attitudes." *European Journal of Criminology* 12(2): 169–187. https://doi.org/10.1177/1477370814551211.

Childs, A., Coomber, R., & Bull, M. (2020). "Do Online Illicit Drug Market Exchanges Afford Rationality?" *Contemporary Drug Problems* 47(4): 302–319.

Childs, S. (2020). "UK Police Can't Search You Just Because You Smell of Weed, Watchdogs Say." (September 11) *Vice*. Available at: https://www.vice.com/en/article/ep4wva/uk-police-cant-search-just-because-you-smell-of-weed-watchdog-says.

Chiswick Herald (2022). "Mayor Announces Chair of First Ever London Drugs Commission." (May 12) *Chiswick Herald*. Available at: https://chiswickherald.co.uk/mayor-announces-chair-of-first-ever-london-drugs-commission-p15156-338.htm.

Chockalingam, V., Wu, V., Berlinski, N., Chandra, Z., Hu, A., Jones, E., et al. (2021). "The Limited Effects of Partisan and Consensus Messaging in Correcting Science Misperceptions." (April) *Research & Politics* 8(2): 1–9. https://doi.org/10.1177/20531680211014980.

Chohlas-Wood, A., Gerchick, M., Goel, S., Huq, A.Z., Shoemaker, A., Shroff, R., & Yao, K. (2022). "Identifying and Measuring Excessive and Discriminatory Policing." *University of Chicago Law Review* 89(2): 441. Available at: https://chicagounbound.uchicago.edu/uclrev/vol89/iss2/6.

Christie, N. (2004). *A Suitable Amount of Crime*. London: Routledge.

Christie, N. (2013). *Crime Control as Industry*. London: Taylor & Francis.

Christie, N. (1986). "Suitable Enemies." In H. Bianchi & R. van Swaaningen (eds), *Abolitionism: Towards a Non-Repressive Approach to Crime*. Amsterdam: Free University Press (pp. 42–54).

Christie, P. & Ali, R. (2000). "Offences under the Cannabis Expiation Notice Scheme in South Australia." *Drug and Alcohol Review* 19: 251–256. https://doi.org/10.1080/713659367.

Chu, Y.-W.L. & Townsend, W. (2019). "Joint Culpability: The Effects of Medical Marijuana Laws on Crime." *Journal of Economic Behavior & Organization* 159: 502–525.

CHSCP (City and Hackney Safeguarding Child Partnership) (2022). "Local Child Safeguarding Practice Review: Child Q." (March). Available at: https://chscp.org.uk/wp-content/uploads/2022/03/Child-Q-PUBLISHED-14-March-22.pdf.

Ciaramella, C.J. (2022). "Biden Signs Executive Order Restricting Chokeholds and Limiting Transfer of Military Equipment to Police." (May 25) *Reason*. Available at: https://reason.com/2022/05/25/biden-signs-executive-order-restricting-cho keholds-and-limiting-transfer-of-military-equipment-to-police.

City of Los Angeles Department of Cannabis Regulation (n.d.). "Eligibility Verification—Identification (Archive)." Available at: https://cannabis.lacity.org/archive/eligibility-verification-individual-archive.

Clarke, R.V.G. & Cornish, D. (1986). *The Reasoning Criminal.* New York, NY: Springer-Verlag.

Clipper, S.J., Morris, R.G., & Russell-Kaplan, A. (2017). "The Link between Bond Forfeiture and Pretrial Release Mechanism: The Case of Dallas County, Texas." *PLoS ONE* 12(8): e0182772. https://doi.org/10.1371/journal.pone.0182772.

Cloward, R.A. & Ohlin, L. (1960). *Delinquency and Opportunity: A Theory of Delinquent Gangs.* New York, NY: Free Press.

Cockburn, H. (2016). "Just One in Four Cannabis Users Are Charged and Arrests Have Fallen by Almost 50% since 2010, New Figures Show." (August 23). *The Independent.* Available at: https://www.independent.co.uk/news/uk/crime/canna bis-arrests-charges-fall-police-giving-drug-policy-uk-a7206036.html.

Cody, D.L. (2006). "Smoke Signals: Cannabis Moral Panics in the United States, Australia & Britain." MA thesis, University of Tasmania.

Coe, K., Kenski, K., & Rains, S.A. (2014). "Online and Uncivil? Patterns and Determinants of Incivility in Newspaper Website Comments." *Journal of Community Health* 64(4): 658–679. https://doi.org/10.1111/jcom.12104.

Cohen, L.E. & Felson, M. (1979). "Social Change and Crime Rate Trends: A Routine Activity Approach." *American Sociology Review* 44: 588–608.

Cohen, S. (1974). "Criminology and the Sociology of Deviance in Britain: A Recent History and a Current Report." In P. Rock & M. McIntosh (eds), *Deviance and Social Control* London: Tavistock (pp. 1–40).

Cohen, S. (1979). "The Punitive City: Notes on the Dispersal of Social Control." *Contemporary Crises* 3: 339–363. https://doi.org/10.1007/BF00729115.

Cohen, S. (1982). *Against Criminology.* New York, NY: Transaction Publishers.

Cohen, S. (1985). *Visions on Social Control.* London: Polity Press.

Cohen, S. (1988). *Against Criminology.* London: Routledge. https://doi.org/10.4324/9781315082875.

Cohen, S. (2001). "Youth Deviance and Moral Panics." In R.C. Smandych (ed.), *Youth Justice: History, Legislation, and Reform.* Toronto, ON: Harcourt (pp. 69–83).

Cohen, S. (2002 [1972]). *Folk Devils and Moral Panics: The Creation of the Mods and Rockers.* London: MacGibbon and Kee.

Cohen, S. (2013). *States of Denial: Knowing about Atrocities and Suffering.* London: John Wiley & Sons.

Cole, M. (2022). "Capacity-Building in Community-Based Drug Treatment Services." *Health and Human Rights Journal* 24(1): 189–202.

Cole, T.B. & Saitz, R. (2020). "Cannabis and Impaired Driving." *Journal of the American Medical Association* 324(21): 2163–2164.

Collins, J. (2020a). "A Brief History of Cannabis and the Drug Conventions." (October 12) Cambridge Core, Cambridge University Press. Available at: https://www.cambridge.org/core/journals/american-journal-of-international-law/article/

brief-history-of-cannabis-and-the-drug-conventions/A8547C998A1D05173
495BCD6012329C0.
Collins, J. (2020b). "A Brief History of Cannabis and the Drug Conventions. Symposium on Drug Decriminalization, Legalization, and International Law." *American Journal of International Law Unbound* 114: 279–284.
Collins, J. (2021). *Legalising the Drug Wars: A Regulatory History of UN Drug Control*. Cambridge, UK: Cambridge University Press. https://doi.org/10.1017/978100 9058278.
Collins, S.E., Lonczak, H.S., & Clifasefi, S.L. (2017). "Seattle's Law Enforcement Assisted Diversion (LEAD): Program Effects on Recidivism Outcomes, Evaluation." *Program Planning* 64: 49–56.
Committee of the Health Effects of Marijuana (2017). "Health Effects of Marijuana and Cannabis-Derived Products Presented in New Report." Washington, DC: National Academic Press. Available at: https://www.nationalacademies.org/news/2017/01/health-effects-of-marijuana-and-cannabis-derived-products-presented-in-new-report#:~:text=The%20committee%20found%20that%20learn ing,who%20have%20stopped%20smoking%20cannabis.
Compton, R. (2017). "Marijuana-Impaired Driving—A Report to Congress." DOT HS 812 440. Washington, DC: National Highway Traffic Safety Administration. Available at: https://www.nhtsa.gov/sites/nhtsa.gov/files/documents/812440-marijuana-impaired-driving-report-to-congress.pdf.
Congress of the United States (2022). "Letter to President Biden." (December 22). Available at: https://blumenauer.house.gov/sites/evo-subsites/blumenauer.house.gov/files/evo-media-document/2022-12-22-letter-urging-recognition-of-merits-of-descheduling-1_0.pdf.
Connley, C. (2021). "Cannabis is Projected to be a $70 Billion Market by 2028: Yet Those Hurt Most by the War on Drugs Lack Access." (July 1) *CNBC*. Available at: https://www.cnbc.com/2021/07/01/in-billion-dollar-cannabis-market-racial-inequity-persists-despite-legalization.html.
Connor, J.P., Stjepanović, D., Le Foll, B., Hoch, E., Budney, A.L., & Hall, W.D. (2021). "Cannabis Use and Cannabis Use Disorder." *National Reviews Disease Primers* 7(1): 16. https://doi.org/10.1038/s41572-021-00247-4.
Conrad, P., Schneider, J.W., & Gusfleld, J.R. (1992). *Deviance and Medicalization: From Badness to Sickness*. Philadelphia, PA: Temple University Press.
Contreras, C. (2016). "A Block-Level Analysis of Medical Marijuana Dispensaries and Crime in the City of Los Angeles." *Justice Quarterly* 34(6): 1069–1095.
Copeland, L.C. (1939). "The Negro as a Contrast Conception." In E.T. Thompson (ed.), *Race Relations and the Race Problem*. Durham: Duke University Press (pp. 152–179).
Copes, H., Tchoula, W., Kim, J., & Ragland, J. (2018). "Symbolic Perceptions of Methamphetamine: Differentiating between Ice and Shake." *International Journal of Drug Policy*, 51: 87–94.
Copes, H., Tchoula, W., & Ragland, J. (2019). "Ethically Representing Drug Use: Photographs and Ethnographic Research with People Who Use Methamphetamine." *Journal of Qualitative Criminal Justice & Criminology*, 8(1): 21–35.

Copes, H., Brookman, F., Ragland, J., & Beaton, B. (2021). "Sex, Drugs, and Coercive Control: Gendered Narratives of Methamphetamine Use, Relationships, and Violence." *Criminology* 60(1): 187–218. https://doi.org/10.1111/1745-9125.12295.

Corbett, Neil (2021). "Lack of Retail Cannabis Fuels the Black Market, Say Store Owners." (January 4) *Maple Ridge News*. Available at: https://www.mapleridgenews.com/news/lack-of-retail-cannabis-fuels-the-black-market-say-store-owners.

Corda, A. (2015). "Drug Policy Reform in Latin America: Discourse and Reality." *The Research Consortium on Drugs and the Law*. Retrieved from http://www.drogasyderecho.org/publicaciones/pub-priv/alejandro_i.pdf.

Cornwell, A.M. (2021). "How Cannabis Can Affect Personal and Professional Relationships." (May 6) *Oracle*. Available at: https://cbdoracle.com/cannabis/how-cannabis-affects-relationships.

Cornwell, B. & Linders, A. (2002). "The Myth of Moral Panic: An Alternative Account of LSD Prohibition." *Deviant Behavior* 23(4): 307–30.

Cort, B. (2017). *Weed, Inc.: The Truth about the Pot Lobby, THC, and the Commercial Marijuana Industry*. Boca Raton, FL: Health Communications Inc.

Corva, D. & Meisel, J.S. (2021). *The Routledge Handbook of Post-Prohibition Cannabis Research*. London: Routledge.

Costa, A. (2010). "Drug Control, Crime Prevention and Criminal Justice: A Human Rights Perspective—Note by the Executive Director." United Nations Office on Drugs and Crime. Available at: https://digitallibrary.un.org/record/681077?ln=en.

Coulton, M. (2022). "Canada's Cannabis Industry Braces for Increased Competition as U.S. Legalization Looms Larger." (April 5) *Financial Post*. Available at: https://financialpost.com/cannabis/canadas-cannabis-industry-braces-for-increased-competition-as-u-s-legalization-looms-larger.

Courtwright, D. (2002). *Forces of Habit: Drugs and the Making of the Modern World*. Cambridge, MA: Harvard University Press.

Cousijn, J., Goudriaan, A.E., & Wiers, R.W. (2011). "Reaching Out Towards Cannabis: Approach-Bias in Heavy Cannabis Users Predicts Changes in Cannabis Use." *Addiction* 106(9): 1667–1674.

Cousijn, J., Wiers, R.W., Ridderinkhof, K.R., van den Brink, W., Veltman, D.J., & Goudriaan, A.E. (2012). "Grey Matter Alterations Associated with Cannabis Use: Results of a VBM Study in Heavy Cannabis Users and Healthy Controls." *NeuroImage* 59(4): 3845–3851. https://doi.org/10.1016/J.NEUROIMAGE.2011.09.046.

Cousijn, J., Toenders, Y.J., van Velzen, L.S., & Kaag, A.M. (2021). "The Relation between Cannabis Use, Dependence Severity and White Matter Microstructure: A Diffusion Tensor Imaging Study." *Addiction Biology*. e13081. https://doi.org/10.1111/adb.13081.

Cowan, R. (1986). "How the Narcs Created Crack: A War against Ourselves." *National Review* 38(23): 26–34.

Cracknell, M. (2021). "The Resettlement Net: 'Revolving Door' Imprisonment and Carceral (Re)circulation." (August) *Punishment & Society* 25(1): 223–240. doi: 10.1177/14624745211035837.

Crandall, R.C. (2020). *Drugs and Thugs: The History and Future of America's War on Drugs*. New Haven, CT: Yale University Press.

Crawford, N. (2021). "We'd Go Well Together: A Critical Race Analysis of Marijuana Legalization and Expungement in the United States." *Public Integrity* 23(5): 459–483. https://doi.org/10.1080/10999922.2021.1955512.

Crean, R.D., Tapert, S.F., Minassian, A., Macdonald, K., Crane, N.A., & Mason, B.J. (2011). "Effects of Chronic, Heavy Cannabis Use on Executive Functions." *Journal of Addiction Medicine* 5(1): 9–15. https://doi.org/10.1097/ADM.0b013e31820cdd57.

Crew, J. (2022). "Black Schoolgirl Strip Searched by Police While on Her Period—Report." (March 15) *Evening Standard*. Available at: https://www.standard.co.uk/news/uk/department-for-education-metropolitan-police-services-scotland-yard-hackney-b988292.html.

Critcher, C. (2003) *Moral Panics and the Media*. Buckingham: Open University Press.

Crockett, D. (2021). "Montreal Councilors Call on City Hall to Ask Ottawa to Decriminalize Simple Drug Possession." (January 21) *CTV News*. Available at: https://montreal.ctvnews.ca/montreal-councillors-call-on-city-hall-to-ask-ottawa-to-decriminalize-simple-drug-possession-1.5273097.

Crowder, M. (2020). "New Appellations Would Celebrate Individual Terroir of Cannabis Strains." (September 22) *San Francisco Chronicle*. Available at: https://www.sfchronicle.com/bayarea/article/New-appellations-would-celebrate-individual-15587030.php.

Cruz, J.M., Boidi, M.F., & Queirolo, R. (2018). "The Status of Support for Cannabis Regulation in Uruguay 4 Years after Reform: Evidence from Public Opinion Surveys." *Drug and Alcohol Review* 37(1): S429–S434. https://doi.org/10.1111/dar.12642.

Currie, E. (1999). "Reflections on Crime and Criminology at the Millennium." *Western Criminology Review* 2(1): 1–13.

Cyrus, E., Coudray, M.S., Kiplagat, S., Mariano, Y., Noel, I., Galea, J.T. et al. (2021). "A Review Investigating the Relationship between Cannabis Use and Adolescent Cognitive Functioning." *Current Opinion in Psychology* 38: 38–48.

D'Souza, D.C., DiForti, M., Ganesh, S., George, T.P., Hall, W., Hjorthøj, C., et al. (2022) "Consensus Paper of the WFSBP Task Force on Cannabis, Cannabinoids and Psychosis." *The World Journal of Biological Psychiatry* 23(10): 719–742. doi: 10.1080/15622975.2022.2038797.

Da Silva, M.T. (2013). "Online Forums, Audience Participation and Modes of Political Discussion: Readers' Comments on the Brazilian Presidential Election as a Case Study." *Information, Communication and Society* 26(4): 175–193.

Dahl, S.L. (2015). "Remaining a User While Cutting Down: The Relationship between Cannabis Use and Identity." *Drugs: Education, Prevention and Policy* 22(3): 175–184.

Daly, M. (2016). "Some Police in the UK Have Stopped Arresting Drug Users." (October 19). *Vice*. Available at: https://www.vice.com/en/article/vdq7b9/drug-decriminalisation-in-uk-narcomania-heroin-crack.

Dandurand, Y. (2021). "Law Enforcement Strategies to Disrupt Illicit Drug Markets." International Centre for Criminal Law Reform and Criminal Justice Policy. Available at: https://icclr.org/publications/law-enforcement-strategies-to-disrupt-illicit-drug-markets.

Daniels, C., Aluso, A., Burke-Shyne, N., Koram, K., Rajagopalan, S., Robinson, I., et al. (2021). "Decolonizing Drug Policy." *Harm Reduction Journal* 18(1): Article 120. https://doi.org/10.1186/s12954-021-00564-7.

Daniels, J. (2019). "Colerado Legal pot Industry Sales Grew 3 Percent in 2018, Top $6 Billion since Recreational Use Began." (February 12) *CNBC*. Available at: https://www.cnbc.com/2019/02/12/colorado-pot-industry-sales-top-6-billion-since-adult-use-began.html.

Daniller, A. (2019). "Two Thirds of Americans Support Marijuana Legalization." (November 14) Pew Research Center. Available at: https://www.pewresearch.org/fact-tank/2019/11/14/americans-support-marijuana-legalization.

Danko, P. (2022). "Exclusive: Portland Cannabis Entrepreneur Nitin Khanna Hits Curaleaf Exec Boris Jordan with $1.5B RICO Claim." (August 22) *Portland Business Journal*. Available at: https://www.bizjournals.com/portland/news/2022/08/22/khanna-jordan-15-billion-rico-claim.html.

Dannenbaum, J. (1981). "The Origins of Temperance Activism and Militancy among American Women." *Journal of Social History* 15(2): 235–252.

Danquah-Brobby, E. (2017). "Comment: Prison for You. Profit for Me. Systemic Racism Effectively Bars Blacks from Participation in Newly-Legal Marijuana Industry." *University of Baltimore Law Review* 46(3): 523–546.

David, M., Rohlof, A., Petley, J., & Hughes, J. (2011). "The Idea of Moral Panic: Ten Dimensions of Dispute." *Crime, Media, Culture* 7(3): 215–228.

Davis, M. (2012). *Jews and Booze: Becoming American in the Age of Prohibition*. New York, NY: University Press.

DeAngelo, G.J., Gittings, R.K., and Ross, A. (2018). "Police Incentives, Policy Spillovers, and the Enforcement of Drug Crimes." (March) *Review of Law & Economics* 14(1): 1–29.

Decorte, T., Pardal, M., Queirolo, R., Boidi, M.F., Avilés, C.S., & Franquero, Ò.P. (2017). "Regulating Cannabis Social Clubs: A Comparative Analysis of Legal and Self-regulatory Practices in Spain, Belgium and Uruguay." *International Journal of Drug Policy* 43: 44–56.

Decorte, T., Lenton, S., & Wilkins, C. (2020). *Legalizing Cannabis: Experiences, Lessons and Scenarios*. New York, NY: Routledge.

Deflem, M. (2020). "Popular Culture and Social Control: The Moral Panic on Music Labeling." *American Journal of Criminal Justice* 45: 2–24.

Degenhardt, L., Hall, W., & Lynskey, M. (2003). "Exploring the Association between Cannabis Use and Depression." *Addiction* 98(11): 1493–1504.

Delgado, R. & Stefanic, J. (2001). *Critical Race Theory: An Introduction*. New York, NY: New York University.

Delgado, R. & Stefanic, J. (2012). *Critical Race Theory: An Introduction*. 2nd edn. New York, NY: New York University Press.

Dellazizzo, L., Potvin, S, Athanassiou, M., & Dumais, A. (2020). "Violence and Cannabis Use: A Focused Review of a Forgotten Aspect in the Era of Liberalizing Cannabis." *Front Psychiatry* 11: 567887. https://www.frontiersin.org/articles/10.3389/fpsyt.2020.567887.

Del Olmo, R. (1991). "The Hidden Face of Drugs." *Social Justice* 18(4): 10–48.

del Pozo, B. (2022). *The Police and the State: Security, Social Cooperation, and the Public Good*. Cambridge, UK: Cambridge University Press.

del Pozo, B., Sightes, E., Goulka, J., Ray, B., Wood, C., Siddiqui, S., & Beletsky, L. (2021). "Police Discretion in Encounters with People Who Use Drugs: Operationalizing the Theory of Planned Behavior." *Harm Reduction Journal* 18: 132. https://doi.org/10.1186/s12954-021-00583-4.

Department of Health and Human Services (2020). "National Survey of Substance Abuse Treatment Services (N-SSATS): 2020: Data on Substance Abuse Treatment Facilities." Available at: https://www.samhsa.gov/data/sites/default/files/reports/rpt35313/2020_NSSATS_FINAL.pdf.

Dertadian, G.C. & Maher L. (2014). "From Oxycodone to Heroin: Two Cases of Transitioning Opioid Use in Young Australians." *Drug and Alcohol Review* 33(1): 102–104.

Dewan, S. (2018). "Caught with Pot? Get-Out-of-Jail Program Comes with $950 Catch." (August 24) *New York Times*. Available at: https://www.nytimes.com/2018/08/24/us/marijuana-diversion-program-maricopa-arizona.html.

Dewey, John (1916). *Democracy and Education: An Introduction to the Philosophy of Education*. New York, NY: Macmillan.

Di Forti, M., Quattrone, D.T., Freeman, P., Tripoli, G., Gayer-Anderson, C., Quig-ley et al. and the EU–GEI WP2 Group (European Network of National Schizophrenia Networks Studying Gene–Environment Interactions) (2019). "The Contribution of Cannabis Use to Variation in the Incidence of Psychotic Disorder across Europe (EU–GEI): A Multicentre Case-Control Study." *Lancet Psychiatry* 6(5): 427–436.

Dickson, D. (1968). "Bureaucracy and Morality: An Organizational Perspective on a Moral Crusade." *Social Problems* 16(Fall): 143–156.

Dobuzinskis, A. (2013). "Former Rep. Patrick Kennedy Leads Campaign against Legal Pot." (January 5) *Reuters*. Available at: https://www.reuters.com/article/us-usa-kennedy-marijuana-idUSBRE9040AF20130105.

Donnan, J., Shogan, O., Bishop, L., Swab, M., & Najafizada, M. (2022). "Characteristics that Influence Purchase Choice for Cannabis Products: A Systematic Review." *Journal of Cannabis Research* 4(1): 1–27.

Donnelly, N., Hall, W., & Christie, P. (1995). "The Effects of Partial Decriminalisation on Cannabis Use in South Australia, 1985 to 1993." *Australian Journal of Public Health* 19: 281–287.

Donohue, Ewing, E. & Peloquin, D. (2011). "Rethinking America's Illegal Drug Policy." In P.J. Cook, J. Ludwig, & J. McCrary (eds), *Controlling Crime: Strategies and Tradeoffs*. Chicago, IL: University of Chicago Press (pp. 215–281).

Donovan, J. (2019). "Canada Must Respect Indigenous Cannabis Laws." (August 1) *Policy Options Politiques*. Available at: https://policyoptions.irpp.org/magazines/august-2019/canada-must-respect-indigenous-cannabis-laws.

Doonan, S.M., Johnson, J.K., Firth, C., Flores, A., & Joshi, S. (2022). "Racial Equity in Cannabis Policy: Diversity in the Massachusetts Adult-Use Industry at 18 months." *Cannabis* 5(1): 30–41.

Dougan, M. & O'Brien, C. (2019). "Reflections on Law and Impact in the Light of Brexit." *Law Teacher* 53(2): 197–211.

Douglas, F. (1845). *Frederick Douglass, 1818–1895: Narrative of the Life of Frederick Douglass, an American Slave.* Boston, MA: Anti-Slavery Office.

Dorling, D. (2016). "Brexit: The Decision of a Divided Country." *British Medical Journal* 354: 1–3. https://doi.org/10.1136/bmj.i3697.

Downey, L.A., King, R., Papafotiou, K., Swann, P., Ogden, E., Boorman, M., & Stough, C. (2013). "The Effects of Cannabis and Alcohol on Simulated Driving: Influences of Dose and Experience." *Accident; Analysis and Prevention* 50: 879–886. https://doi.org/10.1016/j.aap.2012.07.016.

Draaisma, M. (2018). "Don't Drive While High, Canadians Urged in New MADD, Tweed, Uber Campaign." (October 10) *CBC News*. Available at: https://www.cbc.ca/news/canada/toronto/driving-while-high-campaign-madd-canada-tweed-uber-1.4856804.

Dragone, D., Prarolo, G., Vanin, P., & Zanella, G. (2019). "Crime and the Legalization of Recreational Marijuana." *Journal of Economic Behavior and Organization* 159(C): 488–501.

Drake, D. (2012). *Prisons, Punishment and the Pursuit of Security.* Basingstoke: Palgrave Macmillan.

Draper, K. & Macur, J. (2021). "Sha'Carri Richardson, a Track Sensation, Tests Positive for Marijuana." (July 1) *New York Times*. Available at: https://www.nytimes.com/2021/07/01/sports/olympics/shacarri-richardson-suspended-marijuana.html.

Drug Enforcement Administration (n.d.). "Drug Scheduling." Available at: https://www.dea.gov/drug-information/drug-scheduling.

Drug Policy Alliance (2019). "100 Scholars and Clinicians Refute Inaccurate Claims in New Book, Tell Your Children: The Truth about Marijuana, Mental Illness, and Violence." Available at: https://drugpolicy.org/news/100-scholars-and-clinicians-refute-inaccurate-claims-new-book-tell-your/.

Dubois, S., Mullen, N., Weaver, B., & Bédard, M. (2015). "The Combined Effects of Alcohol and Cannabis on Driving: Impact on Crash Risk." *Forensic Science International* 248: 94–100. https://doi.org/10.1016/j.forsciint.2014.12.018.

Duff, C. (2003). "Drugs and Youth Cultures: Is Australia Experiencing the 'Normalization' of Adolescent Drug Use?" *Journal of Youth Studies* 6(4): 433–446.

Duff, C., Asbridge, M., Brochu, S., Cousineau, M.-M., Hathaway, A.D., Marsh, D., & Erickson, P.G. (2012). "A Canadian Perspective on Cannabis Normalization among Adults." *Addiction Research & Theory* 20(4): 271–283.

Dufton, E. (2017a) *Grass Roots: The Fall and Rise of Marijuana in America.* New York, NY: Basic Books.

Dufton, E. (2017b). "Tell Us 5 Things about Your Book: Debating Pot in America." (December 3) *New York Times*. Available at: https://www.nytimes.com/2017/12/03/books/grass-roots-emily-dufton-marijuana-activism.html.

Dufton, E. (2019). "Puff, Puff, Puff, Pass. Lessons from the Defeat of Marijuana Decriminalization." *Perspectives on History*. Available at: https://www.historians.org/publications-and-directories/perspectives-on-history/april-2019/puff-puff-pass-lessons-from-the-defeat-of-marijuana-decriminalization.

Duke, K., Gleeson, H., Dąbrowska, K., Herold, M., & Rolando, M. (2021). "The Engagement of Young People in Drug Interventions in Coercive Contexts: Findings

from a Cross-National European Study." *Drugs: Education, Prevention and Policy* 28(1): 26–35.
Duke, S. & Gross, A.C. (1993). *America's Longest War: Rethinking Our Tragic Crusade against Drugs*. New York, NY: G.P. Putnam's Sons.
Dumitrescu, L. (2018). "The Securitization of East-European Migrants. The Occurrence of Liminal Identities in the European Union." In E. Balica & V. Marinescu (eds), *Migration and Crime: Realities and Media Representations*. London: Palgrave Macmillan (pp. 69–86).
Dunleavy, P. & O'Leary, B. (1987). *Theories of the State: The Politics of Liberal Democracy*. New York, NY: Bloomsbury Publishing.
Duster, T. (1970). *The Legislation of Morality: Law, Dugs and Moral Judgement*. New York, NY: Free Press.
Earlenbaugh, E. (2020). "More People Were Arrested for Cannabis Last Year Than for All Violent Crimes Put Together, According to FBI Data." (October 6) *Forbes*. Available at: https://www.forbes.com/sites/emilyearlenbaugh/2020/10/06/more-people-were-arrested-for-cannabis-last-year-than-for-all-violent-crimes-put-together-according-to-fbi-data/?sh=12b6f591122f.
Earp, B.D., Lewis, J., & Hart, C.L., with Bioethicists and Allied Professionals for Drug Policy Reform. (2021). "Racial Justice Requires Ending the War on Drugs." *American Journal of Bioethics* 21(4): 4–19.
Eastwood, N. (2020). "Cannabis Decriminalization Policies across the Globe." In T. Decorte, S. Lenton, & C. Wilkins (eds), *Legalizing Cannabis: Experiences, Lessons and Scenarios*. London: Routledge (pp. 133–153).
Eastwood, N., Fox, E., & Rosmarin, A. (2016). *A Quiet Revolution: Drug Decriminalisation Policies in Practice across the Globe*. London: Release.
EAT (Equity and Transformation) (2019). "Key Findings: What Is Preventing Black Inclusion in the Cannabis Industry?" (May 29). Available at: https://cf84fce6-8756-40c5-92ef-cd97cbc441f3.filesusr.com/ugd/9c611a_e7455f06dfb04bfe84e3efaa1bbc5cbe.pdf.
Economist Intelligence Unit (2020). "Democracy Index 2020: In Sickness and in Health?" Available at: https://www.eiu.com/n/campaigns/democracy-index-2020.
Edman, J. (2015). "Temperance and Modernity: Alcohol Consumption as a Collective Problem 1885–1913." *Journal of Social History* 49(1): 20–52.
Ediomo-Ubong, E.N. (2021). "'I Cannot Stop Taking Weed Cos It Makes Me Survive': Cannabis Use, Criminal Sanctions and Users' Experiences in Nigeria." *Drugs: Education, Prevention and Policy* 30(2): 196–203. https://doi.org/10.1080/09687637.2021.1972936.
Einstadter, W.J. & Henry, S. (2006). *Criminological Theory*. Lanham, MD: Rowman and Littlefield.
Eliason, A. and Howse, R. (2019). "A Higher Authority: Canada's Cannabis Legalization in the Context of International Law." *Michigan Journal of International Law* 40(2): 327. http://dx.doi.org/10.2139/ssrn.3262773.
Ellingson, J.M., Ross, J.M., Winiger, E., Stallings, M.C., Corley, R.P., Friedman, N.P. et al. (2021). "Familial Factors May Not Explain the Effect of Moderate-to-Heavy Cannabis Use on Cognitive Functioning in Adolescents: A Sibling-Comparison Study." *Addiction* 116(4): 833–844. https://doi.org/10.1111/add.15207.

Elliott, J.C., Carey, K.B., & Vanable, P.A. (2014). "A Preliminary Evaluation of a Web-Based Intervention for College Marijuana Use." *Psychology of Addictive Behaviours* 28(1): 288–293.

Elliott, M.L., Knodt, A.R., Ireland, D., Morris, M.L., Poulton, R., Ramrakha, S., Sison, M.L., Moffitt, T.E., Caspi, A., Hariri, A.R. (2020). "What Is the Test–Retest Reliability of Common Task-Functional MRI Measures? New Empirical Evidence and a Meta-Analysis." *Psychological Science* 31(7): 792–806.

Elmahrek, A. (2020). "L.A.'s 'Social Equity' Program for Cannabis Licenses under Scrutiny." (March 20) *Los Angeles Times*. Available at: https://www.latimes.com/california/story/2020-06-23/cannabis-licenses-social-equity-4th-mvmt#:~:text=But%20the%20city's%20%E2%80%9Csocial%20equity,entrepreneurs%20to%20obtain%20cannabis%20licenses.

ElSohly, M.A., Chandra, S., Radwan, M., Majumdar, C.G., & Church, J.C. (2021). "A Comprehensive Review of Cannabis Potency in the United States in the Last Decade. Biological psychiatry." *Cognitive Neuroscience and Neuroimaging* 6(6): 603–606.

EMCDDA (European Monitoring Centre for Drugs and Drug Addiction) (n.d.). "Cannabis Policy: Status and Recent Developments." Available at: https://www.emcdda.europa.eu/publications/topic-overviews/cannabis-policy/html_en.

EMCDDA (2017a). "Drug Trafficking Penalties across the European Union: A Survey of Expert Opinion." Technical report. Available at: emcdda.europa.eu/publications/technical-reports/trafficking-penalties.

EMCDDA (2017b). "The Netherlands, Country Drug Report 2017." Publications Office of the European Union, Luxembourg. Available at: https://www.emcdda.europa.eu/system/files/publications/4512/TD0616155ENN.pdf.

EMCDDA (2019). *Netherlands Country Drug Report*. Utrecht, Netherlands: Trimbos Institut.

Encyclopedia.com (2018). "Temperance Movement." (updated May 23) *Encyclopedia.com*. Available at: https://www.encyclopedia.com/social-sciences-and-law/sociology-and-social-reform/social-reform/temperance-movements.

Erickson, P.G., & Hathaway, A.D. (2010). "Normalization and Harm Reduction: Research Avenues and Policy Agendas." *International Journal of Drug Policy* 21(2): 137–139.

Erickson, P.G. & Oscapella, E. (1999). "Cannabis in Canada: A Puzzling Policy." *International Journal of Drug Policy* 10: 313–318.

Erickson, P.G., Hyshka, E., & Hathaway, A.D. (2010). "Legal Regulation of Marijuana: The Better Way." In N.A. Frost, J.D. Freilich, & T.R. Clear (eds), *Contemporary Issues in Criminal Justice Policy* Belmont, CA: Wadsworth, Cengage Learning (pp. 109–118).

Erridge, S. (2020). "Real World Data & Patient Registries." (October 19) *Cannabinoid Journal*. Available at: https://centreformedicinalcannabis.substack.com/p/real-world-data-and-patient-registries.

Fagan, J., Geller, A., Davies, G., & West, V. (2009). "Street Stops and Broken Windows Revisited: The Demography and Logic of Proactive Policing in a Safe and Changing City." Columbia Public Law Research Paper No. 09-203.

Fagan, J.A., Geller, A., Davies, G., & West, V. (2010). "Street Stops and Broken Windows Revisited." In S.K. Rice & M.D. White (eds), *Race, Ethnicity, and Policing*. New York, NY: New York University Press (pp. 309–348).

Farley, E.J. & Orchowsky, S. (2019). "Measuring the Criminal Justice System Impacts of Marijuana Legalization and Decriminalization Using State Data NCJ Number 253137." National Criminal Justice Reference Services. Available at: https://www.ncjrs.gov/pdffiles1/nij/grants/253137.pdf.

Farrell, G. (2013). "Five Tests for a Theory of the Crime Drop." *Crime Science* 2(5): 1–8.

Farrell, G., Tilley, N., & Tseloni, A. (2014). "Why Crime Drop?" *Crime and Justice* 43(1): 421–490.

FBI (Federal Bureau of Investigation) Jobs (n.d.). "Eligibility and Hiring: What It Takes to Join the FBI." Available at: https://www.fbijobs.gov/working-at-FBI/eligibility.

Feeley, M.M. & Simon, J. (1992). "The New Penology: Notes on the Emerging Strategy of Corrections and Its Implications." *Criminology* 30(4): 449–474.

Félix, S. & Portugal, P. (2017). "Drug Decriminalization and the Price of Illicit Drugs." *International Journal on Drug Policy* 39: 121–129. https://doi.org/10.1016/j.drugpo.2016.10.014.

Felson, M. (2002). *Crime and Everyday Life*. Thousand Oak, CA: Sage Publications.

Felson, M. & Eckert, M.A. (2018). *Crime and Everyday Life: A Brief Introduction*. Los Angeles, CA: Sage Publications.

Feltmann, K., Gripenberg, J., Strandberg, A.K. Elgán, T.H., & Kvillemo, P. (2021). "Drug Dealing and Drug Use Prevention—A Qualitative Interview Study of Authorities' Perspectives on Two Open Drug Scenes in Stockholm." *Substance Abuse Treatment, Prevention, and Policy* 16(1): 37. https://doi.org/10.1186/s13011-021-00375-w.

Ferguson, C., McFadden, C., Dong, S., & Schapiro, R. (2019). "Tests Show Bootleg Marijuana Vapes Tainted with Hydrogen Cyanide." (September 28) *National Broadcasting Company*. Available at: https://www.nbcnews.com/health/vaping/tests-show-bootleg-marij uana-vapes-tainted-hydrogen-cyanide-n1059356.

Ferrell, J. (1990). "A Critical Criminologist Looks at Critical Criminology: A Review of Stanley Cohen's 'Against Criminology' [Review of *Against Criminology*, by S. Cohen]." *Social Justice* 17(1): 132–135.

Ferrell, J., Hayward, K., & Young, J. (2008). *Cultural Criminology: An Invitation*. Thousand Oaks, CA: Sage Publications.

Fersko, J. (2018). "The Business of Marijuana." (May) *American College of Real Estate Lawyers News & Notes*. Available at: https://cdn.ymaws.com/acrel.site-ym.com/resource/resmgr/news_and_notes/May/2018-05_Fersko_-_Cannabis_Ar.pdf.

Festinger, L. (1957). *A Theory of Cognitive Dissonance*. Palo Alto, CA: Stanford University Press.

Fetterling, T., Parnes, J., Prince, M.A., Conner, B.T., George, M.W., Shillington, A.M., & Riggs, N.R. (2021). "Moderated Mediation of the eCHECKUP TO GO College Student Cannabis Use Intervention." *Substance Use & Misuse* 56(10): 1508–1515.

FFJC (Fines and Justice Center) (2019). "Litigation: Briggs v. Montgomery." (June 18). Available at: https://finesandfeesjusticecenter.org/articles/briggs-v-montgomery.

Firth, C., Davenport, S., Smart, R., & Dilley, J.A. (2020). "How High: Differences in the Developments of Cannabis Markets in Two Legalized States." *International Journal on Drug Policy* 75: 102–111. https://doi.org/10.1016/j.drugpo.2019.102611.

Fischer, B., Russell C., & Boyd N. (2020a). "A Century of Cannabis Control in Canada: A Brief Overview of History, Context and Policy Frameworks from Prohibition to Legalization." In T. Decorte, S. Lenton, & C. Wilkins (eds), *Legalizing Cannabis: Experiences, Lessons and Scenarios*. London: Routledge (pp. 89–115).

Fischer, B., Daldegan-Bueno, D., & Boden, J.M. (2020b). "Facing the Option for the Legalisation of Cannabis Use and Supply in New Zealand: An Overview of Relevant Evidence, Concepts and Considerations." (July) *Drug and Alcohol Review* 39(5): 555–567. https://doi.org/10.1111/dar.13087. PMID: 32436274; PMCID: PMC7383663.

Fischer, B., Lee, A., O'Keefe-Markman, C., & Hall, W. (2020c). "Initial Indicators of the Public Health Impacts of Non-Medical Cannabis Legalization in Canada." *EClinical Medicine* 20: 100–294.

Fischer, B., Daldegan-Bueno, D., & Reuter, P. (2021). "Toward a 'Post-Legalization' Criminology for Cannabis: A Brief Review and Suggested Agenda for Research Priorities." *Contemporary Drug Problems* 48(1): 58–57.

Fisher, G. (2021). "Racial Myths of the Cannabis War." *Boston University Law Review* 101: 933–977.

Fitz, D. & Armstrong, S. (2022). "How Decriminalizing Marijuana Is Reinventing Racism and Poisoning." (May 19) *Counterpunch*. Available at: https://www.counterpunch.org/2022/05/19/how-decriminalized-marijuana-is-reinventing-racism-and-poisoning.

Fletcher, T. (2019). "B.C. Craft Cannabis Growers Wind through Layers of Government." (December 3) *Victoria News*. Available at: https://www.vicnews.com/business/b-c-craft-cannabis-growers-wind-through-layers-of-government.

Fornili, K.S. (2018). "Racialized Mass Incarceration and the War on Drugs: A Critical Race Theory Appraisal." (January/March) *Journal of Addictions Nursing* 29(1): 65–72. https://doi.org/10.1097/JAN.0000000000000215. PMID: 29505464.

Forsyth, M. (2017) *A Short History of Drunkenness*. London: Viking.

Foucault, M. (1979) *Discipline and Punish: The Birth of the Prison*. London: Penguin.

Fox, B. (2018). "Making the Headlines: EU Immigration to the UK and the Wave of New Racism after Brexit." In E. Balica & V. Marinescu (eds), *Migration and Crime: Realities and Media Representations*. London: Palgrave Macmillan (pp. 87–107).

Fox, K.J. (2012). "Redeeming Communities: Restorative Offender Reentry in a Risk-centric Society." *Victims & Offenders* 7(1): 97–120.

Fox, K.J. (2013). "Incurable Sex Offenders, Lousy Judges & the Media: Moral Panic Sustenance in the Age of New Media." *American Journal of Criminal Justice* 38: 160–181.

Fox, K.J. (2014). "Restoring the Social: Offender Reintegration in a Risky World." *International Journal of Comparative and Applied Criminal Justice* 38(3): 235–256.

Fox, K.J. (2015). "Trying to Restore Justice: Bureaucracies, Risk Management, and Disciplinary Boundaries in New Zealand Criminal Justice." *International Journal of Offender Therapy and Comparative Criminology* 59(5): 519–538.

França, L.A. (2021). "How International Should International Criminology Be?" *International Criminology* 1: 46–57.

Frank, D. (2000). "The Devil and Mr. Hearst." *The Nation*. Available at: https://www.thenation.com/article/devil-and-mr-hearst.

Fratello, F., Rengifo, A., & Trone, J. (2013). "Coming of Age with Stop and Frisk: Experiences, Self-Perceptions, and Public Safety Implications." New York, NY: Vera Institute. Available at: https://www.vera.org/publications/coming-of-age-with-stop-and-frisk-experiences-self-perceptions-and-public-safety-implications.

Frisher, M., Crome, I., Martino, O., & Croft, P. (2009). "Assessing the Impact of Cannabis Use on Trends in Diagnosed Schizophrenia in the United Kingdom from 1996 to 2005." *Schizophrenia Research* 113(2–3): 123–128. https://doi.org/10.1016/j.schres.2009.05.031. Epub 2009 June 27. PMID: 19560900.

Frontline (n.d.). "Marijuana Timeline." Available at: https://www.pbs.org/wgbh/pages/frontline/shows/dope/etc/cron.html.

Frydl, K.J. (2013). *The Drug Wars in America, 1940–1973*. New York, NY: Cambridge University Press.

Fuller, T. (2019a). "'Getting Worse, Not Better': Illegal Pot Market Booming in California Despite Legalization." (April 27) *New York Times*. Available at: https://www.nytimes.com/2019/04/27/us/marijuana-california-legalization.html.

Fuller, T. (2019b). "Now for the Hard Part: Getting Californians to Buy Legal Weed." (January 2) *New York Times*. Available at: https://www.nytimes.com/2019/01/02/us/buying-legal-weed-in-california.html.

Fumano, G. (2021). "Regulators Play 'Whac-A-Mole' as Vancouver's Illegal Pot Shops Flourish." (January 9) *Vancouver Sun*. Available at: https://vancouversun.com/cannabis/cannabis-business/regulators-play-whac-a-mole-as-vancouvers-illegal-pot-shops-keep-sprouting.

Gabri, A.C., Galanti, M.R., Orsini, N., & Magnusson, C. (2022). "Changes in Cannabis Policy and Prevalence of Recreational Cannabis Use among Adolescents and Young Adults in Europe—An Interrupted Time-Series Analysis." *PLoS ONE* 17(1): e0261885. https://doi.org/10.1371/journal.pone.0261885.

Gage, S.H., Zammit, S., & Hickman, M. (2013). "Stronger Evidence Is Needed before Accepting That Cannabis Plays an Important Role in the Aetiology of Schizophrenia in the Population." *F1000 Medicine Reports* 5(2). https://doi.org/10.3410/M5-2. Available at: https://facultyopinions.com/prime/reports/m/5/2.

Gagnon, M., Gudiño, D., Guta, A., & Strike, C. (2020). "What Can We Learn from the English-Language Media Coverage of Cannabis Legalization in Canada?" *Substance Use & Misuse* 55(8): 1378–1381. https://doi.org/10.1080/10826084.2020.1741639.

Gama, F. (2016). "The Racial Politics of Protection: A Critical Race Examination of Police Militarization." *California Law Review* 104: 979–1008.

Garland, D. (1996). "The Limits of the Sovereign State: Strategies of Crime Control in Contemporary Society." *British Journal of Criminology* 36: 445–471.

Garland, D. (2001). *Culture of Control: Crime and Social Order in Contemporary Society*. Chicago, IL: University of Chicago Press.

Garland, D. (2008). "On the Concept of Moral Panic." *Crime Media Culture* 4(1): 9–30.

Gasnier, L.J., O'Brien, D., Short, D., McCollum, W., Miles, L., Young, C., & White, T. (1998 [1938]). *Reefer Madness*. St Laurent: Madacy Entertainment Group.

Gavrilova, E., Kamada, T., & Zoutman, F. (2017). "Is Legal Pot Crippling Mexican Drug Trafficking Organizations? The Effect of Medical Marijuana Laws on US Crime." *Economic Journal* 239120: 1–33.

Gaylin, W., Glasser, I., Marcus, S., & Rothman, D. (1978). *Doing Good: The Limits of Benevolence.* New York, NY: Pantheon.

GDPI (Global Drug Policy Index) (2021a). "The Global Drug Policy Index 2021." (November). Available at: https://globaldrugpolicyindex.net/wp-content/themes/gdpi/uploads/GDPI%202021%20Report.pdf.

GDPI (2021b). "The Global Drug Policy Index: Methodology." (November). Available at: https://globaldrugpolicyindex.net/wp-content/themes/gdpi/uploads/GDPI_Methodology_EN.pdf.

Geller, A. and Fagan, J. (2010). "Pot as Pretext: Marijuana, Race, and the New Disorder in New York City Street Policing." *Journal of Empirical Legal Studies* 7: 591–633. https://doi.org/10.1111/j.1740-1461.2010.01190.x.

Gelman, A., Fagan, J. & Kiss, A. (2007). "An Analysis of the New York City Police Department's 'Stop-and-Frisk' Policy in the Context of Claims of Racial Bias." *Journal of the American Statistical Association* 102(479): 813–823.

Gerber, M. (2022). "California Promised 'Social Equity' after Pot Legalization. Those Hit Hardest Feel Betrayed." (January 27) *Los Angeles Times.* Available at: https://www.latimes.com/california/story/2022-01-27/california-pot-industry-social-equity-broken-promises.

Gerster, R. & Bassett, J. (1991). *Seizures of Youth: The Sixties and Australia.* Carlton: Hyland House.

Gham, J. (2019). "How This Company Is Becoming the 'Amazon of Cannabis.'" (June 10) *Mugglehead Magazine.* Available at: https://mugglehead.com/this-company-is-quickly-becoming-the-amazon-of-cannabis.

Gieringer, D.H. (1999). "The Forgotten Origins of Cannabis Prohibition in California." *Contemporary Drug Problems* 26(2): 237–288.

Giffen, J., Endicott, S., & Lambert, S. (1991). *Panic and Indifference: The Politics of Canada's Drug Laws.* Ottawa: Canadian Center on Substance Abuse.

Gittins, R. & Sessa, B. (2020). "Can Prescribed Medical Cannabis Use Reduce the Use of Other More Harmful Drugs?" (January 2020) *Drug Science, Policy and Law* 6: 1–4. doi: 10.1177/2050324519900067.

Gladwell, M. (2019). "Is Marijuana as Safe as We Think?" (January 14) *The New Yorker.* Available at: https://www.newyorker.com/magazine/2019/01/14/is-marijuana-as-safe-as-we-think.

Glasser, I. (2000). "American Drug Laws: The New Jim Crow, the 1999 Edward C. Sobota Lecture." *Albany Law Review* 63: 703–723.

GlobeNewswire (2021). "Cannabis Market Size to Reach $ 128.92 Billion by 2028; Genetic Development and Modification of the Cannabis Boost the Market Demand, States Vantage Market Research." (December 28) *Global Newswire.* Available at: https://www.globenewswire.com/news-release/2021/12/28/2358365/0/en/Cannabis-Market-Size-to-Reach-128-92-Billion-by-2028-Genetic-Development-and-Modification-of-the-Cannabis-Boost-the-Market-Demand-States-Vantage-Market-Research-VMR.html.

GlobeNewswire (2022). "New Frontier Data Projects Annual U.S. Cannabis Sales to More Than Double to $72B by 2030." (March 23). New Frontier Data. Available at: https://www.globenewswire.com/en/news-release/2022/03/23/2408755/0/en/New-Frontier-Data-Projects-Annual-U-S-Cannabis-Sales-to-More-Than-Double-to-72B-by-2030.html.

Goffman, E. (1963). *Stigma: Notes on the Management of Spoiled Identity*. New York, NY: Simon and Schuster.

Goldstein, P.J. (1985). "The Drugs/Violence Nexus: A Tripartite Conceptual Framework." *Journal of Drug Issues* 15(4): 493–506. https://doi.org/10.1177/002204268501500406.

Goldstein, R. & Sumner, D. (2019). "California Cannabis Regulation." *California Agriculture* 73(3): 101–102.

Goldstein, R. & Sumner, D. (2022). *Can Legal Weed Win?: The Blunt Realities of Cannabis Economics*, 1st edn. Oakland, CA: University of California Press. https://doi.org/10.2307/j.ctv2ks6tx4.

Golub, A. & Johnson, B.D. (2001). "Drug of Choice among Youthful Adult Arrestees." (July) National Institute of Justice Research Briefs. US Department of Justice. Available at: https://www.ncjrs.gov/pdffiles1/nij/187490.pdf.

Gonçalves, R., Lourenço, A., & da Silva, S.N. (2015). "A Social Cost Perspective in the Wake of the Portuguese Strategy for the Fight against Drugs." *International Journal of Drug Policy* 26(2): 199–209. https://doi.org/10.1016/j.drugpo.2014.08.017.

Goode, E. (2005). *Drugs in American Society*. New York, NY: McGraw-Hill.

Goode, E. & Ben-Yehuda, N. (2009 [1994]). "Moral Panics: Culture, Politics, and Social Construction." *Annual Review of Sociology* 20: 149–171.

Gopnik, A. (2015). "The Outside Game." (January 5) *The New Yorker*. Available at: https://www.newyorker.com/magazine/2015/01/12/outside-game.

Gornall, J. (2020), "Big Cannabis in the UK: Is Industry Support for Wider Patient Access Motivated by Promises of Recreational Market Worth Billions?" *British Medical Journal* 368: m1002.

Gottschalk M. (2008). "Hiding in Plain Sight: American Politics and the Carceral State." *Annual Review of Political Science* 11: 235–260.

Government of Canada (n.d.a). "Consumer Information—Cannabis (Marihuana, Marijuana)." Available at: https://www.canada.ca/en/health-canada/services/drugs-medication/cannabis/licensed-producers/consumer-information-cannabis.html.

Government of Canada (n.d.b). "Don't Drive High." Available at: https://www.canada.ca/en/campaign/don-t-drive-high.html.

Government of Canada (2019). "Cannabis Legalization and Regulation. Criminal Justice—Cannabis Laws and Regulations." Available at: https://www.justice.gc.ca/eng/cj-jp/cannabis/.

Gracie, K. & Hancox, R.J. (2020). "Cannabis Use Disorder and the Lungs." *Addiction* 116(1): 182–190. https://doi.org/10.1111/add.15075.

Granderson, L. (2021). "The 'War on Drugs' Was Always about Race." (July 21) *Los Angeles Times*. Available at: https://www.latimes.com/opinion/story/2021-07-21/the-war-on-drugs-was-always-about-race.

Grass, M. (2021). "What Is Participatory Disinformation?" (May 26) Centre for an Informed Public, University of Washington. Available at: https://www.cip.uw.edu/2021/05/26/participatory-disinformation-kate-starbird.

Gray, M. (1998). *Drug Crazy: How We Got into This Mess and How We Can Get Out.* New York, NY: Random House.

Green, K.M., Doherty, E.E., Stuart, E.A., & Ensminger, M.E. (2010). "Does Heavy Adolescent Marijuana Use Lead to Criminal Involvement in Adulthood? Evidence from a Multi-Wave Longitudinal Study of Urban African Americans." *Drug and Alcohol Dependence* 112(1–2): 117–125.

Green, K.M., Doherty, E.E., & Ensminger, M.E. (2017). "Long-Term Consequences of Adolescent Cannabis Use: Examining Intermediary Processes." *American Journal of Drug and Alcohol Abuse* 43(5): 567–575.

Greenwald, G. (2009). "Drug Decriminalization in Portugal: Lessons for Creating Successful Drug Control Policies." (April 2) Washington, DC: The Cato Institute. Available at: https://www.cato.org/publications/white-paper/drug-decriminalization-portugal-lessons-creating-fair-successful-drug-policies.

Greer, A., & Ritter, A. (2020). "The Legal Regulation of Drugs and Role of Government: Perspectives from People Who Use Drugs." *Drug and Alcohol Dependence* 206: 107737. https://doi.org/10.1016/j.drugalcdep.2019.107737.

Greer, A., Sorge, J., Selfridge, M., Benoit, C., Jansson, M., & Macdonald, S. (2020). "Police Discretion to Charge Young People Who Use Drugs Prior to Cannabis Legalization in British Columbia, Canada: A Brief Report of Quantitative Findings." *Drugs: Education, Prevention and Policy* 27(6): 488–493. https://doi.org/10.1080/09687637.2020.1745757.

Greer, A.M. & Ritter, A. (2019). "'It's About Bloody Time': Perceptions of People Who Use Drugs Regarding Drug Law Reform." *International Journal on Drug Policy* 64: 40–46. https://doi.org/10.1016/j.drugpo.2018.12.006.

Grierson, J. (2021). "Middle-Class Drug Users Could Lose UK Passports under Boris Johnson's Plans." (December 6) *The Guardian*. Available at: https://www.theguardian.com/society/2021/dec/06/middle-class-drug-users-could-lose-uk-passports-under-boris-johnsons-plans.

Grifel, M. & Hart, C. (2018). "Is Drug Addiction a Brain Disease? This Popular Claim Lacks Evidence and Leads to Poor Policy." *American Scientist* 106: 160–169.

Griffiths, M. (2017). "Foreign, Criminal: A Doubly Damned Modern British Folk-Devil." *Citizenship Studies* 21(5): 527–546. https://doi.org/10.1080/13621025.2017.1328486.

Grinspoon, L. & Bakalar, J.B. (1997). "Missed Opportunities—Beneficial Uses of Illicit Drugs." In R. Coomber (ed.), *The Control of Drugs and Drug Users*. Reading: Harwood Academic Press (pp. 183–212).

Grotenhermen, F. & Russo, E. (2002). *Cannabis and Cannabinoids: Pharmacology, Toxicology, and Therapeutic Potential*. London: Psychology Press.

Grucza, R.A., Vuolo, M., Krauss, M.J., Plunk, A.D., Agrawal, A., Chaloupka, F.J., & Bierut, L.J. (2018). "Cannabis Decriminalization: A Study of Recent Policy Change in Five U.S. States." *International Journal on Drug Policy* 59: 67–75. https://doi.org/10.1016/j.drugpo.2018.06.016.

Grund, J.-P.C. & Breeksema, J. (2013). "Coffee Shops and Compromise." New York, NY: Global Drug Policy Program, Open Society Foundations. Available at: http://hdl.handle.net/1765/50745.

The Guardian (2017). "Uruguay Pharmacies Start Selling Cannabis Straight to Consumers." (July 19) *The Guardian*. Available at: https://www.theguardian.com/world/2017/jul/19/uruguay-marijuana-sale-pharmacies.

Gurminder, K.B. (2017) "Locating Brexit in the Pragmatics of Race, Citizenship and Empire." In W. Outhwaite (ed.), *Brexit: Sociological Responses*. London: Anthem Press (pp. 1–8).

Gusfield, J.R. (1986). *Symbolic Crusade: Status Politics and the American Temperance Movement*, 2nd edn. Urbana, IL: University of Illinois Press.

Habermas, J. (1976). *Legitimation Crisis*. London: Heinemann.

Habermas, J. (1979). *Communication and the Evolution of Society*. London: Heinemann.

Habermas, J. (1984). *Communication and the Evolution of Society*. Cambridge, UK: Polity Press.

Habermas, J. (1985). "Modernity—An Incomplete Project." In H. Foster (ed.), *Postmodern Culture*. London: Pluto (pp. 3–15).

Habermas, J. (1987). *The Philosophical Discourse of Modernity*. Cambridge, UK: Polity Press.

Habermas, J. (1996). *Between Facts and Norms: Contributions to a Discourse Theory of Law and Democracy*. Cambridge, MA: MIT Press.

Habermas, J. (2002 [1981]). "Social Action, Purposive Activity and Communication." In M. Cooke (ed.), *On the Pragmatics of Communication*. Cambridge, UK: Polity Press (pp. 105–182).

Habermas, J. (2006). "Political Communication in Media Society: Does Democracy Still Enjoy an Epistemic Dimension? The Impact of Normative Theory on Empirical Research." *Communication Theory* 16(4): 411–426. https://doi.org/10.1111/j.1468-2885.2006.00280.x.

Haggerty, K.D. (2004). "Displaced Expertise: Three Constraints on the Policy Relevance of Criminological Thought." *Theoretical Criminology* 8(2): 211–231.

Haines-Saah, R.J. & Fischer, B. (2021). "Youth Cannabis Use and Legalization in Canada: Reconsidering the Fears, Myths, and Facts Three Years in." *Journal of the Canadian Academy of Child and Adolescent Psychiatry* 30(3): 191–196.

Haines-Saah, R.J., Johnson, J.L., Repta, R., Ostry, A., Young, M.L., Shoveller, J., et al. (2014). "The Privileged Normalization of Marijuana Use—An Analysis of Canadian Newspaper Reporting, 1997–2007." *Critical Public Health* 24(1): 47–61.

Hall, S. (2012). *Theorizing Crime and Deviance*. London: Sage.

Hall, S., Critcher, C., Jefferson, T., & Roberts, B. (1978). *Policing the Crisis: Mugging, the State and Law and Order*. London: Macmillan.

Hall, W. (2010). "What Are the Policy Lessons of National Alcohol Prohibition in the United States, 1920–1933?" *Addiction* 105: 1164–1173.

Hall, W. & Lynskey, M. (2020). "Assessing the Public Health Impacts of Legalizing Recreational Cannabis Use: The U.S. Experience." *World Psychiatry* 19: 179–186. https://doi.org/10.1002/wps.20735.

Hall, W. & Pacula, R.L. (2003). *Cannabis Use and Dependence: Public Health and Public Policy*. Cambridge, UK: Cambridge University Press.

Halpern, A. (2018). "Marijuana: Is It Time to Stop Using a Word with Racist Roots?" (January 29) *The Guardian*. Available at: https://www.theguardian.com/society/2018/jan/29/marijuana-name-cannabis-racism.

Hamid, A. (1992). "The Developmental Cycle of a Drug Epidemic: The Cocaine Smoking Epidemic of 1981–1991." *Journal of Psychoactive Drugs* 24(4): 337–348.

Hamilton, I. & Monaghan, M. (2019). "Cannabis and Psychosis: Are We Any Closer to Understanding the Relationship?" *Current Psychiatry Reports* 21(7): 48. https://doi.org/10.1007/s11920-019-1044-x.

Hamilton, I., Lloyd, C., Hewitt, C., & Godfrey, C. (2014). "Effect of Reclassification of Cannabis on Hospital Admissions for Cannabis Psychosis: A Time Series Analysis." *International Journal on Drug Policy* 25(1): 151–156. https://doi.org/10.1016/j.drugpo.2013.05.016.

Hamilton, M. (2001). "Drug Policy in Australia—Our Own?" In J. Gerber & E.L. Jensen (eds), *Drug War American Style: The Internationalization of Failed Policy and Its Alternatives*. New York, NY: Garland Publishing (pp. 97–120).

Hamzeie, R., Thompson, I., Roy, S., & Savolainen, P.T. (2017). "State-Level Comparison of Traffic Fatality Data in Consideration of Marijuana Laws." *Transportation Research Record* 2660(1): 78–85. https://doi.org/10.3141/2660-11.

Hand, A., Blake, A., Kerrigan, P., Samuel, P., & Friedberg, J. (2016). "History of Medical Cannabis." *Journal of Pain Management* 9(4): 387–394.

Hands, T. (2018). *Drinking in Victorian and Edwardian Britain: Beyond the Spectre of the Drunkard*. London: Palgrave.

Hannah, A.L. & Mallinson, D.J. (2018). "Defiant Innovation: The Adoption of Medical Marijuana Laws in the American States." *Policy Study Journal* 46: 402–423. https://doi.org/10.1111/psj.12211.

Hansen, B., Miller, K., & Weber, C. (2020). "Early Evidence on Recreational Marijuana Legalization and Traffic Fatalities." *Economic Inquiry* 58: 547–568.

Hanson, V.J. (2020). "Cannabis Policy Reform: Jamaica's Experience." In T. Decorte, S. Lenton, & C. Wilkins (eds), *Legalizing Cannabis: Experiences, Lessons and Scenarios*. Abingdon: Routledge (pp. 375–389).

Hari, J. (2015). *Chasing the Scream: The Search for the Truth About Addiction*. London: Bloomsbury Publishing.

Harm Reduction International (n.d.). "Who We Are: What Is Harm Reduction?" Available at: https://www.hri.global/what-is-harm-reduction.

Harris, C.W. & Wylie, L. (2022). "Drug Testing Policies and Practices: Predicting Successful Outcomes among Juveniles Participating in Pretrial Diversion Programs." *Justice Evaluation Journal* 5(1): 36–52. https://doi.org/10.1080/24751979.2021.1952643.

Hart, C. (2017). "Viewing Addiction as a Brain Disease Promotes Social Injustice." *Nature Human Behaviour* 1: 0055.

Hart, C.L. (2021). *Drug Use for Grown-Ups: Chasing Liberty in the Land of Fear*. New York, NY: Penguin Press.

Hartman, R.L. & Huestis, M.A. (2013). "Cannabis Effects on Driving Skills." *Clinical Chemistry* 59(3): 478–492. https://doi.org/10.1373/clinchem.2012.194381.

Hasin, D.S., Kerridge, B.T., Saha, T.D., Huang, B., Pickering, R., Smith, S.M. et al. (2016). "Prevalence and Correlates of DSM-5 Cannabis Use Disorder, 2012–2013: Findings from the National Epidemiologic Survey on Alcohol and Related Conditions—III." *American Journal of Psychiatry* 173(6): 588–599.

Hathaway, A.D. (2004). "Cannabis Users' Informal Rules for Managing Stigma and Risk." *Deviant Behavior* 25(6): 559–577.

Hathaway, A.D. & Erickson, P.G. (2003). "Drug Reform Principles and Policy Debates: Harm Reduction Prospects for Cannabis in Canada." *Journal of Drug Issues* 33(2): 465–495.

Hathaway A.D., Comeau N.C., & Erickson, P.G. (2011). "Cannabis Normalization and Stigma: Contemporary Practices of Moral Regulation." *Criminology & Criminal Justice* 11(5): 451–469.

Hawk, M., Coulter, R.W., Egan, J.E., Fisk, S., Reuel Friedman, M., Tula, M., & Kinsky, S. (2017). "Harm Reduction Principles for Healthcare Settings." *Harm Reduction Journal* 14: 1–9.

Hawke, L. & Henderson, J. (2021). "Legalization of Cannabis Use in Canada: Impacts on the Cannabis Use Profiles of Youth Seeking Services for Substance Use." *Journal of Substance Abuse Treatment* 126: 108–340. https://doi.org/10.1016/j.jsat.2021.108340.

Hazekamp, A. (2016). "Evaluating the Effects of Gamma-Irradiation for Decontamination of Medicinal Cannabis." *Frontiers in Pharmacology* 7: 108. https://doi.org/10.3389/fphar.2016.00108.

Health Canada (2016). *A Framework for the Legalization and Regulation of Cannabis*. Task Force on Cannabis Legalization and Regulation. Ottawa, ON: Government of Canada.

Hebdige, D. (1979). *Subculture: The Meaning of Style*. London: Methuen.

Hefner, K.R., Starr, M.J., & Curtin, J.J. (2016). "Altered Subjective Reward Valuation among Drug-Deprived Heavy Marijuana Users: Aversion to Uncertainty." *Journal of Abnormal Psychology* 125(1): 138–150.

Hefner, K.R., Starr, M.J., & Curtin, J.J. (2018). "Heavy Marijuana Use but Not Deprivation Is Associated with Increased Stressor Reactivity." *Journal of Abnormal Psychology* 127(4): 348–358.

Heidt, J. (2021). *Tangled Up in Green: Cannabis Legalization in British Columbia after One Year*. Abbottsford, BC: Centre for Public Safety and Criminal Justice Research, University of the Fraser Valley.

Heidt, J. (2022). "Criminological Theory and Criminal Justice Practice: A Visual History." In J. Wheeldon (ed.), *Visual Criminology: From History and Methods to Critique and Policy Translation*. New York, NY: Routledge (pp. 31–51).

Heidt, J. &Wheeldon, J. (2015). *Introducing Criminological Thinking: Maps, Theories, and Understanding*. Thousand Oaks, CA: Sage Publications.

Heidt, J. & Wheeldon, J. (2022). "Data, Damn Lies, and Cannabis Policy: Reefer Madness and the Methodological Crimes of the New Prohibitionists." *Critical Criminology* 30: 403–419.

Heidt, J., Dosanjh, A., & Roberts, D. (2018). *Great Expectations: Perceptions of Cannabis Regulation in Abbottsford, BC*. Abbottsford, BC: Centre for Public Safety and Criminal Justice Research, University of the Fraser Valley.

Henry, B. & Moffitt, T.E. (1997). "Neuropsychological and Neuro-Imaging Studies of Juvenile Delinquency and Adult Criminal Behavior." In D. Stoff, J. Breiling, & J.D. Maser (eds), *Handbook of Antisocial Behavior*. New York, NY: John Wiley (pp. 280–288).

Henry, S. & Milovanovic, D. (1996). *Constitutive Criminology: Beyond Postmodernism*. Thou- sand Oaks, CA: Sage Publications.

Herman, E.S. & Chomsky, N. (2002). *Manufacturing Consent: The Political Economy of the Mass Media*. New York, NY: Pantheon Books.

Hibell, B., Guttormsson, U., Ahlström, S., Balakireva, O., Bjarnason, T., Kokkevi, A., & Kraus, L. (2012). *2011 ESPAD Report: Substance Use Among Students in 36 European Countries*. Lisbon: European School Survey Project on Alcohol and Other Drugs (ESPAD).

Hier, S.P. (2008). "Thinking Beyond Moral Panic: Risk, Responsibility, and the Politics of Moralization." *Theoretical Criminology* 12(2): 173–190. https://doi.org/10.1177/1362480608089239.

Hier, S.P., Lett, D., Walby, K., & Smith, A. (2011). "Beyond Folk Devil Resistance: Linking Moral Panic and Moral Regulation." *Criminology & Criminal Justice* 11(3): 259–276.

High Times (n.d.). "About the High Times Cannabis Cup." Available at: https://www.cannabiscup.com/ab out.

Himmelstein, J.L. (1983). "From Killer Weed to Drop-Out Drug: The Changing Ideology of Marihuana." *Contemporary Crises* 7: 13–38.

Hinton, E. (2017). *From the War on Poverty to the War on Crime: The Making of Mass Incarceration in America*. Cambridge, MA: Harvard University Press.

Hinton, E. & Cook, D. (2021). "The Mass Criminalization of Black Americans: A Historical Overview." *Annual Review of Criminology* 4(1): 261–286.

Hippchen, L.J. (1978). "Some Assumptions and Objectives for a World Criminology." *International Journal of Comparative and Applied Criminal Justice* 2(2): 95–105.

Hirschi, T. (1969). *Causes of Delinquency*. Berkeley. CA: University of California Press.

Hocker, K. (2014). "So 90s: The Gedoogbeleid." (April 17) *Dutch Review*. Available at: https://dutchreview.com/culture/society/90s-gedoogbeleid.

Hodgson, M. (2021). "Santa Barbara County Supervisors Spend Cannabis Tax Funds on Expansion Requests." (April 16) *Lompoc Record*. Available at: https://lompocrecord.com/news/local/govt-and-politics/santa-barbara-county-supervisors-spend-cannabis-tax-funds-on-expansion-requests/article_42d8c7a1-110f-5479-86f7-391e0a5cbd39.html.

Hoffman, A.J. (2016). "Reflections: Academia's Emerging Crisis of Relevance and the Consequent Role of the Engaged Scholar." *Journal of Change Management* 16(2): 77–96.

Hoitink, Y. (2017). "Why the Little Dutch Boy Never Put His Finger in the Dike." (June 30) *Dutch Genealogy*. Available at: https://www.dutchgenealogy.nl/why-the-little-dutch-boy-never-put-his-finger-in-the-dike.

Holden, D. (2019). "Half of Americans Think the Smell of Weed in Public Is a Real Problem." (April 24) *Buzzfeed News*. Available at: https://www.buzzfeednews.com/article/dominicholden/americans-smell-marijuana-public-streets-canada.

Holligan, A. (2021). "Amsterdam Drugs: Tourists Face Ban from Cannabis Cafes." (January 30) *BBC News*. Available at: https://www.bbc.com/news/world-europe-55765554.

Holloway, K.R., Bennett, T.H., & Farrington, D.P. (2006). "The Effectiveness of Drug Treatment Programs in Reducing Criminal Behavior: A Meta-Analysis." *Psicothema* 18(3): 620–629.

Holm, S., Sandberg, S., Kolind, T., & Hesse, M. (2014). "The Importance of Cannabis Culture in Young Adult Cannabis Use." *Journal of Substance Use* 19(3): 251–256. https://doi.org/10.3109/14659891.2013.790493.

Home Office (2021). "£148 Million to Cut Drugs Crime." (January 20) Press release. Available at: https://www.gov.uk/government/news/148-million-to-cut-drugs-crime.

Home Office (2022). "'Swift, Certain, Tough: New Consequences for Drug Possession' White Paper." (updated August 22). Available at: https://www.gov.uk/government/consultations/swift-certain-tough-new-consequences-for-drug-possession-white-paper.

Horsley, M. (2017). "Forget 'Moral Panics.'" *Journal of Theoretical and Philosophical Criminology* 9(2): 84–98.

Howell, A. (2018). *Criminal Conviction Restrictions for Marijuana Licensing*. Los Angeles, CA: Reason Foundation.

Hsu, G. & Kovacs, B. (2021). "Association between County Level Cannabis Dispensary Counts and Opioid Related Mortality Rates in the United States: Panel Data Study." *British Medical Journal* 372: m4957. https://doi.org/10.1136/bmj.m4957.

Huber III, A., Newman, R., & LaFave, D. (2016). "Cannabis Control and Crime: Medicinal Use, Depenalization and the War on Drugs." *B.E. Journal of Economic Analysis & Policy* 16(4): 1–35.

Hudak, J. (2020a). *Marijuana: A Short History*. Washington, DC: Brookings Institute.

Hudak, J. (2020b). "Marijuana's Racists History Shows the Need for Comprehensive Drug Reform." (June 23) Brookings Institution. Available at: https://www.brookings.edu/blog/how-we-rise/2020/06/23/marijuanas-racist-history-shows-the-need-for-comprehensive-drug-reform.

Hudak, J. (2021). "Merrick Garland, Cannabis Policy, and Restorative Justice." (February 24) *FIXGOV*. Available at: https://www.brookings.edu/blog/fixgov/2021/02/24/merrick-garland-cannabis-policy-and-restorative-justice.

Hudak, J. & Wallach, P.A. (2014). "Legal Marijuana: Comparing Washington and Colorado." (July 8) Brookings Institution. Available from: https://www.brookings.edu/blog/fixgov/2014/07/08/legal-marijuana-comparing-washington-and-colorado.

Hudak, J., Ramsey, G., & Walsh, J. (2018). *Uruguay's Cannabis Law: Pioneering a New Paradigm*. Washington, DC: Center for Effective Public Management at Brookings. Available at: https://www.brookings.edu/research/uruguays-cannabis-law-pioneering-a-new-paradigm/.

Hudson, R., DeBeck, K., Socias, E., Lake, S., Dong, H., Karamouzian, M., Hayashi, K., Kerr, T., & Milloy, M.-J. (2020). "Frequent Cannabis Use and Cessation of Injection of Opioids, Vancouver, Canada, 2005–2018." *American Journal of Public Health* 110: 1553–1560.

Huestis, M.A., Mazzoni, I., & Rabin, O. (2011). "Cannabis in Sport: Anti-Doping Perspective." *Sports Medicine* 41(11): 949–966.

Huffman, J. (2022). "Rep. Huffman Introduces Bill to Enable Direct to Customer Cannabis Shipping, Protect Independent Cannabis Farmers." (September 14). Available at: https://huffman.house.gov/media-center/press-releases/rep-huff man-introduces-bill-to-enable-direct-to-consumer-cannabis-shipping-prot ect-independent-cannabis-farmers#:~:text=The%20Small%20and%20Homest ead%20Independent,within%20and%20across%20state%20lines.

Hughes, B., Matias, J., & Griffiths, P. (2018). "Inconsistencies in the Assumptions Linking Punitive Sanctions and Use of Cannabis and New Psychoactive Substances in Europe." *Addiction* 113: 2155–2157. https://doi.org/10.1111/add.14372.

Hughes, C. & Ritter, A. (2008). "Monograph No. 16: A Summary of Diversion Programs for Drug and Drug-related Offenders in Australia." *DPMP Monograph Series*. Sydney: National Drug and Alcohol Research Centre.

Hughes, C., Seear, K., Ritter, A., & Mazerolle, L. (2019). "Criminal Justice Responses Relating to Personal Use and Possession of Illicit Drugs: The Reach of Australian Drug Diversion Programs and Barriers and Facilitators to Expansion." Drug Policy Modelling Program Monograph 27. National Drug and Alcohol Research Centre, University of New South Wales Sydney. Available at: https://ndarc.med.unsw.edu. au/resource/27-criminal-justice-responses-relating-personal-use-and-possess ion-illicit-drugs-reach.

Hughes, C.E. (2020). "The Australian Experience and Opportunities for Cannabis Law Reform." In T. Decorte, S. Lenton, & C. Wilkins (eds), *Legalizing Cannabis: Experiences, Lessons and Scenarios*. London: Routledge (pp. 337–374).

Hughes, C.E. & Stevens, A. (2007). "The Effects of the Decriminalization of Drug Use in Portugal. Discussion Paper." Oxford, UK: The Beckley Foundation.

Hughes, C.E. & Stevens, A. (2010). "What Can We Learn from the Portuguese Decriminalization of Illicit Drugs?" *British Journal of Criminology* 50(6): 999–1022. https://doi.org/10.1093/bjc/azq038.

Hughes, C.E., & Stevens, A. (2012). "A Resounding Success or a Disastrous Failure: Re-Examining the Interpretation of Evidence on the Portuguese Decriminalisation of Illicit Drugs." *Drug and Alcohol Review* 31(1): 101–113. https://doi.org/10.1111/ j.1465-3362.2011.00383.x.

Hughes, L., Schaible, L., & Jimmerson, K. (2019). "Marijuana Dispensaries and Neighborhood Crime and Disorder in Denver, Colorado." *Justice Quarterly* 37: 1–25. https://doi.org/10.1080/07418825.2019.1567807.

Hunt, A. (1997). "'Moral Panic' and Moral Language in the Media." *The British Journal of Sociology* 48(4): 629–648. https://doi.org/10.2307/591600.

Hunt, P., Pacula, R.L., & Weinberger, G. (2018). "High on Crime: Exploring the Effects of Dispensary Laws on California Counties." (May) Rand Corporation. Available at: http://ftp.iza.org/dp11567.pdf.

Hyshka, E. (2009). "Turning Failure into Success: What Does the Case of Western Australia Tell Us about Canadian Cannabis Policy-Making?" *Policy Studies* 30(5): 513–531. https://doi.org/10.1080/01442870902899962.

IDPC (International Drug Policy Consortium) (n.d.). "About Us." Available at: https:// idpc.net/about.

IDPC (2020). "Principles for the Responsible Legal Regulation of Cannabis." (September 9). Available at: https://idpc.net/publications/2020/09/principles-for-the-responsible-legal-regulation-of-cannabis?fbclid=IwAR3LO_YxtqJUCxzG-61RmoKNkd3eeW7uDOgewMut35fTMHeI8ZFFzmTtG84.

Iglesias, M. Saldías, A., & Ross, G. (2018). "Marijuana: Made in Uruguay." (February 19) Wilson Center. Available at: https://www.wilsoncenter.org/blog-post/mariju ana-made-uruguay.

Inciardi, J.A. (2004). "Proposition 36: What Did You Really Expect?" *Criminology & Public Policy* 3(4): 593–598.

Inderbitzin, M. (2011). "Public Criminology." *Oxford Bibliographies*. https://doi.org/10.1093/OBO/9780195396607-0137. Available at: https://www.oxfordbibliograph ies.com/view/document/obo-9780195396607/obo-9780195396607-0137.xml.

Ingraham, C. (2022). "Minnesota's Racial Disparities on Drug Overdose Are the Worst in the Nation." (July 21) *Minnesota Reformer*. Available at: https://minnes otareformer.com/briefs/minnesotas-racial-disparities-on-drug-overdose-are-the-worst-in-the-nation.

INPUD (2018). "Is Decriminalisation Enough? Drug User Community Voices from Portugal International Network of People Who Use Drugs." Available at: https://inpud.net/is-decriminalisation-enough-drug-user-community-voices-from-portugal-2/.

INPUD (International Network of People Who Use Drugs) (2021). "Drug Decriminalisation: Progress or Political Red Herring? Assessing the Impact of Current Models of Decriminalisation on People Who Use Drugs." Available at: https://inpud.net/drug-decriminalisation-progress-or-political-red-herring/.

Intrator, J., Hare, R., Stritzke, P., Brichtswein, K., Dorfman, D., Harpur, T., Bernstein, D., Handelsman, L., Schaefer, C., Keilp, J., Rosen, J., & Machac, J. (1997). "A Brain Imaging (Single Photon Emission Computerized Tomography) Study of Semantic and Affective Processing in Psychopaths." *Biological Psychiatry* 42(2): 96–103. https://doi.org/10.1016/S0006-3223(96)00290-9. PMID: 9209726.

Ioannidis, J.P.A. (2005). "Why Most Published Research Findings Are False." *PLoSMedicine* 2: e124. http://dx.doi.org/10.1371/journal.pmed.0020124.

Irish Penal Reform Trust (2021). "UK: Ethnic Disproportionality in Remand and Sentencing in the Youth Justice System." (January 22). Available at: https://www.iprt.ie/international-news/uk-ethnic-disproportionality-in-remand-and-sentenc ing-in-the-youth-justice-system.

Isaacs, C. (2014). *Treatment Industrial Complex: How For-Profit Prison Corporations Are Undermining Efforts to Treat and Rehabilitate Prisoners for Corporate Gain*. Philadelphia, PA: American Friends Service Committee.

Ishida, J., Wong, P., Cohen, B., Vali, M., Steigerwald, S., & Keyhani, S. (2019). "Substitution of Marijuana for Opioids in a National Survey of U.S. Adults." *PLoS ONE*. https://doi.org/10.1371/journal.pone.0222577.

Jacques, S. (2014). "The Quantitative–Qualitative Divide in Criminology: A Theory of Ideas' Importance, Attractiveness, and Publication." *Theoretical Criminology* 18: 317–334.

Jacques, S., Rosenfeld, R., Wright, R., & Gemert, F. (2016). "Effects of Prohibition and Decriminalization on Drug Market Conflict: Comparing Street Dealers,

Coffeeshops, and Cafés in Amsterdam." *Criminology & Public Policy* 15: 843–875. https://doi.org/10.1111/1745-9133.12218.

JAMA (Journal of American Medical Association) (1945). "Editorial, Marihuana Problems." *Journal of the American Medical Association* 127: 1129.

Jansons, M. (2020). *"The Drug is Not the Problem": The Perceptions of Those Who Have Experienced Substance Addiction on Canadian Drug Policy* (Doctoral dissertation, University of the Fraser Valley).

Jarvis, M., Williams, J., Hurford, M., Lindsay, D., Lincoln, P., Leila, G., Luongo, P., & Safarian, T. (2017). "Appropriate Use of Drug Testing in Clinical Addiction Medicine." *Journal of Addiction Medicine* 11(3): 163–217.

Jay, J. (2001). "Marijuana Australiana: Cannabis Use, Popular Culture, and the Americanisation of Drugs Policy in Australia." South Australia: The Marijuana Australiana Project.

Jesseman, R. & Payer, D. (2018) "Decriminalization: Options and Evidence." *Canadian Center on Substance Use and Addiction.* Available at: https://www.ccsa.ca/sites/default/files/2019-04/CCSA-Decriminalization-Controlled-Substances-Policy-Brief-2018-en.pdf.

Jewkes, Y. (2004) *Media and Crime*. London: Sage.

Jiggens, J.L. (2001) "Marijuana Australiana: Cannabis Use, Popular Culture, & the Americanization of Drugs Policy in Australia 1938–1988." PhD thesis, Queensland University of Technology.

Jin, D., Henry, P., Shan, J., & Chen, J. (2021). "Classification of Cannabis Strains in the Canadian Market with Discriminant Analysis of Principal Components using Genome-Wide Single Nucleotide Polymorphisms." *PloS ONE* 16(6): e0253387. https://doi.org/10.1371/journal.pone.0253387.

JND (Junta National de Drogas) (2019). "VII Encuesta Nacional sobre Consumo de Drogas en Población General." Available at: https://www.gub.uy/junta-nacional-drogas/sites/junta-nacional-drogas/files/documentos/publicaciones/VII_ENCUESTA_NACIONAL_DROGAS_POBLACIoN_GENERAL_2019.pdf.

JND (2020). "Monitoreo y evaluación de la Ley 19.172: Aplicación justa de la Ley y Seguridad y Convivencia." Available at: https://www.gub.uy/junta-nacional-drogas/comunicacion/publicaciones/monitoreo-evaluacion-ley-19172-aplicacion-justa-ley-seguridad.

Johns, A. (2001). "Psychiatric Effects of Cannabis." *British Journal of Psychiatry* 178: 116–122.

Johns, T. (2015). "Managing a Policy Experiment: Adopting and Implementing Recreational Marijuana Policies in Colorado." *State and Local Government Review* 47(3): 193–204. https://doi.org/10.1177/0160323X15612149.

Johnson, B. (2021). "Forward. From Harm to Hope: A 10-Year Drugs Plan to Cut Crime and Save Lives." (updated April 29 2022) London: Ministry of Justice. Available at: https://www.gov.uk/government/publications/from-harm-to-hope-a-10-year-drugs-plan-to-cut-crime-and-save-lives/from-harm-to-hope-a-10-year-drugs-plan-to-cut-crime-and-save-lives.

Johnson, R.M., Fleming, C.B., Cambron, C., Dean, L.T., Brighthaupt, S.C., & Guttmannova, K. (2019). "Race/Ethnicity Differences in Trends of Marijuana, Cigarette, and Alcohol Use Among 8th, 10th, and 12th Graders in Washington

State, 2004–2016." *Prevention Science: The Official Journal of the Society for Prevention Research* 20(2): 194–204. https://doi.org/10.1007/s11121-018-0899-0.
Johnston, L. (1978). "Children, in Test, Buy Drug Trappings Freely at 'Head Shops.'" (March 30) *New York Times*. Available at: https://www.nytimes.com/1978/03/30/archives/new-jersey-pages-children-in-test-buy-drug-trappings-freely-at-head.html.
Jones, S. (2021). "Christopher Rufo and the Critical-Race Theory Moral Panic." (July 11) *New York Magazine*. Available at: https://nymag.com/intelligencer/2021/07/christopher-rufo-and-the-critical-race-theory-moral-panic.html.
Jorge, M.A. (2020). "Short Term Effects of Cannabis Legalization in Uruguay on Crime: An Analysis Using Synthetic Control." *Diem: Dubrovnik International Economic Meeting* 5(1): 9–28. Sveučilište U Dubrovniku.
Jorgensen, C. & Harper, A. (2020). "Examining the Effects of Legalizing Marijuana in Colorado and Washington on Clearance Rates." (October 19) *Journal of Experimental Criminology*. Available at: https://link.springer.com/article/10.1007%2Fs11292-020-09446-7.
Jutras-Aswad, D., Le Foll, B., Bruneau, J., Wild, T.C., Wood, E., & Fischer, B. (2019). "Thinking Beyond Legalization: The Case for Expanding Evidence-Based Options for Cannabis Use Disorder Treatment in Canada." *Canadian Journal of Psychiatry* 64(2): 82–87. https://doi.org/10.1177/0706743718790955.
Kandall, S.R. (1999). *Substance and Shadow: Women and Addiction in the United States*. Cambridge, MA: Harvard University Press.
Kane, H.H. (1882). *Opium Smoking in America and China*. New York, NY: G.P. Putnam's Sons.
Kaplan, J. (1970). *Marijuana—The New Prohibition*. Cleveland, OH: World Publishing Company.
Kaplan, S. (2019). "Surgeon General Warns Pregnant Women and Teenagers Not to Smoke or Vape Marijuana." Available at: https://www.nytimes.com/2019/08/29/health/marijuana-pregnancy-surgeon-general.html.
Kaplan, J. (2023). "Uniform Crime Reporting (UCR) Program Data: A Practitioner's Guide." (March 28). Available at: https://ucrbook.com.
Karch, A. (2021). "Filling a Vacuum: Subnational Governance Amid National Government Inaction." *State and Local Government Review* 52(4): 232–240. https://doi.org/10.1177/0160323X21999585.
Kavousi, P., Giamo, T., Arnold, G., Alliende, M., Huynh, E., Lea, J. et al. (2022). "What Do We Know about Opportunities and Challenges for Localities from Cannabis Legalization?" *Review of Policy Research* 39(2): 143–169.
Kelly, J.F. & Westerhoff, C. (2010). "Does It Matter How We Refer to Individuals with Substance-Related Problems? A Randomized Study with Two Commonly Used Terms." *International Journal of Drug Policy* 21: 202–207.
Kelly, J.F., Dow, S.J., & Westerhoff, C. (2010). "Does Our Choice of Substance-Related Terms Influence Perceptions of Treatment Need? An Empirical Investigation with Two Commonly Used Terms." *Journal of Drug Issues* 40: 805–818.
Kelly, K. (2020). "Prohibition Was America's First War on Drugs." (January 17). Available at: https://www.teenvogue.com/story/prohibition-war-on-drugs.
Kennedy, R. (1997). *Race, Crime and Law*. Cambridge, MA: Harvard University Press.

Kepple, N.J. & Freisthler, B. (2012). "Exploring the Ecological Association between Crime and Medical Marijuana Dispensaries." *Journal of Studies on Alcohol and Drugs* 73 (4): 523–530.

Kerrison, E.M. & Sewell, A.A. (2020). "Negative Illness Feedbacks: High-Frisk Policing Reduces Civilian Reliance on ER Services." *Health Services Research* 52(S2): 787–796. https://doi.org/10.1111/1475-6773.13554.

Keul, A. & Eisenhauer, B. (2018). "Making the High Country: Cannabis Tourism in Colorado USA." *Annals of Leisure Research* 22(2): 140–160. doi: 10.1080/11745398.2018.1435291.

Kiepeka, N., Van de Ven, K., Dunn, M., & Forlini, C. 2019. "Seeking Legitimacy for Broad Understandings of Substance Use." *International Journal of Drug Policy* 73: 58–63. doi: 10.1016/j.drugpo.2019.07.014.

Kilanowski, M. (2021). *The Rorty-Habermas Debate: Toward Freedom as Responsibility*. Albany, NY: State University of New York Press.

Kilgore, A. & Maese, R. (2021). "The Doping Rules That Cost Sha'Carri Richardson Have a Debated, Political History." (July 3). Available at: https://www.washingtonpost.com/sports/olympics/2021/07/03/shacarri-richardson-marijuana-olympics-doping-ban.

Kim, K.M. (2014). "Beyond Justification: Habermas, Rorty and the Politics of Cultural Change. *Theory, Culture & Society* 31(6): 103–123.

King, A. & Maruna, S. (2009). "Is a Conservative Just a Liberal Who Has Been Mugged?: Exploring the Origins of Punitive Views." *Punishment & Society* 11(2): 147–169. https://doi.org/10.1177/1462474508101490.

King, R.S. & Mauer, M. (2006). "The War on Marijuana: The Transformation of the War on Drugs in the 1990s." *Harm Reduction Journal* 3(6): 1–17. https://doi.org/10.1186/1477-7517-3-6.

Kings, A. (2020). "Infarmed Authorizes 5 Companies for Medical Cannabis Purposes." (January 18) *Born2 Invest*. Available at: https://born2invest.com/articles/infarmed-authorizes-5-companies-for-medical-cannabis-purposes.

Kittrie, N. (1971). *The Right to Be Different: Deviance and Enforced Therapy*. New York, NY: Penguin USA.

Klag, S., O'Callaghan, F., & Creed, P. (2005). "The Use of Legal Coercion in the Treatment of Substance Abusers: An Overview and Critical Analysis of Thirty Years of Research." *Substance Use & Misuse* 40(12): 1777–1795. https://doi.org/10.1080/10826080500260891.

Klingemann, H.K., Sobell, M.B., & Sobell, L.C. (2010). "Continuities and Changes in Self-Change Research." *Addiction* 105: 1510–1518.

Klocke, B.V. & Muschert, G.W. (2010). "A Hybrid Model of Moral Panics: Synthesizing the Theory and Practice of Moral Panic." *Research Sociology Compass* 4: 295–309.

Koch, D.W., Lee, J., & Lee, K. (2016). "Coloring the War on Drugs: Arrest Disparities in Black, Brown, and White." *Race Social Problems* 8: 313–325. https://doi.org/10.1007/s12552-016-9185-6.

Koehn, E. (2019). "'Another Level: Race on to Get Over-the-Counter Cannabis Meds to Pharmacies." (September 8) *Sydney Morning Herald*. Available at: https://www.smh.com.au/business/companies/another-level-race-on-to-get-over-the-counter-cannabis-meds-to-pharmacies-20210907-p58pex.html.

Koehn, E. (2021). "'Pot Luck: Australia's $2 Billion Cannabis Stock Sector on a High." (April 10) *Sydney Morning Herald*. Available at: https://www.smh.com.au/business/companies/pot-luck-australia-s-2-billion-cannabis-stock-sector-on-a-high-20210324-p57dkn.html.

Kohut, P. (2021). "Navigating the European market for Medical Cannabis." (January 21) *PharmExec.com*. Available at: https://www.pharmexec.com/view/navigating-the-european-market-for-medical-cannabis.

Kondrad, E. & Reid, A. (2013). "Colorado Family Physicians' Attitudes Toward Medical Marijuana." *Journal of the American Board of Family Medicine* 26(1): 52–60. doi: 10.3122/jabfm.2013.01.120089. PMID: 23288281.

Korf, D.J. (2020). "Coffeeshops in the Netherlands: Regulating the Front Door and the Back Door." In T. Decorte, S. Lenton, & C. Wilkins (eds), *Legalizing Cannabis: Experiences, Lessons and Scenarios*. London: Routledge (pp. 285–306).

Koutouki, K. & Lofts, K. (2019). "Cannabis, Reconciliation, and the Rights of Indigenous Peoples: Prospects and Challenges for Cannabis Legalization in Canada." *Alberta Law Review* 56(3): 709–728.

Kovacevich, N. (2019) "Cannabis Caffes Are Coming." (January 23) *Forbes*. Available at: https://www.forbes.com/sites/nickkovacevich/2019/01/23/cannabis-cafes-are-coming/?sh=74c69c752263.

Kraska, P.B. (2001). *Militarizing the American Criminal Justice System: The Changing Roles of the Armed Forces and the Police*. Boston, MA: Northeastern University Press.

Kraska, P.B. (2006). "Criminal Justice Theory: Toward Legitimacy and an Infrastructure." *Justice Quarterly* 23(2): 167–185.

Kreuz, R. (2020). *Irony and Sarcasm*. Cambridge, MA: MIT Press.

Kroon, E., Kuhns, L., Hoch, E., & Cousijn, J. (2020). "Heavy Cannabis Use, Dependence and the Brain: A Clinical Perspective." *Addiction* 115(3): 559–572.

Kroon, E., Kuhns, L., & Cousijn, J. (2021). "The Short-Term and Long-Term Effects of Cannabis on Cognition: Recent Advances in the Field." *Current Opinion in Psychology* 38: 49–55.

Krout, J.A. (1923). "The Genesis and Development of the Early Temperance Movement in New York State." *Quarterly Journal of the New York State Historical Association* 4(2): 78–98.

Kruger, D.J. & Kruger, J.S. (2019). "Medical Cannabis Users' Comparisons between Medical Cannabis and Mainstream Medicine." *Journal of Psychoactive Drugs* 51(1): 31–36. https://doi.org/10.1080/02791072.2018.1563314.

Kurtz, S.P., Inciardi, J.A., & Pujals, E. (2009). "Criminal Activity among Young Adults in the Club Scene." *Law Enforcement Executive Forum* 9(2): 47–59.

Kurtzman, E.T., Greene, J., Begley, R., & Drenkard, K.N. (2022). "'We Want What's Best for Patients.' Nurse Leaders' Attitudes about Medical Cannabis: A Qualitative Study." *International Journal of Nursing Studies Advances* 4: 100065.

Krissman, Fred. 2016. "America's Largest Cannabis Labor Market." Working Paper. Humboldt State University.

Ksir, C. & Hart, C. (2016). "Cannabis and Psychosis: A Critical Overview of the Relationship." *Current Psychiatry Reports* 18(2): 12–23.

LaFree, G. (2021). "Progress and Obstacles in the Internationalization of Criminology." *International Criminology* 1: 58–69.

Lake, S., Kerr, T., Werb, D., Haines-Saah, R., Fischer, B., & Thomas, G. (2019). "Guidelines for Public Health and Safety Metrics to Evaluate the Potential Harms and Benefits of Cannabis Regulation in Canada." *Drug and Alcohol Review* 38(6): 606–621.

Lammy, D. (2017). *The Lammy Review: An Independent Review into the Treatment of, and Outcomes for, Black, Asian and Minority Ethnic Individuals in the Criminal Justice System*. London: Lammy Review.

LaMotte, S. (2022). "Highly Potent Weed Creating Marijuana Addicts Worldwide, Study Says." (July 15) *CNN Health*. Available at: https://www.cnn.com/2022/07/25/health/marijuana-potency-addiction-study-wellness/index.html.

Lancaster, K., Sutherland, R., & Ritter, A. (2014). "Examining the Opinions of People Who Use Drugs Towards Drug Policy in Australia." *Drugs: Education, Prevention and Policy* 21(2): 93–101.

Lancaster, K. Santana, L., Madden, A., & Ritter, A. (2015). "Stigma and Subjectivities: Examining the Textured Relationship between Lived Experience and Opinions about Drug Policy among People Who Inject Drugs." *Drugs: Education, Prevention and Policy* 22(3): 224–231. https://doi.org/10.3109/09687637.2014.970516.

Langton, J. (2018). "Even with Legalized Marijuana, Organized Crime Isn't Going Away." (January 23) *The Globe and Mail*. Available at: https://www.theglobeandmail.com/opinion/article-evenwith-legalized-marijuana-organized-crime-isnt-going-away.

Laqueur, H. (2014). "Uses and Abuses of Drug Decriminalization in Portugal." *Law and Social Inquiry* 40(3): 746–781. https://doi.org/10.1111/lsi.12104.

Laqueur, H., Rivera-Aguirre, A., Shev, A., Castillo-Carniglia, A., Rudolph, K.E., Ramirez, J., Martins, S.S., & Cerdá, M. (2020). "The Impact of Cannabis legalization in Uruguay on Adolescent Cannabis Use." *International Journal on Drug Policy* 80: 102748. https://doi.org/10.1016/j.drugpo.2020.102748.

Larsen, D. (2019). "The Marijuana Potency Myth." Available at: https://twitter.com/DanaLarsen/status/1167941723969900544.

Lau, N., Sales, P., Averill, S., Murphy, F., Sato, S.O., & Murphy, S. (2015). "A Safer Alternative: Cannabis Substitution as Harm Reduction." *Drug and Alcohol Review* 34(6): 654–659. https://doi.org/10.1111/dar.12275.

Laub, J.H. (2004). "The Life Course of Criminology in the United States: The American Society of Criminology Presidential Address, 2003." *Criminology* 42: 1–25.

Law Enforcement Action Partnership (n.d.). "National Policing Recommendations." Available at: https://lawenforcementactionpartnership.org.

Lawrence, G. (2022). "Interstate Trade in Cannabis Should Begin Immediately." Excerpted from Berke, J., Title, S., Bloomberg, S., Lawrence, G., & Smith, A. (2022). "Regulating Cannabis Interstate Commerce: Perspectives on How the Federal Government Should Respond." *Ohio State Legal Studies Research Paper* 722: 1–11. https://papers.ssrn.com/sol3/papers.cfm?abstract_id=4188089.

Lawson, D. (2020). *Flowers from the Devil: An American Opiate Crisis, the Criminalization of Marijuana, and the Triumph of the Prohibition State, 1840–1940*. Graduate Student Theses, Dissertations, & Professional Papers. Missoula, MT: University of Montana.

Lawson, R.A. & Nesbit, T.M. (2013). "Alchian and Allen Revisited: Law Enforcement and the Price of Weed." *Atlantic Economic Journal* 41: 363–370.

Le Dain, G. (1973). *Final Report of the Commission of Inquiry into the Non-medical Use of Drugs*. Ottawa, ON: Health Canada. Available at: https://publications.gc.ca/collect ions/collection_2014/sc-hc/H21-5370-2-1-eng.pdf.

Lebrero-Tatay, J., Sebag, A., & Ezquerra-Romano, I. (2022). "Asymmetry in Psychoactive Research: A Bibliometric Study on 15 Psychoactive Drugs." *Journal of Drug Issues* 54(2): 509–526. https://doi.org/10.1177/00220426211068439.

LeClair, A., Kelly, B.C., Pawson, M., Wells, B.E., & Parsons, J.T. (2015). "Motivations for Prescription Drug Misuse among Young Adults: Considering Social and Developmental Contexts." *Drugs Education, Prevention, and Policy* 22(3): 208–216. https://doi.org/10.3109/09687637.2015.1030355.

Lee, M.A. (2013). *Smoke Signals: A Social History of Marijuana—Medical, Recreational, and Scientific*. New York, NY: Scribner Publishing.

Lekhtman, A. (2020). "Joe Biden's Unwelcome Plant to Expand Coerced Treatment and Drug Courts." (May 7) *Filter*. Available at: https://filtermag.org/joe-biden-forced-drug-treatment.

Lemert, E. (1951). *Social Pathology*. New York, NY: McGraw-Hill.

Lempert, R. (1974). "Toward a Theory of Decriminalization." University of Michigan Public Law Working Paper No. 209. https://doi.org/10.2139/ssrn.1662653.

Lens (2020). "Black Lives Won't Matter without Major Drug Law Reform." (June 24) Monash University. Available at: https://lens.monash.edu/@politics-society/2020/06/24/1380720/black-lives-wont-matter-without-major-drug-law-reform.

Lenton, S. (2004). "Pot, Politics and the Press—Reflections on Cannabis Law Reform in Western Australia." *Drug and Alcohol Review* 23(2): 223–233.

Lenton, S. & Single, E. (1998). "The Definition of Harm Reduction." *Drug and Alcohol Review* 17(2): 213–219.

Lenton, S., Humeniuk, R., Heale, P., & Christie, P. (2000). "Infringement versus Conviction: The Social Impact of a Minor Cannabis Offence in South Australia and Western Australia." *Drug and Alcohol Review* 19(3): 257–264. https://doi.org/10.1080/713659365.

Leshner, A. (1997). "Addiction Is a Brain Disease, and It Matters." *Science* 278(5335): 45–47.

Levengood, T.W., Yoon, G.H., Davoust, M.J., Ogden, S.N., Marshall, B.D., Cahill, S.R., & Bazzi, A.R. (2021). "Supervised Injection Facilities as Harm Reduction: A Systematic Review." *American Journal of Preventive Medicine* 61(5): 738–749.

Levi-Faur, D. (2014). "The Welfare State: A Regulatory Perspective." *Public Administration* 92(3): 599–614.

Levine, H.G. (1984). "The Alcohol Problem in America: From Temperance to Alcoholism." *British Journal of Addiction* 79: 109–119. https://doi.org/10.1111/j.1360-0443.1984.tb03845.x.

Levine, H.G. (2003). "Global Drug Prohibition: Its Uses and Crises." *International Journal of Drug Policy* 14: 145–153.

Levine, G.H. & Siegel, L. (2015). "Marijuana Madness: The Scandal of New York City's Racist Marijuana Possession Arrests." In J.A. Eterno (ed.), *The New York City Police Department: The Impact of Its Policies and Practices*. New York, NY: CRC Press (pp. 117–161).

Levine, H.G. & Small, D.P. (2008). *Marijuana Arrest Crusade: Racial Bias and Police Policy in New York City, 1997–2007*. New York, NY: New York Civil Liberties Union.

Levinson, C. (2014). "Comey: FBI 'Grappling' with Hiring Policy Concerning Marijuana." (May 20) *Wall Street Journal*. Available at: https://www.wsj.com/articles/BL-LB-48089.

Levinson-King, R. (2019). "Why Canada's Cannabis Bubble Burst." (December 29) *BBC News*. Available at: https://www.bbc.com/news/world-us-canada-50664578?fbclid=IwAR2DSg2tefAFmCSwYNaENWv4nlOkFob43xBFCd7MVd-zt_krwgf_1ke4ymU.

Lewis, H. (2019). "Brexit and the Failure of Journalism." (October 24). Available at: https://www.theatlantic.com/international/archive/2019/10/brexit-journalism-failure/600580.

Lewis, M. (2015). *The Biology of Desire: Why Addiction Is Not a Disease*. Toronto, ON: Doubleday Canada.

Leyton, M. (2019). "Cannabis Legalization: Did We Make a Mistake? Update 2019." *Journal of psychiatry & neuroscience* 44(5): 291–293. https://doi.org/10.1503/jpn.190136.

Ligaya, A. (2019). "Six Months after Legalization, High Prices and Supply Issues Boost Illicit Pot Market." (April 20) *Global News*. Available at: https://www.thestar.com/business/2019/04/20/six-months-after-legalization-high-prices-and-supply-issues-boost-illicit-pot-market.html.

Lilly, R.J., Cullen, F.T., & Ball, R.A. (2015). *Criminological Theory: Context and Consequences*, 6th edn. Thousand Oaks, CA: Sage.

Lin, L.A., Ilgen, M.A., Jannausch, M., & Bohnert, K.M. (2016). "Comparing Adults Who Use Cannabis Medically with Those Who Use Recreationally: Results from a National Sample." *Addictive Behaviors* 61: 99–103.

Lindesmith, A.R. (1938a). "Argot of the Underworld Drug Addict." *Journal of Criminal Law and Criminology* 29: 261–273.

Lindesmith, A.R. (1938b). "A Sociological Theory of Drug Addiction." *American Journal of Sociology* 43(4): 593–613.

Lindsay, S.L. & Vuolo, M. (2021). "Criminalized or Medicalized? Examining the Role of Race in Responses to Drug Use." *Social Problems* 68(4): 942–963. https://doi.org/10.1093/socpro/spab027.

Link, B.G. & Phelan, J.C. (2001). "Conceptualizing Stigma." *Annual Review of Sociology* 27(1): 363–385.

Lira, M.C., Heeren, T.C., Buczek, M, Blanchette, J.G., Smart, R., Pacula, R.L., & Naimi, T.S. (2021). "Trends in Cannabis Involvement and Risk of Alcohol Involvement in Motor Vehicle Crash Fatalities in the United States, 2000-2018." *American Journal of Public Health* 111: 1976–1985. https://doi.org/10.2105/AJPH.2021.306466.

Liu, J. (2009). "Asian Criminology—Challenges, Opportunities, and Directions." *Asian Journal of Criminology* 4: 1–9.

Liu, Y. & Stronczak, A. (2022). "Cannabis Tourism: An Emerging Transformative Tourism Rorm." In A. Farmaki & N. Pappas (eds), *Emerging Transformations in Tourism and Hospitality*. Abingdon: Routledge (pp. 201–215).

Livingston, J. and Boyd, J. (2010). "Correlates and Consequences of Internalized Stigma for People Living with Mental Illness: A Systematic Review and Meta-Analysis." *Social Science and Medicine* 71: 2150–2161.

Lloyd C. (2008). "UK Cannabis Classification: A Flawed Debate." *The Lancet* 371(9609): 300–301. https://doi.org/10.1016/S0140-6736(08)60162-2.

Lockhart, P.R. (2019). "Dozens of Black Partygoers Were Arrested over Less Than an Ounce of Marijuana. Now They're Suing." (March 15) *Vox*. Available at: https://www.vox.com/identities/2019/3/15/18267260/cartersville-70-lawsuit-georgia-arrests-searches-detention-marijuana.

Lodwick, K. (2009). *Crusaders against Opium: Protestant Missionaries in China, 1874–1917*. Lexington, KY: University of Kentucky.

Logan, W.A. (2014). "After the Cheering Stopped: Decriminalization and Legalism's Limits." *Cornell Journal of Law and Public Policy* 24: 319–351.

Long, A. (2020). "Colorado's Summer Cannabis Sales Thrive Despite Collapse of State's Tourism Industry." *MJBizDaily*.

Lorenzetti, V., Solowij, N., Whittle, S., Fornito, A., Lubman, D.I., Pantelis, C., & Yücel, M. (2015). "Gross Morphological Brain Changes with Chronic, Heavy Cannabis Use." *British Journal of Psychiatry* 206: 77–78.

Low, H. (2022). "London Drugs Commission to Look at Legalising Cannabis." (May 12) *BBC News*. Available at: https://www.bbc.com/news/uk-england-london-61416295.

Lowman, J., Menzies, R., & Palys, T. (eds) (1987). *Transcarceration: Essays in the Sociology of Social Control*. Brookfield, VT: Gower.

Lu, R., Willits, D., Stohr, M.K., Makin, D., Snyder, J., Lovrich, N., Meize, M., Stanton, D. Wu, G., & Hemmens, C. (2021). "The Cannabis Effect on Crime: Time-Series Analysis of Crime in Colorado and Washington State." *Justice Quarterly* 38(4): 565–595.

Lucas, P. (2009). "Moral Regulation and the Presumption of Guilt in Health Canada's Medical Cannabis Policy and Practice." *International Journal of Drug Policy* 20(4): 296–303.

Lucas, P. (2012). "Cannabis as an Adjunct to or Substitute for Opiates in the Treatment of Chronic Pain." *Journal of Psychoactive Drugs* 44(2): 125–133.

Luciano, M., Sampogna, G., Del Vecchio, V., Pingani, L., Palumbo, C., De Rosa, C., et al. (2014). "Use of Coercive Measures in Mental Health Practice and Its Impact on Outcome: A Critical Review. *Expert Review of Neurotherapeutics* 14(2): 131–141. https://doi.org/10.1586/14737175.2014.874286.

Lum, C., Koper, C.S., & Wu, X. (2021). "Can We Really Defund the Police? A Nine-Agency Study of Police Response to Calls for Service." *Police Quarterly* 25(3): 255–280. https://doi.org/10.1177/10986111211035002.

Lupton, D. & Tulloch, J. (2002). "'Life Would Be Pretty Dull without Risk': Voluntary Risk-Taking and Its Pleasures." *Health, Risk & Society* 4(2): 113–124.

Lutters, W.G. & Ackerman, M.S. (1996). "Social Relations in Complex Environments: An Introduction to the Chicago School of Sociology." UCI–ICS

Social Worlds Lab #96-1. Available at: https://engagingcolumbus.owu.edu/wp-content/uploads/sites/77/2014/12/1996_Intro_to_Chicago_School_Sociology.pdf.

Luty, J. (2016). "The Beginning of the End of Prohibition: The Politics of Drug Addiction." *British Journal of Psychological Advances* 22: 242–250.

Lux, T. (2019). "The California Cannabis Industry." *Journal of Business Entrepreneurship and Law* 13: 209–244.

Lyman, D.R., Milich, R., Zimmerman, R., Novak, S.P., Logan, T.K., Martin, C., & Clayton, R. (1999). "Project DARE: No Effects at Ten-Year Follow-Up." *Journal of Consulting and Clinical Psychology* 67(4): 590–593.

Lynch, M. (2012). "Theorizing the Role of the 'War on Drugs' in US Punishment." *Theoretical Criminology* 16(2): 175–199.

Lynch, M.J. & Michalowski, R. (2010). *A Primer in Radical Criminology*. New York, NY: Harrow and Heston.

MacCoun, R. & Reuter, P. (2001). *Drug War Heresies: Learning from Other Vices, Times and Places*, Cambridge, UK: Cambridge University Press.

MacCoun, R., Pacula, R.L., Chriqui, J.F., Harris, K., & Reuter, P. (2009). "Do Citizens Know Whether Their State Has Decriminalized Marijuana? Assessing the Perceptual Component of Deterrence Theory." *Review of Law and Economics* 5: 347–371.

MacCoun, R.J. (2011). "What Can We Learn from the Dutch Cannabis Coffeeshop System?" *Addiction* 106: 1899–1910. https://doi.org/10.1111/j.1360-0443.2011.03572.x.

MacDonald, J. (2009). "Medical Marijuana: Informational Resources for Family Physicians." *American Family Physician* 80(8): 782–783.

MacKenzie, A. & Bhatt, I. (2020). "Opposing the Power of Lies, Bullshit and Fake News: The Value of Truth." *Post Digital Science Education* 2: 217–232.

MADD (Mothers against Drunk Driving) Canada (n.d.). "Cannabis and Driving." Available at: https://madd.ca/pages/impaired-driving/overview/cannabis-and-driving.

Mahamad, S., Wadsworth, E., Rynard, V., Goodman, S., & Hammond, D. (2020). "Availability, Retail Price and Potency of Legal and Illegal Cannabis in Canada after Recreational Cannabis Legalisation." *Drug and Alcohol Review* 39: 337–346. https://doi.org/10.1111/dar.13069.

Maier, S.L., Mannes, S., & Koppenhofer, E.L. (2017). "The Implications of Marijuana Decriminalization and Legalization on Crime in the United States." *Contemporary Drug Problems* 44(2): 125–146. https://doi.org/10.1177/0091450917708790.

Majone, G. (1994). "The Rise of the Regulatory State in Europe." *West European Politics* 17: 77–101.

Majone, G. (1997). "The New European Agencies: Regulation by Information." *Journal of European Public Policy* 4(2): 262–275.

Makin, D.A., Willits, D.W., Wu, G., DuBois, K.O., Lu, R., Stohr, M.K., Koslicki, W., Stanton, D., Hemmens, C., Snyder, J., & Lovrich, N.P. (2019). "Marijuana Legalization and Crime Clearance Rates: Testing Proponent Assertions in Colorado and Washington State." *Police Quarterly* 22(1): 31–55. https://doi.org/10.1177/1098611118786255.

Males, M. & Buchen, L. (2014). "Reforming Marijuana Laws: Which Approach Best Reduces the Harms of Criminalization? A Five-State Analysis." Centre on Juvenile and Criminal Justice.

Mallinson, D.J., Hannah, A.L., & Cunningham, G. (2020). "The Consequences of Fickle Federal Policy: Administrative Hurdles for State Cannabis Policies." *State and Local Government Review* 52(4), 241–254. https://doi.org/10.1177/0160323X2 0984540.

Malyshev, A. & Ganley, S. (2021). "The Challenges of Getting Social Equity Right in the State-Legal Cannabis Industry." (July 22) *Reuters*. Available at: https://www.reuters.com/legal/litigation/challenges-getting-social-equity-right-state-legal-cannabis-industry-2021-07-22.

Manderson, D. (1993). *From Mr Sin to Mr Big: A History of Australian Drug Laws*. Melbourne, UK: Oxford University Press.

Manderson, D. (1999) "Symbolism and Racism in Drug History and Policy." *Drug and Alcohol Review* 18(2): 179–186.

Mann, M. (1993). *The Sources of Social Power, Vol. II: The Rise of Classes and Nation-States, 1760–1914*. Cambridge, UK: Cambridge University Press.

Manning, P. (2006). "There's No Glamour in Glue: News and the Symbolic Framing of Substance Misuse." *Crime, Media, Culture* 2(1): 49–66.

Marconi A., Di Forti, M., Lewis, C.M., Murray, R.M., & Vassos, E. (2016). "Meta-Analysis of the Association between the Level of Cannabis Use and Risk of Psychosis." *Schizophrenia Bulletin* 42(5): 1262–1269. https://doi.org/10.1093/sch bul/sbw003.

Marijuanarates (n.d.). "The 5 Most Popular Marijuana Strains Sold in Netherlands Coffee Shops." Available at: https://marijuanarates.com/popular-marijuana-stra ins-netherlands-coffee-shops.

Marin, M. (2022). "Philly Medical Marijuana Dispensary Curaleaf Sued for Allegedly Breaking the City's Fair Workweek Law." (October 26) *Philadelphia Inquirer*. Available at: https://www.inquirer.com/news/curaleaf-philadelphia-fair-work-week-law-medical-marijuana-pennsylvania-20221026.html.

Marqusee, M. (2005). *Wicked Messenger: Bob Dylan and the 1960s*. New York, NY: Seven Stories Press.

Marsh, W., Copes, H., & Linnemann, T. (2017). "Creating Visual Differences: Methamphetamine Users' Perceptions of Anti-Meth Campaigns." *International Journal of Drug Policy* 39: 52–61.

Martins, M. (2021). "News Media Representation on EU Immigration before Brexit: The 'Euro-Ripper' Case." *Humanities and Social Sciences Communications* 8: 11. https://doi.org/10.1057/s41599-020-00687-5.

Martiroysan, S. (2017). "The Decriminalization of Recreational Cannabis in California." *San Joaquin Agricultural Law Review* 27(2): 187–208.

Maruna, S. (2001). *Making Good: How Ex-Convicts Reform and Rebuild Their Lives*. Washington, DC: American Psychological Association.

Maruna, S., Matravers, A., & King, A. (2004). "Disowning Our Shadow: A Psychoanalytic Approach to Understanding Punitive Public Attitudes." *Deviant Behavior* 25: 277–299.

Marwick, A. (2006). "Youth Culture and the Cultural Revolution of the Long Sixties." In A. Schildt & D. Siegfried (eds), *Between Marx and Coca-Cola: Youth Cultures in Changing European Societies, 1960–1980*. Oxford, UK: Berghahn Books (pp. 39–58).

Mastrofski, S.D. (2004). "Controlling Street-Level Police Discretion." *Annals of the American Academy of Political Social Science* 593: 100–118.

Matsueda, R.L. (1992). "Reflected Appraisals, Parental Labeling, and Delinquency: Specifying a Symbolic Interactionist Theory." *American Journal of Sociology* 97(6): 1577–1611.

Matza, D. (1964). *Delinquency and Drift*. New York, NY: Wiley.

Matza, D. (1969). *Becoming Deviant*. Englewood Cliffs, NJ: Prentice Hall.

Mayet, A., Legleye, S., Falissard, B., & Chau, N. (2012). "Cannabis Use Stages as Predictors of Subsequent Initiation with Other Illicit Drugs among French Adolescents: Use of a Multi-state Model." *Addictive Behaviors* 37(2): 160–166.

McAllister, W.B. (2000). *Drug Diplomacy in the Twentieth Century: An International History*. New York, NY: Routledge.

McArdle, T. (2018). "The 'Law and Order' Campaign That Won Richard Nixon the White House 50 Years Ago." (November 5) *Washington Post*. Available at: https://www.washingtonpost.com/history/2018/11/05/law-order-campaign-that-won-richard-nixon-white-house-years-ago.

Mccaffrey, P. (2019). "Drug War Origins: How American Opium Politics Led to the Establishment of International Narcotics Prohibition." MA thesis, Cambridge, MA: Harvard University.

McCormick, C. (2022). *Use of a Visual Criminology Facebook Group in Blended Instruction in Visual Criminology: From History and Methods to Critique and Policy Translation*, ed. J, Wheeldon. London: Routledge (pp. 190–210).

McDonald, J. (2021). "Policing for Profit Targets Low-Income People Who Can't Afford to Fight Back." (November 5) *The Bulwark*. Available at: https://www.thebulwark.com/policing-for-profit-targets-low-income-people-who-cant-afford-to-fight-back.

McGinty, E.E., Samples, H., Bandara, S.N., Saloner, B., Bachhuber, M.A., & Barry, C.L. (2016). "The Emerging Public Discourse on State Legalization of Marijuana for Recreational Use in the US: Analysis of News Media Coverage, 2010–2014." *Preventive Medicine* 90: 114–120. doi: 10.1016/j.ypmed.2016.06.040. Epub 2016 June 30. PMID: 27373208; PMCID: PMC6983281.

McGirr, L. (2016). *The War on Alcohol: Prohibition and the Rise of the American State*. New York, NY: W.W. Norton.

McGrath, J., Saha, S., Welham, J., El Saadi, O., MacCauley, C., & Chant, D. (2004). "A Systematic Review of the Incidence of Schizophrenia: The Distribution of Rates and the Influence of Sex, Urbanicity, Migrant Status and Methodology." *BMC Medicine* 2(1): 1–22.

McLuhan, M. (1964). *Understanding Media: The Extensions of Man*. New York, NY: Mcgraw-Hill.

Mcnamara, J.D. (2011). "The Hidden Costs of America's War on Drugs." *Journal of Private Enterprise* 26(2): 97–115.

McPartland, J.M. (2017). "Cannabis sativa and Cannabis indica versus 'Sativa' and 'Indica.'" *Cannabis sativa L.—Botany and Biotechnology*, 101–121.

McRobbie, A. & Thornton, S. (1995). "Rethinking 'Moral Panic' for Multi-Mediated Social Worlds." *British Journal of Sociology* 46(4): 559–574.

McSweeney, T., Stevens, A., Hunt, N., & Turnbull, P. (2007). "Twisting Arms or a Helping Hand?" *British Journal of Criminology* 47: 470–490.

McWilliams, J.C. (1990). *The Protectors: Harry J. Anslinger and the Federal Bureau of Narcotics, 1930-1962*. Newark, DE: University of Delaware Press.

McWilliams, J.C. (1992). "Through the Past Darkly: The Politics and Policies of America's Drug War." In W O. Walker, III (ed.), *Drug Control Policy: Essays in Historical and Comparative Perspective* University Park, PA: Pennsylvania State University Press (pp. 5–41).

Mead, G.H. (1934). *Mind, Self, and Society*. Chicago, IL: University of Chicago Press.

Media Matters (2019). "Tucker Carlson Suggests Link between Mass Shootings and Marijuana Use." (August 27). Available at: https://www.mediamatters.org/tucker-carlson/tucker-carlson-suggests-link-between-mass-shootings-and-marijuana-use.

Media Jel (n.d.). "Creative Inspiration: The Best Recent Cannabis Ads and Campaigns." Available at: https://www.mediajel.com/blogs/cannabis-ads/?fbclid=IwAR0sAVa8r6MROUFHMiyyoxMwu5gJTdqcYDj6fKZYzBvCnzFUlkvInxwc3U.

Meehan, B., Rusko, C., & Stephenson, E.F. (2020). "(Pot) Heads in Beds: The Effect of Marijuana Legalization on Hotel Occupancy in Colorado and Washington." *Journal of Regional Analysis & Policy* 50: 46–53.

Meeks, D. (2006). "Police Militarization in Urban Areas: The Obscure War against the Underclass." *The Black Scholar* 35(4): 33–41.

Meier, M.H., Caspi, A., Ambler, A., Harrington, H., Houts, R., Keefe, R.S.E., McDonald, K., Ward, A., Poulton, R., & Moffitt, T.E. (2012). "Persistent Cannabis Users Show Neuropsychological Decline from Childhood to Midlife." (October) *Proceedings of the National Academy of Sciences* 109(40): E2657–E2664; https://doi.org/10.1073/pnas.1206820109.

Meier, R.S., Kennedy, L., & Sacco, V. (2001). *The Process and Structure of Crime: Criminal Events and Crime Analysis*. New Brunswick, NJ: Transaction.

Meija, A. (2020). "How Bad Ganja Be? The Indian Hemp Drugs Commission's Discourse on Cannabis." Available at: https://blogs.ed.ac.uk/digitalhumanities2020/research/the-indian-hemp-drugs-commissions-discourse-on-cannabis.

Mejía, A. & Csete, J. (2016). "The Economics of the Drug War: Unaccounted Costs, Lost Lives, and Missed Opportunities." Available at: https://www.unodc.org/documents/ungass2016/Contributions/Civil/OpenSociety/The_Economics_of_the_Drug_War_-_Unaccounted_Costs_Lost_Lives_Missed_Opportunities.pdf.

Melchior, M., Nakamura, A., Bolze, C., Hausfater, F., El Khoury, F., Mary-Krause, M. et al. (2019). "Does Liberalisation of Cannabis Policy Influence Levels of Use in Adolescents and Young Adults? A Systematic Review and Meta-Analysis." *British Medical Journal Open* 9(7): e025880.

Mennis J. (2020). "Trends in Adolescent Treatment Admissions for Marijuana in the United States, 2008–2017." *Preventing Chronic Disease* 17: E145. https://doi.org/10.5888/pcd17.200156.

Mennis, J. & Stahler, G.J. (2020). "Adolescent Treatment Admissions for Marijuana following Recreational Legalization in Colorado and Washington." *Drug and Alcohol Dependence* 210: 107960. https://doi.org/10.1016/j.drugalcdep.2020.107960.

Mennis, J., Stahler, G.J., & McKeon, T.P. (2021). "Young Adult Cannabis Use Disorder Treatment Admissions Declined as Past Month Cannabis Use Increased in the U.S.: An Analysis of States by Year, 2008–2017." *Addictive Behavior* 123: 107049. doi: 10.1016/j.addbeh.2021.107049. Epub 2021 July 15. PMID: 34303941.

Merrill, J. (1988). "The Bible and the American Temperance Movement: Text, Context, and Pretext." *Harvard Theological Review* 81(2): 145–170.

Merton, R.K. (1938). "Social Structure and Anomie." *American Sociological Review* 22: 635–659.

Metropolitan Police Service (2021). "Arrest Data for Cannabis Offenses 2015–2018." Strategy and Insight Unit.

Michalowski, R. (2012). "The History of Critical Criminology in the United States." In W. DeKeseredy & M. Dragiewicz (eds), *The Routledge Handbook of Critical Criminology*. London: Routledge (pp. 32–45).

Mikos, R.A. (2021). "Interstate Commerce in Cannabis." (March 2) *Boston University Law Review* 101: 857. Vanderbilt Law Research Paper No. 21–09. Available at: https://ssrn.com/abstract=3796262.

Mikuriya T.H. (1969). "Marijuana in Medicine: Past, Present and Future." *California Medicine* 110(1): 34–40.

Milanovic, B. (2021). "Is Norway the New East India Company? Gas and Oil, and Opium." (July 23). Available at: https://branko2f7.substack.com/p/is-norway-the-new-east-india-company?r=16uxt&utm_campaign=post&utm_medium=web&utm_source=twitter.

Miller, C. (2019). "An Argument against Cannabis Prohibition in Australia." (November 22). Available at: https://medium.com/everything-is-made-up/a-brief-history-of-cannabis-and-prohibition-in-australia-188ec43d2f0b.

Miller, Richard L. (1996). *Drug Warriors and Their Prey: From Police Power to Police State*. Westport, CT: Praeger.

Miller, Z.J. (2014). "Vice President Joe Biden Not High on Marijuana Legalization." (February 6) *Time*. Available at: https://time.com/5330/marijuana-legalization-joe-biden-pot.

Mills, C.W. (1959). *The Sociological Imagination*. Oxford, UK: Oxford University Press.

Mills, J.H. (2003). *Cannabis Britannica: Empire, Trade, and Prohibition 1800–1928*. New York, NY: Oxford University Press.

Milovanovic, D. (2014). *Quantum Holographic Criminology: Paradigm Shifts in Criminology, Law, and Transformative Justice*. Durham, NC: Carolina Academic Press.

Miron, J.A. (2010). *The Budgetary Implications of Drug Prohibition*. Cambridge: Department of Economics.

Miron, J. (2017). "How to Kill the Marijuana Black Market." (August 11) *Denver Post*. Available at: https://www.denverpost.com/2017/08/11/how-to-kill-the-marijuana-black-market/.

Miron, J.A. & Zwiebel, J. (1991). "Alcohol Consumption during Prohibition." *American Economic Review* 81(2): 242–247.

Miron, J.A. & Zwiebel, J. (1995). "The Economic Case against Drug Prohibition." *Journal of Economic Perspectives* 9(4): 175–192.

Mitchell, O. (2015). "Experimental Research Design." In W.G. Jennings (ed.), *The Encyclopedia of Crime and Punishment*. Malden, MA: Wiley-Blackwell (pp. (602–607).

Mitchell, O. & Caudy, M.S. (2017). "Race Differences in Drug Offending and Drug Distribution Arrests." *Crime & Delinquency* 63(2): 91–112.

Mize, J. (2020). "Reefer Reparations." *Willamette Law Review* 3(2): 1–35.

MJBizDaily (2020). "Dutch Government Seeks to Ease Doubts over Adult-Use Cannabis Trial." (September 25). Available at: https://mjbizdaily.com/netherlands-seeks-to-ease-doubts-over-adult-use-cannabis-experiment.

Moeller, K. & Hesse, M. (2013). "Drug Market Disruption and Systemic Violence: Cannabis Markets in Copenhagen." *European Journal of Criminology* 10(2): 206–221.

Moffitt, T.E. (1993). "Life-Course-Persistent and Adolescent-Limited Anti-Social Behavior. A Developmental Taxonomy." *Psychological Review* 100: 674–701.

Mok, J., Milloy, M.J., Grant, C., Lake, S., DeBeck, K., Hayashi, K., & Socías, M.E. (2021). "Use of Cannabis for Harm Reduction Among People at High Risk for Overdose in Vancouver, Canada (2016–2018)." *American Journal of Public Health* 111(5): 969–972. doi: 10.2105/AJPH.2021.306168. Epub 2021 March 18. PMID: 33734849; PMCID: PMC8033988.

Monshouwer, K., Van Laar, M., & Vollebergh, W.A. (2011). "Buying Cannabis in 'Coffee Shops'. *Drug and Alcohol Review* 30(2): 148–156. https://doi.org/10.1111/j.1465-3362.2010.00268.x.

Montañés, V. (2014). "Rompiendo el Hielo: La Regulación de Cannabis en Países Bajos, Colorado y Uruguay, Donostia/San Sebastián: Fundation Renovatio." Available at: https://idpc.net/es/publications/2014/09/rompiendo-el-hielo-la-regulacion-del-cannabis-en-paises-bajos-colorado-y-uruguay.

Monte, A.A., Zane, R.D., & Heard, K.J. (2015). "The Implications of Marijuana Legalization in Colorado." *Journal of American Medical Association* 313(3): 241–242.

Moon, C. (2013). "Looking without Seeing, Listening without Hearing: Cohen, Denial and Human Rights." *Crime, Media, Culture* 9(2): 193–196.

Mooney, L.J., Zhu, Y., Yoo, C., Valdez, J., Moino, K., Liao, J.Y., & Hser, Y.I. (2018). "Reduction in Cannabis Use and Functional Status in Physical Health, Mental Health, and Cognition." *Journal of Neuroimmune Pharmacology* 13(4): 479–487.

Moore, A. (2015). "The Arc of Reform?: What the Era of Prohibition May Tell Us about the Future of Immigration Reform." *Georgetown Immigration Law Journal* 28(3): 521–554.

Moosavi, L. (2019). "A Friendly Critique of 'Asian Criminology' and 'Southern Criminology'." *British Journal of Criminology* 59: 257–275.

Moreau, J.J. (1841). *Traitement des hallucinations par le datura stramonium*. Paris: Just Rouvier & E. Le Bouvier.

Moreau, J.J. (1845). *Du hachisch et de l'aliénation mentale: études psychologiques*. Paris: Fortin Masson.

Morone, J. (2015). "Book Review: The War on Alcohol." *New York Times*. Available at: https://www.nytimes.com/2016/01/03/books/review/the-war-on-alcohol-by-lisa-mcgirr.html.

Morris, J. (2018). "Does Legalizing Marijuana Reduce Crime?" (September) Reason Foundation. Available at: https://reason.org/policy-brief/does-legalizing-marijuana-reduce-crime/.

Morris, R.G., TenEyck, M., Barnes, J.C., & Kovandzic, T.V. (2014). "The Effect of Medical Marijuana Laws on Crime: Evidence from State Panel Data, 1990–2006." *PLoS ONE* 9(3): e92816. https://doi.org/10.1371/journal.pone.0092816.

Morris, S. (2022). "'Recreational Drug Users Could Have Passports and Driving Licences Confiscated under New Plans in Government Crackdown." (July 18) *Sky News*. Available at: https://news.sky.com/story/recreational-drug-users-could-have-passports-and-driving-licences-confiscated-under-new-plans-in-government-crackdown-12653788.

Moynihan, D.P. (1993). "Defining Deviancy Down." (Winter) *The American Scholar* 62(1): 17–30. Available at: http://www.jstor.org/stable/41212064.

Muncie, J. (2004). *Youth & Crime*, 2nd edn. London: Sage.

Munsch, C.L. (2018). "Correction: 'Her Support, His Support: Money, Masculinity, and Marital Infidelity'." *American Sociological Review* 80(3): 469–495. https://doi.org/10.1177/0003122418780369.

Murch, D. (2015). "Crack in Los Angeles: Crisis, Militarization, and Black Response to the Late Twentieth-Century War on Drugs." *Journal of American History* 102(1): 162–173.

Murkin, G. (2014). "Drug Decriminalisation in Portugal: Setting the Record Straight." Transform Drug Policy Foundation. Available at: https://www.unodc.org/documents/ungass2016/Contributions/Civil/Transform-Drug-Policy-Foundation/Drug-decriminalisation-in-Portugal.pdf.

Murkin, G. (2015). "Cannabis Social Clubs in Spain: Legalisation without Commercialisation." *Transform*. Available at: https://transformdrugs.org/wp-content/uploads/2018/10/Spain_0.pdf.

Murkin, G. (2016). "Will Drug Use Rise? Exploring a Key Concern about Decriminalising or Regulating Drugs." *Transform*. Available at: https://transformdrugs.org/wp-content/uploads/2018/10/Use-report-2016.pdf.

Murphy, E. (1922). *The Black Candle: Canada's First Book on Drug Abuse*. Toronto, ON: Thomas Allen.

Murphy, K. (2019). "Cannabis Is Becoming a Huge Job Creator." (May 20) *Forbes*. Available at: https://www.forbes.com/sites/kevinmurphy/2019/05/20/cannabis-is-becoming-a-huge-job-creator/?sh=2524006049bf.

Murray, G.F. (1986). "Marijuana Use and Social Control: A Sociological Perspective on Deviance." *International Journal of Addiction* 21(6): 657–669.

Murray, R.M., Englund, A., Abi-Dargham, A., Lewis, D.A., Forti, M.D., Davies, C., Sherif, M., McGuire, P., & D'Souza, D.C. (2017). "Cannabis-Associated Psychosis: Neural Substrate and Clinical Impact." *Neuropharmacology* 124(15), 89–104.

Musto, C. (2018). "Regulating Cannabis Markets: The Construction of an Innovative Drug Policy in Uruguay." PhD thesis, University of Kent.

Musto, D.F. (1987). "The History of Legislative Control over Opium, Cocaine, and Their Derivatives." In R. Hamowy (ed.), *Dealing with Drugs*. Lexington, MA: Lexington Books (pp 37–71).

Musto, D.F. (1999) *The American Disease: Origins of Narcotic Control*. New York, NY: Oxford University Press.

Nadelmann, E. & LaSalle, L. (2017). "Two Steps Forward, One Step Back: Current Harm Reduction Policy and Politics in the United States." *Harm Reduction Journal* 14: 37. https://doi.org/10.1186/s12954-017-0157-.

Nadelmann, E.A. (1998). "Commonsense Drug Policy." *Foreign Affairs* 77(1): 111–126. https://doi.org/10.2307/20048366.

National Academies of Sciences, Engineering, and Medicine (NASEM) (2017). *The Health Effects of Cannabis and Cannabinoids: The Current State of Evidence and Recommendations for Research*. Washington, DC: National Academies Press.

National Academies (2017). "Health Effects of Marijuana and Cannabis-Derived Products Presented in New Report." (January 12) News release. Available at: https://www.nationalacademies.org/news/2017/01/health-effects-of-marijuana-and-cannabis-derived-products-presented-in-new-report.

National Archive of South Africa (1923). "Draft Letter, Prime Minister to Secretary, League of Nations." (November 28) SAB BTS 2/1/104 L.N. 15/1SA.

National Commission on Marihuana and Drug Abuse (1972). *Marihuana: A Signal of Misunderstanding*. Washington, DC: National Commission on Marihuana and Drug Abuse.

National Law Review (2023). "Cannabis Lounges Coming to New Jersey." (January 16) *National Law Review*. Available at: https://www.natlawreview.com/article/cannabis-lounges-coming-to-new-jersey.

National Library of Medicine (2017). "The Health Effects of Cannabis and Cannabinoids: The Current State of Evidence and Recommendations for Research. 15. Challenges and Barriers in Conducting Cannabis Research." (January 12) Available at: https://www.ncbi.nlm.nih.gov/books/NBK425757.

https://www.nationalacademies.org/news/2017/01/health-effects-of-marijuana-and-cannabis-derived-products-presented-in-new-report.

NCIA (National Cannabis Industry Association) (n.d.). "About NCIA: Our Mission." Available at: https://thecannabisindustry.org/about-us/mission-values.

Nelson, E.-U. (2021) "'I Take It to Relax . . . and Chill': Perspectives on Cannabis Use from Marginalized Nigerian Young Adults." *Addiction Research & Theory* 29(6): 490–499. https://doi.org/10.1080/16066359.2021.1895125.

Nemeth, J. & Ross, E. (2014). "Planning for Marijuana." *Journal of the American Planning Association* 80(1): 6–20.

Newhart, M. & Dolphin, W. (2019) *The Medicalization of Marijuana: Legitimacy, Stigma, and the Patient Experience*. New York, NY: Routledge.

New York Academy of Medicine (1944). "The Laguardia Committee Report, New York: The Marijuana Problem in the City of New York." Mayor's Committee on Marihuana. Available at: https://rodneybarnett.net/PDF/Laguardia%20Report%201944.pdf.

Ng, S. (2016). "Opium Use in 19th-Century Britain: The Roots of Moralism in Shaping Drug Legislation." *American Journal of Psychiatry Residents' Journal* 11: 6–14.

Nguyen, H., Midgette, G., Loughran, T., & Zhang, Y. (2021). "Random Drug Testing in Prisons: Does a Little Testing Go a Long Way?" *Criminology and Public Policy* 20: 329–349. https://doi.org/10.1111/1745-9133.12543.

NICA (National Cannabis Industry Association) (n.d.). "Our Mission." Available at: https://thecannabisindustry.org/about-us/mission-values.

NIH (National Institutes of Health) (2007). "Alcohol Alert." (January). National Institute on Alcohol Abuse and Alcoholism. Available at: https://pubs.niaaa.nih.gov/publications/aa71/aa71.htm.

Niveau, G. & Dang, C. (2003). "Cannabis and Violent Crime." *Medicine, Science and the Law* 43(2): 115–121.

Nolan, J.L. (2002). *Drug Courts: In Theory and in Practice.* New York, NY: Aldine de Gruyter.

Nolin, P. (2003). *Cannabis—Report of the Senate Special Committee on Illegal Drugs.* Toronto, ON: University of Toronto Press.

Norland, S. & Wright, J. (1984). "Bureaucratic Legitimacy and the Drug Menace: Notes on the Marihuana Tax Act." *Deviant Behavior* 5(1): 239–254.

Nussbaum, A., Thurstone, C., McGarry, L., Walker, B., & Sabel, A.L. (2015). "Use and Diversion of Medical Marijuana among Adults Admitted to Inpatient Psychiatry." *American Journal of Drug and Alcohol Abuse* 41(2): 166–172.

Nutt, D. (2012). *Drugs—Without the Hot Air: Minimising the Harms of Legal and Illegal Drugs.* Cambridge, UK: UIT Cambridge.

Nutt, D. (2015). "Illegal Drugs Laws: Clearing a 50-Year-Old Obstacle to Research." *PLoS Biology* 13(1): e1002047. doi: 10.1371/journal.pbio.1002047. PMID: 25625189; PMCID: PMC4307971.

Nutt, D. (2022). "Why Doctors Have a Moral Imperative to Prescribe and Support Medical Cannabis." *British Medical Journal* 376: o483. doi: 10.1136/bmj.o483.

Nutt, D., Phillips, L., Balfour, D., Curran, H., Dockrell, M., Foulds, J., et al. (2014). "Estimating the Harms of Nicotine-containing Products Using the MCDA Approach." *European Addiction Research* 20: 218–225.

Nutt, D.J., King, L.A., & Phillips, L.D. (2010). "Drug Harms in the UK: A Multicriteria Decision Analysis." *The Lancet* 376(9752): 1558–1565.

Nyika, L. & Murray-Orr, A. (2017). "Critical Race Theory–Social Constructivist Bricolage: A Health-Promoting Schools Research Methodology." *Health Education Journal* 76(4): 432–441. O'Brien, J. (2018). *How to Be Right in a World Gone Wrong.* London: Penguin.

O'Brien, M.S., Comment, L.A., Liang, K.Y., & Anthony, J.C. (2012). "Does Cannabis Onset Trigger Cocaine Onset? A Case-crossover Approach." *International Journal of Methods in Psychiatry Research* 21(1): 66–75.

Ogg, K. (n.d.). "Harris County Criminal Justice Center." District Attorney's Office, Harris County, TX. Available at: https://app.dao.hctx.net/video-misdemeanor-marijuana-diversion-program.

Ogg, K. (2019). "Misdemeanor Marijuana Diversion Program." (April 10). Available at: https://www.kim-ogg.com/marijuana.

O'Grady, C. (2020). "Cannabis Research Data Reveals a Focus on Harms of the Drug." *Science (New York, N.Y.)* 369(6508): 1155. https://doi.org/10.1126/science.369.6508.1155.

Ogrodnik, M., Kopp, P., Bongaerts, X., & Tecco, J.M. (2015). "An Economic Analysis of Different Cannabis Decriminalization Scenarios." *Psychiatria Danubina* 27(1): S309–S314.

Okey, S.A., Castro, S.A., Waddell, J.T., Jones, C.B., Blake, A.J., O'Rourke, H.P. et al. (2022). "Are Recreational Cannabis Laws Associated with Declining Medical Cannabis Program Enrollment in the US? An Analysis of Cardholder Enrollment and Demographic Characteristics from 2013 to 2020." *International Journal of Drug Policy* 100: 103531.

Oldfield, K., Evans, S., Braithwaite, I., & Newton-Howe, G. (2021). "Don't Make a Hash of It! A Thematic Review of the Literature Relating to Outcomes of Cannabis Regulatory Change." *Drugs: Education, Prevention and Policy* 29(5): 439–450. https://doi.org/10.1080/09687637.2021.1901855.

Oleck, J. (2018). "With 40,000 Americans Incarcerated for Marijuana Offenses, the Cannabis Industry Needs to Step Up, Activists Said This Week." (June 26) *Forbes*. Available at: https://www.forbes.com/sites/joanoleck/2020/06/26/with-40000-americans-incarcerated-for-marijuana-offenses-the-cannabis-industry-needs-to-step-up-activists-said-this-week/?sh=266877a7c16f.

Oliphant, E. (n.d.). "Frequently Asked Questions." Erika Oliphant, Prosecuting Attorney, Monroe County, Indiana. Available at: https://www.monroeprosecutor.us/criminal-justice/pretrial-diversion-program/faq.

Ong, J.C. & Cabañes, J.V. (2018). "Architects of Networked Disinformation: Behind the Scenes of Troll Accounts and Fake News Production in the Philippines." https://doi.org/10.7275/2cq4-5396.

Oregon Criminal Justice Commission (2020). "IP 44 racial and ethnic impact statement supplemental document." (August 5). Available at: https://www.theskanner.com/images/stories/2020/August/IP44-REI-Statement-Supplement.pdf.

Oregon State Legislature (2021). "Public Testimony Document." Available at: https://olis.oregonlegislature.gov/liz/2021R1/Downloads/PublicTestimonyDocument/15357.

Orren, K. & Skowronek, S. (2017). *The Policy State: An American Predicament*. Cambridge, MA: Harvard University Press.

Ortiz, A. (2022). "Laura Ingraham Tries to Blame Texas School Shooting on 'Pot Psychosis.'" (June 1) *The Wrap*. Available at: https://www.thewrap.com/laura-ingraham-pot-psychosis-gun-violence-reefer-madness.

Osborne, G.B. & Fogel, C. (2017). "Perspectives on Cannabis Legalization among Canadian Recreational Users." *Contemporary Drug Problems* 44(1): 12–31.

O'Shaughnessy, W. (1842). *The Bengal Dispensatory and Companion to Pharmacopoeia*. London: Allen and Co.

Owen, D. (2017). "The State of Technology in Global Newsrooms. Research Report." Washington, DC: International Center for Journalists. Available at: http://www.icfj.org/sites/default/files/ICFJTechSurveyFINAL.pdf.

Owusu-Bempah, A. & Luscombe, A. (2021). "Race, Cannabis and the Canadian War on Drugs: An Examination of Cannabis Arrest Data by Race in Five Cities." *International Journal on Drug Policy* 91: 102937. https://doi.org/10.1016/j.drugpo.2020.102937.

Owusu-Bempah, A. & Rehmatullah, T. (2023). *Waiting to Inhale: Cannabis Legalization and the Fight for Racial Justice*. Cambridge, MA: MIT Press.

PA News Agency (2019). "Medicinal Cannabis Should Be Treated Like Other Drugs, MPs Told." (March 26) *In-Cumbria*. Available at: https://www.in-cumbria.com/news/17587728.medicinal-cannabis-treated-like-drugs-mps-told.

Pacheco-Colón, I., Limia, J.M., & Gonzalez, R. (2018). "Nonacute Effects of Cannabis Use on Motivation and Reward Sensitivity in Humans: A Systematic Review." *Psychology of Addictive Behaviors* 32(5): 497–507.

Pacula, R.L. & Sevigny, E.L. (2014). "Marijuana Liberalization Policies: Why We Can't Learn Much from Policy Still in Motion." *Journal of Policy Analysis and Management* 33(1): 212–221. https://doi.org/10.1002/pam.21726.

Pacula, R.L., Powell, D., Heaton, P., & Sevigny, E.L. (2015). "Assessing the Effects of Medical Marijuana Laws on Marijuana Use: The Devil Is in the Details." *Journal of Policy Analysis and Management* 34(1): 7–31.

Page, J. & Soss, J. (2021). "The Predatory Dimensions of Criminal Justice." *Science* 15(374)(6565): 291–294. https://doi.org/10.1126/science.abj7782. Epub 2021 October 14. PMID: 34648321.

Pardal, M. (ed.). (2022). *The Cannabis Social Club*. London: Routledge Publishing.

Pardal, M., Queirolo, R., Álvarez, E., & Repetto, L. (2019). "Uruguayan Cannabis Social Clubs: From Activism to Dispensaries?" *International Journal of Drug Policy* 73: 49–57.

Pardo, B. (2014). "Cannabis Policy Reforms in the Americas: A Comparative Analysis of Colorado, Washington, and Uruguay." *International Journal of Drug Policy* 25(4): 727–735.

Pariser, E. (2011). *The Filter Bubble: What the Internet Is Hiding from You*. New York, NY: Penguin Press.

Park, R.E., Burgess, E.W., & McKenzie, R.D. (1925). *The City*. Chicago, IL: University of Chicago Press.

Parker, H. (2005). "Normalization as a Barometer: Recreational Drug Use and the Consumption of Leisure by Younger Britons." *Addiction Research and Theory* 13(3): 205–215.

Parker, H. & Egginton, R. (2002). "Adolescent Recreational Alcohol and Drugs Careers Gone Wrong: Developing a Strategy for Reducing Risks and Harms." *International Journal of Drug Policy* 13(5): 419–432.

Parker, H., Williams, L., & Aldridge, J. (2002). "The Normalization of Sensible Recreational Drug Use: Further Evidence from the N.W. Longitudinal Study." *Sociology* 36(4): 941–964.

Parker, H.J., Aldridge, J., & Measham, F. (1998). *Illegal Leisure: The Normalization of Adolescent Recreational Drug Use*. London: Routledge.

Parnaby, P. (2003). "Disaster through Dirty Windshields: Law, Order, and Toronto's Squeegee Kids." *Canadian Journal of Sociology* 28(3): 281–307.

Pashler, H. & Wagenmakers, E.-J. (2012). "Editors' Introduction to the Special Section on Replicability in Psychological Science: A Crisis of Confidence?" *Perspectives on Psychological Science* 7: 528–530.

Passifume, B. (2022). "Red Tape, Barriers Keeping B.C.'s 'Legacy' Craft Pot Farmers Out of Legal Marketplace." (September 28) *Vancouver Sun*. Available at: https://vancouversun.com/news/local-news/red-tape-keeping-bcs-legacy-craft-pot-farmers-out-of-legal-marketplace.

Patel, J. & Marwaha, R. (2022). "Cannabis Use Disorder." (Updated July 12). *StatPearls* Treasure Island, FL: StatPearls Publishing. Available at: https://pubmed.ncbi.nlm.nih.gov/30844158/.

Paul, B., Thulien, M., Knight, R., Milloy, M.J., Howard, B., Nelson, S., & Fast, D. (2020). "Something That Actually Works: Cannabis Use Among Young People in the Context of Street Entrenchment." *PloS One* 15(7): e0236243. doi: 10.1371/journal.pone.0236243. PMID: 32722721; PMCID: PMC7386570.

Pavlich, G. (2005). *Governing Paradoxes of Restorative Justice*. London: Glass House Press.

Payan, D., Brown, P., & Song, A. (2021). "County-Level Recreational Marijuana Policies and Local Policy Changes in Colorado and Washington State (2012–2019)." *Milbank Quarterly* 99(4): 1132–1161. https://doi.org/10.1111/1468-0009.12535.

Pearlson, G.D., Stevens, M.C., & D'Souza, D.C. (2021). "Cannabis and Driving." *Frontiers in Psychiatry* 12: 689444. doi: 10.3389/fpsyt.2021.689444.

Pedersen, W. & Skardhamar, T. (2010). "Cannabis and Crime: Findings from a Longitudinal Study." *Addiction* 105: 109–118.

Pembleton, M.R. (2017). *Containing Addiction: The Federal Bureau of Narcotics and the Origins of America's Global Drug War*. Amherst, MA: University of Massachusetts Press.

Pereira, I. and Yamada, H. (2021). "Sha'Carri Richardson's Olympic suspension turns to heated debate on cannabis." (July 21) *ABC News*. Available at: https://abcnews.go.com/Sports/shacarri-richardsons-dashed-olympic-hopes-ignite-debate-cannabis/story?id=78635258.

Perlman, A.I., McLeod, H.M., Ventresca, E.C., Salinas, M.G., Post, P.J., & Schuh, M.J. (2021). "Medical Cannabis State and Federal Regulations: Implications for United States Health Care Entities." *Mayo Clinic Proceedings* 96(10): 2671–2681.

Perry, M. (2015). "Milton Friedman Interview from 1991 on America's War on Drugs." (August 6) *AEIdeas*. Available at: https://www.aei.org/carpe-diem/milton-friedman-interview-from-1991-on-americas-war-on-drugs.

Pertwee, R.G. (2006). "Cannabinoid Pharmacology: The First 66 Years." *British Journal of Pharmacology* 147(Suppl 1): S163–S171. doi: 10.1038/sj.bjp.0706406. PMID: 16402100; PMCID: PMC1760722.

Pesta, G.B., Ramos, J., Ranson, J.A., Singer, A., & Blomberg, T.G. (2016). *Translational Criminology, Research and Public Policy: Final Summary Report*. Tallahassee, FL: College of Criminology and Criminal Justice, Florida State University.

Peters, J. (2020). "I Learned to Think Like a 'Warrior Cop.'" (August 28) *SLATE*. Available at: https://slate.com/news-and-politics/2020/08/warrior-cop-class-dave-grossman-killology.html.

Petrescu, D.C., Hollands, G.J., Couturier, D.L., Ng, Y.L., & Marteau, T.M. (2016). "Public Acceptability in the UK and USA of Nudging to Reduce Obesity: The Example of Reducing Sugar-Sweetened Beverages Consumption." *PloS ONE* 11(6): e0155995. https://doi.org/10.1371/journal.pone.0155995.

Philbin, M.M., Mauro, P.M., Santaella-Tenorio, J., Mauro, C.M., Kinnard, E.N., Cerda, M., & Martins, S.S. (2019). "Associations between State-Level Policy Liberalism, Cannabis Use, and Cannabis Use Disorder from 2004 to 2012: Looking beyond Medical Cannabis Law Status." *International Journal of Drug Policy* 65: 97–103. https://doi.org/10.1016/j.drugpo.2018.10.010.

Pinard, M. (2010). "Collateral Consequences of Criminal Convictions: Confronting Issues of Race and Dignity." *New York University Law Review* 85: 457–534.

Pinto C.M. (2010). "Drug Decriminalization in Portugal." (September 10) *British Journal of Medicine* 34l. Available at: https://www.bmj.com/rapid-response/2011/11/03/redrug-decriminalisation-portugal-0.

Piza, E.L. & Connealy, N.T. (2022). "The Effect of the Seattle Police-Free CHOP Zone on Crime: A Microsynthetic Control Evaluation." *Criminology & Public Policy* 21(1): 35–58.

Plecas, D., Dandurand, Y., Chin, V., & Segger, T. (2002). "Marihuana Growing Operations in British Columbia: An Empirical Survey (1997–2000)." Unpublished Paper. Department of Criminology and Criminal Justice, University College of the Fraser Valley and International Centre for Criminal Law Reform and Criminal Justice Policy.

Plunk, A.D., Peglow, S.L., Harrell, P.T., & Grucza, R.A. (2019). "Youth and Adult Arrests for Cannabis Possession after Decriminalization and Legalization of Cannabis." *Journal of the American Association Pediatrics* 173(8): 763–769. https://doi.org/10.1001/jamapediatrics.2019.1539.

Polizzi, D. (2010). "In search of the human in the shadows of correctional practice: A theoretical reflection with Shadd Maruna." *Journal of Theoretical and Philosophical Criminology* 2(2): 158–197.

Pollan, M. (2018). *How to Change Your Mind: What the New Science of Psychedelics Teaches Us about Consciousness, Dying, Addiction, Depression, and Transcendence.* New York, NY: Penguin.

Polson, M. (2019). "Making Marijuana an Environmental Issue: Prohibition, Pollution, and Policy." *Environment and Planning E: Nature and Space* 2(2): 229–251.

Polson, M. & Petersen-Rockney, M. (2019). "Cannabis Farmers or Criminals? Enforcement-First Approaches Fuel Disparity and Hinder Regulation." *California Agriculture* 73(3): 185–193. https://doi.org/10.3733/ca.2019a 0017.

Ponto, L.L.B. (2006). "Challenges of Marijuana Research." *Brain* 129(5): 1081–1083.

Pope, M. (2020). "Pretext Stops Related to the Smell of Marijuana May Soon Be a Thing of the Past." (September 30) *Radio WVTF*. Available at: https://www.wvtf.org/news/2020-09-30/pretext-stops-related-to-the-smell-of-marijuana-may-soon-be-a-thing-of-the-past.

Pope, H., Jr & Yurgelun-Todd, D. (1996). "The Residual Cognitive Effects of Heavy Marijuana Use in College Students." *Journal of the American Medical Association* 275(7): 521–527.

Porter, B.E. & Jacobson, C. (2013). "Report of a Parent Survey of Cannabidiol-enriched Cannabis Use in Pediatric Treatment-resistant Epilepsy." *Epilepsy & Behavior* 29(3): 574–577. doi: 10.1016/j.yebeh.2013.08.037. PMID: 24237632; PMCID: PMC4157067.

Porter, D. (2021). "Cannabis Use Disorder DSM-5, 305.20, 304.30." *Theravive*. Available at: https://www.theravive.com/therapedia/cannabis-use-disorder-dsm--5%2C-305.20%2C-304.30.

Portugal News (2020). "Five Companies to Grow Medicinal Cannabis." (January 17) *Portugal News*. Available at: https://www.theportugalnews.com/news/five-companies-to-grow-medicinal-cannabis/52691.

Price, T., Parkes, T., & Malloch, M. (2021). "'Discursive Struggles' between Criminal Justice Sanctions and Health Interventions for People Who Use

Drugs: A Qualitative Exploration of Diversion Policy and Practice in Scotland." *Drugs: Education, Prevention and Policy* 28(2): 118–126. https://doi.org/10.1080/09687637.2020.1775180.

Pridemore, W.A., Makel, M.C., & Plucker, J.A. (2018). "Replication in Criminology and the Social Sciences." *Annual Review of Criminology* 1: 19–38.

Provine, D.M. (2007). *Unequal under the Law: Race in the War on Drugs*. Chicago, IL: University of Chicago.

Puras, D. & Hannah, J. (2017). "Reasons for Drug Policy Reform: Prohibition Enables Systemic Human Rights Abuses and Undermines Public Health." *British Medical Journal* 356: i6586.

Queirolo, R. (2020). "The Effects of Recreational Cannabis Legalization Might Depend upon the Policy Model." *World Psychiatry* 19: 195–196. https://doi.org/10.1002/wps.20742.

Queirolo, R., Rossel, C., Álvarez, E., & Repetto, L. (2019). "Why Uruguay Legalized Marijuana? The Open Window of Public Insecurity." (July) *Addiction* 114(7): 1313–1321. https://doi.org/10.1111/add.14523. Epub 2019 January 22. PMID: 30536953.

Quinney, R. (1970). *The Social Reality of Crime*. Piscataway, NJ: Transaction Publishers.

Quinton, S. (2022). "Workers Who Legally Use Cannabis Can Still Lose Their Jobs." (February 28) *Stateline*. Available at: https://www.pewtrusts.org/en/research-and-analysis/blogs/stateline/2022/02/28/workers-who-legally-use-cannabis-can-still-lose-their-jobs.

Radzinowicz, L. (1966). *Ideology and Crime: A Study of Crime in Its Social and Historical Contexts*. London: Heinemann Educational Books.

Rahwanji, M. (2019). "'Hash'ing Out Inequality in the Legal Recreational Cannabis Industry." *Northwestern Journal of International Law & Business* 39(3): 333–358.

Raine, A. (2013). *The Anatomy of Violence: Biological Roots of Crime*. New York, NY: Pantheon Books.

Raine, A. & Buschbaum, M.S. (1996). "Violence, Brain Imaging, and Neuropsychology." In D.M. Stoff & R.B. Cairns (eds), *Aggression and Violence: Genetic, Neurobiological, and Biological Perspectives*. New York, NY: Psychology Press (pp. 195–218).

Ramaekers, J.G., Robbe, H.W.J., & O'Hanlon, J.F. (2000), "Marijuana, Alcohol and Actual Driving Performance." *Human Psychopharmacology: Clinical and Experimental* 15: 551–558. https://doi.org/10.1002/1099-1077(200010)15:7<551::AID-HUP236>3.0.CO;2-P.

Ramiz, A., Rock, P., & Strang, H. (2020). "Detecting Modern Slavery on Cannabis Farms: The Challenges of Evidence." *Cambridge Journal of Evidence-Based Policing* 4: 202–217. https://doi.org/10.1007/s41887-020-00052-1.

Ray, R. (2020a). "How Can We Enhance Police Accountability in the United States?" (August 25) *Voter Vitals*. Available at: https://www.brookings.edu/policy2020/votervital/how-can-we-enhance-police-accountability-in-the-united-states.

Ray, R. (2020b). "Setting the Record Straight on the Movement for Black Lives." *Ethnic and Racial Studies* 43(8): 1393–1401.

Raycraft, R. (2021). "The Pros, Cons and Unknowns of Legal Cannabis in Canada 3 Years Later." (October 24) *CBC News*. Available at: https://www.cbc.ca/news/politics/cannabis-changed-canada-1.6219493.

Reddon, H., DeBeck, K., Socias, M.E., Lake, S., Dong, H., Karamouzian, M., et al. (2020). "Frequent Cannabis Use and Cessation of Injection of Opioids, Vancouver, Canada, 2005–2018." *American Journal of Public Health* 110(10): 1553–1560. https://doi.org/10.2105/AJPH.2020.305825.

Rêgo, X., Oliviera, M.J., Lameira, C., & Cruz, O.S. (2021). "20 Years of Portuguese Drug Policy—Developments, Challenges and the Quest for Human Rights." *Substance Abuse Treatment, Prevention, and Policy* 16(1): 59. https://doi.org/10.1186/s13011-021-00394-7.

Reichert, J., Weisner, L., & Douglas Otto, H. (2020). "A Study of Drug Testing Practices in Probation." (January 30) Illinois Criminal Justice Information Authority. Available at: https://icjia.illinois.gov/researchhub/articles/a-study-of-drug-testing-practices-in-probation.

Reid, M. (2020) "A Qualitative Review of Cannabis Stigmas at the Twilight of Prohibition." *Journal of Cannabis Research* 2: 46–58. https://doi.org/10.1186/s42238-020-00056-8.

Reid, M. (2021). "Troubling Claims of Normalization: Continuing Stigmas within Michigan's Medical Cannabis Community." *Deviant Behavior* 43(9): 1068–1087. https://doi.org/10.1080/01639625.2021.1953947.

Reiman, A. (2009). "Cannabis as a Substitute for Alcohol and Other Drugs." *Harm Reduction Journal* 6: 35. https://doi.org/10.1186/1477-7517-6-35.

Reinarman, C. (2009). "Cannabis Policies and User Practices: Market Separation, Price, Potency, and Accessibility in Amsterdam and San Francisco." *International Journal of Drug Policy* 20(1): 28–37. https://doi.org/10.1016/j.drugpo.2007.11.003.

Reinarman, C. & Levine, H.G. (1997). *Crack in America: Demon Drugs and Social Justice*. Berkeley, CA: University of California Press.

Reinarman, C., Cohen, P.D., & Kaal, H.L. (2004). "The Limited Relevance of Drug Policy: Cannabis in Amsterdam and in San Francisco." *American Journal of Public Health* 94(5): 836–842. https://doi.org/10.2105/AJPH.94.5.836.

Release (n.d.). "Regulating Right, Repairing Wrongs: Exploring Equity and Social Justice Initiatives within the UK Cannabis Reform." *Release*. Available at: https://www.release.org.uk/publications/cannabis-regulating-right?fbclid=IwAR2r1Qn7RvKbt_rHPDOsuRXBXI_3EaD_9gUAfOWED3VvMLbDJ_fgrG0_N-E.

Renner, J. (2019). "Counteracting the Effect of Stigma on Education for Substance Use Disorders." *Focus* 17(2): 134–140; https://doi.org/10.1176/appi.focus.20180039.

Reuters (2021). "International Court Backs Probe into Philippines' 'War on Drugs.'" (September 15) *Reuters*. Available at: https://www.reuters.com/world/asia-pacific/international-court-approves-investigation-into-philippines-war-drugs-2021-09-15.

Reyes, E.A. (2021). "L.A.'s Promise of Social Equity for Marijuana Businesses Has Been Painfully Slow for Entrepreneurs." (March 20) *Los Angeles Times*. Available at: https://www.latimes.com/california/story/2021-03-20/la-cannabis-social-equity-frustration.

Ricciardi, T. (2020). "Colorado Won't Stop Employers from Firing Workers for Using Weed off the Clock." (February 19) *Denver Post*. Retrieved from: https://www.denverpost.com/2020/02/19/colorado-legislature-marijuana-employees-fired-2/.

Richards, J.F. (2002). "The Opium Industry in British India." *Indian Economic & Social History Review* 39(2/3): 154.

Riley-Smith, B. (2021). "Priti Patel: Middle-Class Drug Users Will Be Named and Shamed." (October 5) *The Telegraph*. Available at: https://www.telegraph.co.uk/politics/2021/10/05/priti-patel-middle-class-drug-users-will-named-shamed.

Ritter, A. (2021). *Drug Policy*. London: Routledge.

Roberts, C. (2019). "Patented Pot: What Is a Proprietary Marijuana Strain?" (January 11) *Cannabis Now*. Available at: https://cannabisnow.com/patented-pot-what-is-a-proprietary-marijuana-strain/?fbclid=IwAR2l4U4GBoABJobwKLqSUKTo8hM_LSiWJ3hrQxEI8GugXd81HyNl5qpC5tI.

Roberts, C. (2020). "Science Reveals the Cannabis Industry's Greatest Lie: You're Buying Weed Wrong (and So Is Everyone Else)." (June 16) *Forbes*. Available at: https://www.forbes.com/sites/chrisroberts/2020/06/16/science-reveals-the-cannabis-industrys-greatest-lie-youre-buying-weed-wrong-and-so-is-everyone-else/?sh=83265022ee35.

Roberts, D.E. (2017). "Democratizing Criminal Law as an Abolitionist Project." *Northwestern University Law Review* 111: 1597–1608.

Robinson, J.M., Copeland, C., Pilin, M.A., Meyer, A., & Krank, M.D. (2020). "The Impact of Cannabis Legalization in Canada on Adolescents' Perceptions." *Journal of Drug Issues* 50(3): 235–241.

Robinson, M.B. & Scherlen, R. (2014). *Lies, Damned Lies, and Drug War Statistics: A Critical Analysis of Claims Made by the Office of National Drug Control Policy*. Albany, NY: State University of New York Press.

Rodriguez, C. (2021). "German Moves to Legalize Cannabis, Second Country after Malta in Europe." (December 27) *Forbes*. Available at: https://www.forbes.com/sites/ceciliarodriguez/2021/12/27/germany-moves-to-legalize-cannabis-second-country-after-malta-in-europe/?sh=11b0c06b220b.

Rodríguez-Gómez, D. & Bermeo, M.J. (2020). "The Educational Nexus to the War on Drugs: A Systematic Review." *Journal on Education in Emergencies* 6(1): 18–56.

Rogeberg, O., Bergsvik, D., Phillips, L.D., Van Amsterdam, J., Eastwood, N., Henderson, G., et al. (2018). "A New Approach to Formulating and Appraising Drug Policy: A Multi-criterion Decision Analysis Applied to Alcohol and Cannabis Regulation." *International Journal of Drug Policy* 56: 144–152.

Rohloff, A. & Wright, S. (2010) "Moral Panic and Social Theory: Beyond the Heuristic." *Current Sociology* 58(3): 403–419.

Rolles, S. & Murkin, G. (2016). "The Commercial Focus of US Cannabis Regulation Models Should Not Close Our Eyes to Other Options." *Addiction* 111(12): 2092–2094.

Room, R., Fischer, B., Hall, W., Lenton, S., & Reuter, P. (2010). *Cannabis Policy: Moving beyond Stalemate*. Cambridge, UK: Oxford University Press.

Rorty, R. (1979). *Philosophy and the Mirror of Nature*. Princeton, NJ: Princeton University Press.

Rorty, R. (1989). *Contingency, Irony, and Solidarity*. Cambridge, UK: Cambridge University Press.

Rorty, R. (1994). "Dewey between Hegel and Darwin." In D. Ross (ed.), *Modernist Impulses in the Human Sciences, 1870–1930*. Baltimore, MD: The Johns Hopkins University Press (pp. 54–68).

Rorty, R. (1995). "Habermas, Derrida, and the Functions of Philosophy." *Revue Internationale de Philosophie* 49(194): 437–459.

Rorty, R. (1998) *Truth and Progress: Philosophical Papers, Volume 3*. Cambridge, UK: Cambridge University Press.

Rorty, R. (2006). "Born to Be Good." (August 27) *New York Times*. Available at: https://www.nytimes.com/2006/08/27/books/review/born-to-be-good.html.

Rosario, J. (2021). "City Council Members Agree on Even Split of Jersey City Cannabis Tax Revenue between Schools, Social Programs." (July 13) *Jersey Journal*. Available at: https://www.nj.com/hudson/2021/07/city-council-member-agree-on-even-split-of-jersey-city-cannabis-tax-revenue-between-schools-social-programs.html.

Rotermann, M. (2020). "What Has Changed since Cannabis Was Legalized?" *Health Reports* 31(2): 11–20.

Rothman, D. (1972) "Of Prisons, Asylums and Other Decaying Institutions." *Public Interest* 26: 3–17.

Rothman, D. (1975). "An Historical Overview. Behavior Modification in Total Institutions." (February) *Hastings Centre Report* 5(1): 17–24. PMID: 1093999.

Rup, J., Goodman, S., & Hammond, D. (2020). "Cannabis Advertising, Promotion and Branding: Differences in Consumer Exposure Between 'Legal' and 'Illegal' Markets in Canada and the US." *Preventive Medicine* 133: 106013.

Rushton, N. (2018). "There Is a New Drug in the Schedule: The Mysterious Origins of Criminalized Cannabis." Masters' Thesis. Victoria: University of Victoria.

Russell, A. & Keefe, A. (2015). "Burlington's New Police Chief Talks Race Relations, Opiate Issues and Legalizing Marijuana." (September 1) *Vermont Public*. Available at: https://www.vpr.org/vpr-news/2015-09-01/burlingtons-new-police-chief-talks-race-relations-opiate-issues-and-legalizing-marijuanah.

Russo, E.B. (2007). "History of Cannabis and Its Preparations in Saga, Science, and Sobriquet." *Chemistry and Biodiversity* 4(8): 1614–1648.

Ryskamp, D.A. (2020). "As Nuisance Claims Rise, Cannabis Cases May Depend on Expert Witnesses." (June 25) *Expert Witness*. Available at: https://www.expertinstitute.com/resources/insights/as-nuisance-claims-rise-cannabis-cases-may-depend-on-expert-witnesses.

Sabaghi, D. (2023). "What to Know About German's Revised Plan to Legalize Cannabis." (April 13) *Forbes*. Available at: https://www.forbes.com/sites/dariosabaghi/2023/04/13/what-to-know-about-germanys-revised-plan-to-legalize-cannabis/?sh=25875e9c25e0.

Sabet, K. (2021). "Lessons Learned in Several States Eight Years After States Legalized Marijuana." *Current Opinion in Psychology* 38: 25–30.

Sadeghi, M. (2020). "Fact Check: Viral Warning on Marijuana's 'Murderous' Side Effects and Thanksgiving Is Fake." *USA News Today*. Available at: https://www.usatoday.com/story/news/factcheck/2020/11/29/fact-check-viral-warning-marijuana-and-thanksgiving-fake/6441057002.

Sagar, K.A. & Gruber, S.A. (2018). "Marijuana Matters: Reviewing the Impact of Marijuana on Cognition, Brain Structure and Function, & Exploring Policy Implications and Barriers to Research." *International Review of Psychiatry* 30(3): 251–267.

Saitz, R., Miller, S.C., Fiellin, D.A., & Rosenthal, R.N. (2020). "Recommended Use of Terminology in Addiction Medicine." (January/February) *Journal of Addictive Medicine* 15(1): 3–7. https://doi.org/10.1097/ADM.0000000000000673. PMID: 32482955.

Salas-Wright, C.P., Vaughn, M.G., Cummings-Vaughn, L.A., Holzer, K.J., Nelson, E.J., AbiNader, M. et al. (2017). "Trends and Correlates of Marijuana Use among Late Middle-Aged and Older Adults in the United States, 2002–2014." *Drug and Alcohol Dependence* 171: 97–106.

SAM (Smart Approaches to Marijuana) (2018). "SAM Model State Legislation." (October 19) *The New Yorker*. Available at: https://learnaboutsam.org/sam-model-state-legislation.

SAMHSA (Substance Abuse and Mental Health Services Administration) (2020). "Key Substance Use and Mental Health Indicators in the United States: Results from the 2020 National Survey on Drug Use and Health." Available at: https://www.samhsa.gov/data/sites/default/files/reports/rpt35325/NSDUHFFRPDFWHTMLFiles2020/2020NSDUHFFR1PDFW102121.pdf.

Sampson, R. & Laub, J.H. (1993). *Crime in the Making: Pathways and Turning Points through Life*. Cambridge, MA: Harvard University Press.

Sanchez, H.F., Orr, M.F., Wang, A., Cano, M.Á., Vaughan, E.L., Harvey, L.M., Essa, S., Torbati, A., Clark, U.S., Fagundes, C.P., & de Dios, M.A. (2020). "Racial and Gender Inequities in the Implementation of a Cannabis Criminal Justice Diversion Program in a Large and Diverse Metropolitan County of the USA." (November 1) *Drug and Alcohol Dependence*. 216: 108316. https://doi.org/10.1016/j.drugalcdep.2020.108316. Epub 2020 September 28. PMID: 33017750.

Sandberg, S. (2008). "Black Drug Dealers in a White Welfare State: Cannabis Dealing and Street Capital in Norway." *British Journal of Criminology* 48(5): 604–619. https://doi.org/10.1093/bjc/azn041.

Sandberg, S. (2012a). "The Importance of Culture for Cannabis Markets: Towards an Economic Sociology of Illegal Drug Markets." *British Journal of Criminology* 52(6): 1133–1151. https://doi.org/10.1093/bjc/azs031.

Sandberg, S. (2012b). "Is Cannabis Use Normalized, Celebrated or Neutralized? Analysing Talk as Action." *Addiction Research & Theory* 20(5): 372–381. https://doi.org/10.3109/16066359.2011.638147.

Sandberg S. (2013). "Cannabis Culture: A Stable Subculture in a Changing World." *Criminology & Criminal Justice* 13(1): 63–79.

Sander, G., Scandurra, A., Kamenska, A., MacNamara, C., Kalpaki, C., Bessa, C.F., et al. (2016). "Overview of Harm Reduction in Prisons in Seven European Countries." *Harm Reduction Journal* 13(1): 28. https://doi.org/10.1186/s12954-016-0118-x.

Sanders, C. (2013). "Learning from Experience: Recollections of Working with Howard S. Becker." *Symbolic Interaction* 36(2): 216–228.

Santos, M. (2021). "How $1 Billion in Pot Taxes Gets Spent in Washington State." (February 22) *Crosscut*. Available at: https://crosscut.com/news/2021/02/how-1-billion-pot-taxes-gets-spent-washington-state#:~:text=The%20largest%20sin gle%20allocation%20of,who%20lack%20health%20insurance%20coverage.

Santos-Longhurst, A. (2019). "Demystifying the Bong, One Myth at a Time." (August 26) *Healthline*. Available at: https://www.healthline.com/health/how-does-a-bong-work#takeaway.

Santos-Longhurst, A. (2020). "Is There a Safer Way to Smoke Cannabis? How the Methods Stack Up." (April 30) *Healthline*. Available at: https://www.healthline.com/health/healthiest-way-to-smoke-weed#vaping.

Savelsberg, J.J., Cleveland, L.L., & King, R.D. (2004). "Institutional Environments and Scholarly Work: American Criminology, 1951–1993." *Social Forces* 82(4): 1275–1302.

Schencker, L. (2020). "Using Marijuana is Legal—But It Can Still Get You Fired. 'Human Resource Professionals in Illinois Will Have Their Hands Full.'" (January 10) *The Chicago Tribune*. Retrieved from: https://www.chicagotribune.com/busin ess/ct-biz-marijuana-pot-legal-use-workplace-20200110-ynrgpragtfenhilfeg3if2b dta-story.html.

Schirmann, K. (2016). "What It's Like to Be a 'Trim Bitch' on an Illegal Weed Farm." Broadly Vice.

Schissel, B. (1997). *Blaming Children: Youth Crime, Moral Panic and the Politics of Hate*. Halifax: Fernwood.

Schlag, A.K. (2020). "An Evaluation of Regulatory Regimes of Medical Cannabis: What Lessons Can Be Learned for the UK?" *Medical Cannabis and Cannabinoids* 3(1): 76–83.

Schoeler, T., Theobald, D., Pingault, J., Farrington, D., Jennings, W., Piquero, A. et al. (2016). "Continuity of Cannabis Use and Violent Offending over the Life Course." *Psychological Medicine* 46(8): 1663–1677.

Schrad, M.L. (2010). *The Political Power of Bad Ideas*. London: Oxford University Press.

Schroyer, J. (2020). "Divide Opens over L.A. Cannabis Social Equity Licenses, Management Contracts." (July 22) *MJBizDaily*. Available at: https://mjbizdaily.com/dispute-over-los-angeles-cannabis-social-equity-licenses-management-contracts/.

Schuchard, M.K. (1979). *Parents, Peers, and Pot*. Washington, DC: Government Publishing Office.

Schur, E. (1965). *Crimes without Victims: Deviant Behavior and Public Policy: Abortion, Homosexuality, and Drug Addiction*. Englewood Cliffs, NJ: Prentice-Hall.

Schwab, B., Wartenberg, A., & Butsic, V. (2019). "Characteristics of Farms Applying for Cannabis Cultivation Permits." *California Agriculture* 73(3): 128–135. https://doi.org/10.3733/ca.2019a0019.

Schwabe, A.L. & McGlaughlin, M.E. (2019). "Genetic Tools Weed Out Misconceptions of Strain Reliability in Cannabis Sativa: Implications for a Budding Industry." *Journal of Cannabis Research* 1(1): 3.

Schwabe, A.L., Hansen, C.J., Hyslop, R.M., & McGlaughlin, M.E. (2019). "Research Grade Marijuana Supplied by the National Institute on Drug Abuse Is Genetically

Divergent from Commercially Available Cannabis." (March 28) *BioRxiv.org.* https://doi.org/10.1101/592725.

Schwartz, J.C. (2016). "How Governments Pay: Lawsuits, Budgets, and Police Reform." *UCLA Law Review* 63: 1144, UCLA School of Law Research Paper No. 15-23. Available at: https://ssrn.com/abstract=2635673.

SCIE (Social Care Institute for Excellence) (n.d.). "Understanding Common Induction in Social Care." Available at: https://www.scie.org.uk/workforce/induction/standards/cis05_dutyofcare.asp.

Scott, J.G., Matuschka, L. Niemelä, S., Miettunen, J., Emmerson, B., & Mustonen, A. (2018). "Evidence of a Causal Relationship between Smoking Tobacco and Schizophrenia Spectrum Disorders." *Frontiers of Psychiatry* 607: 1–9. https://doi.org/10.3389/fpsyt.2018.00607.

Scott, W.R. (2014). *Institutions and Organizations*, 4th edn. Thousand Oaks, CA: Sage.

Seddon, T. (2007). "The Regulation of Heroin: Drug Policy and Social Change in Early Twentieth-Century Britain." *International Journal of Social Law* 35: 143–156.

Seddon, T. (2020). "Immoral in Principle, Unworkable in Practice: Cannabis Law Reform, the Beatles and the Wootton Report." *British Journal of Criminology* 60(6): 1567–1584.

Seddon, T. & Floodgate, W. (2020). *Regulating Cannabis: A Global Review and Future Directions*. London: Palgrave Macmillan.

Sellin, T. (1938). *Culture, Conflict and Crime*. New York, NY: Social Science Research Council.

Sercombe, H. (1999) 'Boots, Gangs and Addictions: Youth Subcultures and the Media.' In R. White (ed.), *Australian Youth Subcultures: On the Margins and in the Mainstream*. Hobart: Australian Clearinghouse for Youth Studies (pp. 5–15).

Sevigny, E.L., Pacula, R.L., Aloe, A.M., Medhin, D.N., & Greathouse, J. (2021). "PROTOCOL: The Effects of Cannabis Liberalization Laws on Health, Safety, and Socioeconomic Outcomes: An Evidence and Gap Map." *Campbell Systematic Reviews* 17: e1137. https://doi.org/10.1002/cl2.1137.

Sewell, A.A. (2020). "Policing the Block: Pandemics, Systemic Racism, and the Blood of America." *City and Community* 19(3): 496–505. https://doi.org/10.1111/cico.12517.

Sewell, A.A. & Jefferson, K.A. (2016). "Collateral Damage: The Health Effects of Invasive Police Encounters in New York City." *Journal of Urban Health* 93(1): 42–67.

Sewell, A.A., Feldman, J.M., Ray, R., Gilbert, K.L., Jefferson, K.A., & Lee, H. (2021). "Illness Spillovers of Lethal Police Violence: The Significance of Gendered Marginalization." *Ethnic and Racial Studies* 44(7): 1089–1114, https://doi.org/10.1080/01419870.2020.1781913.

Sewell, R.A., Poling, J., & Sofuoglu, M. (2009). "The Effects of Cannabis Compared with Alcohol on Driving." *American Journal of Addiction* 18(3): 185–193.

Shamir, R. & Hacker, D. (2001). "Colonialism's Civilizing Mission: The Case of the Indian Hemp Drug Commission." *Law & Social Inquiry* 26(2): 435–461.

Shanahan, M., Hughes, C., & McSweeney, T. (2017). *Police Diversion for Cannabis Offences: Assessing Outcomes and Cost-Effectiveness*. Trends & issues in crime and criminal justice No. 532. Canberra: Australian Institute of Criminology.

Sheehan, B.E., Grucza, R.A., & Plunk, A.D. (2021). "Association of Racial Disparity of Cannabis Possession Arrests among Adults and Youths with Statewide Cannabis Decriminalization and Legalization." *Journal of the American Medical Association Health Forum* 2(10): e213435. https://doi.org/10.1001/jamahealthforum.2021.3435.

Shepherd, J. (2018). "City of North Vancouver votes to ban Pot Shops." (May 31) *North Shore News*. Available at: http://www.nsnews.com/news/city-of-north-van-votes-to-ban-pot-shops-1.23321301.

Shi, Y., Lenzi, M., & An, R. (2015). "Cannabis Liberalization and Adolescent Cannabis Use: A Cross-National Study in 38 Countries." *PLoS ONE* 10(11): e0143562. https://doi.org/10.1371/journal.pone.0143562.

Shi, Y., Liang, D.I., Bao, Y., An, R., Wallace, M., & Grant, I. (2019). "Recreational Marijuana Legalization and Prescription Opioids Received by Medicaid Enrollees." *Drug and Alcohol Dependence* 194(1): 13–19. https://doi.org/10.1016/j.drugalcdep.2018.09.016.

Shiner, M. (2015). "Drug Policy Reform and the Reclassification of Cannabis in England and Wales: A Cautionary Tale." *International Journal of Drug Policy* 26(7): 696–704.

Shiner, M., Carre, Z., Delsol, R., & Eastwood, N. (2018). *The Colour of Injustice: 'Race,' Drugs and Law Enforcement in England and Wales*. London: Release Press.

Sideli, L., Trotta, G., Spinazzola, E., La Cascia, C.; & Di Forti, M. (2021). "Adverse Effects of Heavy Cannabis Use: Even Plants Can Harm the Brain." *PAIN* 162: S97–S104. https://doi.org/10.1097/j.pain.0000000000001963.

Sifaneck, S.J. & Kaplan, C.D. (1995). "Keeping off, Stepping on and Stepping off: The Steppingstone Theory Reevaluated in the Context of the Dutch Cannabis Experience." *Contemporary Drug Problems* 22(3): 483–512. https://doi.org/10.1177/009145099502200306.

Siff, S. (2014). "The Illegalization of Marijuana: A Brief History." *Origins* 7(8). Available at: https://origins.osu.edu/article/illegalization-marijuana-brief-history.

Silbaugh, K. (2021). "Medical Cannabis and the Age of Majority." *Boston University Law Review* 101: 1155–1171.

Silvaggio, A. (2021). "The Environmental Impact of Cannabis Liberalization: Lessons from California." In D. Corva & J. Meisel (eds), *The Routledge Handbook of Post-Prohibition Cannabis Research*. London: Routledge (pp. 231–242).

Silver, L., Naprawa, A., & Padon, A. (2020). "Assessment of Incorporation of Lessons from Tobacco Control in City and County Laws Regulating Legal Marijuana in California." *Journal of the American Medical Association Network* 3(6): e208393. https://doi.org/10.1001/ jamanetworkopen.2020.8393.

Simon, J. (2007). *Governing through Crime: How the War on Crime Transformed American Democracy and Created a Culture of Fear*. Oxford, UK: Oxford University Press.

Simmons, J.P., Nelson, L.D., & Simonsohn, U. (2011). "False-Positive Psychology: Undisclosed Flexibility in Data Collection and Analysis Allows Presenting Anything as Significant." *Psychological Science* 22: 1359–1366.

Single, E., Christie, P., & Ali, R. (2000). "The Impact of Cannabis Decriminalisation in Australia and the United States." *Journal of Public Health Policy* 21(2): 157–186. https://doi.org/10.2307/3343342.

Sinha, J. (2001). "The History and Development of the Leading International Drug Control Conventions Congress." Available at: www.parl.gc.ca/Content/SEN/Committee/371/ille/library/history-e.htm.

Skliamis, K. & Korf, D.J. (2022). "How Cannabis Users Obtain and Purchase Cannabis: A Comparison of Cannabis Users from European Countries with Different Cannabis Policies." *Substance Use & Misuse* 57(7): 1043–1051.

Slade, H. (2020). *Capturing the Market: Cannabis Regulation in Canada.* London: Transform Drug Policy Foundation and México Unido Contra la Delincuencia.

Slate (2022). "Policing for Profit: Inside a Town Where Law Enforcement Sees Citizens as Dollar Signs." *Slate.* Available at: https://slate.com/podcasts/what-next/2022/01/when-policing-becomes-a-towns-cash-cow.

Smart, A. (2019). "Trend of Low Potency Products Expected in Canadian Legal Recreational Market." (October 7) *CBC News.* Available at: https://www.cbc.ca/news/canada/british-columbia/trend-of-low-potency-products-expected-in-legal-recreational-cannabis-market-1.4853981.

Smart, R., Caulkins, J.P., Kilmer, B., Davenport, S., & Midgette, G. (2017). "Variation in Cannabis Potency and Prices in a Newly Legal Market: Evidence from 30 Million Cannabis Sales in Washington State." *Addiction* 112(12): 2167–2177.

Smart Start New York (n.d.). "The Marijuana Regulation and Taxation Act: Racial Justice Considerations." Available at: https://smart-ny.com/mrta-racial-justice-considerations/.

Smiley, E. (2016). "Marijuana & Other Drugs: Legalize or Decriminalize." *Arizona Journal of International and Comparative Law* 33: 825.

Smith, D.E. (2011). "The Evolution of Addiction Medicine as a Medical Specialty." *Virtual Mentor* 13(12): 900–905.

Smith, J. & Merolla, D. (2020). "PUFF, PUFF, PASS: The Effect of Racial Prejudice on White Americans' Attitudes towards Marijuana Legalization." *Du Bois Review: Social Science Research on Race* 17(1): 189–220.

Smith, R.F. (1917). Report of Investigation in the State of Texas, Particularly Along the Mexican Border, of the Traffic in, and Consumption of the Drug Generally Known as 'Indian Hemp', or Cannabis Indica, Known in Mexico and States Bordering on the Rio Grande River as 'Marihuana'; Sometimes Also Referred to as 'Rosa Maria', or 'Juanita.'" Washington, DC: Department of Agriculture.

Sobesky, M. & Gorgens, K. (2016). "Cannabis and Adolescents: Exploring the Substance Misuse Treatment Provider Experience in a Climate of Legalization." *International Journal of Drug Policy* 33: 66–74. https://doi.org/10.1016/j.drugpo.2016.02.008. Epub 2016 February 16. PMID: 26992485.

Socías, M.E., Kerr, T., Wood, E., Dong, H., Lake, S., Hayashi, K., et al. (2017). "Intentional Cannabis Use to Reduce Crack Cocaine Use in a Canadian Setting: A Longitudinal Analysis." *Addictive Behaviors* 72: 138–143.

Soderstrom, H., Tullberg, M., Wikkelsoe, C., Ekholm, S., & Forsman, A. (2000). "Reduced Regional Cerebral Blood Flow in Non-Psychotic Violent Offenders." *Psychiatry Research: Neuroimaging* 98: 29–41.

Solomon, D. (1968). *The Marijuana Papers*. New York, NY: Signet.
Solomon R. (2020). "Racism and Its Effect on Cannabis Research." *Cannabis and Cannabinoid Research* 5(1): 2–5.
Solomon, R., Single, E.W., & Erickson, P.G. (1983). "Legal Considerations in Cannabis Possession Policy." *Canadian Public Policy* 9: 419–433.
Solowij, N., Stephens, R.S., Roffman, R.A., Babor, T., Kadden, R., Miller, M., et al. (2002). "Cognitive Functioning of Long-Term Heavy Cannabis Users Seeking Treatment." *Journal of the American Medical Association* 287(9): 1123–1131.
Spivakovsky, C., Seear, K., & Carter, A. (eds) (2018). *Critical Perspectives on Coercive Interventions: Law, Medicine and Society*. Abingdon: Routledge.
The Spokesman Review (2020). "State Policies Vary on Accepting Medical Cards." (March 3). Available at: https://www.spokesman.com/stories/2020/mar/03/state-policies-vary-accepting-medical-cards.
Spriggs, A. (2018). "B.C. Missing Big Opportunity in 'Craft Cannabis,' Say Critics." (July 27) *The Tyee*. Available at: https://thetyee.ca/News/2018/07/27/BC-Missing-Cannabis-Opportunity/.
Springhall, J. (1998). "Censoring Hollywood: Youth, Moral Panic and Crime/Gangster Movies of the 1930s." *Journal of Popular Culture* 32: 135–154.
Spyt, W., Barnham, L., & Kew, J. (2019). "Diversion: Going Soft on Drugs?" *Thames Valley Police Journal* 4: 44–58.
Stabile, C.A. (2001). "Conspiracy or Consensus? Reconsidering the Moral Panic." *Journal of Communication Inquiry* 25(3): 258–278.
Stanford Encyclopedia of Philosophy (2007). "Jürgen Habermas." (May 17, updated August 14, 2014). Available at: https://plato.stanford.edu/entries/habermas.
Staniforth, J. (2021). "The 'Cannamons' Parenting with Cannabis." (November 18) *BBC Family Tree*. Available at: https://www.bbc.com/worklife/article/20211116-the-cannamoms-parenting-with-cannabis.
Stanton, D., Mei, X., Kim, S., Willits, D., Stohr, M., Hemmens, C., Wu, G., Lu, R., Makin, D., & Lovrich, N. (2020). "The Effect of Marijuana Legalization on Jail Populations in Washington State." *The Prison Journal* 100(4): 510–530.
Start Smart New York (n.d.). "The Marijuana Regulation and Taxation Act: Racial Justice Considerations." Available at: https://smart-ny.com/mrta-racial-justice-considerations.
Statistics Canada (2019a). "Crime and Justice Statistics." Available at: https://www.statcan.gc.ca/en/subjects-start/crime_and_justice.
Statistics Canada (2019b). "National Cannabis Survey: 3rd Quarter." (October 30). Retrieved from: https://www150.statcan.gc.ca/n1/daily-quotidien/191030/dq191030a-eng.pdf.
Staton, M., Kaskie, B., & Bobitt, J. (2022). "The Changing Cannabis Culture among Older Americans: High Hopes for Chronic Pain Relief." *Drugs: Education, Prevention and Policy* 29(4): 382–392.
Steinberg, J., Unger, J.B., Hallett, C., Williams, E., Baezconde-Garbanati, L., & Cousineau, M.R. (2020). "A Tobacco Control Framework for Regulating Public Consumption of Cannabis: Multistate Analysis and Policy Implications." *American Journal of Public Health* 110(2): 203–208.

Steinfeld, A. (2020). "Debunking Environmental Myths." (Summer) *Insights*. Available at: https://www.bhfs.com/insights/alerts-articles/2020/debunking-the-environmental-myths.

Stevens, A. (2011). *Drugs, Crime and Public Health: The Political Economy of Drug Policy*. London: Routledge.

Stevens, A. (2012). "The Ethics and Effectiveness of Coerced Treatment of People Who Use Drugs." *Human Rights and Drugs* 2 (1): 7–16.

Stevens, A. (2019). "Is Policy 'Liberalization' Associated with Higher Odds of Adolescent Cannabis Use? A Re-Analysis of Data from 38 Countries." *International Journal on Drug Policy* 66(3): 94–99.

Stevens, A. & Zampini, G.F. (2018). "Drug Policy Constellations: A Habermasian Approach for Understanding English Drug Policy." *International Journal of Drug Policy* 57: 61–71.

Stevens, A., Hughes, C.E., Hulme, S., & Cassidy, R. (2021). "Classifying Alternative Approaches for Simple Drug Possession: A Two-Level Taxonomy." *Northern Kentucky Law Review* 48(2): 337–353.

Stevens, A., Hughes, C.E., Hulme, S., & Cassidy, R. (2022). "Depenalization, Diversion and Decriminalization: A Realist Review and Programme Theory of Alternatives to Criminalization for Simple Drug Possession." *European Journal of Criminology* 19(1): 29–54.

Stevens, A.K., Aston, E.R., Gunn, R.L., Sokolovsky, A.W., Treloar Padovano, H., White, H.R., and Jackson, K.M. (2021). "Does the Combination Matter? Examining the Influence of Alcohol and Cannabis Product Combinations on Simultaneous Use and Consequences in Daily Life." *Alcohol: Clinical and Experimental Research* 45: 181–193. https://doi.org/10.1111/acer.14494.

Stickle, B. & Felson, M. (2020). "Crime Rates in a Pandemic: The Largest Criminological Experiment in History." *American Journal of Criminal Justice* 45(4): 525–536.

Stinson, F.S., Grant, B.F., Dawson, D., Ruan, W.J., Huang, B., & Saha, T. (2005). "Comorbidity between DSM-IV Alcohol and Specific Drug Use Disorders in the United States: Results from the National Epidemiological Survey on Alcohol and Related Conditions." *Drug and Alcohol Dependence* 80: 105–116.

Stoa, R. (2018). *Craft Weed*. Cambridge, MA: MIT Press.

Stohr, M.K., Makin, D.A., Stanton, D.L., Hemmens, C., Willits, D.W., Lovrich, N.P., Meize, M., Snyder, J., Lu, R., & Guangzhen, W. (2020a). "An Evolution Rather Than a Revolution: Cannabis Legalization Implementation from the Perspective of the Police in Washington State." *Justice Evaluation Journal* 3(2): 267–293. htps://doi.org/10.1080/24751979.2020.1756378.

Stohr, M.K., Willits, D.W., Makin, D.A., Hemmens, C., Lovrich, N.P. Stanton, D.L., & Meize, M. (2020b). "Effects of Marijuana Legalization on Law Enforcement and Crime: Final Report." Washington, DC: National Institute of Justice.

Stoicescu, C., Peters, K., & Lataire, Q. (2022). "A Slow Paradigm Shift: Prioritizing Transparency, Community Empowerment, and Sustained Advocacy to End Compulsory Drug Treatment." *Health and Human Rights Journal* 24(1): 129–134.

Stop the Violence B.C. (2013). "Breaking the Silence: Cannabis Prohibition, Organized Crime, and Gang Violence in British Columbia." Available at: https://drugpolicy.ca/wp-content/uploads/2011/10/STVBC-Breaking-the-Silence.pdf.

Strike, C. & Rufo, C. (2010). "Embarrassing, Degrading, or Beneficial: Patient and Staff Perspectives on Urine Drug Testing in Methadone Maintenance Treatment." *Journal of Substance Use* 15(5): 303–312.

Stroud, N.J. (2011). *Niche News: The Politics of News Choice*. Oxford, UK: Oxford University Press.

Stuyt, E. (2018). "The Problem with the Current High Potency THC Marijuana from the Perspective of an Addiction Psychiatrist." *Missouri Medicine* 115(6): 482–486.

Subica, A.M., Douglas, J.A., Kepple, N.J., Villanueva, S., & Grills, C.T. (2018). "The Geography of Crime and Violence Surrounding Tobacco Shops, Medical Marijuana Dispensaries, and Off-Sale Alcohol Outlets in a Large, Urban Low-Income Community of Color." *Preventive Medicine* 108: 8–16. https://doi.org/10.1016/j.ypmed.2017.12.020.

Suen, L.W., Davidson, P.J., Browne, E.N., Lambdin, B.H., Wenger, L.D., & Kral, A.H. (2022). "Effect of an Unsanctioned Safe Consumption Site in the United States on Syringe Sharing, Rushed Injections, and Isolated Injection Drug Use: A Longitudinal Cohort Analysis." *Journal of Acquired Immune Deficiency Syndromes* 89(2): 172–177.

Sullum, J. (2015a). "Is Cannabis Causing More Car Crashes in Washington?" (August 21) *Reason Magazine Online*. Available at: https://reason.com/blog/2015/08/21/is-marijuana-causing-more-car-crashes-in.

Sullum, J. (2015b). "Supposedly Neutral Federal Report Stacks Deck against Marijuana Legalization." (September 17) *Forbes Online*. Available at: https://www.forbes.com/sites/jacobsullum/2015/09/17/supposedly-neutral-federal-report-stacks-the-deck-against-marijuana-legalization.

Sunstein, C. (2001). *Republic.com*. Princeton, NJ: Princeton University Press.

Sutton, A. & Hawks, D. (2005). "The Cannabis Infringement Notice Scheme in Western Australia: A Review of Policy, Police and Judicial Perspectives." *Drug and Alcohol Review* 24(4): 331–336. https://doi.org/10.1080/09595230500263947.

Sutton, M. (2021). "Drug Decriminalization in Oregon Officially Begins Today." (February 1) Press Release. Drug Policy Alliance. Available at: https://drugpolicy.org/news/drug-decriminalization-oregon-officially-begins-today/.

Swift, W, Coffey, C, Degenhardt, L, Carlin, J.B., Romaniuk, H. & Patton, G.C. (2012). "Cannabis and Progression to Other Substance Use in Young Adults: Findings from a 13-Year Prospective Population-based Study." *Journal of Epidemiology and Community Health* 66(7): e26.

Swinburne, M. & Hoke, K. (2020). "State Efforts to Create an Inclusive Marijuana Industry in the Shadow of the Unjust War on Drugs." *Journal of Business & Technology Law* 15(2): 235–280.

Syracuse.com (2021). "New York's Marijuana Tax Might Not Be the Nation's Highest Rate But It May Be the Most Complex." *Syracuse.com*. Available at: https://www.syracuse.com/marijuana/2021/05/new-yorks-marijuana-tax-might-not-be-the-nations-highest-but-it-may-be-the-most-complex.html#:~:text=The%20retail%20marijuana%20tax%20will,factors%20like%20weight%20or%20volume.

Szalavitz, M. (2015a). "Genetics: No More Addictive Personality." *Nature* 522: S48–S49. https://doi.org/10.1038/522S48a.

Szalavitz, M. (2015b). *Unbroken Brain: A Revolutionary New Way of Understanding Addiction*. New York, NY: St Martin's Press.

Szalavitz, M. (2021). *Undoing Drugs: The Untold Story of Harm Reduction and the Future of Addiction*. New York, NY: Hachette.

Szalavitz, M. &. Rigg, K.K. (2017). "The Curious (Dis)Connection between the Opioid Epidemic and Crime." *Substance Use & Misuse* 52(14): 1927–1931. https://doi.org/10.1080/10826084.2017.1376685.

Szalavitz, M., Rigg, K.K., & Wakeman, S.E. (2021). "Drug Dependence Is Not Addiction—And It Matters." (December) *Annals of Medicine* 53(1): 1989–1992. https://doi.org/10.1080/07853890.2021.1995623. PMID: 34751058; PMCID: PMC8583742.

Szasz, T. (2007). *Coercion as Cure: A Critical History of Psychiatry*. New Brunswick, N.: Transaction Publishers.

Ta, M., Greto, L., & Bolt, K. (2019). "Trends and Characteristics in Marijuana Use among Public School Students—King County, Washington, 2004–2016." *Morbidity and Mortality Weekly Report* 68(39): 845–850. https://doi.org/10.15585/mmwr.mm6839a3.

TalkingDrugs (n.d.). "Drug Decriminalization across the World." Available at: https://www.talkingdrugs.org/drug-decriminalisation.

Tangherlini, T.R., Shahsavari, S., Shahbazi, B., Ebrahimzadeh, E., & Roychowdhury, V. (2020). "An Automated Pipeline for the Discovery of Conspiracy and Conspiracy Theory Narrative Frameworks: Bridgegate, Pizzagate and Storytelling on the Web." *PLoS ONE* 15(6): e0233879. https://doi.org/10.1371/journal.pone.0233879.

Tanguay, P., Chabungbam, A., & Vumbaca, G. (2022). "Transitions from Compulsory Detention to Community-Based Treatment: No Transparency without Data, No Accountability without Independent Evaluations." *Health and Human Rights* 24(1): 179–181.

Tannenbaum, F. (1938). *Crime and Community*. Boston, MA: Ginn.

Tavares, L.V., GraÁa, P.M., Martins, O., & Asensio, M. (2005). "External and Independent Evaluation of the 'National Strategy for the Fight against Drugs' and of the 'National Action Plan for the Fight against Drugs and Drug Addiction Horizon 2004'." Lisbon: Portuguese National Institute of Public Administration.

Taylor, A.H. (1967). "American Confrontation with Opium Traffic in the Philippines." *Pacific Historical Review* 36(3): 307–324.

Taylor, I., Walton, P., & Young, J. (1973). *The New Criminology: For a Social Theory of Deviance*. Boston, MA: Routledge & Kegan Paul.

Taylor, S., Buchanan, J., & Ayres, T. (2016). "Prohibition, Privilege and the Drug Apartheid: The Failure of Drug Policy Reform to Address the Underlying Fallacies of Drug Prohibition." *Criminology & Criminal Justice* 16(4): 452–469.

Tcherni-Buzzeo, M. (2019). "The 'Great American Crime Decline': Possible Explanations." In M.D. Krohn, N. Hendrix, G.P. Hall, & A.J. Lizotte (eds), *Handbook on Crime and Deviance*, 2nd edn. New York, NY: Springer (pp. 309–335).

Testa, A., Turney, K., Jackson, D.B., & Jaynes, C.M. (2021). "Police Contact and Future Orientation from Adolescence to Young Adulthood: Findings from the Pathways to Desistance Study." *Criminology* 60(2): 263–290. https://doi.org/10.1111/1745-9125.12297.

Thies, C.F. (2012). "The Relationship between Enforcement and the Price of Marijuana." *Journal of Private Enterprise* 28(1): 79–90.

Thies, C.G. & Breuning, M. (2012). "Integrating Foreign Policy Analysis and International Relations through Role Theory." *Foreign Policy Analysis* 8(1): 1–4. https://doi.org/10.1111/j.1743-8594.2011.00169.x.

Thomas, W.I. & Znaniecki, F. (1918). *The Polish Peasant in Europe and America*, Vol. 1. Boston, MA: Badger.

Thomas, W.I. & Znaniecki, F. (1919). *The Polish Peasant in Europe and America*, Vol. 3. Boston, MA: Badger.

Thomas, W.I. & Znaniecki, F. (1920). *The Polish Peasant in Europe and America*, Vols IV & V. Boston, MA: Badger.

Thompson, J.B. (1990). *Ideology and Modern Culture: Critical Social Theory in the Era of Mass Communication*. Cambridge, UK: Polity Press.

Thornberry, T. (1989). "Toward an Interactional Theory of Delinquency." *Criminology* 25: 863–892.

Thornton, M. (1998a). "Perfect Drug Legalization." In J. Fish (ed.), *How to Legalize Drugs: Public Health, Social Science, and Civil Liberties Perspectives*. Northvale, NJ: Jason Aronson (pp. 638–660).

Thornton, M. (1998b). "The Potency of Illegal Drugs." *Journal of Drug Issues* 28(3): 525–540.

Thornton, S. (1994). "Moral Panic, the Media and British Rave Culture." In A. Ross & T. Rose (eds), *Microphone Fiends: Youth Music, Youth Culture*. London: Routledge (pp. 176–192).

Tichenor, D.J. (2002). *The Politics of Immigration Control in America*. Princeton, NJ: University of Princeton Press.

Timber Cannabis Co. (n.d.). "Why the Percentage Doesn't Matter." Available at: https://timbercannabisco.com/why-thc-percentage-doesnt-matter.

Title, S. (2022). "Bigger is Not Better: Preventing Monopolies in the National Cannabis Market." (January 26) Ohio State Legal Studies Research Paper No. 678 (pp. 1–12). Available at: https://papers.ssrn.com/sol3/papers.cfm?abstract_id=4018493.

Thompson, D. (2018). "Toxic Chemicals Found at Most Illegal California Pot Farms." *AP News*. Available at: https://apnews.com/article/6e7d27d687e9428381fa940ccdb0521b.

Tonry, M. (1994) "Race and the War on Drugs." University of Chicago Legal Forum (pp. 25–81).

Tonry, M. (2007). "Determinants of Penal Policies." *Crime and Justice* 36: 1–48.

Tonry, M. (2011). *Punishing Race: A Continuing American Dilemma*. New York, NY: Oxford University Press.

Tonry, M. & Melewski, M. (2008). "The Malign Effects of Drug and Crime Control Policies on Black Americans." *Crime and Justice* 37: 1–44.

Torres-Cortez, R. (2022). "Clark County Oks Cannabis Lounge Rules; Lounges Could Open in 2023." (December 20) *Law Vegas Review Journal*. Available at: https://www.reviewjournal.com/news/politics-and-government/clark-county/clark-county-oks-cannabis-lounge-rules-lounges-could-open-in-2023-2697576.

Tosh, S. (2019). "Drugs, Crime, and Aggravated Felony Deportations: Moral Panic Theory and the Legal Construction of the 'Criminal Alien.'" *Critical Criminology* 27(3): 329–345.

Transform Drug Policy Foundation (n.d.). "Drug Diversion in the UK." Available at: https://transformdrugs.org/drug-policy/uk-drug-policy/diversion-schemes.

Transform Drug Policy Foundation (2017). "Cannabis Legalisation in Uruguay: Public Health and Safety over Private Profit." Available at: https:// transformdrugs.org/cannabis-legalisation-in-uruguay-public-health-and- safety-over-private-profit.

Transform Drug Policy Foundation (2021). *How to Regulate Cannabis: A Practical Guide*, 3rd edn. https://transformdrugs.org/publications/how-to-regulate-cannabis-3rd-ed.

Transnational Institute (n.d.). "The Rise and Decline of Cannabis Prohibition: The History of Cannabis in the UN Drug Control System and Options for Reform." Available at: https://www.tni.org/files/download/rise_and_decline_ch1.pdf.

Tupper, K.W. (2007). "The Globalization of Ayahuasca: Harm Reduction or Benefit Maximization?" *International Journal of Drug Policy* 19(4): 297–303.

Turk, A.T. (1966). "Conflict and Criminality." *American Sociological Review* 31(3): 338–352.

Turk, A.T. (1969). *Criminality and Legal Order*. Skokie, IL: Rand McNally.

Turnbull, P.J. (2009). "The Great Cannabis Classification Debacle: What Are the Likely Consequences for Policing Cannabis Possession Offences in England and Wales?" *Drug and Alcohol Review* 28(2): 202–229. https://doi.org/10.1111/j.1465-3362.2008.00045.x. PMID: 19320707.

Turvill, W. (2020). "'The Legal Stuff Is Garbage': Why Canada's Cannabis Black Market Keeps Thriving." (March 18) *The Guardian*. Available at: https://www.theguardian.com/society/2020/mar/18/cannabis-canada-legal-recreational-business.

Tutenges, S., Kolind, T., & Uhl, A. (2015). "Explorations into the Drug Users' Perspectives." *Drugs: Education, Prevention and Policy* 22(3): 173–174.

Tyler, C. (2019). "Brexit: Hatred, Lies and UK Democracy." *Political Dialogues* 27: 63–82.

Tyler, T.R. & Boeckmann, R.J. (1997). "Three Strikes and You Are Out, But Why? The Psychology of Public Support for Punishing Rule Breakers." *Law & Society Review* 31(2): 237–265. https://doi.org/10.2307/3053926.

Uggen, C. and Inderbitzin, M. (2010). "Public Criminologies." *Criminology & Public Policy* 9: 725–749.

UKCIA (UK Cannabis Internet Activist) (n.d.a). "History of the Development of International Control." Available at: https://www.ukcia.org/research/wootton/apII.php.

UKCIA (n.d.b). "Home Office—Wootton Report: Section VI General Conclusion and Recommendations." Available at: https://www.ukcia.org/research/wootton/sec6.php.

UN (United Nations) (2020). "UN Commission Reclassifies Cannabis, Yet Still Considered Harmful." *UN News*. Available at: https://news.un.org/en/story/2020/12/1079132.

UNCEBC (United Nations Chief Executives Board for Coordination) (2019). "Summary of Deliberations." Available at: https://digitallibrary.un.org/record/3792232?ln=en.

UNDOC (2019). "Summary of Deliberations among Chief Executives Board of Coordination." Available at: https://www.unsceb.org/CEBPublicFiles/CEB-2018-2-SoD.pdf.

UNHCR (United Nations Office of the High Commissioner) (2020). "Portugal at Crossroads of Anti-Racism, Say UN Experts." (December 8) Press release. Available at: https://www.ohchr.org/en/press-releases/2021/12/portugal-crossroads-anti-racism-say-un-experts.

UNHCR (2022). "In Dialogue with Uruguay, Experts of the Human Rights Committee Commend Measures to Address Discrimination and Racial Disparities, Ask about People of African Descent and Prison Overcrowding." (July 1). Available at: https://www.ohchr.org/en/news/2022/07/dialogue-uruguay-experts-human-rights-committee-commend-measures-address.

Unnever, J.D., Cullen, F.T., Mathers, S.A., McClure, T.E., & Allison, M.C. (2009). "Racial Discrimination and Hirschi's Criminological Classic: A Chapter in the Sociology of Knowledge." *Justice Quarterly* 26(3): 377–409.

UNODC (United States Office on Drugs and Crime) (2012). "World Drug Report 2012." Available at: https://www.unodc.org/unodc/en/data-and-analysis/WDR-2012.html.

UNODC (United Nations Office on Drugs and Crime) (2019). *World Drug Report 2019*. Vienna: UNODC.

UNODC (2021a). "Drug Market Trends: Cannabis Opioids." Available at: https://www.unodc.org/res/wdr2021/field/WDR21_Booklet_3.pdf.

UNODC (2021b). "World Drug Report 2021. Book 2 Global Overview: Drug Demand Supply." Available at: https://www.unodc.org/unodc/en/data-and-analysis/WDR-2012.html.

UNODC–WHO (World Health Organization) (2021). "International Standards for the Treatment of Drug Use Disorders." (March 31). Available at: https://www.who.int/publications/i/item/international-standards-for-the-treatment-of-drug-use-disorders.

US Department of Health and Human Services. Substance Abuse and Mental Health Services Administration. Office of Applied Studies (2005). "National Survey on Drug Use & Health: Detailed Tables. Table 1.80B: Marijuana Use in Lifetime, Past Year, and Past Month among Persons Aged 18 to 25." Available at: https://www.datafiles.samhsa.gov/dataset/national-survey-drug-use-and-health-2005-nsduh-2005-ds0001.

US National Commission on Marihuana and Drug Abuse (n.d.). "Marihuana: A Signal of Misunderstanding: Drugs and Social Responsibility—a Final Comment." Available at: https://www.druglibrary.org/schaffer/library/studies/nc/ncrec1_17.htm.

US Supreme Court (2019). "Year-End Report on the Federal Judiciary." Available at: https://www.supremecourt.gov/publicinfo/year-end/2019year-endreport.pdf.

USAID (United States Agency for International Development) (2020). "Police Accountability Mechanisms." Available at: https://2017-2020.usaid.gov/sites/default/files/documents/Police_Accountability_Mechanisms_8.5.2020.pdf.

Valdes-Donoso, P., Sumner, D.A., & Goldstein, R.S. (2019). "Costs of Mandatory Cannabis Testing in California." *California Agriculture* 73(3–4): 154–160. https://doi.org/10.3733/ca.2019a0014.

Valier, C. (2000). "Looking Daggers: A Psychoanalytic Reading of the Scene of Punishment." *Punishment and Society* 2: 379–94.

Valleriani, J., Haines-Saah, R., Capler, R., Bluthenthal, R., Socias, M.E., Milloy, M.J., et al. (2020). "The Emergence of Innovative Cannabis Distribution Projects in the Downtown Eastside of Vancouver, Canada." *The International Journal on Drug Policy* 79: 102737. doi: 10.1016/j.drugpo.2020.102737. Epub ahead of print. PMID: 32289590; PMCID: PMC7308205.

Valverde, M. (2003). *Law's Dream of a Common Knowledge*. Princeton, NJ: Princeton University Press.

Valverde, M. (2008). *Racial Purity, Sexual Purity, and Immigration Policy, in the History of Immigration and Racism in Canada: Essential Readings*, ed. B. Walker. Toronto, ON: Canadian Scholar's Press (p. 175).

Van Amsterdam, J., Nutt, D., Phillips, L., & van den Brink, W. (2015). "European Rating of Drug Harms." *Journal of Psychopharmacology* 29(6): 655–660.

Van Boekel, L.C., Brouwers, E.P., van Weeghal, J., & Garretsen, H.F. (2013). "Stigma among Health Professionals towards Patients with Substance Use Disorders and Its Consequences for Healthcare Delivery: A Systematic Review." *Drug and Alcohol Dependence* 131: 23–35.

Van Green, T. (2022). "Americans Overwhelmingly Say Marijuana Should Be Legal for Medicinal and Recreational Use." (November 22) Pew Research Center. Available at: https://www.pewresearch.org/fact-tank/2021/04/16/americans-ove rwhelmingly-say-marijuana-should-be-legal-for-recreational-or-medical-use.

van Ooyen-Houben, M.M.J., Bieleman, B., & Koff, D.J. (2016). "Tightening the Dutch Coffee Shop Policy: Evaluation of the Private Club and the Residence Criterion." *International Journal of Drug Policy* 31: 113–120. https://doi.org/10.1016/j.dru gpo.2016.01.019.

VANDU, WAHRS, BCAPOM, Maynard, R., & Jozaghi, E. (2021). "The Drug War Must End: The Right to Life, Liberty and Security of the Person during the COVID-19 Pandemic for People Who Use Drugs." *Harm Reduction Journal* 18: 21–22. https://doi.org/10.1186/s12954-021-00474-8.

Varona, G. & de la Cuesta, J.L. (2019): *International Criminology: Concept, History, Developments, and Institutions*. Cambridge, UK: Oxford University Press.

Vitale, A. (2018). *The End of Policing*. New York, NY: Verso Books.

Vitiello, M. (2019). "Marijuana Legalization, Racial Disparity, and the Hope for Reform." Lewis and Clark Law Review 23: 789–821.

Vitiello, M. (2021). "The War on Drugs: Moral Panic and Excessive Sentences." *Cleveland State Law Review* 69: 441–485.

Voelker, R. (2018). "States Move to Substitute Opioids with Medical Marijuana to Quell Epidemic." *Medical News and Perspectives* 320(23): 2408–2410. https://doi.org/10.1001/jama.2018.17329.

Volkow, N. & Li, T.K. (2005). "The Neuroscience of Addiction." *Nature Neuroscience* 8(11): 1429–1430. doi: 10.1038/nn1105-1429. PMID: 16251981.

Wacquant L. (2009). *Prisons of Poverty*. Minneapolis, MN: Univ of Minnesota Press.

Wagner, F.A. & Anthony, J.C. (2002). "From First Drug Use to Drug Dependence: Developmental Periods of Risk for Dependence upon Marijuana, Cocaine, and Alcohol." *Neuropsychopharmacology* 26(4): 479–488. https://doi.org/10.1016/s0893-133x(01)00367-0.

Wagner, L., Bott, M., Carroll, J., Horn, M., & Bonilla, B. (2018). "Small California Pot Farmers Struggle to Survive, Worry that Central Coast Growers Are Using Loophole to Skirt Size Restrictions." (June 25) *NBC*. Available at: https://www.nbc

bayarea.com/news/local/central-coast-pot-growers-exploiting-loophole-to-skirt-size-restrictions-on-grows/186391/.
Walker, S. & Katz, C. (2018). *The Police in America: An Introduction*, 9th edn. (New York, NY: McGraw-Hill Education).
Walsh, J. & Ramsey, G. (2016). *Uruguay's Drug Policy: Major Innovations, Major Challenges*. Brookings Institute. Available at: https://www.brookings.edu/wp-content/uploads/2016/07/Walsh-Uruguay-final.pdf.
Walsh, Z., Callaway, R., Belle-Isle, L., Capler, R., Kay, R., Lucas, P., & Holtzman, S. (2013). "Cannabis for Therapeutic Purposes: Patient Characteristics, Access, and Reasons for Use." *International Journal on Drug Policy* 24(6): 511–516.
Walter, B (2022). *How Civil Wars Start: And How to Stop Them*. New York, NY: Random House.
Wang, G.S. & Post, T.W. (2019). "Cannabis (Marijuana): Acute Intoxication." *UpToDate*. Available at: https://cme.lww.com/ovidfiles/00006565-201911000-00013.pdf.
Wanke, M., Sandberg, S., Macit, R., & Gülerce, H. (2022). "Culture Matters! Changes in the Global Landscape of Cannabis." *Drugs: Education, Prevention and Policy* 29(4): 317–322. https://doi.org/10.1080/09687637.2022.2091301.
Ward, R. (2012). "Print Culture, Moral Panic, and the Administration of the Law: The London Crime Wave of 1744." *Crime, History & Societies* 16(1): 5–24.
Ward, R. (2019). "Alberta Squeaks Out Title as Canada's Top Cannabis Market with $123.6M Sold." (August 26) *CBC News*. Available at: https://www.cbc.ca/news/canada/calgary/alberta-cannabis-sales-1.5259452.
Warf, B. (2014) "High Points: An Historical Geography of Cannabis." *Geographical Review* 104(4): 414–438.
Watson, T.M., Valleriani, J., Hyshka, E., & Rueda, S. (2019). "Cannabis Legalization in the Provinces and Territories: Missing Opportunities to Effectively Educate Youth?" *Canadian Journal of Public Health* 110(4): 472–475. https://doi.org/10.17269/s41997-019-00209-0.
Waugh, P. (2022). "Labour MPs Are Furious with Sadiq Kahn, But His Drugs Policy Could Work." (May 13) *inews*. Available at: https://inews.co.uk/opinion/labour-mps-are-furious-with-sadiq-khan-but-his-drugs-policy-could-work-1629862.
Weed Out Misinformation (n.d.). "About Us." Available at: https://www.weedoutmisinformation.ca.
Weisburd, D.L. & Piquero, A. (2008). "How Well Do Criminologists Explain Crime? Statistical Modeling in Published Studies." *Crime and Justice* 37: 453–502.
Weiss, J. & Morel, O. (2023). "Cannabis in 2023. Here to Stay, but Mayor Challenges Remain." (January 10) *Cannabis Industry Journal*. Available at: https://cannabisindustryjournal.com/feature_article/cannabis-in-2023-here-to-stay-but-major-challenges-remain.
Wesley, J.J. & Murray K. (2021). "To Market or Demarket? Public-Sector Branding of Cannabis in Canada." *Administration & Society* 53(7): 1078–1105. doi: 10.1177/0095399721991129.
Western, B. (2006). *Punishment and Inequality in America*. New York, NY: Russell Sage Foundation.

Western, B. & Pettit, B. (2010). "Incarceration and Social Inequality." *Daedalus* 139(3): 8–19. Available at: https://www.amacad.org/sites/default/files/daedalus/downloads/Su2010_On-Mass-Incarceration.pdf.

Westoll, N. (2018). "'Doobies Make Boobies': York Police Say Officer's Comments on Cannabis are Incorrect." (February 20) *Global News*. https://globalnews.ca/news/4036143/cannabis-york-regional-police-comments/.

Wheeldon, J. (2015) "Ontology, Epistemology, and Irony: Richard Rorty and Re-Imagining Pragmatic Criminology." *Theoretical Criminology* 19(3): 396–415.

Wheeldon, J. (ed.) (2021). *Visual Criminology: From History and Methods to Critique and Policy Translation*. London: Routledge.

Wheeldon, J. & Heidt, J. (2007). "Bridging the Gap: A Pragmatic Approach to Understanding Critical Criminologies and Policy Influence." *Critical Criminology: An International Journal* 15(4): 313–325.

Wheeldon, J. & Heidt, J. (2012). "Contesting Evidence through a Comparative Research Program (or Understanding and Implementing Criminal Justice Reform in an Era of Dumb on Crime)." *International Journal of Criminology and Sociological Theory* 5(2): 922–935.

Wheeldon, J. & Heidt, J. (2022). "The Paradoxes of Normalization: Cannabis as Nuisance Crime, Medicine, and Consumer Good in British Columbia Before and After Legalization." *Deviant Behavior* 44(7): 989–1012. doi: 10.1080/01639625.2022.2125856.

Wheeldon, J. & Heidt, J. (2023a). "Cannabis and Criminology: A History of Race, Addiction, and Inconvenient Research." *Journal of Criminal Justice* 29(4): 426–438. doi: 10.1016/j.jcrimjus.2022.101991.

Wheeldon, J. & Heidt, J. (2023b). *Cannabis Criminology*. Abingdon: Routledge.

Wheeldon, J., Heidt, J., & Dooley, B. (2014). "The Troubles with Unification: Debating Assumptions, Methods, and Expertise in Criminology." *Journal of Theoretical and Philosophical Criminology* 6(2): 111–128.

The White House (2022). "Fact Sheet: President Biden to Sign Historic Executive Order to Advance Effective, Accountable Policing and Strengthen Public Safety." (May 25). Available at: https://www.whitehouse.gov/briefing-room/statements-releases/2022/05/25/fact-sheet-president-biden-to-sign-historic-executive-order-to-advance-effective-accountable-policing-and-strengthen-public-safety.

White, N. (2021). "Black People 12 Times More Likely to Be Prosecuted for Cannabis, New Analysis Shows." (May 28) *The Independent*. Available at: https://www.independent.co.uk/news/uk/politics/black-people-cannabis-prosecutions-b1853669.html.

White, R. & Habibis, D. (2005) *Crime and Society Victoria*. Oxford, UK: Oxford University Press.

WHO (World Health Organization). (2009). *Global Health Risks Mortality and Burden of Disease Attributable to Selected Major Risks*. Geneva: World Health Organization.

Wikström, P.-O. (2004). "Crime as Alternative: Towards a Cross-Level Situational Action Theory of Crime Causation." In J. McCord (ed.), *Beyond Empiricism*. New Brunswick, NJ: Transaction Publishing (pp. 1–37).

Wikström, P.-O. (2008). "In Search of Causes and Explanations of Crime." In R.D. King & E. Wincup (eds), *Doing Research on Crime and Justice*. Oxford, UK/New York, NY: Oxford University Press (pp. 117–139).

Wilkins, C., Rychert, M., Queirolo, R., Lenton, S.R., Kilmer, B., Fischer, B., et al. (2022). "Assessing Options for Cannabis Law Reform: A Multi-Criteria Decision Analysis (MCDA) with Stakeholders in New Zealand." *International Journal of Drug Policy* 105: 103712.

Williams, J. & Bretteville-Jensen, A.L. (2014). "Does Liberalizing Cannabis Laws Increase Cannabis Use?" *Journal of Health Economics* 36: 20–32.

Williams, S. (2018). "Amid Shortages, Black-Market Marijuana Is Thriving in Canada." (November 10) *The Motley Fool*. Available at: https://www.fool.com/investing/2018/11/10/amid-shortages-black-market-marijuana-is-thriving.aspx.

Williams, S. (2019). "Canada's Black Market to Control 71% of Marijuana Sales in 2019." (updated April 18) *The Motley Fool*. Retrieved from: https://www.fool.com/investing/2019/02/09/canadas-black-market-to-control-71-of-marijuana-sa.aspx.

Williams III, F.P. & McShane, M.D. (2010). *Criminological Theory*, 5th edn. Upper Saddle River, NJ: Prentice Hall.

Willoughby, W.W. (1925). *Opium as an International Problem: The Geneva Conferences*. Baltimore, MD: Johns Hopkins Press.

Wilson, P. (2020). "Academic Fraud: Solving the Crisis in Modern Academia." https://doi.org/10.31273/eirj.v7i3.546.

Wilson, S., Bodwitch, H., Carah, J., Daane, K., Getz, C., Grantham, T., & Butsic, V. (2019). "First Known Survey of Cannabis Production Practices in California." *California Agriculture* 73(3): 119–127.

Winterdyk, J. (2021). "Exploring a 'New' Perspective for Criminological Inquiry: Global Criminology." Available at: http://www.maclc.mk/Upload/Documents/J.%20Winterdyk.pdf.

Wogen, J. & Restrepo, M.T. (2020). "Human Rights, Stigma, and Substance Use." *Health and Human Rights* 22(1): 51–60.

Wright, H. (1909). "The International Opium Convention." *American Journal of International Law* 3(3): 648–673.

Wu, G., Boateng, F.D., & Lang, X. (2020). "The Spillover Effect of Recreational Marijuana Legalization on Crime: Evidence from Neighboring States of Colorado and Washington State." *Journal of Drug Issues* 50(4): 392–409. https://doi.org/10.1177/0022042620921359.

Yakowicz, W. (2022). "Cannabis Investors Feel 'Emotional Whiplash' around Dashed Prospects of SAFE Banking Act." (December 7) *Forbes*. Available at: https://www.forbes.com/sites/willyakowicz/2022/12/07/cannabis-investors-feel-emotional-whiplash-around-dashed-prospects-of-safe-banking-act/?sh=b792fa975d81.

YorkWilliams, S.L., Gust, C.J., Mueller, R., Bidwell, L., Hutchison, K.E., Gillman, A.S., & Bryan, A.D. (2019). "The New Runner's High? Examining Relationships between Cannabis Use and Exercise Behavior in States with Legalized Cannabis." *Frontiers in Public Health* 7: Article 99.

Young, J. (1971). *The Drugtakers*. London: Paladin.

Young, J. (2011). *The Criminological Imagination*. Malden, MA: Polity Press.

Yücel, M., Solowij, N., Respondek, C., Whittle, S., Fornito, A., Pantelis, C., & Lubman, D.I. (2008). "Regional Brain Abnormalities Associated with Long-Term Heavy Cannabis Use." *Archives of General Psychiatry* 65(6): 694–701.

Zakrzewski, W., Wheeler, A.P., & Thompson, A.J. (2020). "Cannabis in the Capital: Exploring the Spatial Association between Medical Marijuana Dispensaries and Crime." *Journal of Crime and Justice* 43(1): 1–15. https://doi.org/10.1080/0735648X.2019.1582351.

Zimmer, L. & Morgan, J.P. (1997). *Marijuana Myths Marijuana Facts: A Review of the Scientific Evidence*. New York, NY: Lindesmith Center.

Zimring, F. (2007). *The Great American Crime Decline*. New York, NY: Oxford University Press.

Zinberg, N. & Robertson, J. (1972). *Drugs and the Public*. New York, NY: Simon and Shuster.

Zoorob, M. (2020). "Do Police Brutality Stories Reduce 911 Calls? Reassessing an Important Criminological Finding." *American Sociological Review* 85(1): 176–183.

Zraick, K. (2022). "N.Y. Prisons Punished 1,600 Based on Faulty Drug Tests, Report Finds." (June 4) *New York Times*. Available at: https://www.nytimes.com/2022/01/04/nyregion/ny-prisons-faulty-drug-tests.html.

Zuardi, A.W. "History of Cannabis as a Medicine: A Review." (2006). *Brazilian Journal of Psychiatry* 28(2): 153–157.

Zürcher, K., Dupont, C., Weber, P., Grunt, S., Wilhelm, I., Eigenmann, D.E., et al. (2022). "Use and Caregiver-Reported Efficacy of Medical Cannabis in Children and Adolescents in Switzerland." *European Journal of Pediatrics* 181(1): 335–347. https://doi.org/10.1007/s00431-021-04202-z.

Index

For the benefit of digital users, indexed terms that span two pages (e.g., 52–53) may, on occasion, appear on only one of those pages.

Tables, figures, and boxes are indicated by an italic *t*, *f*, or *b* following the page/paragraph number.

abstinence policies
   harm reduction, and 184
accountability mechanisms
   policing of cannabis 194–95, 242
Adbusters 253–54
addiction 197–99
alcohol
   anti-alcohol activism 39–41
American Magazine 62
American Society of Criminology 17
amotivational syndrome 12
Anslinger, H. 44, 46–47, 47*f*, 62–63, 150
arrest rate trends of cannabis possession by race
   between decriminalization, legalization, and no-policy-reform states 253, 253*f*
assumptions 21–22, 266–67
   diversion 22, 266–67
   policing of cannabis and racially unequal outcomes 21–22, 42, 266
   stigma around cannabis use 21, 266
Australia
   regulatory models of cannabis policy 99–101

Bauden, M. 141–42
Beatles 49
Becker, H. 63–64, 75
Belackova, V. 121
Bender, S. 97–98
Bennett, J. 140–41
Ben-Yehuda, N. 65
Berenson, A. 12–13

Berke, J. 230
Bermeo, M. 9
Beweley, D. 45
Beweley-Taylor, D. 77–78
Bhatt, I. 85
Biden, J. 113, 145–46, 195
"Big Cannabis" 212
Boeri, M. 12
Boyd, S. 62
Brown, W. 188–89
Burnett, J. 129

Caine, W. S. 41
Campos, I. 76
Canada
   legalizing the cannabis supply chain 51–52
   regulatory measures, impact of 142–43
   regulatory models of cannabis policy 101–3
cannabis candy 227–29, 228*f*
cannabis criminology 11, 11*f*, 250–52
   duty of care 255–56
   engaging people who use drugs 251–52
   insights, interrogation, and imagination 263–66, 267–68
   pragmatism, and 256–57, 258–59, 260–62
      moral pragmatism 259–60
   translational criminology 252–55
   updating public criminology 255–56
   see also eras of cannabis research
cannabis culture 240
   credible concerns 247–50
   stigma at the macro-level 241–43
   stigma at the meso-level 243–45
   stigma at the micro-level 245–47
   supporting and building 240–41

cannabis liberalization
  legal, moral, and cultural
    re-negotiation 6–8
  lenses of 13–15
  see also limits of liberalization
cannabis use disorder (CUD) 135–36, 153–55, 159, 160–61, 196
Caron, C. 156
categories of cannabis policy 178, 182f, 182–83
  criminalization 178, 179–80
  depenalization 178, 180–81
  legalization 178–79
Christie, N. 10
citizens' jury model 261
Clockwork Orange 199
coffee-shop culture 50, 97, 141
Cohen, S. 15–16, 17, 19–20, 23–25, 64–65, 72, 125–28, 134–35, 137, 139–40, 143, 146, 148, 190, 250, 258–60
colonization of drug control 42
Comeau, N. 43–44, 54
commercial model of cannabis policy 96–97, 115, 168–69
Community Justice Centers (CJCs) 199–200
Conrad, P. 94–95
consumer cannabis model 96–97, 115, 168–69
  harm reduction and benefit maximization 221–24
control and coercion 134–39
Cooper, Z. 12–13
Cornwell, B. 68–69
"corporate capture" 227
Corva, D. 213
counterculture movement 49
criminalization of cannabis 178, 179–80
  goals of 31
  moral panics 74–76
crises in criminology 5–6
critical race theory (CRT) 98
crusaders 64

Dad Grass 231–32
David, M. 68, 69
Decorte, T. 144
decriminalization 177, 180–81, 182f, 182–83
  decriminalization "*in media res*" 181
  decriminalizing and destigmatizing cannabis use 182, 189

key questions for jurisdictions considering decriminalization or legalization 190–91, 191t
  "thin form of" 190–91
defining deviance down 127–28
deliberative democracy 18–20, 260–61
del Pozo, B. 192–93
depenalization 178, 180–81
diversion programs 22, 123–24, 126, 136–39, 196–97, 266–67
Dolphin, W. 12, 153, 158–59
Donohue, J. 178
Doonan, S. 170–71
Douglass, F. 40
drug prohibition
  effect on cannabis use 6, 9, 10
drug scheduling 48, 148–49, 152
drug testing 120, 132–33, 139
drug users, support and input of 214–15, 251–52
Dufton, E. 56–57, 239
duty of care
  cannabis criminology 255–56

Eastwood, N. 124
Ehrlichman, J. 151
El Guindy, M. 77–78, 149–50
elite-engineered moral panics 66
environmental concerns over cannabis production 82
eras of cannabis research 148–49, 171–72
  cannabis criminology and regulatory models of governance 162
  consumer cannabis 168–69
  medicinal model 167–68
  public health 164–66
  public safety 162–64
  drug war (1973–2017) 152–55
  early cannabis prohibition (1961–1972) 150–52
  funding research 153
  post-prohibition research (2018–present) 158–60
  prohibition-based policies 149–50
  reform, media, and the New Prohibitionists (2012–2017) 155–58
  social and racial equity 169–71
  studying legal cannabis 160–62
Erickson, P. 43–44, 54
"evil weed" 62–63

INDEX

Fagan, J. 131
Fischer, B. 8, 92
Fisher, G. 61–62
Floodgate, W. 9, 27, 50, 100
"folk devils" 65, 70, 71
Foucault, M. 127
Fox, K. 199–200
Friedman, M. 234–35
funding research 153

Garland, D. 55, 68, 70–71, 127–28
gateway theory 12, 43–44
Geller, A. 131
geographic diffusion of cannabis 34*f*, 34
Gladwell, M. 156
global criminalization of cannabis 43, 44–49
Global Drug Policy Index (GDPI) 124–25
godly society 36
Goffman, E. 32–33
Good Brands Cannabis Company 233
Goode, E. 65
Granderson, L. 10
grassroots moral panics 65–66

Habermas, J. 19, 260–61
Hall, W. 209
Hamilton, M. 81–82
harm reduction 14–15, 183–84
    abstinence policies, and 184
    concept of 183
    harm reduction and benefit maximization 206–9, 220–21
        expanding consumer cannabis 221–24
        racial and social justice 224–26
    public health, harms of 185–86
    public safety, dangers of 185
    racial justice, reconciliation and 186–87
Harm Reduction International (HRI) 183
Hathaway, A. 43–44, 53–54
Hicks, B. 246
Hier, S. 70
Highsman Cannabis 233–34
Hughes, B. 100–1
human rights 14

illusory reform 15–16, 127–29
    control and coercion 134–39

legalization and regulation 139–45
predatory policing 129–34
impaired driving 93, 235–36, 242
insanity
    moral panics 62
interest-group moral panics 67
International Drug Policy Consortium (IDPC) 211–13

Johns, A. 154

Kaplan, C. 106, 245–46
Kaplan, J. 5
Kavousi, P. 141, 164–65, 167, 168–69, 170, 229
key concepts 23–25
    pragmatism 23–24
    responding to the failures of the past 24
    visions 24
Klocke, B. 72–73, 75–76, 78, 80
Koutouki, K. 102–3

Le Dain Commission, 151–52
legalization 178–79
    key questions for jurisdictions considering decriminalization or legalization 190–91, 191*t*
    "thick form of" legalization 190–91
legalization and regulation 139–45, 205–6
    harm reduction to benefit maximization 206–9
"legalize-and-privatize" model 179
Lempert, R. 78–79
Levine, H. 49
lifespan of moral panics 60–61, 71–73
    cultivation 72–74
    dissipation 73, 80–82
    operation stage 73, 74–80
limits of liberalization 120–25, 145–46
    illusory reform 15–16, 127–29
        control and coercion 134–39
        legalization and regulation 139–45
        predatory policing 129–34
    international comparison of regulatory models 122*t*
    "soft end of social control" 125–27
Linders, A. 68–69
Lofts, K. 102–3
Lu, R. 163
Lucas, P. 208

MacKenzie, A. 85
Marconi, A. 157
Marley Natural 233
McAllister, W. 39–40
McCormick, C. 244–45
McSweeney, T. 186
media
 framing of cannabis 11–12
medicalization of cannabis use 94–95
 moral panics 77–80
medicinal model of cannabis policy 95–96, 115, 167–68
Meisel, J. 213
Miss Grass 232, 232*f*
monikers that exist to describe cannabis 34
moral dissonance 78–79
moral entrepreneurs 63–64
 crusaders 64
 rule enforcers 64
moral panics 56–57, 60, 67, 86–88
 attributes common to 65
 criminalization of cannabis 74–76
 critiques of the concept 68–71
 dramatization of evil 63
 elite-engineered moral panics 66
 "evil weed" 62–63
 grassroots moral panics 65–66
 insanity 62
 interest-group moral panics 67
 lifespan of 60–61, 71–73
  cultivation 72–74
  dissipation 73, 80–82
  operation stage 73, 74–80
 medicalization of cannabis use 77–80
 "moral panic today" 66*f*
 multiverse of moral panics 82–83, 84
 participatory disinformation and "informational cocoons" 83–86, 87*f*
 "popularization" of cannabis use 76–77
 processes that lead to 64–65
 racializing cannabis use 73–74
 stigma, and 61
 White youth, threat to 61–62
"moral pragmatism" 19–20, 259–60
Murray, K. 143
Muschert, G. 72–73, 75–76, 78, 80

National Academy of Science, Engineering, and Medicine (NASEM) 157

Netherlands
 coffee-shop system 50, 105–6, 106*t*, 141
 regulatory models of cannabis policy 104–6
Newhart, M. 12, 153, 158–59
"New Prohibitionists" 12–13, 149, 155–58, 171, 180, 250–51
New York Academy of Medicine 150
New York Times 227–28
Nixon, R. 151
no-knock search warrants 195
normalization 33, 49–52, 56
 legalizing the cannabis supply chain 51–52
 popular culture, developments in 51
 "privileged normalization" 50–51, 54–55
 relationship between stigma and normalization 54, 55–56
"nuisance" crime 133–34
Nutt, D. 184

Oldfield, K. 213
opium
 restrictions on 37–38
 uses of 37
origins and uses of cannabis 35–36
 decline in usage 36

Pacula, R. 209
Parker, H. 33
participatory disinformation and "informational cocoons" 83–86, 87*f*
paternalism 13
"perversions of restorative justice" 244–45
Pesta, G. 252
policing of cannabis 192–95, 241–43
 accountability mechanisms 194–95, 242
 defining and diverting problem drug use 195–97
 input from the police 214
 predatory policing 129–34
 racially unequal outcomes, and 21–22, 42, 266
 reshaping officer attitudes and beliefs 192–93, 194
 threshold limits 193–94
polymorphic governance 209–13, 236–37
 barriers to reform 226
  economic barriers 229–34
  legal barriers 234–36

political barriers 227–29
consumer cannabis, expanding 221–24
decriminalization to legalization and regulation 214–15
drug users, support and input of 214–15
edicts to guide policymakers 215–19
guiding principles 211–12
harm reduction and benefit maximization 220–21
expanding consumer cannabis 221–24
racial and social justice 224–26
input from the police 214
issues to consider 215, 216t
public support 214
Portugal
regulatory models of cannabis policy 103–4
post-prohibition cannabis research programs 8–9
pragmatism 23–24
cannabis criminology, and 256–57, 258–59, 260–62
moral pragmatism 259–60
predatory policing 129–34
Pridemore, W. 5
"privileged normalization" 50–51, 54–55
"prohibit-and-punish" model 180
prohibition culture jamming 253–54, 254f
public health model of cannabis policy 94–95, 114–15, 164–66
harms of 185–86
public safety model of cannabis policy 92–93, 114–15, 162–64
dangers of 185

racializing cannabis use
moral panics 73–74
racial justice model of cannabis policy 97–99, 115, 169–71
harm reduction and benefit maximization 224–26
reconciliation and 186–87
racially unequal outcomes, policing of cannabis and 21–22, 42, 266
arrest rate trends of cannabis possession by race
between decriminalization, legalization, and no-policy-reform states 253, 253f

Reefer Madness 62
regulating aversion 239–40
decriminalization and destigmatization policies 189
regulatory models of cannabis policy 91–92, 114, 162
commercial model 96–97, 115, 168–69
international comparison
Australia 99–101
Canada 101–3
Netherlands 104–6
Portugal 103–4
United Kingdom 106–8
United States 110–14
Uruguay 108–10
medicinal model 95–96, 115, 167–68
public health model 94–95, 114–15, 164–66
public safety model 92–93, 114–15, 162–64
racial justice model 97–99, 115, 169–71
rehabilitation 186
Reid, M. 53, 87, 166, 245
Reynolds, J. R. 35–36
Ritter, A. 14, 260, 261
Rodríguez-Gómez, D. 9
Rogan, S. 246–47
Rorty, R. 19, 261–62
Rothman, D. 127
rule enforcers 64

Sandberg, S. 241
Sear, K. 101
Seddon, T. 9, 27, 50, 100
Sheehan, B. 170, 253
Shiner, M. 130–31
Sifaneck, S. 106, 245–46
Sisley, S. 80–81
Smart Approaches to Marijuana (SAM) 155, 227
Social Care Institute (UK) 255
social construction 52–53
social control 15–16
"social worlds" 165–66
Solomon, R. 187
Staniforth, J. 247
Steinberg, J. 134
stereotypes of cannabis users 43–44
Stevens, A. 124, 155, 180–81, 256

stigma associated with cannabis use 21,
    31, 32–33, 42–43, 44, 53–56, 87–88,
    192, 266
  decriminalizing and destigmatizing
    cannabis use 182, 189
  managing the stigma 53–54
  moral panics, and 61
  relationship between stigma and
    normalization 54, 55–56
  stigma at the macro-level 241–43
  stigma at the meso-level 243–45
  stigma at the micro-level 245–47
Sunstein, C. 85

Tannenbaum, F. 63
taxonomy of sanctions 180–81
Taylor, A. 37
temperance movement 36, 38, 39–41, 42–43
  anti-immigration movements 41–42
  cannabis, and 41
"thick form of" legalization 190–91
"thin form of" decriminalization 190–91
threshold limits
  policing of cannabis 193–94
Title, S. 223
tolerance 187–89, 190, 207, 239–40
translational criminology 252–55
"treatment-industrial complex" 12, 16
Tyson, M. 234

UN Commission on Narcotic Drugs
  (CND) 99

United Kingdom
  Lambeth Cannabis Warning Scheme
    (LCWS) 130
  regulatory models of cannabis
    policy 106–8
United States
  expected cannabis legislation in
    2023 209, 210*t*
  regulatory models of cannabis
    policy 110–14
Uruguay
  cannabis social clubs (CSCs) 109–
    10, 144–45
  legalizing the cannabis supply chain 51–52
  regulatory models of cannabis
    policy 108–10
utilitarianism 13–14

"visions" 24
Vitiello, M. 7
voluntary and community-based support
  services 199–201, 267

Wanke, M. 165–66
"war on drugs" 9, 10, 55, 125, 149, 151
Wesley, J. 143
White youth, threat to
  moral panics 61–62
Wootton Report 151
World Anti-Doping Agency (WADA) 81

Young, J. 6, 263–64